My Life over the Rainbow

My Life over the Rainbow

*Judy Garland's Story
as told to
Lorna Smith*

VANTAGE PRESS
New York / Washington / Atlanta
Los Angeles / Chicago

To my three children, Liza, Lorna and Joe, with all my deepest love and in gratitude for the love they still have for me, and to my friends Lilian and Stanley, who have been so kind to me in my present life.

Judy

Preface

I first met Judy in October 1957, having already enjoyed her work in the movies and on stage for nearly twenty years, and I came to know and to love her personally during the years that followed. We last met on 16 June 1969, at her rented home in London, only six days before she died there.

Her sudden loss to the world came as a shock to the many who had known and loved her personality and talent. Yet in the weeks and months that followed, little that appeared about her in the public media handled her passing in the right manner, and little that was written about her bore much resemblance to the person I had known, either as a human being or as a performer. Only a few recognized and remembered her true worth. My increasing anger at the way her memory was being mishandled brought about the decision to write my own account of her life and talent, and, early in 1970, I set about this task.

My biography of her, which was called *Judy—with Love*, was accepted for publication in England only after being considerably reduced in length, and I was instructed to avoid any inferred criticism of anyone still living, irrespective of how much he or she may have been contributing to the public misconception of Judy's whole nature and actions. After much delay, it was published in a much shortened form in August 1975, but received little publicity in the face of the numerous longer and more sensational-sounding accounts that had been emerging and that continued to emerge.

During the latter part of 1970, I also commenced enquiring into the question of psychic phenomena and the possibility of a life continuing elsewhere after death on earth. I attended lectures and public demonstrations of clairvoyance, as well as reading books on the various aspects involved, and I began to be convinced

vii

that such continuance was true. In January 1971, I actually received a fairly detailed message from Judy through a well-known medium. She seemed to know what I was doing for her and to be pleased and grateful, and I was delighted and relieved to hear from her. For the next two years, I occasionally went to lectures on psychic matters, but I was mainly concerned with trying to complete the book with its subsequent editing problems, as well as maintaining my full-time job. However, during this period, I began to be aware of psychic activity around me, although I was not in any way seeking personal psychic development. Having had it "thrust upon me," I saw no alternative but to try and learn how to handle it correctly. Over a period of years the situation gradually stabilised and strengthened until I became able to correctly receive direct communications from those who had passed from this world to their continuing life in the next, including Judy. I assure you I have tested this comparatively "late-in-life" ability in many ways before acting as the medium through whom Judy has now provided the book which follows.

As my own psychic development has been closely linked with Judy's progress in her present life, she has included much of how this all came about in her own narrative. There you will also find a detailed explanation of how we came to work together and how this book came to be written. In offering this account to you, she hopes that those of you who may have felt and acted as she did when on earth will find some comfort and interest in finding out a little of what may lie ahead, although each one will have his or her individual problems and experiences. She is grateful to have been helped by others in her present world to formulate the material into the shape and method by which it has been related to me, and she explains later on why it may not often seem much like her manner of expressing herself when on earth. She jokingly asks me to explain that it has been largely "ghosted" for her, but that in transferring it to me, she has been "the main 'ghost' "!

As the account Judy gave to me of her present life includes some references to her life on earth, I have preceded her story with a brief outline of her life as "Miss Show Business" for the benefit of those readers who may be less familiar than some with when these incidents occurred.

Lorna Smith, 1985

Introduction:
"Miss Show Business"

Frances Ethel Gumm was born on 10 June 1922, in Grand Rapids, Minnesota, U.S.A., to two vaudeville performers, Frank and Ethel Gumm. She had two older sisters, Virginia and Susan. When she was only three years old, she joined the family act, which continued until 1935, by which time her sisters had left to get married and her beloved father had died. She had already been recognised in *Variety* as the only talent in the family, and, with her name already changed to Judy Garland, she was toured by her mother around the vaudeville circuit as a single act. Many of these engagements were before very rough audiences, and she had a hard time overcoming her fears of singing alone before such audiences without any visible affection or interest from her mother.

By 1936, Judy had begun a film career as a child performer with Metro-Goldwyn-Mayer. During the next fourteen years, she made twenty-nine pictures for that studio, including *The Wizard of Oz* (1939), *For Me and My Gal* (1942), *Meet Me in St. Louis* (1944), *The Harvey Girls* (1946), *Easter Parade* (1947), and *In the Good Old Summertime* (1949). She became an acclaimed and exceptionally popular international star after the success of *The Wizard of Oz*, when she was seventeen. All her pictures from then onwards were guaranteed money-makers for the studios.

Judy had a very loving and sensitive nature, and, despite her successful career, she felt very lonely inside. She felt she was of interest to people, including her mother, only as a means of making money. This caused her to have insomnia when she was only seventeen. Since the studios required her to remain slim and she had a natural tendency to plumpness, she faced severe slimming diets. These, in her case, meant eating hardly any food at all. She was also prescribed pills to aid the slimming. When she could not sleep, she was prescribed sleeping pills, and, when these two factors caused her to become easily overstrained and emotional, she was prescribed sedatives. When these mixed reactions caused her to feel tired and depressed, she was prescribed more pills to ease this situation. All these medicines, added to her continuing feeling of inner loneliness, brought about several nervous collapses during the last seven years of her work for the studio, and, in 1950, she was informed that her contract with the studio would not be renewed.

In 1941, when she was nineteen, Judy married thirty-one-year-old orchestra leader David Rose in the hope of finding a happy marriage that would end her loneliness. Rose, however, was mainly away on orchestra tours or in the army, and, by 1943, he had asked her for a divorce, telling her that she was too immature in her outlook to be his wife. The after effects of this feeling of failure accentuated her first nervous breakdown.

In 1945, Judy married film director Vincente Minnelli, who was more than twice her age. Their daughter, Liza, was born in 1946. Judy found that her husband's ideas of marriage were far more sophisticated than hers. Her feeling of loneliness remained, and her nervous problems continued and escalated. They separated, at his request, and were divorced in 1951.

Shortly after leaving the film studio and separating from Minnelli, Judy met Sidney Luft, a former test pilot who had recently separated from his wife. They became engaged in July 1951 and married in 1952, when both divorces had become final. Their daughter, Lorna, was born in November 1952, and their son, Joseph Wiley, was born in March 1955.

In April 1951, Judy had returned to the stage taking as her signature tune the very famous song "Over the Rainbow" from her film *The Wizard of Oz.* Thereafter, she was always expected to sing it; no Garland performance was considered to be complete without it, and few who saw her singing this song over the many years will ever be able to associate it with anyone else. By October 1951, she had already established herself in the eyes of the public as an even greater performer on stage than she had ever been on the screen. She became widely acclaimed, both by the general public and by her fellow professionals, as "Miss Show Business," and many who experienced her stage work during the next twelve years recognised her as one of the most, if not *the* most, exciting and best-loved performers within living memory.

In 1953, Judy returned to the screen to make her most famous film *A Star is Born*. This, along with *The Wizard of Oz*, remains the picture with which she is most widely associated, despite the popularity of many of the others. Although nominated for an Academy Award for her role in *A Star is Born* and regarded by the professional critics and public alike as wholly deserving of it, Judy lost to Grace Kelly for her performance in *The Country Girl*. The public made their feelings known, in both America and Great Britain, by voting Judy "Actress of the Year," and by a large majority, in independent polls.

When Judy left the film studios in 1950 and became happily married to Sid Luft, she discarded many of the medications that had been prescribed for her by the studio's doctors and managed to keep going mainly on sleeping pills and sedatives. Despite remaining comfortably plump and no longer slimming, she was still liable to become easily overstrained and overreactive as a result of her past severe breakdowns and so continued to use sleeping pills and sedatives. When, in November 1959, she nearly died from a rare form of hepatitis and the doctors thought it had been caused by the build up in her system of the many years of sedatives and sleeping pills, she tried hard not to return to these after she left the hospital. Although she had been informed that she would never be strong enough to work again and would remain a semi-invalid for the rest of her life, Judy felt able to return to her concert work in August 1960 and, during 1960–1961, produced her most exciting work of all, singing on stage for almost two and a half hours at each performance. In 1961 she won a "Show Business Magazine" Award as "Performer of the Year" for her tremendous work on stage. During that year she also acted in two dramatic films, *Judgment at Nuremberg* (for which she was nominated for an Academy Award) and *A Child is Waiting* (in which she worked with mentally retarded children).

During 1961, Judy and her husband vaguely parted company for a while, and their reconciliation at the end of the year was short-lived. When she made a film in England during the summer of 1962, called *I Could Go On Singing*, she found herself facing the unhappy possibility that further reconciliation was becoming less likely, and her whole outlook was unsettled by this throughout the filming. When Judy and her husband again reconciled in April 1963, it was less easy to adjust, and they separated again shortly before she began a television series of twenty-six shows.

These shows were completed between July 1963 and March 1964, during which time Judy had sung three hundred songs and shared the programs with more than fifty guests. She had previously starred in several highly praised television specials, and her 1962 special had won the Rose Award for the best musical show on international television. The special undertaken earlier in 1963 had also been highly commended. At the outset of the 1963 series, Judy had been included in the preliminary discussions. She had been led to believe she would be given some say in what was to be undertaken and would be working in her usual manner within a set format. She had also been assured that there would be set hours, and, therefore, no difficulties would arise in spending plenty of time with her children. In the event, she faced many changes in format, in her co-workers, and in producers. Most of these arbitrary decisions were undertaken with hardly any discussion or warning. She was also given the personally demoralising information that the sponsors were not pleased with her way of working. In the midst of all these changes and upsets, with working hours that were, as a result, far longer than ever envisaged, she was approached by her husband for custody of the children on the grounds that she was hardly ever at home. Judy agreed to them seeing their father whenever they wished, but objected to losing legal custody. She was feeling desperately lonely and felt there was nowhere to turn for any friendly support or advice. When her husband then started a sensational court case in an attempt to gain custody of Lorna and Joe, Judy felt that was the final let down and that he had clearly lost all love for her. Her health was already cracking. As a result of deep distress and personal loneliness, accentuated by this public action, and in order to accomplish all that was being demanded of her, she returned to the sleeping pills and the sedatives and was also prescribed a medicine called Ritalin to help her to keep going through all the long hours of working. By the time the series had ended, she had lost all stamina and all peace of mind. As a result, when she undertook to perform some concerts in Australia in May 1964 in order to keep herself occupied, she became so ill that she collapsed with bronchial pneumonia and pleurisy and nearly died again. This time she was saved, after being in a coma for fourteen hours, by a tracheotomy, which enabled her to breathe. The aftermath, however, was that her vocal cords became affected, as did her general health, and, during the last five years of her life on earth, Judy had to contend with increasingly failing health and voice. These handicaps in turn affected her financial position, and her hard-won earnings of recent years dwindled to nothing.

When, in November 1965, she married actor Mark Herron after her divorce from Sid Luft had taken place, it was to try and establish a family unit again for herself and her children. They had been friendly for eighteen months, and she had always felt calm and happy in his company. He had been carefully attentive without being intrusive, and she had liked his quiet manner and swift sense of humour. When he left her only six months later, assuring her it was not in any way her fault, Judy felt she had lost the only adult person who had seemed to care what happened to her. Having regained her health to some extent during the past year, she began to not eat or sleep. By early 1967, she was far too underweight and was facing the world with failed health and voice and no money. She had to sell her house to meet back taxes, and she spent the rest of her life almost constantly changing hotel rooms. Eventually, during 1968, she even had to face letting her beloved children, Lorna and Joe, go to stay with their father for a while as a break from her ill health and troubles.

Although she remained in the public eye as a performer, Judy was unable to work as well as she used to do, and her reputation as a great performer took some severe knocks. This brought some adverse publicity from those who did not realise the truth behind her changing demeanour and failing voice, and a lot of people misunderstood her and the reasons behind her actions. This became accentuated when those few people who had been her friends during former years began to turn away from her and leave her alone. As a result less reliable factions gathered around her, and her last few years were sad, lonely, and demoralising. As she so often said: "It's lonely being 'a legend' ."

In December 1968, Judy became engaged to a New York discotheque manager, Mickey Deans. They were married in London in March 1969. She had welcomed his cheerful company and his assurance that, if they married, he would look after her and she would not have to work again unless she really wanted to do so. Sadly, her new marriage came too late to help her failing health, and she continued not to eat enough to keep her well. She was found dead in their rented home in London on 22 June 1969. A post-mortem revealed she had the equivalent of six Seconal sleeping tablets in her system and no food. This, together with her generally frail condition, was considered to have been sufficient to cause her death, although she had survived similar accidentally high quantities in the past.

Her husband flew her body back to New York, and twenty thousand people filed past her casket in the Memorial Chapel. One newspaper headlined it as "Judy's People Didn't Forget" and later as "All Night Vigil for Judy." One critic who had known her work for many years correctly commented: "She has left a void that will never be filled." A year later, Sir Richard Attenborough ended a speech to Judy's memory with these words: "She brought something that no one else has ever equalled. She brought something in her way which was unique and our profession will never, ever be quite the same because she was a member of it. All who follow her have to bear that very, very, very hard comparison of Judy Garland—anybody who sings, anybody who holds an audience in the palm of their hand with such consummate ease, with such magic, with such sincerity, with such love and such truth. She is, was, always will be 'Miss Show Business'."

My Life over the Rainbow

Chapter 1

I woke up in a hospital ward. I could not imagine how I came to be there, because I could not remember being ill, and I wondered: *What on earth am I doing here? What has happened to me now?*

The surroundings were extremely beautiful for a hospital. I cannot really describe the walls, except that the whole atmosphere was diffused with softly beautiful colours and there were flowers and soft perfumes everywhere. There seemed to be a number of people in various parts of the room, and in each instance someone seemed to be bending over the occupant of a bed to see how they were. From time to time, someone came and bent over me. I felt so relaxed and sleepy that I did not feel I had it in me to say anything. I just kept drifting away and drifting awake and drifting away again. Somehow, although I vaguely wondered how I came to be there, it did not seem to matter very much, except that I was sleeping.

After I seemed to have drifted asleep and awake, on and off, for I do not know how long, I next awoke to find a very kindly lady leaning over me. She asked how I was feeling. I replied, "Very well, thank you," which must have seemed a little foolish, otherwise why was I in hospital? She said to me, "Are you feeling a little more wide awake now?" and I said, "Yes, I think so. Why am I here?" She said to me, very gently and carefully, "I have to explain to you, my dear, that you have passed into the spirit world. You are no longer on earth."

My God! I thought, *How did I get here? What has happened? I don't remember an accident!* Then she explained to me that I had simply passed over.

My next question was, "My God! Mickey and my kids! What are they going to do? What can I do about them?" She told me not to worry, that they were being looked after as well as possible and that there was nothing I could do except to relax and get better.

"But I'm not ill!" I exclaimed. "I feel quite all right!"

Then she told me that I had been very unwell for a very long time and that quite often in my sleep I had, in fact, already been partly visiting the spirit world. I did not remember any of that, and I thought, *This sounds a load of nonsense.*

"No, my dear," she said. "You see, you have several layers of consciousness and that part of you that has always remained in the spirit world has been visiting here more clearly and closely than you can, at the moment, recollect. Because your whole body has been so tired for so long, we have been expecting you. Several times in your sleep, for quite a long period, you have almost reached us but have woken up again."

I found this extremely difficult to believe or to understand. I began to wonder whether I was in the middle of a confused dream. It was not an unpleasant dream, because everything around me seemed to be restful and beautiful, but what she was saying did not make any sense, and I began to think, *Garland, either you are having a strange dream or you are going off your head!*

I tried to take it quietly and slowly, and I tried hard to absorb all that was happening. I looked around me and asked, "Who are all these people?" I was told, "They are others who have passed here in circumstances similar to yours. You have all come here after long periods of extreme tiredness and weakness. Therefore, you have all come here in a very gentle way and, in a gentle way, you will be getting better. Some people who come here by a violent, unexpected death have to be looked after in a different way and in a different kind of place. As you have all come peacefully and gently, without realising what has happened, your body has been preparing you for this for quite a long while. So your transition from earth life to spirit life has been a gentle one, and all you have to do now is to go back to sleep until you feel really rested and then you will feel fine."

I felt fine there and then, except that I was concerned. I was

2

concerned for Mickey, I was concerned for my children, and I was a little bit concerned for myself, because I had not visualised coming here for a very much longer time than this! I had just started out on a new life with Mickey. I was about to have a visit from my daughter, Lorna, whom I had been longing to see for such a long time. So what was I doing here, and what could I possibly do here, and why had I come? All these questions kept going around in my mind. Yet somehow, although I kept asking them and I kept wanting answers, part of me kept on saying, "Don't worry, dear! Don't worry, dear! Just go back to sleep." Whether it was my subconscious saying, "Don't worry, dear. Go back to sleep," or whether it was the healing forces that were around me, I don't know, but back to sleep I went, and I was later told that it was for a number of months of your time on earth.

When I fully awoke I had completely lost the former tiredness, and I felt a need to be moving and asking questions.

I found that I seemed to be wearing a sort of floating garment that had all sorts of beautiful, shimmering colours and looked very different from the little cotton nightie I remembered I had been wearing when I went to bed on earth. I thought, *Why am I wearing this; how did I get here and what do I do now?*

I knew that I had not been feeling too well just recently, but I had not been feeling all that awful, and I had been having a fairly easy time. Mickey and I had been out and about visiting people and going to parties. I had been feeling a little bit tired, but no more than I had been feeling for some while, and I could not understand how I could have "passed over." I began to think back as to what I might have been doing. I recollected that I had gone to bed earlier than usual because I had a sore throat and a headache and I thought that it would be better to try and sleep it off. I had left Mickey downstairs with friends, I thought when I looked back. Then I realised that I must have fallen asleep, because I seemed to remember waking up in bed and feeling absolutely terrible. I did not quite know what I wanted to do, so I thought I had better head straight for the bathroom, which I did. When I got there, I stood undecided between the toilet and the hand basin. I think that is when I must have passed out and, possibly, passed here, because I do not remember anything more. I began considering how I could have passed out in the bathroom

3

when I had been feeling comparatively all right when I went to bed. I decided this had to be the first thing to try and find out about myself before I went any further.

I looked around for the lady who had tried to reassure me each time I had woken up, and I found that she was already by my side. "We have to wait for you, my dear, to decide when you are ready to start asking questions," she explained to me very kindly. She smiled at me and nodded towards what I could now see was a doorway. We went through this doorway, and I found myself in an absolutely beautiful world of nature at its most perfect. It was peaceful, birds were singing, the trees seemed to be a vibrant and almost translucent green, the atmosphere was soft and slightly perfumed. It was neither hot nor cold; it just felt perfect. There were flowers growing, there were little furry animals going about their daily activities—and no people. At least, when I say "no people," there did not seem to be any people. But the moment I thought "no people," I began to see that there were more people around me than I had previously noticed. They were wearing similar garments to mine, but their colours were intermingled differently. Each one was individual in some respect and everyone seemed to be as confused as I was as to what they were doing, where they were going, and why they were here. I was told that they were all souls who had recently awakened, as I had done, from their beds in the spirit world hospital, where we had all recovered our health, and that they, like myself, were all on their way to their first "voyage of discovery."

I felt I could not begin to go anywhere until I had found out how I got there from going into the bathroom. Then it was explained to me that, just as I had done so many times before, I had inadvertently taken too many sleeping pills. I tried to remember whether this could have been so. I could recall going to bed, and I could remember taking my usual two pills. I could also remember that I did not seem to be doing too well with them, but I could not recall taking any more. I tried going back in my mind and then realised that I might have woken up and thought that I had not been to sleep and taken two more pills. The lady nodded kindly at me. "In fact, my dear, you took three lots of pills in your confusion."

I looked at her, staggered. "I don't remember doing that!"

"You have done that in the past, my dear. If you recall, there have been a number of occasions when you have slept for very many hours and people have been concerned about you."

"Yes," I said, "but that has only been because I have slept a bit longer than usual."

"Not necessarily, my dear," she explained. "There have been a number of occasions when you have not remembered waking up and taking more pills. You have gone back to what has been, in your confusion, a very, very heavy sleep. This is why you have sometimes slept for a longer time than usual. When you have woken up, you have felt so much better for your long sleep because, fortunately, your system had become so accustomed to your sleeping pills that it did not react too badly against them. But they were too strong for you, much too strong for you to have taken so many. In the past, your body succeeded in overcoming them, but this last time—and it was not the first time you have taken so many of those pills on an empty stomach—it was just too much for you. That is how you came to pass here. It had a much too severe reaction on your internal organs, and it brought you to us, as it did, in fact, nearly bring you to us several times before in recent months."

You can imagine my reaction to this information! I thought, *My God! They're going to say I've committed suicide. My poor kids! What can I do about them?* The lady said to me, "My dear friend, do not be concerned. Your children know you far too well to accept that you would ever have taken your own life. They know you have made past mistakes with your pills. They will know that you may have done it again. They will not blame you in any way, and as long as your children know that you are in good hands— and they will because they do each have their beliefs—you need not worry."

That's all very well, I thought to myself. *That's what I have always been told in my life. Don't worry, it will all work out all right in the end.* But I had found in the past that, whenever I was told not to worry, there was usually a king-size headache on its way, and I began to wonder what was going to hit me this time. After forty-seven years of being told not to worry and nearly always finding there was really a very good reason to worry, I began to wonder what this next worry was going to be! With that attitude, I decided that the best thing to do would be to try and forget about it for the moment but to be prepared.

"Well, where do we go from here?" I asked. My friendly lady explained, "I have been appointed to help you through your first stages here. If you would like to come with me, I would be only too pleased to show you some of the beauties of our world before I start showing you your first steps toward your future life." With that she took me beyond the little glade in which we were standing out into what seemed to be open sunshine.

As I stood and gazed at a continuously unfolding vista of mountains and valleys and trees and all the other beauties of a perfectly beautiful countryside, I could occasionally see people walking on the paths and I realised that there did not seem to be any effort or physical fatigue to their walking.

As I walked farther out into the sunshine, I felt slightly different from the way I had felt when I had emerged from the hospital. I could not explain in what way I felt different. It was not that I felt any better or happier or healthier or more relaxed, I just felt slightly different. I asked my companion and she explained to me that I was gradually being adjusted to the different vibrations on which I would be existing in "the world of the spirit." This word *vibrations* did not mean very much to me, and I suppose I must have looked as confused as I felt. "I do realise how difficult this must seem to you, my dear, but I will try and explain to you, as basically as possible, the manner in which we all exist here.

"On earth you think of *vibration* in the way, perhaps, you can tap a tuning fork and listen to it *vibrating*. If you watch it vibrate, it looks a little different while the sound of the vibration is coming from it, because it is, in itself, vibrating. All life vibrates all the time. The human body is vibrating, although you are not aware of it. An animal is vibrating, a tree is vibrating, a plant is vibrating. You cannot see it, but it is happening. We exist here, as you existed in the physical world, on a vibrational level, but the vibrations are different. Ours here are very much lighter, higher, quicker, faster, however you like to put it.

"Your own personal vibration on leaving the hospital was an intermediary vibration of leaving the earth and waking up in the spirit hospital. As you spent your period of time sleeping and gradually recovering in the hospital, your vibrations changed, and as you now leave the hospital to take your first steps forward into the world of the spirit, your vibrations change slightly again. You will find that, as I take you through the different parts of our world, from one environment to another, you will change your vibrations slightly in order to exist comfortably in that area.

"In the physical world, for example, you would put on a coat to go from a hot room into a cold street, or you would take off your coat to come from a cold street to a hot room. This is similar to what you do here. We do not have extreme heat and cold here in the way you know it in the physical world, but we have different areas of existence. Some people can exist very comfortably in some areas that would not be so comfortable for you. Therefore you may have to put on some form of protection to go through an area in which others are, possibly, quite comfortable. You have just moved from an area of transitory sickness into an area of health. Therefore, you have lost one small item of protectiveness. As I take you further forward, you will gradually be adjusting to each environment to which I take you; and I shall be taking you through many, many environments in order to give you some idea of the different kinds of existence that there are here."

As there was little I could do about my present situation, I decided that, for the time being, I would have to try and make the best of it. This was something that, of course, I had been doing for the larger part of my life. There were many highs and lows in my earth life, a great deal of happiness and a great deal of unhappiness. Sometimes the one seemed to exceed the other. There were times in my life when I felt that all I had been through in the past was a build up for something happier and better that had arrived in my pathway at a certain juncture in my life. But I usually found that I had not gone very far along that pathway before something else happened to stop me short, knock me down, and once again, I would be back to a feeling of desperation and despair and "where do I go from here?" The fact that I had thought that I was happy with my new life with Mickey, that I was about to be reunited with at least one of my children and, hopefully, with the others before too much longer, and then I suddenly found myself transported to this unexpected situation was something to which I was finding it difficult to adjust; the more so because, despite the fact that everything around me was very peaceful and beautiful and I had a very kindly and gentle companion, I felt totally lost. I was not in my usual clothes; I was not in my usual place of being. It was a lot to accept, as were some of the things I was being told, yet I was about to embark on being shown a whole new world. I had always hoped, in my heart, that when we died, we would all continue to be individual, intelligent creatures, but I had also been a little fearful of what might be over my famous rainbow. Now here I was over it and about to be confronted with it! I had a peculiar feeling. I know this must sound strange to you, considering I had left my physical body in your world, but I can only describe it to you as a strange feeling in the pit of my stomach as I set forth on what was to prove to be the strangest adventure that I had ever encountered, even as Dorothy on the way to Oz.

II

The scene below me gradually began to change as my guide and helper took me forward with her.

As we walked along a path which took us past trees and streams and birds, I became aware of other things. I had heard birds on earth and had thought that some of them were lovely little creatures, but I had never been much aware of their backgrounds and why they were singing. I came to realise, as I walked along here, that the birds were trilling melodies that not only sounded very beautiful but that seemed to have thoughts and purposes behind them that I could understand. I found this incredible. There was a joyousness and a beauty that I had never before experienced in nature. Even the flowers that we encountered as we walked through a woodland glade seemed to be vibrating music. This was not loud or intrusive, but I somehow became aware of the inner soul of the flower as I also did with the trees and the little animals that were scurrying around. I began to see the animals in a different way, as though they were individuals and not just some furry little balls that were moving around on the ground. I suddenly realised that I felt in tune with all these songs and sounds and beauties of nature in a way that I had never been able to feel in tune with anything surrounding me in my life on earth.

Suddenly we came upon a little stream, and my friend said to me, "Walk in the water." I did not fancy this idea very much. I had only just started on my journey, and what was the point in getting my feet wet? Then I realised that I had not got any shoes on my feet, so I walked into the water and it was beautiful. It was soft and warm and yet refreshing. We walked gently through the stream for a little way until we came to a place where the stream and the pathway divided. My guide left me to decide which way we were to go, which was a bit confusing because I had no idea! As I stepped out of the water I realised that my feet were no longer wet. I began to wonder whether this was all a dream and whether I was in Oz after all instead of the next world! Then my helper, whose name I later discovered was Doreen, explained to me that, in our present world, although everything looked very much as it was on earth, everything had its own dimension, its own vibration of existence. Once I had removed myself from a particular item, such as the water, I was no longer sharing the water's vibration, and therefore, although I could still see it and hear it, I had removed my form of existence from its form of existence and so I no longer had it with me. I stopped and thought about that, and I tried to assure myself that, yes, that did make some sense. But, although it made sense on the one hand, I was still feeling very confused about it on the other, and now I had to make a decision as to which way we were going to go!

One path led us into a more deeply forested area and the other into a very bright sunlight. That brought me up short because, on earth, if I spent a lot of time in bright sunlight, my skin usually came up in bumps. On the other hand, I loved to see the sunshine, without the prickly heat, and I was not too happy at going into a dark forest; I stood and dithered until my guide—and friend as she was by now—explained to me, "Try and make the decision by forgetting all the hang-ups that you had on earth. Remember that sunlight will not bring out any skin irritations here. It is not hot sunlight, it is just a brighter light."

That made up my mind for me. There was no way I was going into that darker area if I could avoid it and go out into the light and not get burned. So I said, "Right! We'll go that way!" and she replied, "You have just made one of your first decisions here and it happens to be the right one." She went on to explain

9

to me that, had I gone into the darker area, I would have gone into a much heavier vibration and would have had to immediately put on a different cloak of protection around me from the one that I was already wearing. Let me explain here that she referred to the invisible protection that she had mentioned earlier. So we turned towards the bright light and went out into it.

After the comparative shade in which we had been, it was like walking out into a blinding, golden light of intense sunshine. There was a form of glare, against which I had to shade my eyes for a few moments, but there was no intense heat. It was still a warm, comfortable, perfumed atmosphere, and as my eyes became adjusted to the light, I realised that I was not actually adjusting my eyes to the glare, as I had originally thought that I was doing. I tried to decide what it was that I was adjusting. My friend Doreen explained that I was, in fact, adjusting my whole vibration to the brilliant light. She took me across to where others were sitting or walking and quietly talking in little groups in this very bright place, and she suggested that we sit and wait for a few moments for what was about to take place.

As I adjusted to my surroundings, I looked around and tried to decide where we might now be. I had got to the stage where almost anything could happen, and, frankly, I could not help but, to some degree, compare my present situation with that of Dorothy in *The Wizard of Oz*. I began to wonder whether I had, somehow or other, gotten myself into some fantastic dream as a result of my sleeping pills or, possibly, the temperature that I had been running when I went to bed. I did not feel like talking to anybody at that point, so I just sat there and looked at the others. Then I realised that they seemed to be equally bewildered. Some were talking to each other, but I came to realise that, probably, they were talking to someone who had befriended them in much the same way as Doreen had befriended me. Nobody seemed to be particularly familiar with his surroundings. Then I realised that we were forming a semicircle and that, apart from the doubts and the bewilderment that I picked up from the others who seemed to be sharing my situation, there was an air of expectancy on the part of our guides and helpers.

In the film of *The Wizard of Oz*, Dorothy wakes up over the rainbow, having been hit on the head on earth. She is confronted, amongst other things, with the sight of a large coloured ball of light coming towards her. When the ball stops, she is suddenly confronted with the vision of a very beautiful good witch, who is played in the film by Billie Burke. When an exceptionally strong light seemed to appear in the distance in the atmosphere of the already strong light in which we were and began to come towards us, I could not help thinking to myself, although I did not say anything to anybody, *Here comes Billie Burke!*

As the strong light came to rest in our midst, I could see that there was a very beautiful person in that light. I can only try and explain it to you in what I feel to be inadequate words. The visitor was a human being, but everything about the person radiated intense love, intense purity, intense wisdom. This person seemed to be neither male nor female, and I say that in the nicest possible way. It was almost like seeing one of the gods in mythology, but it was not as basic as that, and it transpired that we were being visited by an exceptionally high teacher in the world in which I now was.

He greeted us all and told us that we had all reached the point of having come through the transition from one life to the next and that we were about to go on our individual pathways of experience. He went on to explain, "There has been a time, a long time ago, I cannot say how long because time does not exist here as it does on earth, when I was sitting where you are now sitting and I had to make all the decisions and all the discoveries that you will have to encounter in your different ways. I gradually reached a point where I had to make a big decision as to whether I was going to remain in the world to which I had now become adjusted or whether I was going to take a big step forward towards yet another world. I came to discover, as I experienced and experienced and changed and experienced further, that there are innumerable worlds of existence in this land of the spirit. It will very much depend on how each one of you handles your experiences here as to which world you remain in and for how long. I come from a very, very long way away from the world in which you are now presently existing, and I have to come through many forms of existence to reach you as I speak to you.

"When I leave you, I will be returning to the world in which I now exist and which is very different from the one in which you now are. I assure you, that need not worry you at all, because it is exceptionally beautiful. It is even more beautiful than the one you are presently experiencing, and I have come to be where I now am only as a matter of personal choice. You will each adjust to, and remain in, the world in which you now are just as long as you wish to do so. It will not be, as it was when you departed from the land of earth, at an unexpected time, a time that some of you will have waited overlong for and from which others will have been removed quicker than expected or even wanted. Any changes that you experience here, from one area of existence to the next, will come about through your own efforts and your own wishes and decisions. That, my dear children, removes from all of you the biggest burden that hangs over any human being on the world of earth.

"I give you my blessing and my love, and I know that each and every one of you, in the time that lies ahead, will go through a tremendous number of changes and decisions and interests. Knowing from here the kind of people that you all are, which is why you are gathered together in front of me as a unit at this time, you are all people who have suffered in the earth world in similar ways to each other, who had similar natures in the earth world, and who will adjust similarly here.

"There are other people who come here from the world of earth who have had different attitudes, different natures, less sensitivity, whom I could not, at this time, even begin to approach. I could not reach the depths in which they are mentally, and they could not possibly see me. I would say to you that you are all people who, in the world of earth, were born with exceptionally sensitive natures, with exceptionally loving natures. You gave a lot of love, you expected a lot of love, and when you did not get it, you struggled with it, and you tried to live with it in your own individual ways. The manner in which some of you tried to live with it was often misunderstood, often caused you a great deal of heartache and sometimes, unintentionally, caused heartache to others. But the fact that it was unintentional means that you have come here with your souls intact. You do not have to go through, as so many human beings have to do when they come here, a period of readjustment to help you to be removed from all the erroneous thoughts that you have pulled around you during

12

your time on earth. You are able to step immediately forward into the pure, clear light and air of our world and to begin immediately to progress to your future life.

"Sadly, there are many human beings who are unable to do this. In the world of earth they cause deep distress to their fellow human beings with their lies, with their violence and their viciousness and their wish to harm others, with their greed, and with their complete selfishness. Most of you have, in your own way, created beauty in the world of earth. Some of you have been public figures in various professions, who have tried to uplift and help your fellow citizens. There are others among you who were never famous, but you worked and toiled in a small way, largely unknown, to help others, to bring a smile here and a helping hand there. Here, in this world, the famous and the unfamous mingle together on similar vibrations, and nobody here is treated any differently. The only way in which you are treated is how you are in your soul. You souls who are before me now are beautiful within. With that as a start, you should not find any problems ahead of you that you cannot surmount.

"I will visit you all again when you have had more experience here. In the meantime, I give to you the love and the blessing and the encouragement of all those beings in the world of the spirit who have at one time stood where you are now standing and who are now in far higher places." With that, he gradually faded back into the distance, or perhaps I should say he faded away. That is the only way I can put it.

I sat there completely dumbfounded. I thought, *I don't think I could have dreamed all that eloquence.* I turned round to Doreen, who was smiling at me in an amused way.

She said, "I got your thought about *The Wizard of Oz*. I'm not so far removed from your recent world not to know what you are talking about, and I suppose it must have looked like that to you. But you will find, as we go along your pathway, that it will be a very, very different experience from all those problems you encountered in Oz. But, you know, when Frank L. Baum wrote that classic story for children, he was not so far wrong, because each of those characters were seeking for something that they already had without realising it; and you, my dear friend, have in you all that you will ever need to succeed here.

13

"You succeeded on earth, in many ways, far beyond the average. Where you feel that you failed and where, possibly, you did fail, was because your inner sensitivity could not cope with the harshness of the realities of the world of earth. This caused something inside of you to snap. Where that snap, or breakage, occurred within your soul, it meant that you always had the conflict of one part of your soul rubbing against the other. That caused you many of your difficulties, and although, on the surface, many of your difficulties were caused by others, it was this inner division within yourself that caused you the greatest difficulties. In order to help you to go forward here in the way in which I know you can, we have to show you how some of those difficulties arose, how you coped with them, and how, in some ways, you did not cope with them. Because until you have this picture of your inner self completely clear, you will find it less easy to communicate and experience here and also to go forward here.

"Now, my dear, I do not wish to make you feel that you are going to spend the larger part of your existence here in soul searching. You are not. You will be going forward with me to see other parts of this world. You will be meeting all sorts of people. You will be sharing their experiences. You will be creating with and for others. But each time it seems an appropriate moment for you to stop and look back and regard and consider one of the things that may have confused your earth life, that is when I will encourage you to stop and spend time thinking until you have got that particular aspect clearer in your mind and can put it behind you and be ready for the next step forward. Having said that to you, I think you have had enough to try and understand for the time being. I will leave you to digest what I have said and to have a little rest. Then I will take you forward to your first individual step towards your future."

III

My friend and companion, as she had become, left me in what appeared to be a small glade. There was sunlight filtering through light foliage. There were grass and flowers, and I noticed what appeared to be little, bell-like flowers. As I touched them

14

gently, they seemed to respond by vibrating towards me, and I felt better for having touched them.

I began to take stock of myself. I had already noticed that I had no shoes on my feet and that I was wearing a different kind of garment from the one I had been wearing on earth, which was probably just as well as I could hardly have mingled with all those people just wearing a little cotton nightie! We all seemed to have been wearing similarly shimmering garments. My own, as I looked at it again, seemed to be a shimmering, glistening mixture of different shades of pink, blue, yellow, green, silver, and gold. It was really very beautiful. My feet looked as they had always done; so did my hands, and I felt complete and solid. Yet I realised I could not be as I had always been because, surely, I had left my physical body behind on earth, as we all do! But it was a big relief to me to find that I still resembled myself as I was used to being. The world around me seemed to be something that I could accept and recognise, despite it having its variances. I had never felt better, except that I still felt mentally confused and a little bit lost. After all, I had left my children and my new husband behind on earth, and so what was the point of being here at this juncture of what appeared to be a continuing life?

It was then that I stopped to consider. *Well, if you're here, Judy, and all those other people are here, your parents must be here. Your sister Susie must be here. All those people whom you have known in the past who have died must be here!* I thought, *Jack Kennedy will be here! I wonder whether I could ask to see him?* He had been a strong influence in my life at a time when I needed someone to turn to for advice. Although he had become president of the United States of America and had died in November 1963 in such a terrible way, by assassination, he had always said to me, "Judy, just because I have become president, it doesn't mean that I cease to be a friend. If there is anything I can do for you, at any time, please call me." He had even arranged for any telephone call from me to be put directly through to him at the White House. "Just ask for me and you'll be put through," he had said, and his advice had always been sane, common sense during a time when everything else around me had been like living in a mad house. He was the only person who had kept me sane during a very bad period, until he had died so tragically. When he died, I felt I had lost the one reliable person to whom I could turn. It seemed a good idea to ask whether I could see him now.

When Doreen returned she was greeted by me with the request: "Would it be possible for me to see Jack Kennedy?" She looked a bit surprised at this blunt request. I went on to tell her that he had been a well-known politician in my country, that he had become president of the United States of America, but that he had remained a personal friend, and that, as his judgment in the past had always seemed very sound and sensible, I wondered whether I could discuss my present situation with him. "Well, dear," Doreen explained kindly, "I am sure he will be pleased to see you when the time comes, but I really do not think this is the point when you should be asking him for his advice. There is a lot for you to learn and discover about this world of the spirit that he may not yet be in a position to understand himself. I think it will be wiser for you to come with me a little bit further along the way." She went on to ask me whether there were any others I would like to meet.

"My parents are here and my sister Susan. . . ." I said hesitantly.

"Well, dear, we'll have to see what can be done. In the meantime, I would suggest that the next thing for you to do is to stop and consider why you arrived here."

"I've already done that," I replied, "and you've told me it was because I took too many sleeping pills on an empty stomach."

"Yes," she replied, "but what caused you to get into that state in the first place? What caused you to be taking sleeping pills? What initially caused the condition which brought you here as soon as it did?"

I felt a little bit confused by this. "What do you mean?" I asked her. "I came here because I had been taking sleeping pills and because I had not been eating. You told me that yourself. Otherwise, I don't know how I did come here!" I exclaimed a little bit truculantly, because I felt she was not being particularly helpful at that point.

"What I want you to do, my dear," she said, "is to sit down quietly and say to yourself, 'How did I come to be taking sleeping pills in the first place?' "

"That's easy!" I said. "I was given sleeping pills when I was only sixteen years old by the doctors for MGM."

"Well then," she said, "I think this is where you have got to start in your rethinking. Get back to those years and say to yourself, 'Why did they give me sleeping pills? Why was it necessary for me to have them?'"

"Overwork," I told her without any hesitation.

"Overwork from what?" she asked me.

"Filming schedules," I said. "Too much work, too little play, too little food. I couldn't sleep. They gave me sleeping pills."

"The first thing I want you to ask yourself," Doreen went on, "is why you could not sleep. Not that you were overworked, that you got overtired, but why could you not sleep?"

I thought it was very strange for me to be asked, at this stage in my arrival in the next world, why during my early years at MGM, I started not to be able to sleep. It had always seemed so obvious to me that I had not been sleeping because I was over-worked and overstrained in a number of ways.

I said as much to my companion, who went on to explain to me that, in order to make any progress in the world in which I now was, I would have to go back in my mind to find out what started all my troubles. She went on to remind me that I had been a relatively happy little girl with my family. Admittedly, I had not had any outside friends, and that had made me a lonely child in many respects, but I had, basically, not been consciously un-happy until I reached the age of around sixteen years, which was when girls start to come towards maturity and to have different views from those they have had before.

She reminded me that it had been made more difficult for me by the fact that during those formative years from when I was about thirteen to fourteen years of age, I had been removed from any parental guidance and put under the firm disciplinarians of the film studio, and whereas some parents might have objected, my own mother had let it happen. This had meant that I had not really had anyone to whom I could turn and this had begun to cause within me, to a far sharper degree, the feeling of insecurity that I was developing as I reached the tender teenage years to-wards maturity.

She recollected that by the time I was fifteen or sixteen years of age, I was beginning to feel increasingly unhappy because the

17

friends I had at the studios, such as Mickey Rooney and Freddie Bartholomew and Lana Turner, were just that little bit older than I was. They were going out and seeking lives of their own and being allowed to do so, whereas I was being restricted by the studio chiefs in order to try and keep me as a little girl, with a little girl look and a little girl image, as long as possible. This was brought about, to some extent, by the need to use me in *The Wizard of Oz* as a little girl when I was already reaching the age of seventeen years, so that the studios needed to keep me younger longer than some of the others. Because of this and all the restrictions that were being imposed upon me, it began to form in my own mind a very confused image of myself. I did not quite know what age group I was supposed to be in, and that began to form a feeling of insecurity and, to some extent, instability within me. I knew it was no good going to my mother with my problems, and there was nobody at the studio with whom I could particularly discuss them. It all began to churn up within me, and that, she explained, was why I began not to sleep well in the first place.

"It was, of course, aggravated by the way you were being kept on a strict slimming diet and not being allowed to have as much food as your body required. It was also aggravated by the work schedules on an empty stomach and no sleep. But it basically stemmed within yourself from the fact that you were, literally, not being allowed to develop in the way anybody else in your age group should have been allowed to develop.

"Because of your kind of personality and your own very refreshingly innocent outlook, you were kept as a child longer than some of the other child performers who were allowed to move towards more sophisticated, mature roles.

"It was this feeling of indecision and insecurity within yourself which contributed, in later years, to you not really knowing where you belonged or with whom you belonged. There were people who came into your life who had seen you on the screen, acting as a child, and who expected that kind of personality from you. There were others who, moving in the sophisticated show business world and anticipating the kind of sophisticated background that they presumed you to have had at the studios, expected you to be far more mature than you had actually been allowed to become.

18

"Between these two approaches and the confusion and uncertainty yourself, there developed within you a complex and an attitude to life that confused you and others for the rest of your earth life and was the basic cause of almost all of your future problems.

"Having said that to you, my dear, I would like you to stop and consider for a moment how it is that you have managed to come to this world without a blemish on your soul, on your character, even on your outlook, because, although your outlook is, at the moment, blindfolded and to some extent confused, it is not in any way vicious or malignant or hurtful to others.

"Within yourself you feel deeply hurt, and you feel you have been very badly let down. Over the years, you have been badly hurt and badly let down. As a direct result of these hurts and let downs, you have often struck out at others in a feeling of desperation and loneliness and let down, but whatever you have said and whatever you have done has never been caused by an inner viciousness within yourself. It has been caused by your need to feel that you had to try and defend yourself, to try and not let those people hurt you any more.

"It has not been, in the way some people have come here, with a deeply inset viciousness that has been allowed to creep within your soul. That is why you are in the position you are now in, to go forward immediately into a more beautiful life. But we have to get deep down within the inner troubles that started your early life problems before we can begin to peel away from your innermost being the kind of things that have cramped your soul in so many ways. Then you will find, my dear, that all the facets and beauties that lie within you will begin to become much more clear to those around you.

"You have looked at the garment you are wearing and you have said to yourself 'this is a very beautiful thing, whatever it is.' It is your soul, my dear, and the beauties that lie within you creates those colours. If you think it is a beautiful garment now, it is nothing compared with the garment that you will be wearing in not so long a time, when you have finally managed to work through in your mind all the different problems that cramped your soul in your earth life.

"I would also like you to stop and consider for a moment

whether, now that I have explained to you the cause of your lack of sleep and the tensions and also the misunderstandings that began to follow, you can accept that explanation or whether you have anything else you would like to ask me before we go any further."

I felt dumbfounded and confounded by this woman, whom I had never seen before until I opened my eyes in the hospital, who seemed to be able to read my thoughts and who knew so much about me. She later explained to me that she had no wish to intrude upon my life and feelings but that she was trying to help me, and, in so doing, she would have to try and penetrate my thoughts to some extent in order to steer me through my confused reactions and onto the right pathway.

I said to her, "Well, the only thing I can think of is that, having failed to get my feelings across to my mother and to the studio, I began to feel that I had to try and find somebody that I could express myself to and be understood. I think it was that which started me wondering whether it would not be a better idea to try and find myself a reliable husband who could be turned to for advice and understanding. But the studios were insisting that I go out only with those people they had chosen for me as escorts, and I began to feel so completely trapped within myself.

"I think I can go back now and realise that this idea of being trapped was beginning to form a feeling of claustrophobia within me, so that I didn't know who I was or who I was expected to be. Looking back now, I think this is probably why my first marriage failed, because the studio was wanting to keep me as an ingénue and my husband expected me to behave as a mature person. I really did not know who was the real me, and I think this may possibly have been the beginning of my problems, although I had started not to be able to sleep long before I met my first husband, David Rose. I think that, probably, by the time I had met David, I was already reaching the point where I was beginning to be highly strung to some extent, but it was probably not already obvious to most people at that time. I know that when, shortly after our marriage, he accused me of being too immature and the studio later told me not to have the child that had been conceived on my honeymoon, as it would go against my public image that they had created around me, I felt torn inside, deeply

20

mortified, and deeply divided in my emotions.

"I did not know who to blame for all the trauma. I did begin at that time to blame my mother for, once again, simply referring me to the studio chiefs, and I began to blame David for not supporting me in my wish to have a child. I just felt that everything was crumbling away and falling apart within me. So when they started advising various tranquillisers, I accepted them, because I did not know what else to do. I couldn't think clearly."

"That, my dear," interrupted my friend Doreen, "was the beginning of your life's problems from then on."

"Well, that's pretty obvious," I said to her again, somewhat hurtfully I think, because I thought *Why is she just taking me through something that I know already?*

"I have to ask you to go back, my dear, because in the years that followed, you became so embroiled in all your nervous breakdowns and all the things that were happening around you that, over a period of time and without realising it, you began to see things slightly differently. Thus they became a little distorted in your mind and, therefore, as a memory. I have to try and get you back to just how things really were at that original period of time so that you can say to yourself, 'Where did all the faults lie? Was it all my fault or was it someone else's fault?'

"Having got you to go back and think of that period of time when you felt that the studio was cramping you, that your mother was being unhelpful, that your husband was not appreciating you, and when you had lost your first child and all the atmosphere that was being created around you left you with a feeling of acute loneliness, a feeling of having failed the child that you did not have, of having failed the husband you had hoped would love you beyond everything, we have reached your first complete nervous breakdown. It was from then onwards that you were unable, at certain periods of your life, to see things clearly. At times you saw things from a point of nervous hysteria in a way that was very different from that of another person who was able to view things more dispassionately.

"Having said that to you, I would now ask you to say to yourself, 'Why did my mother not listen to me? Why did she always refer me to the studio chiefs, and why did I always feel that it was my father to whom I could have turned had he lived?'

21

Because that *is* what you said to yourself for many years and that is why you tended to turn to men that you met who were older than you were and who you quite often wanted to take no more than a fatherly interest in you. You hoped you could discuss a problem with them. All too often they misunderstood and thought you were taking a personal interest in them as a future man in your life, which was not at all your thoughts and feelings. This was something you came up against over the years, yet it is something from which you never really learnt and which caused you to be misunderstood over and over again by some people. So go back to that period when you felt that your mother had failed you."

I had been asked where I had gone wrong with my sleeping habits so many times before, when I was on earth, by the various psychiatrists to whom I had been sent during my years at the studios when I had begun to feel so ill, so confused, so alone and so completely unable to cope with all that seemed to be happening around me that I sometimes began to feel that maybe I belonged in a mental institution instead of simply being sent to the rest home I had gone to from time to time ever since my first nervous breakdown.

I went, at that time, to a hospital in Boston, to which I returned at various times during the rest of my life. On each occasion, my visits there had been simply to try and overcome my nervous tensions and my sometimes hysterical reactions to things that were happening, to try and understand myself, to try and calm down my nervous hysteria, and to try and find out why it was that, every so often, I had these breakdowns in health. Although I had put it down to some extent to the fact that I was on a strenuous work program along with a strict slimming diet, I did realise that others at the studio were coping with equally strenuous schedules. Although not necessarily subjected to dieting, they were subjected to long hours and strenuous rehearsal periods, and I did wonder what it was within me that caused me to have these bad reactions. That is why I always willingly put myself into the hands of those who were accomplished doctors and psychiatrists in the hope that they would get to the bottom of my problem.

Of course, they had all started off with why did I go onto sleeping pills in the first place, and why did I blame my mother and the studios? We had all been through it so many times before without any particular conclusions having, in my opinion, been reached. I wondered why I should now, one more time, be asked to go back to that period.

Having come to the conclusion that the lady might possibly have a point, I thought I'd better try and cooperate. I tried to take myself back and, to my surprise, began to realise it was comparatively simple. Whenever I had done this before, I had always been a little confused about the whole situation, unable to recall everything clearly and, therefore, probably misleading the psychiatrist just as much as I had been misleading myself. I had never before had a really clear recollection of how it all began. This time, when I got myself back in my thoughts to when I was about seventeen years of age, which was around the time *The Wizard of Oz* was about to be released, I found that I could recollect my personal feelings at that time very vividly.

To me this was amazing. I had never, when I was on earth, ever believed it would be possible to go back in one's mind and see things completely clearly ever again, despite the fact that, every so often, there would be this, that, or the other individual who claimed to have the ability of total recall. I never did. Of course, in going back through my life, as I have now done here, I realise that there is not one living person in your world of earth who is truly capable of complete, total recall, although some do delude themselves that this is possible. In fact, they only recall what their own mind has seen and felt and heard. It is not necessarily as things happened to them, but only what they think they remember seeing, feeling, hearing. However, I digress now, because, in order to get my mother more clearly in focus, I have to go back to when I was around sixteen or seventeen years old, the period I was actually making *The Wizard of Oz*, after which I became, in the words of the studio, "a hot property."

It was around that period that my mother met her future husband. He was some years her senior, a not unpleasant man, but she was completely carried away with him and lost all interest, I thought, in me. We had never had what I felt was a close relationship. I had always felt that I had received far more love and understanding from my father, and, when my mother took me on stage tours on my own, she was very unkind to me. A very abrupt woman, she seldom went into any explanation or any endearments, and she always made sure that I was kept to a very rigorous and vigorous routine. Although we had never had a very stable family life, always moving from place to place, seldom staying anywhere for very long and seldom much in the way of money or comforts, I had always felt part of the family and happy until my dad died and my sisters left to get married. When I was left alone with my mother, she showed so little affection for me that I began to form the opinion that she did not really care for me at all. The fact that my father had always been very demonstrative to me showed, I felt, that he was the one, and not my mother, who truly loved me.

When I got to the studio and she simply handed me over, almost, to those in charge, although I went home to her every night, I really did not feel that I was getting much in the way of affection or even interest from her. I did try to get her interested, but she always seemed absent-minded about it all and not really to care, despite my explanations of what we had been doing all day at the studio.

When she met the man that she eventually married, when I was seventeen, she seemed to lose all interest in me. She was never there when I got in, and she was hardly ever there most of the times when I needed some sort of help. When they married and he moved in with us (he was some sort of engineer with not much money of his own and so he just moved in with mother and me), I felt as though I had been pushed out of my own home, because everything was geared to the new husband. The fact that it was my money that was maintaining the home did not seem to occur to either of them, and they still treated me very much as though I was a child and not entitled to any personal feelings. I was often told, "We're very lucky that you've found yourself a soft place at the studio. What have you got to complain about?" Whenever I mentioned my father, my mother would shut up like a clam, as though I had mentioned an unpleasant smell. I could never understand this, because, from where I had seen things as a child, he always seemed to be a happy, easy-going man, and it was my mother who had always been the serious one who would not let us do things that we wanted to do.

Looking at it with the gift of hindsight, I decided that that was, possibly, why I had not been sleeping. I just had not got anybody at all who truly loved me or who seemed to be showing any interest in me. I would lie awake at night and wish that my father was still living and that my mother had not remarried and that she would show a little more interest in what I was doing. I would ask myself where I could find somebody who would be more interested in me as a person. I think that started the sleepless nights, plus the tensions caused by the severe slimming diets when I was not allowed to eat at all, sometimes only liquids, and the very long working hours. Yes, I decided, that was probably where all my troubles started, and so I blamed my mother.

It was at this point that Doreen interposed with: "Why did you always feel that your father loved you more than did your mother?"

I said, "Well, he was always far more demonstrative. He would put his arm around me and cuddle me and kiss me on the top of the head. He would say things that made me laugh, and we would have long talks together. My mother never did any of those things."

"Yes," said Doreen, "but if you look at your life that followed, would you not say that, as you went through life, there were many people who wanted to put their arms around you and kiss you and make a fuss of you? But were they not, quite often, the people who found it easy to be demonstrative? Did you not often find that, when you really needed them, they were not there with the friendship that you thought they had for you? Whereas, there were others who did not demonstrate much at all, but, when you did turn round in trouble, they were more likely to be there."

I thought about this carefully. I had lived the sort of life where everyone seemed to fling themselves at me one moment and to disappear the next. I never really did know who truly loved me, who I could trust, who just loved the name "Judy Garland" or who really loved "Frances Gumm," which was my real name before it was changed to "Judy Garland" for professional purposes.

"You do have a point there," I acknowledged. "I do realise some people are more demonstrative than others and that I was always getting into trouble for being too demonstrative to people. But I was an outgoing person, and I just went towards people. I think, perhaps, my father may have been like that."

25

"Yes," interrupted Doreen again, "but you must stop and consider it from your mother's viewpoint before you go any further, because you have built up, in your heart and in your thoughts, a rancour against your mother which is more exaggerated than you realise, and far more distorted in your memory than you realise. I must ask you now to go back to the period when your father was very ill with meningitis, from which he subsequently died. Was it not during this period that you felt your mother was lacking any sort of sympathy or affection or understanding towards you, or even towards your father when he was so unwell?"

"That's it!" I said to her. "I remember now. I used to visit my father at the hospital. If my mother came, she didn't say anything. She used to stand there with me and not say anything to my poor father, who was lying in bed so ill. I used to try and put my arm round him and hold his hand and kiss him on the cheek, and she didn't do any of those things. She just walked away, silently. He wasn't able to say very much, because he was so ill and had a sort of fever, but I kind of felt that if I held his hand and kissed him, he'd get something from it. Even at that young age, I felt that that was possible, and I still feel that that is the sort of thing one should do to people you love, when they are unhappy or uncertain about life in any way. My mother never did that. She was always very upright and firm and quiet. I never got a word out of her when we left the hospital. I used to try and hang onto her hand sometimes, or her arm, and she usually shook me away and said, "Don't be silly." I found that very hurtful. I was missing my father and not getting any affection from my mother, who did not seem to be showing anything for my poor father."

"Yes," said Doreen. "Now I have to tell you something that you probably have not stopped to think about before. All you could think about, as a child, was what you saw and heard and, as a result, what you felt. But, you see, just as in later life, you found you were being misunderstood by many people, so were you, at that time, misunderstanding your mother and even your father. What you have to realise, my dear, is that, although your father was very demonstrative to you personally, it was because you were demonstrative to him. Because you loved him and you wanted to show him that you loved him, you always found it easy to go up to him and put your arms round his neck and kiss him. Because you did that to him, he returned your demonstrativeness.

"Your mother was a very undemonstrative woman, and your father was seldom demonstrative to her. He was not as demonstrative to your sisters as he was to you, but they did not need it, and, therefore, he did not offer it. He gave it to you because you clearly needed it, and he was the kind of person that could switch on and off towards someone. If he felt that that was the way they wanted it, that was the way he would provide it.

"It was this ambivalence in your father that upset your mother. She resented him giving you so much demonstrative love and affection and giving her so little. This built up a resentment within your mother against your father and, to some extent, against you. *She* was not going to fall all over you, no matter what happened, and she was not going to fall all over your father either, if he did not seem to want her love!

"At the time of your father's passing, they were really quite separate from one another. They had remained together in a very uncommitted sort of way, but they were not happy together, and you had not stopped to think of that. They had stayed together because, in those days, people did not separate as easily as in later years, but they were not happy together, and that turned your mother against you to some extent when you seemed to be getting all the love from your father that she felt she ought to have been getting."

I had never thought of it from that point of view, and I said, "Yes, but what about after my father had gone and there was just Mother and I touring around together? Why could she not have been a little more demonstrative then? I did try and be demonstrative to her, but she did not seem to want me to be. That is why I stopped and why I began to feel so repressed within myself, that there wasn't anybody who really cared about me."

"Your mother was a strange person in many ways. She had an in-built reserve. She was hurt at the way you had given all your love to your father, and she did not see why you were suddenly going to give it to her after he had gone. She felt that she was being used as second best. She also felt that the correct thing was to discipline a child who was on the stage. She felt she

27

had to make sure you did perform every night, no matter how you were feeling. She felt it should be imbued in any performer to be 'a trouper.' She did not think, as she should have done, that you were feeling the loss of your father very badly, that you were having to go out onto the stage alone, that is was no fun to face the sort of audiences you were facing, and that you needed some support and affection to go out there and perform.

"That is something, Judy, that endeared you to all the audiences you met in the years that lay ahead of you, that, whatever they gave you in the way of love, and they gave you a great deal of love, you could always respond to that love, even when you were feeling dreadfully unhappy and physically ill. You could pull something out of yourself and give it to those audiences because of the love that they poured out to you. What you needed to get you out onto any stage was someone in the wings who loved you. If your mother had loved you, or shown that she loved you, you would have gone out there and sung your heart out just to show her that you were doing it for her, irrespective of what was out there. That is what you did many times in later years, but it all stemmed from those years. You needed someone beside you and behind you to show you that they cared before you could go out there and perform to the best of your ability.

"Now then, when you got to the studios and your mother, as you felt, handed you over to the studio chiefs, it was simply because she felt that, as they were managing your career, they should take you over completely. It relieved her of a lot of responsibility that she did not feel she was capable of assuming, because, although your mother was basically an honest woman, she had no head for business any more than you had a head for business. She felt it was better to leave you in the hands of those who knew. When she met her next husband, it was something that carried her away mentally from you towards something she had been longing for for a very long time. Therefore, she tended to shut herself away from you and open up to the person who, she felt, was giving her the kind of loving attention she had wanted for such a long time and that she had not been receiving from your father for a number of years before he died.

"I am not saying that your mother was not at fault. She was at fault in a number of ways, but it does not make her into the gorgon that you built up in your mind. I am not asking you to do this at this moment, but, before we go much further, I would like you to let me arrange for you to see your mother, because I fully and firmly believe you would each gain something from meeting again and facing the situation more clearly as it appears from here. But, before you meet your mother again, I think one of the first things we ought to do is to try and help you to find your father. Would you like me to do that?"

That question came to me out of the blue and I thought to myself, *Judy! You're the biggest fool ever! Why didn't you think of this before? Why did you bring Jack into it when the first person you should have thought of is your father?* I said, "Yes, of course I would! Why didn't I think of that before?"

Doreen replied, "Because you are having to go back in your mind over so much that your first thought was of somebody whom you had known more recently to give you some sound advice. You had learned to put your father in the back of your mind as the years went by, although he was so predominant in your life in your early years. I think the first thing we must do, before we go any further, is to make our way gradually along the road towards your meeting your father. I want you to have a few experiences first. Then, when you meet him, you will have had some opportunity to assimilate more of the world in which you are now living, and it will also be helping your mind to adjust to the way you have to communicate here.

"You will have probably already realised that we tend to communicate in a slightly different way to the manner in which you communicate on earth. I can, if I wish, read your mind, and you could, if you wished, read mine, unless either of us are fully prepared to put up the kind of mental barrier that will prevent somebody from reading our minds. That is what we have to learn to do here by certain processes. If you happen to be with somebody with whom you have a very close understanding, you will probably be quite prepared to let them read part of your mind, but you may not be prepared to let them read all of it. Therefore, you have to learn to put an element of restraint on your mental processes so that your companions can only penetrate these as far as you want them to penetrate.

"Because I have been appointed to help you, I have vigorously penetrated only as far as is necessary in order to help you. I certainly would not have done so without the express permission of those who are in charge of your expansion here, because that would be tantamount to peeping through keyholes or listening at doors on earth. So, before we go much further, I want you to sort out your various thinking processes and the way you are going to manage your thoughts in future, because here thought is used far more frequently than words. You will find, after you have been here for some while, that you will not be forming words so completely and laboriously as these are formed on earth. You will simply flash a thought to somebody, and they will know precisely what you mean. You will not need a complete sentence or paragraph. The flashed thought will enable you to communicate precisely what it is you wish to convey, and a thought can be flashed back to you. Our communication processes here are so much easier and quicker than on earth. This is why, when you are in the right environment for your state of being, you are more in harmony with those around you in this world than ever on earth. If you say something to somebody on earth, it is so easy for you to be saying one thing and thinking or feeling another. You may be feeling particularly hurt over something and be unable to put it into words. Somebody thinks you have snapped at them, whereas you are really feeling very hurt or very lonely, or, possibly, you love somebody and you cannot actually tell them in a way they would understand. Here in this world, all those feelings come through without any difficulty and, therefore, there is less opportunity for misunderstanding each other. This is why, in order to live in any form of harmony, every individual here has to exist within the environment which is the most compatible to them.

"In saying that to you, I would explain that the environment is which you are at the moment is your environment, to which I am attuned in order to help you. That is why you are feeling so comfortable and peaceful and not unhappy, despite feeling confused and a little bit lost and wishing you had not left your husband and children behind you. In order to reach your father, you will have to move into a different environment to the one in which you are currently existing, because he is, basically, not so close to your state of being. Now, I am going to leave you to rest for a while and to think over all that we have been discussing."

IV

After Doreen had left me I decided that the best thing I could do was to go slowly through it all in my mind, so that I could adjust myself to the thought of meeting my father again for the first time after what had to be, in earth time, at least thirty-four years.

I realise there are many on earth who will not have met their relations for as long a time as that, including relations who are still on earth, and perhaps it is not such a shaking experience as it might seem. But to me, at that moment, when I realised that, after all that I had been through, I was about to meet my father again, it came as something of a surprise to find that, although I had welcomed the idea, I really had so little deep reaction to the suggestion.

Had I been approached with it in my twenties, I would have been so delighted I would have felt over the moon that at last I was going to be able to discuss everything with my father—"my dear dad," as I had thought of him in my mind—and get back to where I had been all those years ago, back with someone in whom I could put my complete faith and trust.

As the years had gone by, I had found that each other person in whom I had put my complete faith and trust had decided, after a period of time with me, that they had had enough and they wanted out. I felt that this was one thing that my father would, possibly, never have done. Then, as I got to my late thirties and early forties, I began to see life somewhat differently to the way I had seen it before. My complete trust in various people had taken so many severe knocks that I found it difficult, at times, to really feel I could put my complete trust in any human being that I encountered in my life.

Although I had begun to feel that, I had still, nevertheless, continued to put my trust in certain individuals who came into my life. I had hoped that they would prove to be as faithful and sincere as they had promised to be, but I no longer felt certain

31

that they would. I gave each of my husbands all the love that I had in me, and I hoped that they would give me theirs in return. But, latterly, I always had in the back of my mind the feeling of doubt that it would last.

The very word "husbands," in the plural, gives an impression of faithlessness to some extent, and I would like to say that, at no time in my life did I ever consider leaving my husband for another man. It was always my husband who had decided, for some reason or another within themselves, to leave me. I remained faithful to each man in my life. I had no extramarital relationships with anyone, and I always had a very strong belief in marriage vows.

It was only because, for one reason or another, my husband had left me and I faced the world alone again—and I found it exceedingly difficult to face the world alone—that I ever considered marrying again. It was only after I felt that it was absolutely certain that there was no hope left of reconciliation with my husband that I ever considered marrying another, and, when I married, I always married in the hope and belief and faith that, this time, it really would last. Yet, each time, except for my most recent marriage, which had taken place only a few months before I had suddenly come here, I had always found that my partner had failed me. When I say "my partner failed me," I do mean that, because, no matter what differences of opinion we may have had over the years, I did always make it completely clear that I loved them and needed them, that they were the most important thing in my life except for my three children, whom I also loved deeply and sincerely and whom, I am so glad to say, I find even from here, still love me.

But at the time I had been left by Doreen to consider my life generally, before setting off along the road towards meeting my father, I very much felt that, given the gift of hindsight, I would probably have been far better off not to have been so devoted to my father originally, now that I had had certain things explained to me by Doreen about my mother. Because I did hold him up as my idol for very many years, only to find that something that my mother did tell me, only shortly before she passed here, shook my faith even in my father. It seemed he had not been quite the man that I had thought he was. Although I still felt, in my heart,

32

that he had been devoted to me, I had come to realise that he had not been the firm base on which we had all leaned to such an extent, as I had originally thought as a child. Therefore, although I was delighted at the prospect of meeting him again, I was not in quite the same frame of mind in which I would have been had I been given the same offer in my twenties, before my mother had spoken to me in a little more detail.

Doreen had left me in what seemed to be the usual place to leave me—a pretty, quiet, gladelike place. A beautiful light was filtering through the leaves. I could hear the stream in the background. There were pretty little flowers amongst the grass on which I was standing. Then I thought, quite suddenly, *why was I standing?* Normally, one would sit down to think. Then I realised that sitting or standing seemed not to make any difference. I felt equally relaxed. No feeling of tiredness or tension. Everything around me seemed so relaxed and beautiful. However, having realised that I was standing, I decided to sit down and I began to go back in my mind over all that we had been discussing.

Gradually, from all this going back, a resolution formed within me to try and see whether, before I met my father, I could try and find out precisely where I had gone wrong in some of the things I had been presuming during the years that we had been discussing. I decided this would be the next thing I would ask Doreen when she returned to me. It was in this mood that I think I must have drifted into some form of sleep, because I only gradually became aware that Doreen was with me again and seemingly waiting for me to become in full possession of my faculties.

"It is quite all right, my dear," she assured me kindly, as I looked at her confusedly and was obviously not quite clear where I was for the moment. "We all find, when we first leave earth to come to this world, that we experience tiredness and drifting away."

"But I wasn't tired! I just seemed to be thinking one moment and to have drifted off the next!"

"You were not consciously tired," she said, "but you were mentally tired. This is a very familiar experience for people when they first come here, until they have fully adjusted to their change of condition. Now, have you got any questions to ask me before we go on our way?"

"Well, yes, I have got a few, and I thought one of the first things I would like to do before I meet my father again is to try and find out more of where I might have gone wrong over the years that we have been discussing."

"I am exceedingly delighted to hear you say that, my dear. So many people assume that everyone else has been wrong and that they have always been right, and they make no attempt to remedy the situation. This means they tend to stay in one place here for much longer than they need to do. The fact that you have voluntarily considered that you may have been wrong and that you may need to put things right is a big step forward, and I do congratulate you!"

"Well," I said to her, "I have always realised in my heart that I must have made a tremendous number of mistakes in my life. Sometimes I have only realised, too late, that I have made them. Sometimes I have been so confused and nobody has been prepared to discuss it with me, so that although I might have been prepared to admit that I could have made a mistake, I haven't been given the opportunity to find out where I have been wrong or to try and put it right.

"I have never been the sort of person who thought that everyone else was wrong and I was the only one who was right, but I always found it difficult to find people who were prepared to discuss it with me. They either shouted at me or slammed out of the room or ignored me completely or walked out on me and never came back. Those who came back, later in my life, only came back for their own reasons. They didn't stay very long or very thoughtfully. They just came back because they thought they might get something out of me in one way or another, and I'm afraid it made me feel very bitter on some occasions, so that, I do realise, it made me snap more than I would have done at some other poor soul who, probably, hadn't caused me any offence at all! Then, if I tried to explain to *them* later on, I found that they had also walked away and had not come back. I do realise that everybody would not have walked away and not come back if I had not been largely at fault. It was just that I was not always too clear where I had gone wrong, and I would like to try and get some of this sorted out in my mind."

"As I said before, dear," said Doreen, "I do congratulate you, and I think you have just made a flying start towards what is bound to be for you, I think, a very considerably quicker progress here than a lot of others will experience. Nevertheless, the first thing I want you to do, before we go back again into any part of your life, is to get hold of this problem of communication here in the manner that I have recently explained to you. Now then, let us try a little exercise."

She led me out from the little glade into the brighter light. I am going to call it sunlight, because that is how it seemed to me. That is what it still seems to me, although we are not, of course, dependent upon the physical sun in the same way as you are on earth. But it is, nevertheless, an emanation of light of different gradations, according to where we are. Here, as I was walking out into the warm, bright light and looking across the countryside, there were gentle hues of pale mauves and greens and pale pinks, a shimmering light and softly rounded hills and mountains stretching before me. In the far distance, something was glistening white. It seemed to have a form, but I could not make out what it was.

Doreen said to me, "Now, my dear, I want you to stand here beside me and look at that white object in the far distance. It is one of the cities we have here, and I want you to concentrate very hard upon it. Do not put any mental strain on yourself. Simply look at it, concentrate upon it and say to yourself, 'I very much want to go there. I very much want to go there.' "

Once again, I pulled up short in my mind. I thought back to the closing scenes in *The Wizard of Oz*, where Dorothy, wearing the famous ruby slippers, was told to click her heels three times and say over and over again, "There's no place like home." In the movie, Dorothy woke up away from Oz, in her own little bed in the prairie home she shared with her aunt and uncle. For one shaky moment I thought, *Here we go again!* I almost felt that I should be surrounded by the Cowardly Lion, Tinman, and Scarecrow, as I was in the movie.

Doreen laughed at me and said, "I'll have to try and get you away from *The Wizard of Oz* if we're going to get any further in this world!" But she only said it jokingly, and I couldn't help laughing with her.

"It's all very well for you," I said to her. "You haven't spent

35

the larger part of your life on a movie set wondering what is going to happen next. I almost expect the camera boom to come looming over me at any moment!" However, I tried to quieten my mind and to take it seriously and do what she had asked me to do.

I stood and concentrated on this gleaming white shape in the far distance. After a moment or two, it seemed to come shakily towards me, as it might have done had I looked at it through a telescope. But then it receded again and was no clearer than it had been before.

"What I want to explain to you now," said Doreen, "is that when you are a little more used to being here, you will be able to concentrate on that city and will be able to transfer yourself from where you are standing to the centre of the city simply by a strong thought process."

I looked at her quizzically. "What did you say about me not being in Oz?" I said to her, and we both laughed again.

"I am not exaggerating. It is quite true. It is done by a concentrated thought process, but you are clearly not ready for it yet, so I propose to take you on foot. Remember, you will not feel the least bit tired, because you are no longer in your heavy, physical earth body, which used to require a lot of food and nourishment and rest in order to keep it going."

"Well, I never seemed to have much nourishment or much rest," I said to her, "and if I did, I got overweight and felt easily tired anyway. So this will be something of a treat!" Laughing together, we set off along the pathway to which she led me. This time I did not have to make my own decision as to which path we were taking. Doreen took me along a gentle, winding path on one of the lower mountains. There was a river sparkling in the valley. I was aware of the trees and the birds, and I could also see people when I stopped to think about it.

Doreen said, "The first thing I am going to do, because you have a great love for them, is to take you to a centre where we receive the children who come here from earth in sudden and somewhat shocked circumstances. I would like you to see how they are being helped and handled, and I would like you to see whether you find it easy to communicate with them. Remember, my dear, that they have not learned our way of communicating any more than you have, and so you should be able to talk with them in the ways of earth and find it quite easy."

V

When Doreen told me that she was going to take me to meet some children, I felt this was, possibly, somewhere where I could be useful sometime in the future when I was a little more sure of myself here, because I have always had a very sincere love for children, quite apart from my own three whom I adored each in their own way. I had always found it so much easier to relate to children. To my mind, they always seemed less critical than adults. They had the sort of minds that I could reach more easily. I could talk and joke with them and play with them, quite happily, for long periods of time, and I always felt they were responding to me. They had been several periods when a child had come into my life and made life so much happier and, somehow, more secure, because he or she needed me and I needed to be needed.

In each of my marriages I had always felt that I needed my husband more than my husband needed me. This had come through to me to some extent even in my last marriage to Mickey Deans because, although I loved Mickey very much and I did believe, while I was on earth, that he did also need me more than I had been needed by anybody for a very long time, I had also come to realise that my need to be loved was greater than his need. When I look back at it now from here, I suppose the kind of love that I offered to almost everybody in my life, including my husband, was a form of childish love, because it was the kind of love where I always wanted complete devotion in return. I wanted them to be everything to me, and I wanted to be everything to them. In saying that, I include my three children, because in some ways, I needed them in the same way I needed my husband. I needed someone with whom I felt comfortable, someone who trusted me and who needed my trust and devotion and to whom I could turn for trust and devotion.

Once or twice in my life on earth I had been given the opportunity of working with handicapped children. There was an occasion when I was in the hospital in Boston, to try and get my own nervous system going again, when I met and befriended a very strange little girl, who had been ill-treated by her family and who had consequently not spoken for at least six months. After a while, that little girl, who would not respond to any of the nurses and doctors and certainly not to her own family because of the fear they had instilled in her, responded to me. I would talk to her, and she would smile and listen, and finally I managed to break through her silence. She flung her arms around me, burst into tears, and said, "Don't leave me! Don't leave me!" Unhappily, I had to leave, because I had to return to the studio to make another movie. I had no right to remove her from the doctors and nurses who were caring for her, as I had no means of caring for her properly if I was going back to full-time work on a movie set. In fact, I still felt I had not been completely cleared of my own problems. But it had shown me that I was capable of reaching out and touching the heart of a little girl that nobody else had succeeded in reaching and, believe me, it was a marvellous feeling. When, years later, I got involved in some work for handicapped children as a result of my friendship with the Kennedy family, I realised how rewarding it was to try and reach these children who had such a simple attitude to life and who seemed to need only a friendly glance, a kindly word, to give them the confidence that they needed.

At one point in my life, I made a movie in which I actually worked with handicapped children. I found it to be one of the most rewarding experiences of my entire life to be able to reach out and communicate with and feel part of the lives of these children, to have touched their lives and to have made them laugh and seem happier than they had been before I had spoken.

Therefore, to find that I was now being taken to meet children who had come from earth under difficult circumstances was something to which I felt I could respond. In my heart, I realised that I had always remained partly childlike in my approach to people, in the devotion that I gave to my husbands, and in the friendships that I offered to other adults who had sometimes abused the perhaps foolishly childlike trust that I had placed in their offers of friendship. I therefore felt I could respond to these children who might have come here under somewhat abused circumstances.

I was telling all this to Doreen as we walked along. She nodded every so often, as though she already knew what I was telling her, and I realised and recalled what she had told me earlier, which was that she had been allowed to reach into part of my mind in order to help me.

"I hope I am not boring you with all these stories," I commented with a rueful smile, as we walked. "I have always been a great talker. I often used to wonder how many people were truly listening to what I was saying, because so often, after I had told them something or other, they seemed to think that I was telling them something out of the wish for adulation or pity instead of only telling them a simple fact."

"I fully realise, my dear, all the hurts you have had in your life," Doreen responded kindly. "I would not be with you now and helping you in the way that I am if those here who are trying to help you did not all feel very strongly that you have to be handled just as kindly and carefully as do those poor children. That is why I am beginning your experiences in this world with a visit to the children. You have a lot in common. You did remain largely childlike in your approach for the whole of your life. It caused you numerous difficulties, because so many people were unprepared to accept that your approach was as guileless as it appeared to be. They were not free of guile. Their minds were working in very different channels and they automatically presumed that yours was too, that you were conniving to get their sympathy and attention, not that you were seeking it truly and idealistically.

"That is the reason why you have been so misled by people, why your actions have been so misinterpreted by them, and, in turn, related and misrepresented and exaggerated to and by others. They have, in their turn, gossiped and distorted it even further from the recollection of what they had been told. You have had to try and exist on earth through all this mass of misunderstanding and misinterpretation until you were completely hemmed in by an absolute well of misunderstandings. Even those people whom you had liked and who gave every appearance of liking you were not seeing you as you truly were but as they thought you were. You had to step only a little bit out of line from what they expected from you for them to react violently against the fact that you had not said or done something they had expected you to say or do. Then they would in their way misinterpret and misrepresent you to others.

"But here, my dear, you are seen completely as you are, and I can say to you most sincerely and straightforwardly that you have always retained within you the heart of a child. That is, quite often, how you viewed your life, despite trying to see it with the eyes of an adult. You were sincere in your heart and guileless and outgoing. When you tried to overcome it, you lashed out at people verbally and sometimes physically in attempts to cope with it all through your feelings of hurt and let-down and confusion.

"That is how a child frequently reacts, particularly a disturbed child, and you, my dear, to your last day on earth, remained in your heart, deep down inside of you, a disturbed, hurt, wounded child. That is how you have always been seen from here, but that, unfortunately, was not how you were seen by the majority of people who surrounded you. They put around you a thick blanket of misunderstanding that you, particularly during the second half of your life even more than the first, had to continuously try and struggle through to emerge in your true light.

"Here you are emerging again in your true light, but those on earth who were around you during your life there have created in their minds a very different person from the one that you are. I have to show that to you later on because, although you are aware at the moment that you have been largely misunderstood in many instances, you are not as aware, as you will eventually have to become, of just how much you have been misunderstood. That will be part of your evolution from your present chrysalis to the beautiful butterfly that you will be able to become.

"Now, when you reach these children, I want you to react to them in your normal, spontaneous manner, and I think you will find that you will be able to bring to them a light and a beauty that they have sorely needed for a very long time."

Even as she said this to me, I became aware of the voices of children, some of them happily at play, and we gradually came to an area that I can only describe to you as one of the most beautiful places that I had seen in this world and certainly far more beautiful than anything I had encountered on earth. It was almost as if Disneyland had come to life, except that the animals and birds and fishes and trees that I saw were all in their natural beauty. The children were playing with these animals and, somehow or other, communicating with them, and the animals were communicating with the children in a way that I would have previously thought to have been totally impossible.

As I stood there and looked at them, I realised I was understanding what the animals were communicating to the children as well as what the children were saying to the animals. I did not say anything to Doreen because this time it was so beautiful, and the feeling around me so beautiful, that I did not even feel capable of going back in my mind and jokingly mentioning Disneyland. Doreen was standing there quietly, not saying anything, letting me absorb the scene, and I suddenly realised that my vibration had slightly changed again. I felt drawn forward to where all the laughter was at its height.

It was a group of children, a mixture of boys and girls who seemed to me to be around four or five years of age, playing with a big roly-poly kind of dog. I am not very good at breeds of dogs, but he was very large and fluffy with golden-coloured fur. He was almost as large as one of those huge mountain dogs, but he did not seem to be that breed. He not only seemed to be joining in the fun, but it was almost as if he was saying, "Well, come on then, do this to me!" or "Bet you can't catch me here!" I found myself standing next to a youngish girl, around nineteen years of age, who was dressed in a nurse's uniform. She smiled at me in welcome and said, "We'll be finished in a moment and then I'll introduce you to the children."

Shortly afterwards everyone subsided and sat down on the turf, and the young nurse said, "My name is Sheila. I'll introduce you to the others." I was taken round to each one and was introduced, and I said, "My name is Judy. Can I join you?" I sat down and before long we were laughing and talking together. I was talking to the dog as well, and he was wagging his tail and giving me a "pleased to meet you" sort of look, and we all got along fine together. Eventually, I looked up and found that Doreen had joined me but was standing a little further back. I think she must have sent me a thought, because as I looked at her, she said, "I'm sorry to drag you away, Judy, but I would like to take you to another part of this section of our world." So I said good-bye to the children, who all gathered around me and touched me and laughed, and I touched their heads as I moved away. I said goodbye to Sheila and to the dog, whose name, I gathered, was Patty.

"I want to take you to another place," said Doreen as we left the happy children behind us. The next thing I knew I was being taken into a darkened room. As I went in, the atmosphere struck me as chill and dark and there was an unhappy feeling. I shivered. "Wait a moment," said Doreen, "before you go any further." As I waited and my sight adjusted to the gloom, the chill left me, but I still felt repressed and confined, and I began to feel unhappy. Doreen took me to a bed where a nurse was standing. There was a child on the bed, and when I looked at her I felt shocked and horrified by how emaciated she was. She had long, golden, wavy hair, but her face was gaunt and pallid, and there were dark rings under her eyes. Her arms were like sticks. I could not see her legs as there was a coverlet over her. I felt incapable of movement as I stood there with a feeling of acute horror and revulsion rising up in me for whatever had caused this poor child to be in this condition. Doreen took me by the arm and guided me back towards the door. Out we went, back into the bright and warm light.

"I think I feel sick," I said to Doreen, "despite not having my earth stomach with me."

"On earth," said Doreen, "if ever you had an emotional shock, or a worry, or you were getting 'het up' over something, it invariably went to your stomach, didn't it?"

"Yes, it did." I agreed.

"Well, your emotions are used to having that physical reaction, and, until you are completely used to being here, away from earth's vibrations, you will find you are getting the same physical reaction to your similar emotional reaction."

Even as she was explaining it to me the feeling of nausea subsided, but the feeling of shock remained. "That poor child," I said, "whatever has she been through?"

Doreen led me to a quiet place, and we sat while she explained to me. "That child, believe it or not, has come here from having been tethered, literally tethered, to a bed and shut away in a room and left for weeks on end by her so-called parents, in the hopes that she would die. They had come to the conclusion that she was not right in her mind, and instead of taking her, as they should have done, to consult a doctor and get medical advice, they decided, of their own choice, to let her die. They shut her away and tethered her and left her without food and water. They have not even been near her."

I looked at Doreen as though she was telling me a horror story. I said, "Surely such creatures don't exist?"

"I assure you they do, my dear. This is only one of a number of children who come here to us from earth in similar circumstances, and you would be surprised and horrified to know some of their backgrounds. If they had come from a part of the earth world where there has been a lack of education, a lack of what you and I have come to regard as civilisation, and had been brought up with a lot of what are now out-of-date attitudes, there might be some excuse. But this child, like so many, has come from what appears to be, on the surface, a normal suburban American home.

"The neighbours have been told that the child has gone away to stay with an aunt, and this has been allowed to happen. Both parents, I have to say, although it is not all that obvious, are slightly mentally retarded. They are not completely and fully aware of the agony of mind and body to which they have put their child. They have what is called 'diminished responsibility,' but they have, nevertheless, put the child through one of the most agonising processes that you can possibly imagine for a child. She had been shut, immobilised, in this darkened room without food or drink or human contact for many weeks before she came here. She lived in a conscious world of terror and acute discomfort and then pain for ten or more days before falling into a delirious state and then into a coma before she eventually passed here. During the years before this took place, she had sustained many beatings from her parents. She had been starved for days at a time as punishment for something that she did not know that she had done, and so she had always lived a life of terror and hatred.

"Her problem, my dear, was that she was deaf and dumb. The parents, already having an element of diminished responsibility, regarded her as an idiot but did nothing about taking her anywhere. They kept her mainly shut away. She never played with other children. She was unable to receive any form of communication from her parents, who just ignored her once she had

43

got to an age of two years and should have been responding. When they realised they were not getting any response, they assumed they had borne an idiot and they did nothing about her. That child has lived her life like that.

"What you picked up, when you walked into that atmosphere, was the sort of creature that she has been turned into as a result of these two parents and as a result of what she has most recently experienced. It is going to take a very, very long time of her being in our world before we will be able to reach her and to even start to make her better. It is far beyond anything you or I could attempt to do. Even with my experience here, I have not had the kind of experience that child needs in order to help her, and you cannot possibly be expected to help her. But I did want you to see the two extremes of the children who have arrived here in normal circumstances and those that have not. Having faced you with the two extremes, there are many other children existing here in many, many varied circumstances and this is where I will be taking you after we have had another little rest."

There is little that can be said by way of compensation for the fact that the poor child, who had been through so much, was now going to have to go through another period of soul-searching in order to find her self underneath all that had happened to her. That, I have now learned, is what has to happen when people come to this world in a terrible state of mind. No matter how innocent their own actions may have been on the world of earth, if they have been in any way mentally injured or impaired, if they have had a lot of cruel treatment which has distorted their outlook, they come here with that outlook and they have to be helped to work their way through it before they can find their true selves.

This is something that Doreen explained to me while we were sitting and quietly discussing what I had recently experienced. That, she went on to explain to me, is why the people in the spirit world who visit close to earth to try and help those who are still undergoing earth's experiences will always try their very hardest to try and dissuade any human being, no matter how sick at heart they may be feeling, to ever attempt to destroy their own earth life. If they do that, they only bring with them all the problems that they have been suffering on earth, because most of those problems are mental.

Of course, there are exceptions, where people are in such acute physical pain that they feel they cannot stand it any longer and wish they could end all the pain. "But," I was told by Doreen, "even those people, if they decide that that is what they will do, go through an element of physical suffering here. They have left their physical body behind but have ejected their spirit body from their earth body before that spirit is ready to depart. This action can have a devastating effect on the finer spirit body that they bring with them to the world of the spirit.

"This means that they may still go through a form of illness, of physical pain and mental confusion, before they are able to adjust themselves to being here and take their rightful place in this world."

This is why Doreen wanted me to see the two extremes of children who had arrived here before taking me to see any adults. She told me that, after we had been to see some of the other children who had arrived here in more moderate circumstances, she would be taking me to see parts of the Animal Kingdom so that I could see the way some of the animals were being helped. She told me that animals can, and often do, arrive here in the same mentally confused states. Domesticated animals, having been close to humans, often pick up the confused states of minds of the humans with whom they reside. This can rub off on the animal and cause them to have illnesses and hang-ups that wild animals are less likely to experience.

As Doreen was explaining all this to me I began to feel that existence here sounded just as complicated and horrific as existence could be on earth. But Doreen explained that, in this world, once we have been helped, we can go forward without the fear, and often it is a fear, of ever being hurt and mishandled and misunderstood again in the future. Once we have unravelled our problems, found our true selves, and become the sort of person we were always intended to be, or had always hoped and meant to be, we would then be able to go forward with the certainty that we would never have to backtrack.

So many times on earth we go through a terrible period, then just begin to feel that we have surfaced and can go forward again hopefully only to find that something else has come from around the corner to knock us down again. I certainly felt that almost the whole of my life was spent picking myself up, dusting myself down, only to be knocked down again and to have to start all over. I used to wonder whatever was going to happen next, and I used to caution my children, "Don't ever feel, where your mama is concerned, that anything is ever going to be straightforward, because there is always something round the corner to trip us up." And I do say "us," because my kids were always close to me and with me as often as possible, so that we did all seem to go through my experiences together. Although I, as their mother, tried to shield them from a great many of the hurts and the unhappiness that happened to me and always tried to turn it into a joke in front of them, I know there was many a time when they realised their mama was joking only on the surface, and they did feel sorry and even protective towards me.

It may sound very strange that a ten-year-old boy and a twelve-year-old girl could feel protective to their mama, who was already reaching the age of forty, but it did happen, and I appreciated it even then. Looking back from here on my earth life, as a result of the many experiences I have now had here, I can only say, from here, how deeply grateful I am to have had three such wonderful kids as I did have and how much I love them. I loved them then and I love them from here, more than ever, for loving me as much as they have continued to do.

I know that many of the things that happened to me in my life must have rubbed off on them to some extent, although I did try to shield them from my problems, but I say here and now that I did always try to be a good mother; I always loved them deeply and sincerely, and I always tried to give them good advice. I always tried to show them that the pathway they should take in life was the honest and straightforward pathway. I am happy and proud to say that my children have lived up to what I tried to instil in them. Admittedly, some of them are making their own mistakes, but that is how we all develop in life. We have to make our mistakes in order to find our character.

When they come here they will find that they will be just as well received as I have been because, in their hearts and minds, they have remained good people. I am assured that nothing so dire is likely to happen to change them. I shall be here to greet them and to give them all the love and to share all the love that we did always share together. We loved each other, laughed together, and sometimes we cried together, too, but it was always a happy, comfortable feeling when we were together.

We will be together again and I can't wait to tell them, from the bottom of my heart, how much they always meant to me. I hope that, one day, they will at least be able to read this book and realise how deeply and sincerely their mother still loves them and suffers with them and for them and wishes with all her heart that they could find the deepest happiness that always seemed to elude me. But I also want them to know that I have found happiness here. I shall go into that in more detail later on, but I did feel that, as Doreen and I were sitting there and discussing the children we had seen, and I started to tell her about my childhood and my own children's childhood, that it seemed as good a point as any here to make my little speech to my children. If I have digressed again, I apologise to my readers but I hope that, somewhere in what I have said, they have recognised a little bit of themselves, a little bit of their children; or, if they have not, that at least they have seen what it might have been like to have had children and not to have found, perhaps, when they reached this world of the spirit, that they have been loved as much as I found I had been loved.

How grateful I was to realise that, for once in my life, I had not been wrong when I thought that somebody loved me. So often in my life, I did think this, that, or the other person had an affection for me, which in the end proved to have been false. But my children always retained their love for me, and that is a wonderful thing and not to be taken for granted. You have to earn that love. You cannot expect to have it just because you are their parent. They did not ask to be brought into the world. They did not ask to have to put up with their parents' vagaries and misunderstandings and problems. So, the least one can do is to give them as happy and contented a life as possible and, most of all, be prepared to listen to them. That, I am told, is something that I was always able to do as far as my children were concerned. I confess I did not always listen to what other adults were trying to tell me, but I did always listen to my kids, and, in the end, it brought us together with a deep love for each other that has survived the years of my passing here, and I am so grateful.

Having said all that, I think I had better get back to where Doreen and I were sitting together in the usual little glade.

I said to Doreen, "How is it that, no matter where we have been, we always seem to finish up in the same place for our discussions and for my rest periods?" Doreen explained that it was a particularly harmonious place in which to be and that was why we always returned to it: "because the vibrations are right for you to rest and to consider."

She then went on to tell me that one of the things that had always "rung little bells of pleasure" in the world of the spirit was the great love that I had for my children and that my children had for me. "You have always had guardians who have been keeping an eye on you while you were on earth. They have not always been able to reach you to impress upon you the right action to take, but they have not been far away from you. They have seen what you have been through.

"They have seen your highs and your lows, your triumphs and your disasters, and you, my dear, have had more than your share of both in your short earth life. But one of the things that always brought pleasure to those who were trying to guard you was the very deep and sincere love you had for your children and the love they returned to you. From here it was beautiful to see, and it brought with it such a beautiful light. If you stop and consider, my dear, that even from earth it was producing a beautiful light here, you will realise just how beautiful that light will be when you eventually meet together again here.

"Of course, the kind of love that you have for each other will change to some extent, because you have left behind two very immature children and one young lady. When they come here, they will all be mature people who have had their own problems in life, who have met and loved other adults, who may even have children of their own. Therefore, you will be meeting, after quite a long period, people who will have changed in many ways. They will still love you, but slightly differently, and you will find that your love for them will be slightly different.

"On earth it was the love between a mother and her children. Here, they will no longer be your children, they will just be individual souls who will love you, not because you happen to be their mother but because there will be a spark of soul recognition between you. That is something that does not always occur. We often find, when parents and children meet again here, that although they have been together in their physical life on earth, they have absolutely nothing in common here, and they drift away from each other. You will not do that. You will always be able to feel close to each other and always love each other. That, I feel sure, my dear, is something that you must be very grateful to know."

"I am indeed," I said. "I hadn't really got around to thinking about it yet, but after a little while here, I probably would have. It is good that you forestalled me. I can start looking at my life with that knowledge, and it gives me a very cosy, warm feeling inside."

"I knew it would," said Doreen. "That is why I chose this moment to explain it all to you, because I feel that, when you reach your father, you may be somewhat disappointed. I already know, from having examined the situation, that you and your father are not in the least alike any more than you and your mother are alike. I am telling you now so that you can begin to adjust to that idea, and, when you meet him, you will not be so terribly disappointed that you act wrongly.

"Having said that, I think it will be as well to take you back to the children so that I can introduce you to a few who have come here from different disturbed circumstances. Certainly their lives were not as horrific as the one you have recently experienced, but they will have had some problems in their lives, and I think it will be helpful and interesting for you to find out a little bit about how they are being helped here."

"Yes, I would like to," I agreed hesitantly, because I felt I had already had a little more than I could easily take at the moment. It was not that I felt selfish about it, but the atmosphere that surrounded that poor child was so appalling that I had not completely disentangled myself from it, and I was not at all sure that I was, at the moment, quite up to meeting anybody else who had arrived here in any kind of distress.

Doreen, of course, picked up those thoughts immediately and explained to me, "It is because you have not been here long, my dear, that you did not completely protect yourself before I took you into that atmosphere. Possibly I should not have taken you there at that time, before you had become sufficiently used to adjusting yourself to the change of conditions. But, having led you to that extreme, I feel that if I take you back now and warn you a little more carefully before you go forward in each instance, you will be able to handle the situation very much better and not have any sad after-effects.

"It is possible to view what people are experiencing here without becoming emotionally involved. You can feel sorry for them, you can sympathise with them and have a sincere wish to help them, but it need not leave you feeling permanently sad or appalled and injured. When you have had a little more time here you will learn that each and every one of those souls will be helped, and they will eventually find themselves and go forward to a happy life, something that could not have been promised to them on the world of earth. If you feel you are sufficiently rested and can accept that what I have told you is the truth, I would now like you to come back with me to see some of the other children."

"Yes, if you think that's best," I agreed, still somewhat reluctantly, and we set forth once again into the sunlight.

As we walked back towards the children, Doreen took me through a slightly different area. This time it was to show me some very pretty little streams that had various brightly coloured fishes in them. I had not noticed fishes properly before. Doreen said that that was because, in the previous areas, the fishes were not so colourful. These were the more brightly coloured varieties that had existed, on earth, around the regions of China and Japan. Here, Doreen explained, we can have all the forms of life in almost any area that is suitable for their vibrations, because they are no longer dependent upon the kind of food and climate that they needed when on earth. Here they can exist anywhere that the correct vibration is supplied.

As we stopped and looked at them, to my amazement and delight even the fishes seemed to be emanating a form of musical enjoyment. That is the only way I feel I can put it. I almost felt as though I was swimming around with them. It was so delightful that I felt just like a child with a new toy, and I said this to Doreen.

"That is because you have a childlike quality within you, my dear," she replied. "Those people who are not susceptible to

50

beauty, whose thoughts in your world were only of materialistic things and who had cast their minds away from the joys and pleasures of nature and had not given any thought for their fellow creatures on the planet earth, would not be able to see or feel or appreciate any of these natural beauties that we are easily enjoying. Because you have always had an innocent approach in many ways, you are able to appreciate immediately all these beauties that are available here.

"These fishes would have lived simple lives in a simple environment, unaware of any particular unhappiness or impending danger to themselves, even if they were, as they often were, captured and used by humans for various purposes. As they were unaware of it, they went happily about their lives and, as that was their existence, so they are giving off beautiful harmonies."

I partly understood the explanation, but I felt it was getting a little bit too deep for me at that point, and Doreen could see that I was only partly with her in her explanation.

"I think I had better go into this more deeply when I take you to the Animal Kingdom, but I wanted you to see these little fishes while we are on the way to the children because it will help to clear you of the unhappy vibrations you have had around you since we saw that unfortunate child."

I began to realise that I did, indeed, feel much happier and refreshed. It seemed incredible that so much could have been taken away on the one hand and returned on the other simply by watching these beautiful little creatures with whom I appeared not to have any mental connection. Yet as we walked along the pathway towards the children, I realised I felt much happier and brighter than I had been feeling before. I even felt like bursting into song, but refrained from shattering the peace of the local surroundings in that way.

Doreen looked at me quizzically. "You will be able to sing again here, you know."

"I hadn't really thought about that," I said. "I just felt like singing a moment ago and then thought nobody would want to hear my loud voice bursting over the peace of these lovely surroundings!"

"You will find you will be able to make beautiful music here, my dear child," Doreen told me as we approached the children.

"In fact, you may even be able to sing to the children, which will bring them a great deal of pleasure."

I was not sure about that, because in the last few years of my life, I realised that I had not been singing as well as I used to. I had lost a lot of the power, and I could not get the notes or hold them. In fact, I could not put across what I had wanted to put across half as easily as I had at one time been able to do.

"Don't worry about that," said Doreen, reading my thoughts. "It will all come back to you here and far, far better than ever before."

"There will certainly be room for improvement," I said to her ruefully, "because my voice was a very unreliable instrument, especially in the last few years. But I always had trouble with it; I was always getting laryngitis."

"That was because you were straining your vocal cords in many different ways," said Doreen. "But here you will be using a totally different way of projecting your voice and on completely different vibrations. You will find a far greater flexibility and purity of sound than you could ever believe is possible."

By this time we had reached the children again, and I was taken to a little girl who was playing on her own with a cuddly doll. She looked up at me as I approached. I smiled at her and she smiled back and held the doll out to me. I sat down beside her, put my arm around her, and took the doll.

"My name is Judy. What is your name?" She told me that she was Sally. At this juncture, a young nurse joined us and sat down and said, "Sally hasn't been with us very long, have you Sally?"

Sally said, "No." Then, looking at me, she continued: "I left my mommy behind and I can't find her."

"Perhaps you'd like me to be your mommy for a little while until we find yours," I replied. She smiled at me a little hesitantly, but I saw a warm smile in her eyes, as if to say, "that's not such a bad idea," although she did not say anything.

The nurse went on to explain to me, "This little girl has come to us as a result of a car accident. She was killed instantly, but her mother is in hospital with various broken limbs and she has not yet been told that her little girl has passed here. They want her to get over the shock of the accident before they tell her. When she is told, there will be such a deep distress within her that, if we are not careful, it might reach Sally and disturb her. But, if we can keep Sally from thinking too much about her mother, the distress will not reach her. So, we have to keep her occupied here as much as possible to try and keep her mind on what she is doing here and who she is with here and not let her keep thinking back to her mother. If she does, it will not help her mother but it will hurt Sally. So I am very pleased to hear you say that to her. If she feels that she can identify with someone here, it will keep her mind away from her mother."

"How long will this be for?" I asked a little hesitantly because, although I felt drawn towards this child and I wanted to cherish her and put my arms around her and talk with her, I was not sure about Doreen's plans.

"It has to be until the mother has got over the initial shock of it," replied the nurse. I looked round for Doreen, who was nowhere to be seen.

"Well, can I help in any way?" I asked. "I have just been brought here by my friend, and I haven't been in this world very long myself. I am a bit confused as to whether I am saying the right thing. I don't want to intrude, and I don't want to cut across any plans that my guide and friend has for me, but if I can help in any way, I would be only too pleased."

"I think you've made a very good start with Sally already," said the nurse. "Why don't we all go together and see what some of the other children are doing?"

I stood up and took Sally's hand in mine while the nurse held Sally's other hand. We strolled slowly towards a group of children who were sitting together and quietly listening to a story that was being told to them by another young nurse. We three sat down and joined in listening to the story, Sally's hand remaining peacefully and dependently in mine.

After a while the story was finished and Sally's nurse suggested that we might all like to have a little singsong and said, "Sally might like to suggest a song and start it off." She took Sally and pushed her gently into the centre of the group. Sally stood there shyly, twisting her little skirt in her hands, and looked towards me.

"What songs do you know, Sally?" I asked her. She thought

she knew "Baa, Baa, Black Sheep." Sally, I might add, was around three years old. She seemed a little shy at singing on her own, so I said to her, "Would you like me to start off the singing for you?"

"Yes, please," she said, running back to me and sitting on my lap. We sat facing the group and I, cradling both my arms around her, started singing something I remembered from one of my early movies, a song called "They're Playing Ten Pins in the Sky," and that seemed to go down very well. I asked Sally whether she had thought of another song she would like to sing.

"No, thank you," she replied quietly, putting her arms around my neck. She had established a contact in the world where she now was, and I felt completely involved in the thought of keeping this little girl away from the distress that might be reaching her.

Some of the other children were a little bit older, and they all knew songs that they called out, and we sang them together. We were not all in tune, but it did not matter and we had a wonderful time. My little girl was contented to just sit there listening to them all, with her finger in her mouth and her eyes round with wonder as I held her closely in my arms and gently rocked her to the rhythm of the songs we were singing.

"You're a natural for this sort of thing," said the young nurse, looking at me.

"Well, I've always had affection for children and always felt that we got along well together. I would be more than happy to help in a place like this when I get the opportunity. But I haven't been here very long, and my friend, Doreen, is taking me around the different parts of this world to show me how things work and to try and get me adjusted to the way of living here."

"Yes, it does take a while to get used to everything," agreed the young nurse. "I found I had to go on a long journey around before I was able to come back and help the children. When you do feel able to do so, you will be more than welcome here, and I am sure you will be a great success."

By this time the little girl had fallen asleep in my arms. "I think this is the moment to take her and put her to sleep for a while," said the girl. "She has come here very abruptly, so abruptly that she hasn't slept. She has been worrying about where her mother is, but you have got her to a situation where she was able to fall asleep. This means we will now be able to keep her asleep until she is well past the problem time of her mother's distress signals coming to her. So you have done your bit for the moment; but if you would like to come back and meet Sally again later on, I am sure she will be delighted to see you again. In the meantime, you will have had the opportunity to have gone further with your guide."

"Thank you, I'd like to." I smiled at her and she smiled back.

Suddenly, Doreen reappeared. "Where have you been?" I asked.

"I thought it was better to leave you with Sally for a while," replied Doreen. "Now I will take you to see some more of the children."

As I left Sally in the hands of the kindly young nurse and walked forward with Doreen towards another group of children, I had a mixture of feelings within me: a feeling of gladness and warmth that I had helped a little child to feel more reassured, but a feeling of distress in my heart for the young mother who had lost such a beautiful child so suddenly and so tragically young. I had a strong feeling within me: If only we could reach that mother and reassure her that Sally was alive and well and, I felt sure, going to be happy.

Doreen looked at me and said, "I know what you are thinking, my dear. We often feel here that it is very sad so many people on earth either feel that they cannot communicate with us here or, for some reason or another, that they should not communicate with us. But that is a different subject that we will be looking into a little later on. Now, let me show you these children."

We entered a small place which resembled a schoolroom, except that there were no walls. We were still in the open with the trees and the birds and the flowers, but there was a blackboard of some sort on which something was being drawn. These children, it was explained to me, had been blind when on earth and had come here without having previously seen anything. Where you or I would recognise a fish or a tree or a bird or another human being, they had not been able to recognise anything. It was, of course, joyous for them to realise they were seeing, but it also came as something of a shock to them suddenly to be able to see all these wonders and so they were being taught what these were. It would not take them very long to adjust to their new situation. Of course, they were also having to learn how to communicate in the same way as I was having to learn, with thoughts rather than words, and also how to close themselves down, although this aspect was not so vital with them as they would be remaining in their present element for some long while and so would have more time to learn that sort of thing. Nevertheless, they had the additional problem of not only concentrating on what they were looking at but of also discovering at what they were looking.

"It may seem an easy task, but it is a very specialized task to teach those children who have come here from being blind," said Doreen.

"I should imagine so," I replied. "In fact, I don't think I'd know how to begin."

"You will do, if you want to," said Doreen, leading me away towards another group who were listening to music.

"These children were deaf and dumb," Doreen explained. "They are having to find out how to communicate here and how to relate to each other. They know what they are looking at, because they have all been to schools for the handicapped. Now they have to learn how to interpret the sounds and also how to communicate their thoughts. This, again, needs a different approach, because the kind of words they were using were, in many ways, differently expressed from ours. Some of them knew sign language. Others had not acquired it, although they will have learned how to read. They have to be trained here how to communicate in our way, but, of course, by a different approach to the way the blind children are being taught. But they make amazingly good subjects on which to work and, when we have completely taught them how to see and communicate here, it is a joy to see the pleasure on their little faces that they can take part in everything around them along with all the normal children who have arrived here and be exactly the same as them after a short while. It is a special joy to them to realise all the sights and the sounds and the beauties of this world in which we live."

I found that emotional tears were running down my face as I watched these children. I had always felt a deep sympathy within my heart for anyone who was deaf or dumb or blind, but especially for a little child, because I felt one could not explain it to them.

It was a wonderful feeling to realise that, after a while, everyone who arrives here, in no matter what state of mind or attitude of mind, no matter what mental or physical impairments they may have had on earth, can eventually, here, be restored to full health and full benefit of all their senses plus far more highlighting of those senses than one could ever realise or understand when on earth.

"I think you have had more than enough for the present," said Doreen. "I think it is time you returned to your little glade for another rest."

I must confess that, although I had felt emotionally uplifted from all that I had experienced, I was more than ready for that rest and I nodded silently to her as we walked away and back to the glade.

VI

As I rested with Doreen and we discussed my experiences with the children, I came to realise how lucky I had been, really, in my own childhood. I had always been healthy and, although I had suffered some hang-ups over my mother, these had not amounted to the same things some poor children had had to endure and try to overcome. But the loneliness and the heartache and the hurts that I had experienced in my childhood relationship with my mother had caused me to make up my mind that any child of mine would never suffer the same feeling of lack of interest of lack of love that I had been through. When my Liza was born to me, during my marriage to Vincente Minnelli, I began to feel that, at last, I could contribute something towards a child and give her what I felt I had never had.

At the time I married my second husband, Vincente, I had been divorced from David Rose for almost eighteen months. I had felt during the whole of that period that I was lacking something in my life that I badly needed, which was a strong person to whom I could turn with my troubles and problems and also for love and laughter and almost, one would say, a religious experience. I felt that marriage to someone who loved you beyond everything and whom one could love beyond everything in return would be a beautiful and almost God-fulfilling experience and

57

something which should be able to take one through all of life's problems.

When I met Vincente it was as a director for one of my pictures for Metro-Goldwyn-Mayer called *Meet Me in St. Louis*. He was older than I was and, during the filming, I had reason for feeling unhappy in general and we did not get along too well. When I was about to make *The Clock*, I realised he would be the best director for it and I put his name forward during a conference about the picture. We got along much better this time, because I was recovering a little from all my unhappiness surrounding my divorce from David Rose and feeling better able to cope with the filming. We were a happy partnership this time, and he seemed the sort of person one could turn to for friendly advice. We became attached to one another, and he asked me to marry him. When he first asked me, I hesitated a little. He was twice my age and I felt this was a bit too much older, although my first husband had been almost twelve years older than I was. But Vincente was more than persistent and so I felt he would be the sort of person I could turn to for all the caring and loving that I felt I badly needed.

When we had been married for only a short time and I was pregnant with Liza, I found I had married someone who would be very kind to me in many ways but who felt that he had the right to continue living his life in the way he had always done before our marriage and to continue to have other women in his life. This fact had never occurred to me, and I felt deeply unhappy as well as deeply mortified that I should be expected to share my husband with another woman at any time at all and least of all so shortly after we had begun our baby. Although Vincente assured me that he loved me and that I was more important to him than anyone, he also said that I was not to expect him to change his already established life-style and there was no cause to feel that I lacked his loving interest. By the time Liza was born, I was already unhappy over the situation, but we both loved her so much that I decided to try and make the best of things until she was older and we had had a chance to see whether Vincente changed his attitude.

I never felt able to discuss this problem with anyone at the time of our marriage and not for some long time after it had ended six years later. Most people considered that we were a very happy couple, except for my continuous breakdowns in health which kept occurring during almost the whole of our marriage. A lot of those nervous troubles were blamed by me on the busy work schedules in conjunction with the studio's insistence on very strict slimming diets almost all of the time, causing insomnia and a highly strung condition generally. But I also knew the main problem was the fact that I seldom felt I had the whole of my husband's love and interest, and I felt torn apart inside that I seemed unable to find anyone who loved me as completely as I needed to be loved.

I did feel, however, that one very beautiful thing came from our marriage and that was our daughter, Liza. She was a lovely little girl, with huge brown eyes and a warm and affectionate nature. I gave her a lot of love, and we had a lot of fun together. We gave parties for all the children around, and I kept these as free as possible from any sophistication, even though there were always some children there who belonged to my co-workers at the studio. Also, I made it clear that Liza was going to have as normal a childhood as possible and not be pressed into any film work, as I wanted her to have all the love and happiness that I felt I had so sorely missed. We did let her have one brief appearance as my daughter in the closing scene of *In the Good Old Summertime*, but she was only seen for a moment and had no lines to speak. Vincente accepted the stipulation and it was agreed she would be allowed to remain an ordinary little girl with lots of ordinary children as playmates.

When Vincente later said we should separate and divorce, since we were no longer getting along well together, it hurt me deeply. I had accepted his bohemian attitude towards our marriage, although I was unable to accept it for myself, and I had tried to be happy with the arrangement. The fact that I had spent several periods away in a sanitorium for my nervous tensions was, I did realise, something that put an additional strain on our marriage, and I also had periods of deep unhappiness and emotional reaction. This was partly due to the overwork I was experiencing throughout the many long filming schedules, but it was also partly due to realising that my husband was often elsewhere during the periods I was home as well as when I was away. Nevertheless, I still felt that we owed it to Liza to try and stay together, because I had hoped to keep her free of our troubles and felt she needed a father as well as a mother. Eventually we did separate, and I took Liza with me, but I always tried to remain friendly with Vincente so that we could meet together from time to time and still give our Liza the love and interest from us both.

Looking back over those six years with Vincente, I realise he tried to be a loving husband and father, and, in his way, he felt he was being a good and caring husband, but the feeling of emptiness and failure within me that was caused by the knowledge that I had not got all of my husband's love and interest contributed a very great deal to my nervous distresses. I do feel these would not have reached the proportions they did had I been able to have more faith in our marriage and felt able to go to my husband for everything and not always feel that there was somebody else in the background who was taking his love away from our marriage.

This has taken me a long way away from where I have just been with the children, but I found it coming into my mind as I was about to discuss Liza with my friend Doreen. She said to me, "My dear child, it has come into your mind because it is part of your deepest repressed feelings. It was these deep hurts within you, who still had, in many ways, the emotions of a child, that caused all your nervous problems. It was not the overwork at the studios at the outset—you could have handled that in the earlier days. Latterly, you did become overstrained by it. In those earlier days, if you had had the right person with you, beside you, you would not have had all the problems you experienced later.

"I am asking you to go back in your mind over this period and to get it out of your system before we go any further. You have faced the fact now that a lot of your problems stemmed from that period. It added to your feelings of hurt and insecurity and it affected your life forever after, despite the fact that you tried to put it behind you and did not discuss it with anybody until many years later.

"At the time you separated from your husband, everybody thought it was because you had had many rows, but it was far more than that within you. As I understand it, it was shortly after you had separated from your husband, Vincente, that you met the man whom you thought would truly be the rock in your life that you had been seeking. He was a rock in many ways for a number of years. We know that, when that rock left your side, it was, for you, the beginning of the end of your life, because so many other things were linked with that loss from which you could never, ever, completely recover.

"Having brought you to that, my friend Judy, I am going to take you now to a little place that is set aside for people such as yourself, who have had this kind of upset. I want to show you something because I think it may affect the way you are able to look at life here. Just come with me a little way along the path that lies ahead, and I think I will be able to show you something that will surprise you more than you, at the moment, could possibly realise."

Doreen led me beyond the glade once again. This time we seemed to be walking along a sea-shore. I was walking on sand. There were gulls flying. There were a few tropical-looking trees, and the rollers were breaking on the shore. I said to Doreen, "This is how I've always imagined the Caribbean, although the nearest I've been to it was playing a part about it in a movie called *The Pirate*."

Doreen replied, "This is not dissimilar, but I am bringing you here for a particular purpose. I want you to look across the water into the far distance and tell me what you see."

The waves seemed to be glinting in the sunlight as I looked across the expanse of water and saw a thin, purple haze that was not unlike the sort of haze one might see in certain light conditions on earth. Through the haze, a little golden light was twinkling.

My companion asked, "Can you see anything, Judy?"

"There is a little golden light twinkling," I replied.

"Are there any others?" she asked me.

I looked again more carefully and decided. "Not really. There is a kind of yellow-golden haze around that golden light, but it is just like a strong star twinkling except that it is daylight."

"Well that, my dear Judy," went on my friend Doreen, "is the kind of love coming towards you which you have always sought and never found amongst those you took as your husbands. That is the light of someone who loves you, not as a wife or as a famous name or as somebody who might do something for them because of your name or your position, but who sympathises with you for all that you have been through in your life, for all the hurts that she saw you receiving, because she had enough

61

knowledge of you within her own soul, without ever realising herself that she had that knowledge, to be able to understand you no matter what you said or did or how much you may have been misinterpreted by others or lain yourself open to being misunderstood. She understood you because, deep down in her innermost being, she is very similar to you.

"She has lived a very different life from yours. Had you discussed it together you would both have agreed that you really seemed to have little in common, yet she has a deep love for you, and it is a very pure love. She never asked anything from you, she did not want anything from you. She did not understand why it was that she made excuses for you as often as she did, but she always found it easy to make an excuse for you. Even when she did not make an excuse for you, she simply shrugged it off and said, 'That's all right. She didn't mean it.'

"Later on I am going to tell you who that person is, but at the moment I just want you to know there is someone on earth, other than your children who all love you very much as their mother, who loves you in the way you wanted to be loved. Because there is no marital, physical relationship involved, it can, in many ways, be a much more abiding love and respect than anything you can get from a marriage.

"In saying that, I am not wishing to mislead you. There are many marriages between men and women on earth that are, indeed, made in heaven. They are twin souls who love each other sincerely, irrespective of being man and wife, and when they come here they continue together here. On the other hand, many of the people married on earth who have been brought together through various circumstances and for various reasons are not always mentally compatible, and they often, without realising it, tear each other apart emotionally. When they come here, they find it very difficult to stay together. They might still be fond of each other and like to see each other, but they do not necessarily go along the same pathway.

"What you have coming to you from someone who is still on earth is the very sincere friendship of someone who would never have considered you as a partner when you were together on earth despite the fact that you knew each other and liked each other, and she is not thinking of you as a partner at this moment.

Yet, what you are seeing when you look far ahead of you is the golden, loving light of somebody who loves you just as you are—for yourself—with all your mistakes, with all your confusions, with all the heartache that you drew around you and some of the heartache that you yourself unintentionally dispensed. Beyond all that, she loves you.

"There is a saying on earth that she has sometimes quoted, which is 'A friend is someone who knows all your faults and loves you just the same.' That is what you have always wanted from your husband. That is what you did get, for many years, from the man you married after Vincente Minnelli, and we all know, my dear, that you never wanted to lose him. When he seemed to lose his love for you, you really did feel that life would never be the same for you again, and, indeed, it was not. Before much longer I will have to ask you to go back in your mind over the years of your marriage to Sidney Luft and to ask yourself where that went wrong."

I looked at Doreen while she was telling me all this, totally aghast and confused, and I thought, *Where the hell are we going now?* I went back in my mind and thought, *We've been visiting the children, we have just discussed my Liza, we've dismissed my marriage to Vincente in a few words, and now we're going straight on to Sid!* I asked her, "What's all this with Sid? Aren't we supposed to be going to meet my father?"

"You will be meeting your father," replied Doreen. "But, my dear child, before you meet the man who you thought you were seeking in others, you need to go back through your life and see yourself more clearly. Yes, you will meet your father and also your mother and your sister and all those others you have known on earth, but see yourself more clearly first."

VII

My third husband, Sidney Luft, had come into my life at what seemed to me to be a supreme moment for a complete change in my life pattern.

Having separated from Vincente, I took my little girl, Liza, to New York for a holiday, and there I met, at a party given by friends of us both, my future husband, Sidney Luft. We immediately felt companionable. We seemed to have a similar sense of humour and the same attitude, in some ways, to Hollywood and all that it stood for. He was feeling let down and with an element of rancour in his life, having recently separated from his wife, Lynn Bari. I was feeling lonely and uncommitted, having separated from Vincente and also having left the film studio where I had worked for so many years of my life, and not at all sure where I could possibly go or what I wanted to do to make life bearable. He was feeling somewhat the same way, and he invited me to be his dinner guest for an evening.

During the dinner discussion, I told him about my lack of direction and how undecided I was as to what to do next. He suggested to me that, as I seemed to have "a God-given talent," as he described it, I should endeavour to do something with it on the stage. This, I felt at that time, was something that would be completely beyond me. I thought back to my vaudeville days and all that had been involved then and decided that I had really got too far away from that kind of life, having spent so many years in front of the Hollywood film cameras. But Sid told me that he had always felt, when he had been watching me in movies, that I had the kind of talent that would do well on the stage if given the right direction.

He also told me a little of his life before we had met, and he seemed to be as unhappy and lonely a person in his own heart as I was. Before long we had become regular companions. I introduced him to Liza, who seemed to like him straightaway, and he had a warm, fatherly affection towards her.

When we decided to marry, it seemed to me that I had at last found somebody who was going to lead me towards a different kind of life, because he did not like Hollywood any more than I did. I had come to dislike it mainly through my ill health and my disillusionment over David Rose and Vincente Minnelli. He disliked it because it had never really been his background. He had been in the United States Air Force and was subsequently a test pilot before drifting into Los Angeles and meeting and marrying Lynn Bari, who had asked him to remain with her as her secretary and manager. He gave up his flying, feeling he was, in any case, getting to be a little bit too old for a test pilot.

Sid was thirty-six years of age when I met him, nearer to my own age. He was thirty-eight and I was twenty-nine when we married in 1952, six months before our daughter, Lorna, was born to us. Here, I would like to explain that, when Sid and I became engaged in 1951, he was having to wait for his divorce from Lynn Bari to become final and I was also waiting for completion of my divorce from Vincente Minnelli. When we got to the early part of 1952 and we were loving each other very much and the divorces were not yet final, I accepted his suggestion that we should live together as man and wife until such time as we could be officially married in the eyes of God and, I suppose I should add a little ruefully, in the eyes of the general public. Because I loved him and trusted him I agreed to the suggestion and so, although we were not able to marry until the May of 1952, our daughter was born to us, to our great mutual joy, in November of 1952. She brought us all the love and the radiance that I felt should come from the marriage of two human beings who love each other.

When our little boy, Joe, was born to us in 1955, I felt that, no matter what went wrong in future in my career, I had at last found a secure and happy family life. Admittedly we had our rows and our arguments, because Sid was a hot-tempered person and I was not the calmest in the world, but I was feeling physically better than I had been for a very long time. I was away from the pressures of the studio, and I was allowed to be my normal weight, which some people might have called plump but which I quite honestly called fat. I was not particularly happy at being so over-weight, but Sid kept urging me to let well enough alone since I was feeling so much better: "You need all the strength you can get, Judy, to keep going in your stage work." By this time I had become established as a successful singer back on the stage where I had begun my life.

During the years from 1951 to 1961, many of our differences stemmed from the fact that my Sid continued to be the heavy gambler he had always been before our marriage. This caused me a number of problems and heartaches because it disrupted our life together when he got heavily in debt on a number of occasions and we did not know where the money could be found to settle those debts nor those that had been incurred on my behalf. Nevertheless, I had a deep love for my Sid and felt that he also loved me deeply in return, and no matter how many times we parted in anger, we always came together again.

When I had been taken dangerously ill with hepatitis towards the end of 1959, the doctors told Sid I might not survive it, and if I did, I would never be well enough to work again. He stayed by my side through all the weeks in the hospital until I was well enough to leave and return home to the children, who were thrilled to have their mama back again and also their daddy. When he later obtained a responsible job in an aircraft factory so that he would be able to support me and the children, I felt doubly secure in our marriage and had seldom felt happier. During the months in the hospital, where the doctors thought that my sleeping pills and sedatives and also some of the stimulants that I had been prescribed from time to time may have caused the illness, I had been completely free of all outside stresses and exertions. Despite having become greatly overweight as a result of all the fluids created in my body due to the illness on top of my usual tendency to being overweight for my height of just five feet, I felt completely relaxed and also reassured in my general outlook. I felt that I was about to enter a new phase in my life, and I determined not to return to any more pills.

We had decided to try a new life in England, where I had gone for a holiday in the summer of 1960 and to record some songs for a double album to be issued by Capitol Records. I was feeling so fit and well. I rented a house in London, where Sid and the children joined me, Sid having to commute back and forth between London and his job in America. I loved England so much that I wanted to remain there and we did seriously consider it. By the end of the summer, I had felt well enough to resume my concert work, despite some doubts on Sid's part. I was singing onstage for nearly two and a half hours at a time and even revelling in the stimulating work and the loving responses from the audiences.

When, in January 1961, I returned temporarily (as I then thought) to New York to consider some work offers, we found that much higher taxation would arise if we made our home in England. So I reluctantly agreed to remain in America for at least a while to see how we made out and to spend more time with Sid, since his work really needed his more regular presence there.

Around this time, when we were considering our future actions, I received an offer of a new management from two theatrical agents whom I had known previously as part of the vast MCA Organisation and who had decided to establish their own agency. Sid agreed willingly enough at the time. When his job at the aircraft factory ended, in March 1961, he asked me to leave the new managers so that he could resume management of my career. I felt this was not a fair or easy thing to do at that time, as I had already signed various contracts which took me through 1961 and almost into 1962. We had a strong argument, and Sid said that if he could not be my manager and had nothing else to contribute to the family, he had better leave. This came as something of a shock to me at the time, because I felt I had always made it completely clear that I loved and needed him. I felt unhappy at this unexpected rift at a time when everything had otherwise seemed all right, but I put it all down to a surge of pride as well as anger within Sid, and I expected that he would soon return to his family. He did come and see us occasionally during 1961, but he was always vague when the children asked him why he stayed away so much, and I began to feel some doubts creeping into my mind about our marriage.

By the end of 1961, I had completed a year of highly successful concert tours; I had co-starred with Burt Lancaster in a film about retarded children, called *A Child Is Waiting*, which I had felt to be a worthwhile project; I had managed to pay off all the past debts and to keep some money in the bank for the first time in years, and I had agreed to make a film in England in the Spring of 1962. When, at the end of 1961, Sid returned to the family, I felt we would be able to settle down to a more secure future. Unhappily, the many months of separation seemed to have changed the atmosphere of our marriage. Sid was not as loving as he had been before, and I felt he was there for the sake of the children rather than to be with me. I was still with my new managers and Sid felt at a loose end, but I did arrange for him to be a part of the production team on the picture to be made in England and had hoped that this would succeed in bringing us closer together again.

I had also begun to diet in order to get as slim as possible for the British film in which I was supposed to be the heroine. I had not seen a completed script, but I gathered I was supposed to be a young boy's mother as well as a stage star, and despite my own weight being acceptable to my concert audiences, I felt that, some-how, this would not be as acceptable in the cinema. I realised afterwards that this did not really matter at all and that I might have had a better picture, and certainly a better time, had I re-mained my usual weight. Sid was right when he got angry and told me I was being foolish to risk my health again with severe dieting just to make a film. I always got highly strung and easily upset and also easily angry when on a starvation diet, and this did not help our marriage. At that time I did not see it like that, although I did later on.

We had more rows, and although Sid had originally accepted the offer to act for me as my personal manager on the picture, he left home again after he discovered that the job was not as respon-sible and active as he had originally supposed. When he then tried to prevent me from taking the children with me to England, saying he would have a court order taken out to prevent me, I rushed the children onto an earlier plane then planned and we reached England to a blaze of publicity. Sid followed us, and we had several angry scenes at the house that the studios had rented for me. The children were upset by it all and the studios had an injunction placed on Sid that refused him access to the children at that time.

During the whole of the weeks of the filming, although Sid had eventually returned to America, I faced court orders and numerous long-distance telephone calls with threats of legal action for the children when I returned. I was already feeling excessively tired and easily upset, and when I faced this almost continuous harassment on top of the many problems that arose at the studios, I found it extremely difficult to remain calm on the set. It soon became clear that English filming methods were far removed from those I had experienced in Hollywood. The script proved to be terrible and was being largely rewritten. The director soon angered me because he frequently left me to my own decisions over the dramatic scenes, when some guidance would have been helpful, yet imposed his own decisions on the way I moved and sang the songs in the picture despite the fact that I had been singing songs for the whole of my life! No doubt my nervous tensions caused some unpleasant moments that might otherwise have been av-oided, but it was, as usual, my feeling of loneliness without Sid and his seeming lack of love for me that caused the insomnia, which I had managed to lose during the past two years, to return.

My co-star was Dirk Bogarde. We had both looked forward to making the picture together as much as I had also looked forward to working again in England. Dirk and I had become friends when we were introduced at a Hollywood party in 1957. I had stayed at his house in England once or twice during recent years, where he had made me feel very welcome, and he was an amusing person to be with. He always made a fuss over me and had often said he would like to work with me. At the outset of the picture he was a great help to me. He lent a friendly ear to all my complaints and he even helped to rewrite one of the scenes to enable me to get something worthwhile across.

We were both affected, however, by the lack of cohesion in the script and also on the set, and we had several arguments of our own. He did try to act as my father confessor from time to time, but he eventually told me that he had his own problems and he could not always be listening to mine. The result was that, by the end of the picture, our friendship had lost some of its old rapport, but we parted as friends. Although, in the years that followed, we saw little of each other, due to our mainly living and working in very different places, I always felt we had retained our friendship. He was his usual pleasant self when we saw each other daily during the four days I was in England for the première of the picture in March 1963, and he told me that he was so pleased that Sid and I had recently become reconciled. We only met once after that, when, in 1965, he called to see me at my house during a brief visit he was making to the United States. He was living and working abroad by the time I next returned to England in 1969, but I always respected his friendship as he seemed to be one of the few people who was prepared to tell me the truth.

When I returned to America at the end of the filming in July 1962, I was allowed to retain custody of the children. I felt, however, that Sid had lost all feeling for me, and so, in October, I filed for divorce. The inner loneliness I had been feeling during the past months all welled up within me and it seemed the only thing to do. On that occasion it seemed to bring Sid back to me because, shortly before the divorce proceedings were due to be heard early in 1963, he contacted me and said that, for the sake of the children, we should try again. I willingly agreed and deeply hoped we would be able to remain together this time.

I had already agreed to undertake a television series, and it was to begin in July 1963 for twenty-six shows. Sid was offered a job as my personal manager for the series and, once again, I hoped this would help to bring us closer together, as it had up to 1961. It would also provide the personal shoulder I always needed to lean on when facing new work. But Sid complained that I was getting to be difficult to live with due to my continuing dieting for the series. I was also feeling a lack of love for me, and that made me feel so unhappy inside that it was also affecting my attitude to Sid. When he left me again shortly before I was about to begin the series, I felt I would probably not ever manage to save the marriage I had needed so much and still needed deep down within me. I needed Sid as my partner in every possible way, including that of manager, as I had missed terribly that additional personal interest in connection with my work as well as our personal life together.

When the television series ran into production problems, largely due to the sponsors disagreeing with the format, and there were many sackings, so that I never seemed to know with whom I would be working from week to week, and I was also being constantly told that I needed to change my own style of working, I missed Sid more than ever. My managers were not taking much interest, having more or less handed me over to the television managers. It was a medium in which I had not had a great deal of past experience despite a few very successful specials, and I felt I needed at least one friendly shoulder on which to lean, but there was nobody. I could not sleep. I was not eating.

The constant changes in format produced extremely long working hours. I was forbidden to have the children visit the studios during rehearsals, something they had always previously been used to be able to do while their mama was working, and I was not getting home in time to see them. They were becoming lonely and unhappy, and so was I. Had Sid approached me with a request to see more of the children at that time I would have agreed, but, in the midst of all these problems, Sid chose to apply for their legal custody once again. I took the usual legal steps, and, because I was so extremely tied up at the television studios,

I had to leave it all in the hands of the lawyers. I was already feeling that I was living and working in a mad house. Discussing the whole series afterwards with others, I have been assured that, quite apart from my own personal anxieties and strains and difficulties in remaining calm, it would have been a horrendous experience even for a calmer person than I ever managed to be.

When Sid's lawyers phrased an affidavit on his behalf to the effect that I had made nineteen suicide attempts, my own lawyers immediately had this withdrawn as the abominable lie that it was, but it was headlined in the newspapers and it had a most unpleasant effect on the television sponsors and the whole crew as well as on the general public. I felt sure then, as I do today, that it was partly this cruelly unjust publicity that contributed to the failure of the series when it ended in March 1964. It certainly contributed to the failure of my marriage.

Although Sid did apologise to me afterwards, saying that it had been intended only to make me stop and realise the need to discuss the whole situation and that he had never intended such an allegation to become public property, I felt that he could not possibly have any love left for me at all if he could even suggest such a thing in any legal statement. I had never previously felt so lonely or so demeaned, and it all came at a time when I had nobody at all with whom I could sit down and quietly discuss anything. The only person on the television series with whom I had found any rapport was the original director, George Schlatter, and he had been fired by the sponsors very early in the series. Afterwards there were constant changes, and I moved in a seeming nightmare. My good friend, President John F. Kennedy, had been my sole support during the autumn of 1963. He listened to my problems with sympathy and understanding and also constructive advice and common sense during my long-distance telephone calls to him at the White House. This lasted until his tragic death in November 1963, when he was taken from his wife and family as well as his country in such a terrible way, by assassination.

During my years with Sid, from 1951 to 1961, I really had felt loved as I had never been loved before. Despite his own problems and his gambling and his inability to keep any money for very long, so that our family constantly lived on the edge of a financial precipice, I felt that he loved me and the children and we all loved him. Looking back, I think those years with Sid were the happiest in my life. I deeply regretted that we ever separated. I did not choose to separate from Sid. He chose to be separated from me. Life was never quite the same for me afterwards. Although I did remarry in an attempt to find a happier life than I would have had if I had remained alone, something I was never good at being, I could never, ever understand how it was we came to lose our marriage. It had all been an escalating nightmare to me, and I missed Sid very much. I would never have married anyone else if I had felt there was the slightest chance of regaining a happy life with Sid, but by the end of March 1964, I had completely lost faith in our marriage and all that I had hoped it was. (As I was relating this to Doreen, who simply nodded from time to time, I felt all the past deep emotions churning up within me.)

I was feeling completely miserable over the loss of my husband and over the failure of the television series when, shortly before I was due to travel to Australia to perform concerts there in May 1964, I met actor Mark Herron at a local party in Hollywood. He had a quietly smiling personality with a quick sense of humour. He was a pleasant person to be with and I felt at ease in his company. I was pleased when he chose to become part of the small group of people who set out for a brief holiday on the way to Australia. When I was taken ill there and this was followed by my nearly dying in Hong Kong from bronchial pneumonia and pleurisy, he was exceedingly kind and we became good friends. Despite the fact that the newspapers spread some extraordinary stories, we were never lovers, only good friends, but Sid heard all the rumours and again tried for custody of the children. This time I had to face the public allegation of being a heavy drinker, something that was unfair at any time. It was particularly incongruous that, during the period alleged, I was being exceptionally careful after my hepatitis and was restricted to short drinks of tea or water. Once more the public were reading all sorts of peculiar stories surrounding my illness, my friendship with Mark, and now the alleged heavy drinking.

During the years 1964 and 1965, Mark and I did remain constant companions, and he spent time at my home with the children while we decided what we were going to do. He was always a kind and caring sort of person and I had come to depend upon his companionship, although I had also come to realise that there were reasons against us marrying. However, we were truly fond of each other and, after a lot of careful discussion and heart-searching, we did decide to marry at the end of 1965, so that we could form a regular family unit for the children, who liked him very much. There was every reason to believe there would be a good chance of at least having a responsible and caring friendship on a permanent basis after all the months of carefully considering our situation. It came as a great shock when, less than six months later, Mark told me that, due to circumstances he had not anticipated, he felt he should leave. He assured me it was in no way my fault but that, in the circumstances in which he found himself, it would be better if he left.

Because of the continuous strains arising in the period I was making the television series in 1963 and 1964, I had had to return to all the pills I had discarded after my hepatitis—the sleeping pills, the sedatives, and even the strength-giving Ritalin. I had deeply regretted this in case they affected my health again, but I had no choice if I was to get through those tremendously exhausting months of my contract. Although I had reduced my weight prior to undertaking the series by my usual process of severe dieting, I had continued to lose it latterly due to the overwork, the strain, the shocks, and the deep loneliness. During the two years I had known Mark, I had regained a lot of my lost peace of mind and with it my lost weight. I was now overweight again, and, this time, I decided there was no way I was going to destroy my health again, having nearly died in a coma as a result of the pneumonia and pleurisy I had in May 1964.

During 1965 I had several bad colds that affected my breathing. On one occasion, I tried to perform with a temperature of 104 degrees. I had also had to accept that my voice was becoming an unreliable instrument, having sustained some damage due to my last illness, but I had otherwise been feeling well and also contented in the midst of the family. With Mark's departure I felt I had really lost the last chance of any real friendship or happiness for myself despite still having the love of my children. They tried so hard to be loving to their mama, and I loved them for their love. Although I always tried not to let them see me when I felt at my most miserable, I probably only partly succeeded, although I did always try and turn my personal disasters into jokes for them.

VIII

I related all this to Doreen at far more length than I can possibly attempt here. She took me quietly by the hand and led me back through it all, slowly, carefully, and thoroughly, until I could see more clearly where and why and how some of the things happened that were to have such a disastrous affect on my whole outlook, both mentally and physically, for the last three years of my life on earth. I felt so ill, so lonely, and so deeply and desperately unhappy for almost the whole of that time until I remarried, for the last time, in March 1969.

According to Doreen, what had primarily caused Sid to leave me during 1961 were his feelings of failure. He had regretted the loss of his job at the aircraft factory, and unless he could resume management of my career, he felt useless. He would have returned by the summer of 1961 had I not clearly been doing so well professionally without his support and seemed well able to support myself without him. I immediately told Doreen that there had never been any doubt before that I needed him by my side irrespective of any professional success. She then informed me that I had seemed very self-possessed and assured during that period and had given him glowing accounts of my two new managers. He had felt unwanted. To some extent, he had also thought there would be a time when I would feel unsure again, so he preferred to let me ask him to return.

"But I did tell him how we all missed him!" I told Doreen.

"Nevertheless," she replied, "you have to face the fact that he felt useless. By the time he did feel able to return, in December 1961, he was also feeling exceedingly lonely, as you were, but neither of you actually admitted it to the other. You each wanted the other to make that move, and neither of you did."

"But I had always made it clear to Sid before how much I loved him. When he said he was coming back and then seemed not to be so loving towards me as he had been before, although he still got along so well with the children, I felt unsure inside. I hoped that he would see this and try to reassure me."

74

"Judy," said Doreen, "you also had the one big fault of assuming everyone else should know what you were thinking. They did not. Because you felt unsure of Sid at that time, after he had been away for so many months, you were a little more reticent than usual. Sid felt it and saw you as being more interested in your new managers than in him. You seemed to refer all the various plans to them instead of discussing them with him, as you had once done."

"Well, that had become a regular practice during the months he had been away, but I did discuss the filming plans with him, and we did both agree he would try and come with me," I explained.

"You discussed these first with the managers, and only after you had done that did you suggest to Sid that he be on the unit in England. But, most of all, you were easily overwrought, and you failed to stay calm. So he got angry and walked out again. In the past you would probably have both got over it within a few days. Now, however, you had the filming on your mind and felt somewhat nervous about it, despite your original interest in the idea. When you got there, you over-reacted and so did he, and you were both at fault. The children had always wished to be with you. Had their father given that more thought, all the unpleasantness would have been avoided.

"I want you to realise that, when you were making the picture in England, you were far less pleasant to almost everyone in the production than you would normally have been had you been eating and sleeping properly and not feeling so desperately hurt by your husband's actions. Some of his actions were justifiable, because he did feel incensed that you had rushed the children to England when he was feeling concern over the climate not being good for your son's health. But his own actions were extreme and unnecessary, and so you were both to blame. He still loved you then, underneath his anger, and he was unhappy when you were going your separate ways. It was only because he had a strong temper as well as strong pride that he stayed away.

"When you reacted so strongly each time he approached you, you actually succeeded in making the rift worse. The same problem arose again during 1963, when you separated again shortly before starting the television series. We saw it happening from here, and we all tried so hard to get you to calm down more. The sad thing is that, when people on earth most need our help, it is usually the most difficult for us to extend any calming influence.

"Those responsible for making the television series were partly to blame, and, indeed, the way they constantly changed their minds over the format and the songs to be rehearsed and the sackings of many of the people on the unit would have shaken the strongest. But, in your case, you were never able to stay calm under stressful working conditions. You have always needed some strong faith and guidance and somebody to rely upon, but you had nobody with you at the time who cared for you. Those who tried to be friendly were not your sort of person. You tried to fit in with them only to find they were gossips and unreliable. Your natural reactions to all the changes caused you to get easily upset, and your health rapidly deteriorated, so that you reached the stage of seldom seeing the problems very clearly in any case.

"Then you faced the shock of the assassination of your friend President Kennedy. This came on top of all the changes taking place on the television series and the complaint that your own approach to your work was wrong. Moreover, you had to face the appalling public accusation of all those so-called suicide attempts. It is a wonder you got through it all as well as you did. The return to your pills after three years of steadfast refusal to do so was understandable. The suicide allegation was one of several suggestions put forward by Sid's lawyers, and had he realised the outcome in advance, he would never have agreed to have it made. He did sincerely regret that it all went too far. Even then he still had some feelings for you, although not so much as previously.

"We all saw you desperately trying to cling to some faith in your life, and we all saw you drifting along towards a doubtful decision. We love you here for seeing Mark as somebody who also needed careful companionship, and we do understand why you felt so drawn to his company. His presence in your life helped you overcome your past troubles and another illness and gave you back your confidence as a person. While we understood it all, we nevertheless deeply regretted your decision to marry, as we felt it would be asking too much from each of you in view of your individual egos.

"In saying 'egos,' I mean your innermost feelings. You have always felt the need to be demonstrative, and Mark was unable to respond to your demonstrative nature, although he was kind and thoughtful. He was very lonely and exceedingly pleased to have your warm and happy personality with him. He liked being accepted as your friend and possible future partner, as well as being accepted and liked by your children, who all called him 'Uncle Mark.' We all saw the strain a marriage ceremony would put on your, so far, excellent companionship, and this was really the crux of the situation that developed some few months later. Although he was more to blame than you were, because he failed in his promise to you, you must also accept that, had you not been prepared to make a compromise in order to, as you saw it, regularise your family unit, you need never have lost his friendship and would have, at least, had a fairly reliable friend and frequent companion."

I listened to all that Doreen was saying and knew in my heart it was true. I had fooled myself, really, in believing Mark and I would succeed where others had failed. I felt I had lost my faith in human nature.

"You had good cause to feel let down, Judy, and you were, but it does take two to make a mistake. Although it was a completely loving, innocent mistake, you paid for it, as usual, with the unpleasant publicity that followed your separation. Once again, the world at large got a peculiar image of you and misjudged you accordingly."

IX

I felt exceedingly hurt and exceedingly bitter during the months after Mark left me. The children remained at my side, constant in their own kind of love for their mama. It was not, however, like having a responsible adult with whom I could discuss things generally or turn to for advice and loyal interest or to be escorted socially in an area where an escort was essential.

I had regained my lost weight during the past two years. When Mark left me so suddenly, I felt so shocked and miserable that I just stopped wanting to eat. By the November of 1966, I was far thinner than I had ever been, and without even trying to be. I was also lonelier than I had ever been. Because I was not at all well, I had not worked much and the money was running out. People whom I had thought were my friends did not seem to be around any more.

It was during this exceedingly low period in my life that I met a young man called Tom Green, who was introduced to me as a theatrical agent. He seemed to like my company, and I was pleased to accept his invitations to various social events in preference to staying home and feeling lonely and overlooked. I never took our acquaintance seriously, however, until he asked me to marry him. I told him that, although I felt honoured that he had asked me, I felt no interest in that way and that, also, he was far too young. He was very persistent, so, eventually, feeling that he was the only person who seemed to be caring a damn about me, I did agree to become engaged, but only on the understanding that we had a longish engagement. I needed time to consider my feelings and the whole situation as I felt we were unlikely to be sufficiently compatible.

We became engaged in March 1967, and I ended the engagement, after numerous arguments and tiffs, in May 1968. I had always felt him to be a really ineffectual person, although I had tried to see him otherwise. We had little in common. He was serious, while I always liked to see the humourous side of life, even in its darker moments. He clearly cared for me sincerely, but he never seemed able to understand me, and we spent almost all of the period of our engagement going from one misunderstanding to another.

When, in May 1967, Sid came to me and suggested he arrange a short concert tour for me in which I would be joined on stage by Lorna and Joe, I welcomed the idea. I was completely broke by this time and had even had to sell my home. The children loved the idea of having their father around for a while as well as their mama. It worked well and a further tour was arranged, which I hoped to be able to make despite getting very easily tired and my voice failing far more than previously. But I caught a very severe chill early in the autumn tour that affected me so badly that I hardly knew how to complete the tour. I could not afford to cancel it, as I would have been held legally responsible for paying for each cancelled concert, and I had no money left with which to pay. I hardly knew how to set foot on stage on almost every occasion, and I got very poor receptions and very poor reviews on many of those evenings. It was terrifying and it was demeaning to have people calmly accusing me of being drunk on stage when the bald truth was that I was feeling desperately ill and severely handicapped by my failing voice.

The children were back in school. Sid had left the scene in August when I found the financial position was not as good as I had been led to believe and that we did not get the money I had anticipated. Managements tended to have been influenced by the adverse publicity about me and to presume that it was correct. I felt desperately, horribly alone. Those few people who did seem to still take an interest in me were welcomed, but they were mainly people who had been fans of mine and who, I later realised, had really only been interested in the name "Judy Garland," not the human being. When I could not always live up to my image, they had also turned away and left me alone again. Only my kids remained constant.

When, in July 1968, I had to return again to hospital, having returned there several times during the past two years to try and keep my health going, there was no alternative but to send my kids, Lorna and Joe, to stay with their father in California. I spent several weeks in the hospital in Boston between the months of July and November 1968, trying to improve my health, but the hospital doctors told me there was really nothing more that they could do for me. They explained that a lot of my problem stemmed from not eating enough to nourish me and that this, in conjunction with overstrain, were the two main problems. Needless to say, they recommended a complete rest for at least a year and that I eat regular, sustaining meals. I had no money at all—in fact I had an accumulation of unpaid bills, despite trying to work to pay them off—and no home of my own, so I had to leave Lorna and Joe with their father. Those months were deeply and terrifyingly lonely until I met the man who became my last husband, Mickey Deans.

Mickey was a night manager at a New York disco that was managed by Sybil Burton and was a popular place with show business people. We had been acquainted for two years, as I had visited there from time to time and had taken Lorna along with me sometimes, and I had always liked his happy attitude.

When I visited the disco again, towards the end of November 1968, it was with a young man whose songs I had recently sung on a television show. He had been very kind and appreciative and had taken me to meet his family, who had asked me to stay with them for a few days. It was so good to feel that ordinary people could take an interest in "that terrible Garland woman," but it also accentuated my own lack of any family with me, and I longed to have my kids back with me.

When I met Mickey again and he made me laugh a lot—in fact we spent the whole evening laughing—I accepted his suggestion that I visit there again soon as he would be there every evening. This I did and we were so happy in each other's company. Before long he had asked me to marry him and I had accepted. I had never reacted to anyone so hastily before, but I had been feeling so lonely and unwanted. When Mickey showed an interest in me and told me that if I married him he would take care of me and that I need never work again unless I really wanted to do so, I felt happy and needed for the first time in a very, very long while. I fell in love with him, although in a different way to Sid, and I felt I was clutching at my last chance of happiness. I tried to overlook the fact that he was ten years younger than I was. In fact, when I was with Mickey, it did not seem to matter. We spent a lot of our time together laughing, and I loved living my life with laughter, despite all the problems that usually erupted around me.

Although we had intended to marry in London in January 1969, we had to delay our marriage until March because the legal formalities of my divorce from Mark Herron had never been properly completed. Mickey was concerned for me when we reached London because there were several problems arising around my prearranged engagement to sing there for five weeks at a popular night-spot called Talk of the Town. He therefore remained in London and lost his job as a result. When we found that our marriage ceremony had to be delayed for a while because of a failure on my part to ensure that the divorce from Mark Herron had been finally concluded, I felt terribly guilty. Mickey suggested, and arranged, a special blessing in a church, so that I would feel better about pre-empting our legal union, and this did make me feel less uncomfortable about it.

In my innermost thoughts, I would have waited until we

were able to be legally married, but the fact that Mickey cared enough for me to have lost his job and now arrange a church blessing brought me the confidence I needed for our future together. When we did marry in March 1969 and he was trying hard to arrange for a reunion with my children, I felt and hoped I had made a correct decision in marrying Mickey. We did have several bad rows during the six months we were together, and once or twice these had gone beyond immediate reconciliation, but he had told me he cared for me and we had made it up. I deeply and sincerely regretted having been taken from Mickey after such a short and seemingly happy marriage, and I told all this to Doreen.

X

Needless to say, I spoke to Doreen in far greater detail than I am able to do here. I felt it all pouring out of me, all the loneliness—all the horror I had felt at the adverse publicity I was receiving during those weeks of the autumn tour on top of all the past adverse publicity, all the rudeness and calculated insults that I received from some of the managements for whom I appeared, the insults that I also received from members of the audiences who took it upon themselves to shout out rude comments to me and even to come onto the stage and take the microphone out of my hand while I was trying to get my breath back enough to complete the song. Looking back through those years of 1967 and 1968, I had never before felt so demeaned, so horribly ill and lonely and unwanted during the whole of my past life. I was unjustifiably accused of actions that I would never have dreamt of undertaking. All those alleged actions became increased and further distorted in the newspaper accounts of my life and work, so that all the beauty and love that I had tried to pour into my work and to create between myself and my audiences seemed to go for nothing. Few people mentioned the fact that my past years of working had been so rapturously received and so highly commended. I was reduced, in my eyes as well as in the eyes of the general public, to somebody who was living and working as an empty shell and who should no longer be appearing before the public.

I was facing a number of difficult circumstances. My health

and my voice were going from bad to worse. I had absolutely no money that I could call my own, and the debts were rising to a horrible degree. Each time I tried to live somewhere, even if it was the smallest hotel room, I was faced by hotel staff telling me that I had not paid my last hotel room bill and so they were not prepared to accept me without some payment in advance. There were even occasions when I had my suitcase of clothes taken away from the room during my absence from the hotel and held as a deposit against unpaid bills. Therefore, when I met Mickey again at the end of 1968, I really was in the most deplorable circumstances that anyone could be in; yet I was still regarded as a famous name and someone who was expected to live up to the life-style of a famous name. It was just too impossible for any human being to do.

Even Mickey was, at the outset, under the impression that I had far more money than I actually had, but I alerted him to it all before we married, so that he fully realised I had nothing to offer him at all except my love for him and my name. This is something I would like to make clear, because some people have tried to imply that Mickey may have married me for what he could get out of me. He knew I had no money whatsoever and that I had not been working much just recently because my health had not been good. Yet he had said to me that he cared enough for me to want to make a home for me and to look after me and that I need never work again unless I wanted to do so. This meant a great deal to me and was one of the reasons why I felt I was doing the right thing to let Mickey come to London with me at the outset in the hopes of marrying there. I felt that, after so many years, I had at last found someone to whom I could turn for a feeling of assurance and dependency.

As I explained all this to Doreen, as I have previously said, in far more detail than can be expressed here, she had, from time to time, stopped me and interjected some explanations. In each instance where I was mentioning a particular let-down or a particular hurt, she was able to show me the viewpoint of each of the other individuals concerned as well as my own, and I began to get a very different picture of me as a human being than I had before.

I would like to say here that, in all the years of my life, even including the last few years when everything seemed to go even more wrong than ever before, I had never failed to realise that a lot of the faults were caused by my own actions. I did realise that I could be easily hurt within myself, that I became far too overemotional in my dealings with others so that I became overwrought and shouted unkind things at them or else dissolved into hysterical tears. I realised I was frequently being too extreme, but I could not stop it happening. Something inside me just got worked up and overwrought and I was away! When it was all over and it had subsided, I sometimes did not clearly remember just what I had said and done, but I sometimes had the feeling that the fault had been partly, if not wholly, mine. On other occasions, I used to feel quite certain in my heart that the fault had lain with the others concerned and not with myself.

This is how I always got confused in my attitudes over all those years. When Doreen had taken me through it all, I did realise where, in many instances, I had been at fault. But there were still also many other occasions where others had been at fault, and, had I been able to remain calm, I would have been able to resolve the problem to my advantage better than I had ever succeeded in doing.

She also explained to me how it was that, sometimes during those last few years, I had pushed away from me well-intentioned, genuine people who had been trying to help me. Because I had not been seeing things clearly (mainly as a result of not eating enough, which had resulted in a kind of malnutrition that was affecting my mind so that I was seeing things in a distorted way), I over-reacted to their kind attempts to be helpful and so pushed them away from me.

There were others, she said, who had taken me for a ride, inasmuch as that they had approached me with a great deal of seeming love and affection but were really only wishing to be with "Judy Garland." They did not really care for me as a human being. They just wished to be with a famous name. They did everything in their power to ruin my reputation with others that they met as a result of having passed time with me. They lied about me in the most abominable way and helped to create, in the minds of others, a Judy Garland who had never existed on the surface, least of all in my innermost thoughts. They were responsible, to a large degree, for the derisive attitude that began to arise around me in the audiences and among managements, because, as I went on tour, they were spreading lies and more lies. People were coming to see me with those lies in their minds and looking for me to support them with my actions, which, quite often, I did seem to be doing. When I stood on the stage and either did not say anything at all for some while or else talked for far too long while I tried to regain my breath and my voice, people either saw me as drugged or full of alcohol, whereas it was simply that I was feeling exceedingly ill and tired and breathless.

Out of all the muddle that we discussed between us, there came two things that Doreen felt I should stop and think about before we went to meet my father as she had originally promised.

"Judy, I have to first of all discuss with you your last husband, Mickey Deans, and to tell you that, when he first asked you to marry him, he was deeply, strongly attracted to you because of what you have always had—a swaying back and forth between the adult woman that you tried to be and the child that remained within you during the whole of your life. Both of these aspects drew Mickey towards you. But when it came to actually living with you as your husband instead of just seeing you from time to time as he had done before, he came to realise that you were far too dependent upon him for almost everything, and this he had not anticipated. You expected him to be not only your husband and your father but also your stage manager, your financial director and all the other jobs you felt should be his as your partner. He began to feel a little overwhelmed and to some extent out of his depth in matters in which he had had no previous knowledge. This is why, despite his sincere efforts to help you during the weeks you spent together in London at Talk of the Town, he failed in a number of ways to fulfil all your expectations.

"You, in your turn, were becoming more and more exhausted by having to sing every night for five weeks in an exceedingly smokey atmosphere, which was bad for your already poor health. You were becoming more and more unwell and slowing down more and more as a result. You also became less and less clear in your own mind as to what was taking place. This added to your problems and to his. It also added to the management's problems and to those of others who came around you at that time to try and be helpful.

"The image you created from the stage was very similar to the one you had created during your recent performances in America. Again, the press and the public were being turned against you. Mickey was well aware that you were not the sort of person that was being written about in the newspapers. He did sympathise with your reactions against the articles that were appearing and against the comments that were being called to you by some of the noisier members of your audiences, but he did not know how to cope with the situation any more than you did. He failed to explain to you where you were failing. You went on stage each night in ignorance of where you were failing. All you knew was that you were often failing to establish the kind of rapport you had previously achieved with English audiences. Between the two of you, the whole engagement went terribly wrong.

"During the few months that you were married to Mickey, he began to get more and more confused about your confusion. He realised that, in many ways, you were trying to be a good wife and companion to him. He also realised that, in some ways, you were not well. What he did not realise, and could not be expected to realise because of the lack of any knowledge of you in the past, was just how much the deep down hurts of the past and your current lack of strength and lack of food were all affecting your whole mental outlook. When you became difficult to handle, as you did on many occasions, he saw it as a childish outburst, as an ego-trip, and as a lack of consideration for him and others around you. It was all unintentional on your part, but he could not see this, and really, we do not, from here, blame him for not seeing this.

"Therefore, Judy, I do have to tell you that the happy days of your marriage to Mickey were becoming numbered. He was beginning to feel more easily irritated, more easily angry. He was beginning to feel frustrated that he was seemingly unable to get you towards a better state of health. He could see that your condition was becoming more run-down and he was concerned for you, but he did not know what to do about it. Someone who was older and better acquainted with you in the past would have handled the situation differently. In his ignorance, Mickey pushed you into doing things socially that you did not really feel up to

85

doing. He was blaming you for being unsociable in not wanting to go. Normally, you would have loved to have gone to all the places where he wanted to take you, but at that point in your life you felt you could not always manage to keep up."

While Doreen was telling me all this, I began to realise that it had probably been very unfair of me to marry Mickey, who was a vigorously healthy younger man, when I was feeling so unwell. I told her so.

"No, Judy, we are not blaming you for that. He came along to you like a lighthouse through a fog, and we understood why you turned to him at that time in your life. You did not have anywhere to go. It was a desperate time for you, and we are not blaming you.

"What we are doing is trying to help you to see that you did not really have much of a future with Mickey. Although you laughed a lot together and you liked him a lot, you were very different from each other in so very many ways. It would not have been very much longer before you would both have come to the conclusion that you were not getting along as well as either of you had hoped. We do not really forsee that your marriage, as much as you would have wanted it to be successful, as much as you would have thought that you were trying hard to preserve it, would have had any real future. In saying that, we are not blaming you or Mickey. You were two people who came together at what seemed to be the right moment for each of you. In fact, it was not.

"You were married to somebody who loved you in his heart but who could not have coped with your outlook as it was then or even your true outlook had you become well, because you were so different in your individual ways. You just enjoyed laughing together. That is what it really comes down to, Judy. So, in leaving Mickey behind as you have now done, you have really only shortened your happiness together by a few months or maybe a year."

I felt completely shocked, yet again, as I considered this statement of Doreen's. I went back in my mind over the months that I had known Mickey. I had always realised, of course, that our interests were very different. We also saw life differently in so many ways, although we shared a similar sense of humour. I suppose, after a period of being together, this would have begun

86

to affect our feelings for each other. But it was difficult for me to see it as clearly then as I have come to see it since.

I do now fully realise what it was that Doreen was trying to tell me. But before I leave this part of my story to go further into my experiences here, I would like to say to all those people who thought that Mickey and I were doing something ridiculous when we married—and I know that many people did—that those few months with Mickey were happier than any I had had for a number of years. I felt I was being cared for and thought about and that I was no longer alone.

Although I do realise from here that perhaps Mickey and I would not have had a long future together, I am exceedingly grateful he came along when he did. I thank him for the love he tried to give me. I thank him for the way he cared for me when I came here, because he took my body back to America and tried to have it decently interred. It was not his fault that, when the time came, he did not have the money to have me interred in the manner that he had wished for me and that, eventually, my final interment had to be paid for by my daughter, Liza, who arranged things a bit differently from Mickey's idea for me.

In his heart, he wanted me to have a "special place" somewhere, but away from Hollywood and its tourist routes, because he knew that I had come to dislike it so much. He knew that I had liked New York in the days that I felt happier there, and he had felt that my final resting place should remain close to there. I thank him for what he tried to do for me in his heart, even if he did not manage it in fact. I send him my love from here and my hope that the rest of his years on earth will be happy ones. I also hope that, when he comes here, we will meet again as friends, even though it will not be as permanent companions.

I would also like my children, Lorna and Joe, to know that, from here, I do appreciate all that their father did for me during those ten years that we remained man and wife. Although some of his actions since then have turned me from him in many ways and continue to turn me from him, I still retain the memory of the happy years we spent together, and, when he comes here, I hope that we can also meet as friends and at least regain a little of the lost companionship that we had. Because we all make mistakes as we go through life. I made many mistakes in mine

87

and my mistakes contributed to some of Sid's mistakes as much as they contributed to Mickey's mistakes and as much as they contributed to the mistakes of others with whom I came into contact during my life on earth.

XI

"There is one more thing I would like to tell you before we go to meet your father," continued Doreen. "In speaking as we have been doing of your life on earth, I am well aware that I have destroyed within you any faith that you have anyone beyond your three children who could continue to have any permanent love for you. I am also aware that there is a feeling of doubt within you that you even had as much of Liza's love for you, towards the end of your life, as you had once felt that you had. This was mainly brought about by her insistence on trying to make her career without being overshadowed by yours and by the usual changes of outlook that are aroused in all teenagers reaching adulthood and by their need to be completely independent.

"In some ways Liza adored you, and in other ways she resented always being seen as 'Judy's daughter Liza.' She resisted your attempts to make her see where you saw her repeating some of your previous mistakes, and she took herself away at a time when your own attitude of mind, during 1967, made you extremely difficult to be with at times.

"But she still did, and she still does, love you. She sees you more clearly each day, as her own life experiences bring her closer to understanding how your problems took you over sometimes. In assuring you of that, let me bring you back to something I mentioned to you earlier, because I am aware that, apart from your children's love, I have now, after all our discussions, made you feel more lonely than before."

"You have," I said to her. "I am aware that, in going back over all this with you, I have obviously churned up all my past loneliness, but I can't help thinking now that we have gone through it all, that I have really not achieved any permanent love for me as a human being on earth, other than from my children. I realise Mickey is still fond of me. I realise that in his heart Mark is sincerely sorry that he did what he did. But I do not seem to have suceeded in finding the kind of truly permanent loving companionship that I always wanted to find almost more than anything else." I looked at her ruefully and said, "I suppose there aren't any chances of finding it here?"

"This is exactly where you will find it," said Doreen, "because in this world, although it is possible to continue marital relations if people wish to do so, there is a tendency not to do so once you get to our level of existence. It is a very earth-bound link. It is something that is normally brought about by being in the physical body, which exists on a different vibration to the spirit body. The kind of partnerships you find on our level of existence, especially as you progress forward, are of a very different nature. But most of us do need to feel that somebody loves us for ourselves as individuals.

"I want to take you back to something that I tried to explain to you earlier when I told you that there is someone on earth who has loved you over many years in the way you have wanted to be loved, purely for yourself, for your soul one could almost say. She loved you first for your personality and your talent. During the years she came to know you personally, she continued to love you for your public personality and for your talent, but she also developed, deep within her, a love for you as a human being. She seemed to know, instinctively, how you were feeling and why you did some things and why you reacted in certain ways.

"She could see where some people were misleading you or lying to you and not understanding you. She could see, at times, where you were failing in your approach to others even when you did not always realise it. She tried to explain you to some of those people, and she tried to make allowances for you when you sometimes spoke sharply to her without any just cause.

"She is not somebody who would be subservient to you simply because you are Judy Garland, but she frequently allowed you to get away with certain actions that, had she experienced them from anyone else, she would normally have spoken out against straight away. She is not someone who did not speak to you because she was afraid of what would happen, but she is someone who did not answer back because she did not want to upset you just as you were about to undertake a performance. She had enough common sense to realise that what you needed most before going on stage to perform was an element of quiet support and friendship. This she tried to give you, although you were not always aware of it. Even when you were aware of it, you did not always acknowledge it in the way that you possibly could have done or should have done."

While Doreen was telling me this, an image began forming in my mind. It was an incredible image, really, in one way. Yet, when I stopped to think about it, in my heart of hearts it did not seem to be quite so incredible after all!

"Do you know," I said to her, "I think I am beginning to tune in to you, because I have just got a very strong image of Lorna Smith! She helped me a lot when I was at Talk of the Town. She used to come and be with me and Mickey at the hotel, and we used to travel together to the theatre. She used to stay with me in my dressing room, and she stood in the wings and came with me to the dressing room afterwards, and we spent time chatting together every night."

"Well," said Doreen, "although it may seem a little strange and unusual to you, that is who I am talking about."

"That's not the person you mentioned earlier when you said there was always somebody who loved me in their heart?" I asked Doreen.

"Yes, it is," she replied.

"But I only saw Lorna occasionally, from time to time," I responded.

"Yes, I know you did," said Doreen, "but don't forget that she saw you more frequently than you saw her. She was often backstage or standing on one side at the various studios or watching you from the wings or alongside when you were approached by various people back stage or at parties and receptions. She saw you and heard and understood and felt for you far more than you ever saw her.

"Although she began her interest in you as a fan, she subsequently stayed by your side as a friend. She felt for you during those years she saw you going downhill and with nobody to whom you could turn. Although she was not always with you, she heard what was happening and understood what was happening. When you came together from time to time—and each time she saw a change in you—she wanted so very much to help you more than she could do, because you were always putting more faith and trust in others around you. Although you always liked her and always made it clear to her that you liked her, you seldom asked her for anything more than superficial help, and you failed to listen sometimes when she tried to be helpful."

"Well, I always thought of her as my fan club secretary, at the outset, but I did also always feel with Lorna that I was receiving kindness and friendliness. She was a little bit quiet and shy, but I always felt that I was in safe hands when I was with Lorna."

"You were in safe hands," said Doreen. "You are still in safe hands, because she is still trying to put it right for you on earth. She is still telling people and writing to people, trying to clarify their misconceptions of you. She is arguing against newspaper and magazine articles. She is writing to the fans who write to her to try and put it right for you. Ahead of her she has a far more gigantic task than either of you could recognise at the moment, but I will tell you more about that later.

"I just wanted to let you know, before you go any further, that there is one person on earth, other than your children, who cares for you and understands you and makes allowances for you, and who is very much like you deep down in her own soul. Although it will be many years before you are reunited here, she is someone to whom you will be able to go to share long discussions and to laugh with and to even travel around with during your activities here. But I will go into that in more detail later on.

"The next thing is to take you through the animal kingdom, which we shall be visiting on the way towards meeting your father. While we are on the way there, we will be able to discuss further what we have been going over recently, and you will gradually see yourself and others very differently. Any confusion you may still feel within yourself at present will be alleviated to some extent as we approach and enter the animal kingdom. But before we go, Judy, I think it is time you had a rest. I will leave you again to think things over and I will be back for you in a little while."

XII

After Doreen had left me in what seemed to be my regular little glade, I felt so mentally exhausted and confused and unsettled and unhappy about all that we had been discussing that I felt totally incapable of going through it any further at that point. In fact, I felt desperately tired. I think I must have nodded off to sleep because it seemed no time at all before Doreen was beside me and asking me whether I felt better for my rest.

I had to stop and think how I was feeling. To my amazement, I really felt quite relaxed. All the unhappiness and the emotional churning that I had been through seemed to have subsided.

I said to her, "Do you know, Doreen, for almost the first time in my life, after being through an emotional upheaval—because that is what I was finding our discussions to be—I have been able to sleep as though nothing had happened, and I am now feeling very, very relaxed and even happy within myself! I can't imagine why, because most of the things that we have been discussing seem to have had a negative effect. I don't understand how I can suddenly feel so relaxed and at peace within myself, but I do!"

"That, my dear Judy, is because you have been able to face it all in the right manner. You have accepted that a lot of the faults were yours, but that by no means were they all yours. You have recognised that the relationship you had with each of your husbands was fulfilling to some extent, despite the fact that each one ended in unhappiness, as your last marriage with Mickey would have, had you had the opportunity for it to have lasted longer than it did.

"In his case, it has ended in an element of unhappiness because, looking back at your months together, he does feel that he had a lively and happy time with you despite your illness and despite your arguments. He loved your sense of humour. He loved you yourself, and although he was feeling very worn down and beginning to feel a little bit exhausted at trying to work his way through a lot of the emotional situations that were created by much of your confusion, he does miss you, and he very sincerely regrets that he did not succeed in achieving the results in your marriage that he had hoped he could have done. But he will get over it; he is a very resilient young man. In fact, he is already able to play your records, to discuss you with people, and to act in a happy and cheerful manner about you. So this is something that you need not regret.

"In fact, although on the surface Mickey is regarded by most people as not having loved you as much as he might have done, otherwise he could not have got over it as quickly as he has, he has always been the sort of person who has looked at life, much as you also tried to do, as a case of 'Well, that's over and finished, and now I've got to go ahead with my life.' That is what he is doing. You used to tell yourself that. The difference between you two is that Mickey is able to go forward with his life without any backward glances. You, on the other hand, used to do that on the surface, but every so often, within yourself, those past hurts and disappointments would well up within you and cause the disturbance within your soul that created the tensions that, in their turn, caused you to become easily overemotional and easily overwrought.

"This is something you have always had within you, and it is something that would have also persisted here had I not, at this early stage of your arrival, asked you to please try and go back through all those years of emotional reaction. By asking you to face it all so early after your arrival, you will now be able to go forward with an element of peace within you.

"It is something that human beings on earth are often told by psychiatrists to try and do, but it seldom has a lasting effect. Here, the fact that you are away from earth's vibrations and all that life on earth did to you means that, once you can bring yourself to sort it all out in your mind, once you can see where you were wrong and where others were wrong, once you can manage to come to terms with all of that and realise that there is a future here where that sort of thing can be avoided, that the relationships and friendships you will form here will be on a different vibrational level, so that you will be able to see what they are really thinking about you and whether or not they truly like you, you will find it will be very much easier to keep yourself in a much more relaxed and happier frame of mind."

"That was one of my big problems before," I said to Doreen. "I never really knew who truly liked me and who was around me simply because of what they thought they could get out of me. I always hoped they liked me for myself, but I often found, after a period of time, that they only wanted my company for what they could get. In the end, I felt very uncertain of almost everybody. Even with those in whom I did try hard to place my trust, I would sometimes find myself reacting against them and doubting.

"It did make life exceedingly difficult to be almost always

93

regarded as 'Judy Garland' and seldom as myself. I did believe that Mickey was trying to treat me as an ordinary person. He used to try and persuade me to do housewifely tasks that I was not very good at doing despite the fact that I had always felt in my heart that I would like to try to do them or to be given the opportunity to do them. Sometimes he said, 'Just because you're Judy Garland on stage doesn't mean that you're not Mrs. Deans at home, and Mrs. Deans has got to learn to do the sort of jobs that any other housewife would do, as far as I'm concerned.' I don't think he meant to treat me as a slavey, but he did feel that I should be interested in trying to do little things about the home. Possibly, if I had been feeling more myself and less tired and confused, I might have taken more interest than I did.

"Looking back, I can see now why he might have got a bit exasperated. But I don't think I would ever have been any good at those sorts of things. I had spent too many years being 'Judy Garland' and just being expected to sing. The fact that I was no longer singing too well and might not be performing in the future as much as I used to do was something with which I had not yet come to terms. I liked the idea when Mickey said I need never work again unless I really wished to do so, but I think that, eventually, I would probably have found it difficult not to try and sing from time to time, even if I was no longer able to sing as much as I had done some years before."

"The main thing," said Doreen, "is that you have now been able to see everybody's point of view. You have been able to see that life here holds a future for you and that there will be people coming along with whom you will feel able to be happy. It should not be very much longer before you take your place among all those people who are of your disposition, because that is what happens here. We live and work with those who are closest to us in their own natures. If, for any reason, we have to visit people who are different from us in outlook, we use the protective cloak that I have previously mentioned to you.

"Now, dear Judy, it is time to take you to see the Animal Kingdom, where you will not need any such protection because, although you will be aware of them they will hardly be aware of you. It is something which is done to keep them as close to their own environment as possible. When they are approached by humans, it is for the express purpose of trying to help them to get well again in whatever way is necessary. Those who are not used to being with humans will remain where they are. Those who are used to being with humans and would like to return to being with humans, at least from time to time, will be helped to do so. Having explained that to you, I think you will find a lot to interest you and a lot to amaze you, but at no time will you find it necessary to use any protection." With that, we once again left the glade and set out along the path.

XIII

"You know," I said to her, "I really haven't had much experience with animals. I have had various dogs in my life. When I was younger, at the studios, I was given a dog from time to time, but for some reason or other we never seemed to be able to keep them for very long. There are some pictures of me with various dogs, but they usually belonged to the studios, and I only had them for publicity purposes because they felt that I should have animals. I had not chosen them for myself.

"My mother and I were not used to having animals because we had always been travelling with my dad and my sisters and we could not easily have had an animal travelling with us on the road. The few dogs that I had in my young days I was fond of in a way, but I never became deeply attached to them.

"Later on I had a few puppies around for the children, but after a while we'd be moving away or doing something or other that meant we had to part with the puppy, and it would have to be given away. So I never had a lot of opportunity to form a deep attachment to any animal except for one dog I had in the early 1950s. He was a collie-sheepdog called Sam. I was very fond of Sam, but I lost him to an illness when he was seven years old. I did feel sad about Sam, but the others just came and went. Does that sound very shallow?"

"Not really, dear," replied Doreen. "People have different attitudes towards their domestic pets. In some ways, we feel here that it is a pity domestic pets ever became a form of existence on earth. Originally, of course, there were no such things. Then various tribes adopted wild dogs, and from those came tame dogs

95

and gradually, over the planet, it became accepted for human beings to have tame dogs. The same thing can be said for cats. It is a complicated process that I cannot possibly go into here, but it has meant that there has been an imposition on those animals of human outlooks and human thinking that has, to some degree, restricted their own growth in their natural way of existence. Over the centuries, of course, those animals, particularly dogs and cats and horses, have gradually become 'toned down' to such a degree that they are able to live alongside human beings, but it is usually in a subservient capacity, dependent upon human beings.

"Those that have been treated well by their human caretakers will retain an affection for those caretakers and be happy to be with them here from time to time. There are others who have been neglected and in some cases put through acute pain and torture. To them a human being is anathema, particularly the person who should have been caring for them. There are others who have given their devotion to their human caretakers, despite the ill-treatment and pain handed out to them, and they have retained their devotion beyond any call for it. They have to be helped in their way.

"So you have the different kinds of domestic pets or tamed creatures, including, for example, parrots and parakeets, as well as those we've already mentioned. Then there are the other parts of the Animal Kingdom where you have the untamed creatures such as lions, tigers, cheetahs, bears, porpoises—you name them, we've got them!" said Doreen laughingly. "Those humans who appreciated such creatures while on earth can visit them and see them existing together in harmony and peace. If the human has sufficient love and the animal is receptive, it is possible for a human to approach a lion or a tiger or a bear and communicate with it. If the animal does not wish the human to approach it, it simply dismisses that human from its mind and cannot be approached."

I said to Doreen, "If it hadn't been for the experiences I've already had with those fishes and also the dog playing with the children, I would begin to think that I was back in Oz again!"

"I was wondering when I would next hear from you about Oz," said Doreen, laughing again. "But I realise that you have been gradually accepting your new surroundings and gradually getting away from your fears and doubts and the thoughts that you may be hallucinating."

"For some reason that I can't explain to you," I replied, "I feel a part of this existence already. I feel calm within myself, and I am very much looking forward to visiting all those animals and increasing my knowledge a little bit, because I feel totally ignorant of them in so many ways. I used to see some of the wild animals in movies and think how beautiful some of them were, but I would not have wanted to be near them. In fact, I was always terrified of being near a horse. They always seemed so big and liable to rear up at any moment, and I was most unhappy when I had to work near horses in a couple of my pictures. I kept away from them as much as I could, but there were times when I had to be near one and I wasn't too happy about it, although I do think they are very handsome-looking animals."

Discussing animals generally, we made our way towards their part of this extraordinarily beautiful world.

Chapter 2

I

Our approach to the Animal Kingdom must have been a gradual one. Doreen and I were talking much of the way, and I suddenly realised that the scenery we had been passing through, which had been very much like the kind to be found in New England in America, was gradually changing to what seemed to be the open prairies or plains, with just a few trees here and there. But whereas, on earth, the trees in that kind of environment would have been stunted and distorted, these were luxuriantly beautiful.

Doreen had to draw my attention to the kind of life that was there, possibly because, in my ignorance, I did not know what to tune into. But gradually I became aware of all the wild creatures I had previously seen only in photographs or in movies. There were the animals we had already discussed; there were panthers, antelopes, little baby fawns as well as adult deer; there were numerous brightly coloured birds, and there were also rivers and streams and ponds.. Then I became aware of buffalo and bison and some animals that Doreen described to me as water buffalo, as distinct from the buffalo I had recognised from America.

The light was very bright, but I did not have to adjust to it as I had done before when I had been taken to hear the teacher shortly after my arrival. Doreen explained that this was because it was a different kind of bright light. "This light is here because the animals existed on earth in this kind of light on the plains. Before, you were in the kind of bright light that assisted the teacher to reach you. It was a more spiritual brightness than this."

"It does get complicated," I commented.

"Yes, I realise that it must sound complicated, but we have different kinds of light here, depending upon the vibrations in which each creature exists."

As we progressed, we left the open plains behind and came to woodlands and forests. On that earlier occasion when I had been asked to make a decision as to whether or not we should go into the dark forest I had rejected it, but this kind of forest was different. The other one had been heavy and oppressive. Here, although we had tall trees, there were monkeys swinging from branch to branch, and there was a lot of general activity up in the branches. What looked like sunlight was filtering through, and it was all very cheerful and happy, yet also peaceful. I began to recognise all kinds of creatures who live in the trees, and there were some on the ground that I recognised, such as opossums and raccoons and little squirrel-like creatures, that we Americans know as chipmunks. There were many others that I cannot recall at present, but the main thing, Doreen explained to me, was for me to see and understand how these creatures existed. So, from time to time, we would stop and I would concentrate upon them.

I must confess that I had not previously taken much interest in these kinds of creatures. My life had been showbiz, showbiz, and more showbiz. I had spent most of my life in towns and cities, with little opportunity to go out into the American countryside, let alone travel to the other countries where many of these creatures existed. I seldom watched nature programs on television. I would sometimes watch an animal program with the children to keep them company and we would discuss the different animals, but I confess that they had never been an important part of my existence. So I was a little hesitant to even begin to approach them at this stage, and I said so to Doreen.

"Judy," said Doreen, "there is only one thing that I have to explain to you before we go any further. You have always, in your heart, had it in you to be a friend to all your fellow creatures. You have never intentionally hurt another living thing in your earth life. When it comes to children, you have given them a great deal of your love, even those that you did not know too well. If they came towards you to approach you, you always reached out in a friendly way to the average adult human being who approached you, not wishing to appear offhand or unkind. It was only when your nerves caused you to have acute anxiety complexes from time to time that it became difficult for people to be with you.

"We have been through all that. But it was never in your true nature to be unkind or hurtful to any living creature, and this includes animals. It was just, as you have already said, that you did not have much opportunity to mix with them. You would never have hurt an animal, and I believe that had you had people around you who were interested and who gained your interest, you would have been only too happy to have been included in visits to the countryside to see the different creatures. You were always prepared to be interested in other things if the situation was right, but you were so seldom away from the cities, and almost all of your companions, throughout your life, were also city-oriented. This meant that you had no particular incentive to take much interest in these creatures.

"The very fact that you would never have been intentionally unkind to any of them and the fact that you have now expressed your willingness to learn by going through their kingdom with me indicates that you are a very good subject. There are many others who have arrived here who have merely dismissed them and said that they 'did not want to be bothered with those.' Therefore, they have not even been through this part of our world.

"If they did but realise it, they are missing a great deal of pleasure. Animals are basically simple-hearted creatures. On earth they frequently had to fight to survive in the wild. Those that did not live in the wild and who were dependent upon human beings often had to fight to survive if people were not kind to them. Some, of course, suffered from excessive kindness to such a degree that they were overfed and underexercised, and their health was ruined accordingly. Many lost a lot of their individuality, their personalities, when they submitted to their human caretakers. Again, a lot of people, simply by treating another creature in the same way they would treat a human being, have sometimes killed it with kindness, as the saying goes.

"You are someone who, had you been given the responsibility of caring for an animal, would have done what you could to fulfil the task. You would never have left it to starve or to get unclean. You would have tried to give it some attention. The fact that you have that kind of behaviour within you means that you will not have much difficulty in relating to your fellow creatures here. It is simply that, up to this moment, you had little opportunity to think much about it, and so the idea had not crossed your mind. Now that I have implanted it there and you have shown some interest, you will not have anything to worry about, as you will see."

With that, she drew me hesitantly forward to a young deer that seemed to be grazing at the side of the path. "Animals are used to being able to fend for themselves for their food. It is an in-built characteristic of this young fawn, even though it was taken from its mother early in its life. It instinctively knew how to feed itself, and, because it is young and has not been here very long, it is still using the instincts that were in-built when it was born on earth. Although it failed to survive for long, because it was found and killed by a cheetah, it is now continuing here much in the same way as it would have continued on earth.

"Its body is the same as ours here. What has been technically known as the 'etheric' body of the creature will gradually grow to adulthood, just as the human children you have already seen will also grow and mature to adulthood. By the time it reaches its full size it will be a fully antlered male deer, but it will no longer need to mate and produce young, and so it will no longer need to fight its fellow deer. Because no creature here needs to eat, it will not be attacked by any of the wild creatures here that would have attacked it in the wild on earth. It will also no longer need to feed and so will cease to graze as it is now doing. It takes a period of adjustment for all creatures who arrive here, and this is just one example.

"Now then, this little creature was not on earth long enough to be afraid of human beings. He does not know what you are, because he has not experienced a human being. But if you extend your thought out to him and offer him your friendship, you should be able to impinge on his young, inexperienced mind sufficiently for him to respond to you if he wishes to do so." With that, she put her hand out towards the fawn and stood there.

"You come and do the same thing," she said to me, "and mentally say to him that you are feeling friendly towards him."

I did what Doreen asked. I had no objection to putting my hand out to the little creature; in fact, I felt that I wished to do so. It was the suggestion that I had to send out a thought at which I balked for a few moments! Then I realised that the very fact that I liked the idea of putting my hand out to the little fellow seemed to have the desired effect, because he immediately came towards us and we both stroked his flank. He put his warm, soft nose into my hand and nuzzled it, and I found myself getting down onto my knees and putting my arms around his neck while I put my cheek against the soft, sleek fur. Doreen stood there beaming at me. "For somebody who doesn't know what to do with animals, you've just made a remarkable recovery!"

We both laughed, and I said, "Well, it just seemed the instinctive thing to do. I have always felt like doing this with children. I never thought I'd do it to a deer."

We stayed with the little fellow a while longer and then made our way further along the path.

The next thing that registered with me was a giraffe. I looked up in wonderment as it stood there calmly surveying the scene. "I don't think I shall be able to put my arm round its neck, no matter how friendly it may be," I laughed to Doreen.

"No," she said, "and I would not attempt it if I were you, because it has not been here very long. I can tell by its attitude, and I don't think it will be feeling particularly friendly, because it has come here from a part of Africa where there was a lot of poaching, and it is used to running away from humans. It will not harm you, but I do not propose to disturb it by concentrating upon it. There is a baby giraffe over here," she added, leading me towards a considerably smaller version.

"This one," she said, "was born in a zoo. It is very tame, as it was treated well and was sometimes taken to the children's part of the zoo. Unfortunately, although they were very careful with it, its mother contracted some disease that meant she was not producing the right kind of milk for the little chap. Before they could find out what to do about it, he passed here. He'll be gentle and tame because he is used to being with humans who had been kind to him."

So we went over and stood beside him and, baby as he may have been, I stood there looking up at his beautiful, curling eyelashes and the soulful eyes. "Those eyes and lashes," I commented, "are better than any movie star's I've ever seen!"

Doreen laughed and stepped forward to put her hand gently on its flank and stroke it. I was standing slightly further away. He looked at me and, after a few moments, bent his head. Then he too nuzzled my hand. I stroked his nose and also that part of his neck that was nearest his head, while Doreen continued to stroke his flank. Then he removed his nose from my hand and gently nuzzled Doreen before walking slowly away.

"Well, that's two successes for you," smiled Doreen.

"Yes," I said to her in some surprise. "I didn't know I had it in me!"

Laughing, we made our way towards a clump of small trees by some water. There, yawning at me from the water, was a huge creature that even I recognised as a hippopotamus. "Aren't they dangerous?" I asked Doreen, a little apprehensively.

"On earth, yes, except occasionally you hear of a comparatively tame one in a zoo allowing its keeper to go up to it and even put his head in its mouth."

"Oh, my God!" I recoiled at that thought.

"But here it will not hurt you. I can tell that this fellow has been here quite a long time and he was a good age when he came here. He is used to being here now, and he is used to having humans approach him. He was never in a zoo. He was amongst those who were in the wild in Africa. He died of old age, and now he's a very placid old fellow."

"I think I'll take your word for that," I told Doreen.

"You don't have to. Why not take your courage in your hands and find out for yourself?"

Very, very slowly indeed, I walked towards this huge animal. He blinked at me in an unruffled manner, his nostrils just slightly above the surface of the water, as I approached the edge of the pool.

"Go into the water and talk to him," Doreen urged me.

I thought of those pictures I had seen of hippopotamuses on earth, where they always seemed to be almost up to their necks in exceedingly muddy water, but I now realised that the water in which he was standing was completely translucent. Remembering the water of the stream that I had stood in before, I took the chance of walking a little way into this pool and I found it to be beautifully soft and soothing. So I slowly approached this huge animal, who continued to blink at me in what almost seemed to be a benevolent manner, if a hippopotamus can be described as looking benevolent! He snorted a little, and the water cascaded, but he did not move, although I stood still to wait and see what happened next.

As I stood there looking at him, I felt myself, in some extraordinary way, drawn towards him, as though I felt that it would be rather pleasant to put my hand on that huge nose. In the end, to my own amazement, I did! I walked slowly forward—by that time I was almost floating in the water, and it still felt beautiful—and I put my hand on his nose. He still did not move, but he eyed me in a friendly manner. It was almost as though he was saying, "Hello! I'm glad you like me!" or something to that effect. I realise this must sound ridiculous, but it was a kind of welcome that he gave me. He was not effusive, but he did not reject me either, and he seemed quite pleasant and welcoming.

As I patted him on the nose, I could not help thinking back to my kids and how, a few years ago, when they had a bit younger, they would have loved to be able to do something like this. By this time in their lives, of course, they would probably have been as scared as their mama had been at the thought of doing such a thing. I laughed to myself to think that here I was, neck deep in water and patting the nose of a hippopotamus! How incredible can you get? Anyway, we both tired of this arrangement after a few moments, and I gradually made my way back to dry land and Doreen. Just as on the previous occasion when I had stepped out of the stream, I was completely dry the moment I had left the pool.

"What an experience!" I gasped. "I never thought I'd ever do anything like that!"

"How did it feel?" asked Doreen.

"Extraordinary! I can't explain it to you!" I said to her. "I did get a feeling of friendliness coming from that animal. I got a feeling of pleasure from stroking it on the nose, and he seemed to get a similar feeling of pleasure from me wanting to do that! It sounds ridiculous, absolutely ridiculous, and yet, do you know, I feel as though I have just had a marvellous experience."

"Well, you have," said Doreen. "You have made a friendly contact with a creature that you have never met on earth and that you were unlikely to meet, and you find that you can each get pleasure from having spent a little time in each other's company. That is how it should be. This is how the truly receptive humans have a much happier time when they come here than those who feel they have no time whatsoever for any creature who exists beyond themselves."

As Doreen and I wended our way along the various pathways, she continued to draw my attention to different birds and animals and even some fishes that we saw in the streams. Each and every one had its fascination, its individual personality, its different vibration. The fishes emanated music, as had those I had encountered earlier, and the birds were singing their beautiful songs. With the mammals, it was not so much that they were making any particular sounds other than the occasional roar or chittering as we passed by, but that each seemed to be surrounded by a colourful aura almost in the same way as we humans were wearing various colours in our clothing. Although the animals were still in their fur and looking as they had on earth, they somehow had shades of colour and light around them.

As Doreen drew my attention to this, she explained to me how one could learn to read the mood of that particular creature. Indeed, as we moved along, I began to respond to their different auras (as I learned that these colours and light were called), and I could see one lion who had had quite a bad time in the past. There was a darkness around him, but there were lighter shades beginning to penetrate the darkness. Doreen explained that he had not been long in our world. He had been exceedingly poorly treated in a circus in Central Europe, and when he died it had

104

been from some form of infestation of the intestines that nobody had discovered, as they had not had him examined by a vet. He had been beaten when he had refused to respond, and the reason he had not responded was that he was unable to digest any food and had felt lethargic and in great pain. He had died in acute agony and, when he had first arrived here, had lain for a while in darkness. This had lasted until he had been reached by those in our world who were prepared to help a creature in that kind of distress until he could be returned to the surroundings in which he now was.

Although it was still taking him some time, he was on the way to recovery, and he would eventually be completely drawn out of his present condition and into the brightness of his fellow creatures. She showed him to me as only one of numerous similar disaster cases that arrive here all the time, and she told me that he was only one example of numerous creatures who had been mistreated on earth by human beings.

Doreen went on to tell me that, during her earlier days of being in our world, she had undertaken to help some of the creatures who had arrived here in distress. She related to me the case of a small capuchin monkey that had been in the possession of a small boy and his mother, having been purchased from a pet store. They had simply been told by the owner of the pet store to feed it on bananas and grapes. This they had done for many months without any variation of this diet. Consequently, the poor monkey developed internal problems and a lot of his fur came out.

The family could not understand why this was occurring. They thought they were being kind to it, and the little boy cuddled it when they went out along the street. They did not realise that the monkey could not survive the temperatures, particularly the outside temperatures into which they were taking it during the colder months. It went from warm room to cold street without any external wrapping beyond a small wool jacket. This did not keep it as warm as it needed to be, having been in their country only a short time and having been brought from a hot climate. It developed pneumonia, which, on top of its internal problems, caused it to pass to our world.

Because it had been treated kindly by the little boy's family it did not arrive here in a mentally distressed state, but it was in such a poor physical condition that it took a while before its etheric body could be made strong again. It was then able to be returned to an area where it could join its fellow monkeys. After that, of course, it blossomed into a very happy creature. Nevertheless, through ignorance on the part of its human caretakers, it had suffered unnecessarily on earth, and it had come to this world much more quickly than it would have done in other, more natural, circumstances.

Doreen went on to explain that, when creatures come here after only a short earth life, particularly where they have been held in conditions which are not their natural conditions by birth, they arrive here under a handicap. They need time to overcome that handicap and to form a natural existence here with their fellow creatures in the Animal Kingdom.

"I know this must be a difficult thing for you to understand, Judy, but just as human beings have to learn to develop and to expand their consciousness in so many ways, so do the mammals, the birds, and the fishes. They each, in their own way, progress to different levels of existence as we humans progress to different levels of existence. They do not progress in the same way as we do, and, after a period of time, we tend to progress away from them as much as they have always been partly away from humans. But while we are in certain levels of our existence here and in certain levels of progression, we get a great deal of pleasure and delight from being with and seeing the animals. They, in their turn, can be given on element of progression, provided we meet them in the proper manner. But beyond that there is no permanent contact.

"They continue to progress, and they continue to increase their intelligence and their understanding in many ways. However, I do abhor those teachings that are sometimes given to humans on earth by people from here that suggest that an animal, having increased its knowledge and intelligence beyond a certain level here, will eventually become a human being. That is utter nonsense and should never be taught. I sincerely hope those that teach such nonsense will eventually be prevented from doing so. Unfortunately, it is sometimes beyond the control of others here to stop them saying such things. I will go into that at a later time, when I discuss with you the ways in which people here can, in certain circumstances, communicate with those who are still on earth."

"I have often wondered about that!" I exclaimed. "It has intrigued me for years, but I never felt able to find out more about it. I always felt a little bit scared. I used to go along sometimes, at parties, with those who wanted to tell fortunes or to read my palm or even to look into the crystal, but I never really took it at all seriously. Yet, in the back of my mind, I felt that such possibilities truly do exist, but that it would probably be better not to find out any more about it."

"I know what you mean," acknowledged Doreen. "There is such a lot of controversy and fallacy and misunderstanding that has built up around the whole subject over very many centuries that, although a light is beginning to break through, it is still only a tiny light compared with what we could do in the right conditions if only people could be brought to understand the seriousness of the whole matter and to handle it all correctly. Again, Judy, that is something I will have to discuss with you later on, because you have more than enough to understand at the moment without me going into something that is going to involve you very much indeed in the future."

I looked at her in some surprise. "Why would that involve me?" I asked her.

"Well, that is something that comes a little later on. I do not want to fill your mind with that sort of thing until we have got you past your present series of experiences."

II

Presently she brought me to a little gate set into a hedge that was growing in wild and colourful profusion. She took me through the gate and along a little winding path to a front door, where she sent out the thought (it was only a thought, but I picked it up): *Would it be all right to come in? This is Doreen and a new friend!*

The door was opened by an elderly gentleman who had a round, pleasant face with bright blue eyes and a mass of white hair. He was in his shirt-sleeves and a waistcoat and trousers and shoes, much as he would have been on earth, and I wondered how it was that he did not have all the colours around him that

107

Doreen and I had. He smiled at us and motioned us into what looked like a small workman's cottage. The floor, which was made of flagstones, was bare. There were a few plain wooden chairs standing around, and there was a polished wooden table in the centre of the room. There were pictures on the walls and a fireplace with a mantle. There were various items on the mantle, including candlesticks and a clock, and it was somewhat cluttered.

"How are you?" asked Doreen.

"Very much better, thank you," he answered, motioning us to sit down, which we did.

"I thought I would bring my new friend along because, as you see, she has already got those beautiful colours around her and she has only recently arrived."

He smiled and nodded at me in a friendly fashion and came over and shook hands. I smiled back, and he returned to his seat.

Doreen went on to tell him, "This young lady has come here after a very difficult life on earth. But because she has always retained her honesty and a certain cheerfulness of outlook and a feeling of love within her for people, despite sometimes feeling very bitter over some of the things that happened to her, she has immediately been accepted on a vibrational level that has put all those colours around her that you can see. I want you to understand, my dear friend, that this is all because of her own mental outlook.

"You have it within you to move in the areas where she has been moving. We have reached you via part of the Animal Kingdom, and she has already been talking and playing with the children. They all loved her, and she is now on her way to experience more of the animals before she moves on to meet those of her family and friends who are already ahead of her here. As I have told you before, you have a loving sister and your mother and father waiting to meet you here, but you cannot meet them until you are happier in your mind than you were when you arrived here, because what you had drawn around you would hurt them. It will not hurt you at the moment as much as it would hurt them, but it is hurting you and keeping you in the area where you are at the moment and preventing you from moving to better places and feeling far happier.

"I wanted you to meet this young lady because I want you

to realise that she has been through not just some of the hurts that you went through, but far more of those hurts than you experienced. Yet she has retained a beautiful life within herself, which immediately took her to a beautiful place here. It is within you to do the same, if you could only learn to bring yourself out of the dark frame of mind into which you had let yourself be drawn.

"I can see from the light in this room that you are beginning to feel a little bit better. I will be along to see you again soon, and there will be others coming to see you, but I just wanted to introduce you to my new friend and for you to realise how easy it really is for you to bring yourself into happier circumstances. I will not keep you any longer as I have a lot to show Judy. We are on our way to see another part of the Animal Kingdom, but I wanted to see how you were, and I wanted to let you see my friend, who is such an example to you of how you could be."

Ted, as I learned his name to be, eyed me reservedly, as if to say, "Who the hell is she that I should get this sort of ticking off!" Something within me, that I could not explain at that precise moment, made me go over to him. I took both his hands in mine and looked him straight in the eyes as I smiled at him and said, "Ted, I don't know anything about you. All I know is that my name is Judy and I came here very suddenly. At the time I came here I did feel that I was loved by somebody, but I'd had many years of feeling that I hadn't been. I can only say to you that, although that brought a lot of unhappiness, a lot of uncertainty, and some bitterness, I always was prepared to try and believe in the next person who came along and told me that they loved me. They didn't always love me, but some people who said it meant it.

"Doreen has shown me all of this and where I went wrong and where they went wrong. I can only tell you that although I am sad in some respects, because I have left three children behind me whom I love very much, I know that they are all right and that I shall be seeing them again eventually. I am trying to adjust myself to my new surroundings here. I have already found a lot of beautiful things, and I hope you will find them, too, before much longer."

With that, I squeezed his hands more tightly, kissed him on the forehead and stepped back towards Doreen, who also smiled

109

at him and said, "Well, Ted, that was a surprise for you, wasn't it? None of your previous visitors have done that to you!"

He stood there looking dumbfounded. I saw tears come into his eyes, and for some reason that I could not understand, tears came into mine. But they were not sad tears. I felt that I had made some sort of breakthrough, without quite knowing what I had done or how I came to act quite the way I had done.

"We must go now, Ted," said Doreen. "Someone will be along to see you before much longer."

He came to the door and watched us go along the path to the gate, where we turned and waved to him. He did not wave back, but he looked at me long and hard, and then he winked. I winked back, before turning the corner to continue on our way.

"Judy," said Doreen, "that is the first time that any of the people whom I have taken to see Ted have gone up to him in that manner."

"Well, I don't really know why I did it!" I said to her. "Mind you, I did always have this kind of reaction to people who came up to me, but this was usually because they knew I was Judy Garland. They came up and fell all over me for one reason or another, or else they were looking shy or uncertain, and I always felt that taking their hand would give them some form of confidence. I have always done that, and I used to get told off for it sometimes. I was told that I was too emotional and too demonstrative, and there were many times when I was misunderstood for reacting that way to people."

"Yes, I know you did, dear," responded Doreen. "That was one of the reasons you were so easily hurt, because people did not understand when you went forward in friendliness and sympathy. They used to have all sorts of peculiar ideas about your impulsive nature. But let me tell you that what you have just done has been a big step forward, a breakthrough, for that man. He did have a difficult life, but he turned very bitter in his mid-forties. He let that bitterness grow around him and completely enclose him. The reason he is looking the way he is at the moment is because we have not been able to break him away from his earth surroundings. This is why he is still in his original clothes and his original cottage."

"On earth?" I said to her, in some surprise.

"No, dear. He is no longer on earth, but we have had to create around him his original surroundings to give him the sort of vibration in which he can comfortably exist here until we can break him out of that bitterness. He was in a darker place when he first arrived, but we have managed to get him this far, so that he is now in his original surroundings, which look a little more pleasant than they did on earth. We cannot get him to be his true self until we have removed all that bitterness. I could see, the moment you went towards him and spoke to him in that way, that a layer of bitterness peeled away from him. Some of it is still there. Even the way he winked at you showed that he had not completely understood your approach, and it was good of you to wink back."

"I didn't really know what it was all about," I explained to her. "I had this impulse to go forward and be nicer to him. Then, when we got to the gate and turned back and he winked, I began to think that maybe I had done the wrong thing. But I knew that you and I were walking away, and so, for some reason that I cannot explain, I decided I would wink back and hope that my wink would not be misunderstood. It was just my quick way of trying to escape without feeling too embarrassed."

Doreen laughed heartily at this. "I do understand your predicament. I felt your amazement throughout the entire session, but I can tell you that something within you caused you to act in the right way. You acted impulsively, but it was the right action, and it did show, as I have felt and said all along, just how much love and goodness you have in you if it can possibly be steered into the right direction."

I looked at her a little ruefully. "I'm not quite sure I like that phrase 'in the right direction'," I said to her.

"Well, dear, I only say that because you did give a lot of love to certain people when you were on earth, and it was not always appreciated. Others who would have appreciated it did not receive as much of it as, possibly, you could have given them."

"I have gathered that from some of our past discussions," I said to her, "but I have always been an impulsive person and I have not always stopped to think too clearly."

"That has been part of your trouble," said Doreen, "and that is one of the things that I have to try and help you overcome.

111

Nevertheless, you have just scored a victory for yourself, and you have just helped one very lonely and embittered old gentleman to take one step further forward to the better existence he will eventually come to enjoy. Now let us continue to see more of the animals."

III

As we walked along the road, we saw other creatures that I had not met before, including at one point a baby walrus in a large pool of water. He was a fat little creature with soulful eyes, and I had no difficulty in bending down to him by the edge of the water and patting him on the head. Doreen said he was an example of a baby walrus who had been born in captivity but had not survived for long. He had not been harmed in any way; he had simply not succeeded in surviving long in the environment in which he had been born. He was happy little creature, and he would shortly be joining his fellow walrus.

She told me that, of all the creatures who come to this world from earth, some of the sea animals are considered to be the most highly developed of all the animals in the Animal Kingdom. She said, "You will probably not be too surprised to learn, Judy, since there has been a lot of publicity about it in your world, that the most highly developed of all the sea creatures is the bottle-nosed dolphin. All dolphins are highly intelligent creatures, but the bottle-nosed dolphin has the highest intelligence of them all.

"It has long baffled human beings as to how it uses its extrasensory perception, and it has long been a matter of sadness here that so many of these highly intelligent, highly sensitive creatures are kept in captivity at all. Although we realise they have an extreme fascination for humans, it is a deep unkindness to them to keep them in captivity. Their natural intelligence is to some extent impaired by the closed surroundings in which they are kept, although they give every indication of enjoying the tricks they are asked to perform. In some ways they do enjoy performing, because they are friendly and communicative creatures and they are doing something that demonstrates that they have intelligence and because it seems to please those land creatures who are around them.

112

"But captivity does, unfortunately, have a bad effect upon them. Their sonar impulses, which are their ways of communicating and hearing, can be affected in much the same way as a continuous battery of noises on a human eardrum can render that human being either totally deaf or almost totally deaf. Also, just as if you put a very high-pitched and loud screeching sound into the ear of a human being over a prolonged period, that human being could be reduced to madness, confined surroundings can have similar effect on the poor dolphin. The sonar noises that he emits can bounce back off the walls of the pool where he is kept and so confuse and confound him, sometimes reducing the poor animal to hysteria.

"It is important to understand this may depend on where the dolphin spends the larger part of his time, but many dolphins are kept in totally unsuitable and confining places. This is why we are so sad here that these highly intelligent and sensitive creatures, who love to leap and swim for many miles at a rapid pace through the oceans of the world, are ever caught and brought to captivity. That is why so many of them fail to survive in captive surroundings irrespective of how extensive their human captors think those surroundings to be.

"There is not such a dire effect on walrus and seals, as they have not got the same high intelligence as the dolphins and they have not got the same extrasensitive system of communication, so their state of mind and hearing does not get affected in the same way. It does, however, also restrict their activities. They are all strong swimmers and they like to swim for many, many miles in the seas. None of these creatures are able to so do when they are confined to a pool. It is just like confining a human being to a prison cell for the rest of his or her life.

"The effect is the same on all creatures who are born to be free. The birds, the apes, the great cats are all born to be free and not caged, but they are caged, and however well fed they may be, however kind their captors may try and be, their restriction can only have a demoralising effect on their whole mental attitude to life. It is claimed that, on the savannas in Africa, for example, lions are normally lethargic, lazy creatures and that they do not travel very far other than to look for food. It is claimed that, in captivity, their food is provided and they remain lethargic and so they are not missing very much. But any living creature who is deprived of its natural environment, who is deprived of any freedom of will and movement, has to be affected in a detrimental way.

"Why is it that, when human beings are put into prison, their form of punishment is a restriction of their freedom and sometimes solitary confinement? How often do human beings restrict animals and also ban them to solitary confinement? They do not see it as such, but it is just the same. The animals may be fed and watered, but they are frequently left alone for very many hours of the day and night without any companionship.

"Even those people who claim to love their own domestic pets, such as dogs and cats and parakeets and rabbits, keep them away from their own kind, and leave them alone in the house or in the kennel or a hutch for many hours each day while the humans go out all day and possibly for the evenings as well. Yet, they expect the animals to remain docile and happy. How can a poor creature with any sort of mind of its own—and they do all have individual personalities and minds—live a truly happy and fulfilling existence? It cannot be, especially among the naturally gregarious creatures.

"Many such creatures who come here have to be helped by us to adjust mentally to their new existence, and the task can be just as long and hard as it is for a human being who comes here from a lot of deprivation in various ways.

"People who keep a bird in a cage for the whole of its existence should stop to realise that it is, for the bird, like a human being never, ever going out for a walk along the street or in a park, let alone for a walk through the woods or along the coast. Even a caged bird that has been born in captivity and knows no other life and would probably be afraid of the outside world if it were let out of its cage, can be harmed by confinement. Of course, some are cheeky little creatures that fly away at the earliest opportunity, but they are not primed for living outside with nature or oriented to fend for themselves. They often die, although some do manage to survive and breed and adapt themselves to the outside world. Others remain cramped, both mentally and physically, by their cages. They pull out their feathers in frustration. They grow lumps. It is nearly always because they are not living the life they were meant to lead. Of course, in the case of caged birds, there is frequently too much inbreeding, just as there is often too much inbreeding in pedigree dogs. This often produces highly strung creatures with far less stamina than their mongrel counterparts.

"All this has to be coped with here. The first hospital we are going to see is for some of those creatures who have come here from homes of people who loved them and felt they were doing the right thing for them. I would like you to see, my dear Judy, the effects of some of that love on some of those creatures.

"Now then, this is where I am going back to my original discussion with you regarding protection. On the whole it is not necessary, as I have said before, to protect yourself when walking through the Animal Kingdom. Most of the animals that you have already seen are back in their normal environment. Even that lion was on the way to recovery, and you had no unhappy impingement on your aura.

"The old gentleman I took you to see was just outside and beyond the Animal Kingdom, but he is in a place where he can be shown the animals as soon as he feels he wishes to do so. His vibration has now reached the point where it is not harmful to such as you or I or the animals. When he first came here, he was exceedingly bitter. Both of us, as well as the animals, would have needed to be protected from the bitterness that he was giving off. Now he is in a much, much happier frame of mind, which is why there was hardly any necessary change in our vibrational level when we met him, although I did give you an imperceptible cloak of protection without mentioning to you that you needed it."

"I must confess, I didn't even think about it. I just walked in! I didn't know, of course, what I was walking into. I felt strange all the time I was there, as though I didn't know what it was all about or what I ought to be saying or doing. What I did say and do was completely impulsive, without any real thinking! But, yes, now you mention it, how is it that, if he was not wearing similar colours to those we are wearing, I didn't need protection?"

"There is a very fine dividing line, sometimes, between seeing and not seeing a person's aura. His will start to be visible before very much longer. Because he is now on the way to recovery and he is no longer being belligerent or deeply unhappy, very little protection was needed by us. Now, as we approach the animal hospital, it is not so much in the early stages that you will need any protection against the animals attitudes. Most of them, having come from places where they were not specifically unloved, will not be giving off any vibration that will be harmful to you. Later on, when we encounter creatures who have arrived here in different circumstances, you will need a stronger element of protection, and that I will explain to you when we get there. At present, we are approaching a reception centre, for want of a better word, for those creatures who have come here from domestic homes, who have not been intentionally hurt but who have, nevertheless, sustained an element of damage to their outlook."

IV

We entered what seemed to me to be a small paddock. Standing in the corner, with a look of utter dejection, was a donkey. Mind you, those few donkeys that I had ever seen in my life on earth had always seemed to give off an air of dejection. It seemed to me it was usually the way that they stood, with their four legs slightly splayed and their head down, as well as having a shaggy coat. Doreen led me up to the little fellow, who had the most beautiful, chocolate-coloured fur. It was shining and glistening, not rough and ill-kept, as the donkeys I had seen on earth. I instinctively put one hand onto his neck and the other hand onto his muzzle and his soft, velvet nose. He blew gently into my hand and softly scraped the ground with one of his front hooves.

"Hello, Neddy," I greeted him, without having any idea what his name really was, but the donkeys in my children's books always seemed to be called Neddy!

"He was among some donkeys who used to give children rides," explained Doreen. "His owner fed him regularly on hay, gave him apples and oranges from time to time and groomed his coat once a week. In the winter he was stabled with the other donkeys, and all through the summer months they were left to roam in the field. Unhappily, never at any time did the owner examine their hooves. This little chap got some sort of disease of the hooves. His fetlocks became swollen and inflamed, the hooves began to get some sort of fungus, and every hoof became distorted. He walked in great pain, and it was not until he had walked and

116

limped in pain for some long time that his owner realised that whatever it was was not going to go away. He then called the vet.

"At least this owner did call the vet, who immediately diagnosed it as something which was now beyond any chance of recovery because it had been left for so long. The animal had to be put down. In this instance it was ignorance rather than intentional lack of interest on the part of the owner. He had eventually called the vet, and he had accepted the advice to put it down. But there are many other instances where the owners do not care. When the animal cannot work, they either beat it or they leave it to starve or leave it in the fields to take its own course, and the animal will often die in acute agony. One of these you will probably be seeing as we journey through. But this little chap came here after a number of painful months, and sooner than he need have done, simply due to the ignorance of his owner.

"Anybody who keeps any sort of creature should find out in advance what they ought to be doing. The first thing this man should have done was to have checked each donkey's hooves at least once each week in order to see whether anything had got into a hoof, whether any sort of disease may have started. Had he checked them properly in the early days, this would have been a very minor thing for the vet to have handled. The donkey is fine now and it will not be long before he joins his fellow donkeys."

We moved across the field towards a horse. He was a huge animal and seemed to tower above me. He was a glistening chestnut colour with a white, starlike, marking on his forehead, and he had a beautifully flowing mane and tail. I found that I was no longer nervous of being close to a horse.

"He was a racehorse," explained Doreen, "who broke his leg and was shot. There was nothing else wrong other than the broken leg. In many instances, it is not always possible to mend a broken leg of a horse, and it is sometimes decided that the animal should be shot. I am not going into that outlook at this stage, but this is a horse that fractured its leg around the knee. It could have had surgery that, in time, would have restored its leg to at least a comfortable walking function, although he would never have been able to race again. It was also a gelding—in other words it could not have been used for breeding. The immediate decision of the owner, therefore, was that, as it could only be sold for very little

117

indeed, it should be shot to avoid the expense of the veterinary fees. So it was shot.

"This creature has come here from a comparatively confined life. Physically, it was well cared for because people wanted to make money from it. It was groomed daily; it was exercised and fed all the right food. It was regularly checked by a vet and kept in perfect physical shape. But its mental attitude included an element of frustration. It was not consciously deeply unhappy, but it led a very regulated life. It knew precisely when it was going to be exercised and when it was going to be fed. It was shut in the stable when it was not being exercised or fed. He could hear his fellow horses in the other stalls, but he was not close enough to have their companionship. He was lonely, he was frustrated, and his outlook was very restricted.

"When he came here so suddenly, we had to cope with two things. First was the fact that an otherwise healthy animal had been suddenly ejected from his physical body by the shot, thus damaging the etheric body of the animal. When he came here, therefore, he was not glossy and gleaming as you now see him. He was surrounded with a complete darkness because it had happened so suddenly and his fairly simple mind could not understand what had happened. His etheric body was so thin, so unable to withstand the vibrations that would be his normal vibrations of existence, that he had to be restricted to special surroundings. It is difficult to explain this in a way that is easy for you to understand at present, but he had to be kept in the spirit world equivalent of a darkened room until his etheric body became sufficiently strong to withstand the light into which he is now emerging.

"His mind was running along a comparatively narrow track, and this is now also gradually opening out and blossoming. When he is returned to the complete freedom that will soon be his, with a strong body and a gradually blossoming mind, he will be able to live comfortably and happily and in freedom, side by side with his fellow creatures. His mind will gradually develop and expand in the way it would have started to develop had he lived a completely free life on earth.

"Now, over here," she said, leading me to yet another part of the field, "is a little horse who was used by a tinker."

I looked at her blankly and she explained that this tinker had lived in England in the city. He had kept this horse with a cart and had travelled from house to house collecting old furniture and old clothing, and so on.

"You may call him something different in America. Not too many still trade," Doreen went on, "but this little horse was kept in a shed in the man's backyard in the middle of the city. He was taken out daily with the cart, and he got used to moving in the traffic. He was given a regular feed of hay and oats, and he was fairly comfortable in his shed. He had straw, and a small heater was also left there for him in the winter months. The man had a dog, a little black and white mongrel, who shared the shed with him from time to time.

"But it was hardly a natural environment for a horse. He never saw a field or a fellow horse. He and the dog shared an element of companionship, but it was a very unnatural existence. He came here from old age. The man, to give him his due, did not overwork him, and he let him live out his days in the shed, but the horse was not, in the end, getting much of a life, and it had never been very much of a life. The man was fond of his horse and he did what he thought was the best for it. But, of course, what would have been the best was for it to be in a field and able to run in freedom with his fellow horses.

"Now he has come here with his etheric body impinged upon by a feeling of being cramped, because he never experienced the environment that he should have been allowed to experience. He is placid and docile, but he is mentally slower than he should be, and there is no joy in him. There is a feeling of lassitude, a lack of interest in everything around him. He was so used, over the years, to wearing blinkers in the street, to having nothing else around him but concrete and noisy vehicles, and to then coming home to his little shed, that he has turned right in on himself mentally and he has to be drawn out of that. He is very much better than he was, but he still lacks interest in anything that is going on around him. He now has to be helped to develop his mind and his body so that he can eventually join his fellows."

We then came to a little gate in what looked like a part of a farmyard, and I saw that there was a pig lying on its side, looking very pink and placid and well scrubbed.

"Now, this old pig," said Doreen, "was kept by a farmer for

producing piglets. She was not among those that were killed or taken to market, and so, in her way, she had a comparatively easy time of it. But every season she produced piglets, and every season she lost them after a few weeks and was left on her own again. That did not have a bad effect on her, really. However, in the end she got too old to bear any more piglets. She was regarded as an additional expense to feed, and having been treated for years in a quite kindly way by the farmer and his family, having often been petted by the children, she was suddenly disposed of as an unnecessary expense and her throat was cut. That was such a mental shock to her that she has lain here in a state of shock for quite a long while. She is not taking any interest in anything that is going on around her, and she has to be helped to try and find the interest to get back on her feet when, believe it or not, she will eventually join the group soul for pigs."

"The group soul? What do you mean by the group soul?" I asked.

"I suppose I put that rather abruptly," said Doreen. "A pig does have an individual personality in some ways, but it cannot think for itself very clearly and because of that it does not retain a strongly individual personality after it has been here for a while. Therefore, she will probably join her fellow pigs who have come here in similar circumstances, and they will all be together and think together and exist together as a group. They will not stand out in an individual way, as do a lot of other creatures who have higher intellects. Do you follow me?"

"Yes, I think so," I said a little hesitantly. "Give me time to think about that!"

"Right!" said Doreen, smiling.

"Now," she said, becoming serious again, "I want you to protect yourself against where we are going, not because you will come to any real harm but, knowing the sadness you experienced and absorbed when with that poor child, you may have a similar reaction to where I am now taking you."

She led me towards a much darker area, and I felt myself being enclosed in what seemed like a heavy blanket. It literally did feel heavy and dark upon me as we entered the atmosphere that Doreen warned me contained a number of animals who had come here from exceedingly unhappy circumstances.

"This area that we are now entering, Judy," explained Doreen, "is largely the area where we receive the domesticated animals. These animals have been dependent upon mankind during the whole of their existence. They have been tamed or trained and used, and frequently abused, in so many different ways. They come here in a terrible state, poor creatures, and those humans here who are prepared to spend time doing so will do all they can to help them regain their natural selves as soon as is possible. Some of them come here having been beaten unmercifully, having been starved, having been confined without any signs of kindness or understanding from the humans on whom they had no alternative but to depend.

"Human beings have a tendency to say that this, that, or the other person who they think is terrible 'behaves like an animal.' I would like to say, as would all of us who work here with animals, that no animal behaves to its fellow creatures in the abominable way that some human beings behave towards animals or even to other human beings."

She led me over to a very dark corner of an area that, as I looked around me, seemed to be a stable. In the corner was a little donkey, if you could call it that. It was lying on its side. I could see it was the shape of a donkey, but all around it was darkness, and it gave off a cramped and dehydrated feeling. The animal had got a complete etheric body, but I could feel only a very, very faint sign of any life coming from it. Doreen explained that it had developed trouble in its hooves in a somewhat similar way to the little donkey that we had already met. In this instance, however, the owner had not called for a vet but had merely shut it in a shed without food or water and had left it to die without any attention whatsoever. The poor dumb animal had been left in a filthy condition in filthy surroundings to die of starvation, with the disease that had already affected its hooves gradually creeping further up its legs towards its body. The whole of his legs had been inflamed. His body had swollen and distended and become bloated beyond all belief due to starvation, until dehydration had set in and the poor animal had gradually shrivelled.

This donkey suffered and died rather like the poor child I had previously seen who had been treated so abominably by its parents. It was, according to Doreen, to some extent going through

121

a similar process to the child, and Doreen tried to explain to me where the differences arose.

"Here you have a creature with a comparatively simple mind. If treated kindly, it will respond in a simple and kind manner to whoever is handling it. Although it is incapable of completely understanding all that is going on around it, it did go through untold physical agony. Although its mind could not comprehend precisely why it was in such agony, it still suffered a very great deal of totally unnecessary pain. Because of that, it is taking us some while to get it out of the frame of mind in which it was when it eventually passed here.

"The child had, of course, been hampered by having been deaf and dumb, and, therefore, her mind has not expanded as much as would the mind of a child who had not been so hampered. But she had a sufficiently developed mind to realise that she was being ill-treated by her parents and that she had been locked in a room without any attention whatsoever. Both she and the donkey suffered the same amount of pain. The child's agony of mind was greater because she had the ability to think a little bit further than the donkey, but he had the additional inflammation to his legs.

"It does not alter the fact that human beings inflicted this terrible carnage on the physical being of two living creatures and that the donkey deserved to have the right treatment just as much as the child deserved to have it. Because you have a strong cloak of protection around you, you will not be so affected as you were by the emanation from the child. If you had not got this protection around you you would feel the acute physical pain of this poor little creature who did no harm to anyone other than to get a disease of his hooves that he would not have got had he received proper attention. He will get better eventually, but it is going to take a long time."

With that, Doreen led me further along to where there was a dog lying on its side. He reminded me of my Sam. He was a collie, and Doreen explained that he had been owned by some people who had gone on holiday and left it shut up in the house with all the windows closed. They had not arranged for anyone to visit the poor animal to feed it or to let it outside or to exercise it. They had simply put down various bowls of food and water in different parts of the room and also a box of earth which they supposed it could use for its toilet. It had been shut up in the house for two weeks during an intensely hot period of the year. The sun had streamed through the windows on this poor creature, and there was a lack of oxygen as the days went by. The food went mouldy, and the water dried up.

When they returned home, he was in a terrible condition. He had lost a great deal of weight. His tongue was swollen in his mouth. His eyes were glazed, and he could hardly stand up. His coat was filthy and matted because he had had no alternative but to excrete in the room. They took it to the vet, who said the dog had to be put down because there was nothing he could do for it.

He reported the family to the authorities, and they were banned from keeping another animal. He has not been here long and we will be able to get him back on his feet before too much longer, but, again, a perfectly healthy animal came here, after a terrible two weeks, simply because its human caretakers had so little thought for it, so little intelligence or caring for it, that they treated it in that manner."

We then moved to the next stall where there was a dark patch. Doreen asked me to concentrate on it, and I eventually saw there was a rabbit in this dark patch.

"Look closely at that rabbit. What colour would you say it is?"

"It looks grey," I replied.

"Look again," said Doreen. As I concentrated through the darkness, I realised it had fluffy white fur.

"This poor creature," she said to me, "had originally been in a pet store as a juvenile rabbit. It was bought by some people who wanted to use it for its fur. Because of this, it was kept away from other creatures and well fed so that it grew large and its coat remained in good condition. When they felt it was ready for their purposes, they simply hit it on the head and cut into it with a knife. But they had not successfully killed the poor creature. It began to come round while its fur was being removed. When they realised what was happening, they tried to wring its neck but did not immediately succeed in that attempt. The poor creature went through an agonising time, what with having the incision into its flesh to remove its fur and then being strangulated in a not very professional manner, before it actually passed from its physical body. Here it is in darkness until we can get it out of its state of acute shock.

"Rabbits are comparatively simple-minded creatures, but they are very gregarious. They like to live together in a group. This rabbit had been taken from its mother at a young age and sold. Having been kept in isolation and then treated in that manner, we are having to combat here both the isolation and the agonising death.

"What a lot of these brutal human beings do not care to think about is that every living creature on earth feels pain. Some have not got the intellect of the higher creatures, but they all feel pain and hunger and thirst. They all feel extreme heat and extreme cold. They all suffer if they are not kept in the right conditions, just as human beings suffer. Each one of God's creatures deserves to be allowed to live in its own environment in a state of dignity."

I was then led further along towards a seething mass of darkness. It looked revolting in the way that it just seemed to seethe in darkness. I felt rather than actually smelt a terrible stench. I said to Doreen in horror, "My God! What have we got here?"

"This," she said, "is part of a group soul. These were battery chickens. They were kept in close, cramped quarters to provide eggs in quantity, and then they were slaughtered. They were kept in such cramped conditions, as are most battery chickens, that they were nearly all badly deformed. They were unable to walk about or scratch around on the floor and peck for their food, as a chicken does in normal circumstances. Their beaks were clipped to stop them pecking each other, and this produced some difficulty in feeding. Their wings frequently became broken or distorted. They could hardly stand up. They spent their short life in that condition, and then when they were slaughtered, it was done by factory methods that were not always successful.

"The way they were mishandled in their death as well as in their life has caused them to come here in this state. A chicken has an extremely simple mind. It would never have stayed here as an individual for any length of time any more than that pig will do so. But it can still feel pain and discomfort, and this is how a group of chickens from a battery house have come here. Before they can join their group soul, they have to be helped to emerge from this terrible condition."

124

Protected as I was, I still began to feel sick inside again as this appalling atmosphere began to reach me, "We'll leave this now, Judy, otherwise it will affect you. Let us move along," said Doreen, taking me outside again into the light. "We will have a little rest, dear, before I take you any further."

At that point, I felt unable to comment. I just felt appalled. I had always been aware that these things were taking place on earth, and I had felt exceedingly sorry for those creatures that I had read about as having been kept in some of these conditions. I had not stopped to think, however, how they might have existed beyond their earth death. I had never had a very clear idea in my mind as to how it would be for anybody. I had not even been clear as to whether I was likely to continue to exist, and I had been even less clear about animals. Now that I had faced these various creatures and seen their conditions as they now were as a result of the different ways that they had been handled on earth, the whole appalling situation left me speechless.

There is nothing I can say from here that will really explain to you how I felt. One had to stand and feel the atmosphere that was coming from each of these poor creatures to realise what had been inflicted upon them and what they had suffered within themselves at the hands of people who called themselves human beings.

"Are you feeling a bit better now?" asked Doreen after a while.

"Yes, I think so," I said. "I am just so appalled by it all."

"I would like you to come over to this shed now," said Doreen. As we approached it the atmosphere darkened once more and I found myself facing a row of what I thought to be cows until Doreen told me that they were bullocks. In each instance there was a darkness around them and a feeling of fear, but there was not the feeling of horror I had felt from the animals that we had just seen.

"These creatures," said Doreen, "have come here from the slaughterhouse. They were kept in open fields until the time came for them to be taken to the market, and they lived a comparatively normal life considering that many generations of cattle have become used to such circumstances. But the darkness you see around them and the feeling of fear that you get from them was the outcome of entering the slaughterhouse where they immediately picked up the stench of death and the fear of those who had gone before them. This had been picked up in their auras by the time their turn came to be killed, and this is what you feel around them now. Because it was a comparatively short experience, it will only take a comparatively short time here to revive them sufficiently to join their group soul. But it does at least show you, Judy, the effect such an end has on the condition of such a simple creature."

We then moved to another shed. Here I was faced with an overwhelming feeling of revulsion, similar to that I had felt around the chickens, but this was even more overpowering, and it really hit me badly despite the fact that I was getting very strong protection. I felt it to such an extent that I recoiled from it.

"Doreen, I'm sorry, but I must get out of here!" I gasped at her.

"All right, dear, we'll go outside again." And out we went.

"I'm sorry," I said to her, "but it just caught me, and I felt that I couldn't stay there another moment. My God! Whatever happened there?"

"That, my dear Judy, are some of the calves that are kept for veal. Like the chickens, they are kept in close, cramped, quarters. They never see daylight. They cannot turn round or sit down. They are fed food that keeps their flesh white, which means they get insufficient nourishment so that their bones and organs fail to develop as they should and they are very weak and sickly during the whole of their short lives. They are usually allowed to exist between six to eight weeks, and during the whole of that time they are kept in that cramped condition. At the end of that time, it depends upon where they are kept, because some places slaughter them quickly. In many other instances, however, they are tied by their back legs and hung down, head first and alive, while their throat is only partly cut so that the blood can drain from them while they are still alive. This is because it produces whiter meat.

"Although they have only a limited intelligence, they are aware of feeling cramped and painful and unhappy. They can feel the presence of their fellow calves, but they cannot reach any of them, although they would normally keep together. They are already wretchedly weak creatures, and then they have the additional agony of that prolonged death. Some fall into a coma or are stunned before they are completely killed. Mostly, the job is

126

finished off while they are hanging upside down. They have enough mentality to suffer a great deal of agony, and that is what you picked up in there, dear Judy."

"I just feel sick at the thought of it," I said to her. "I had no idea, no idea at all, that such an appalling thing could happen to an animal."

"Unfortunately," said Doreen, "it happens all the time and in some parts of the world there continues to be a great demand for veal. It is still considered to be a great delicacy in many countries, and while there is still a demand for it that kind of thing will continue to take place. There are groups of people who are trying to speak out for the animals and have these kinds of practices stopped. Unfortunately, too many people sweep them aside as cranks and do not wish to listen. It is going to take us a long time to get through to them and begin to help them not to continue to live in that feeling of agony."

I felt myself shivering. Despite the fact that there is no such climate here, I was literally shivering from what I had picked up from those poor creatures.

"I think you have had enough for the time being," said Doreen.

"I don't want to sound like a baby," I said to her. "I do understand why it is necessary for me to see all this, and I wish there was something I could do to help them. I do feel that I shouldn't turn my back on any of it, but it is just that I need time to get over my reactions. I don't know why I am shivering but I do need time to get over it."

"Well, let me take you to another area for a little while," Doreen replied.

V

While we were still outside in the warm light, she took me over to a beautiful, translucent pond with fishes swimming around in it. They were not emanating any music or joy, as had the other fishes I had seen. They were simply swimming around silently, but they seemed placid enough.

"These fishes have recently arrived here from the trout farms. Trout farms are kept much in the same way as other farms. These fish were born and reared ready to be killed for food. These creatures lead boring existences because they do not fend for themselves. They are kept in close waters and are fed regularly until they are considered to be large enough to be caught, stunned, and killed. Trout, left to their own devices, have extraordinarily agile minds considering the kind of creatures that they are.

"Fishes only have a comparatively limited intelligence, but they have more intelligence than human beings often credit them with having, and the trout is a particularly intelligent fish. It does not compare with a dog or a cat, but it does have a reasonable intelligence. Therefore, when it is confined with its fellow trout in a trout pool, not having to extend its abilities at all, and then it comes here by a sudden death, it needs a period of time to shake off its confined surroundings and its sudden propulsion here before it can find itself. I do, literally, mean 'find itself,' because it is rather like emerging from a mental chrysalis. It will emerge, and it will begin to give off beautiful colours and gradually absorb the joyfulness that is in the water here. It will, in itself, become joyful. Can you understand that, Judy?"

"Yes, I believe I can," I said to her. "I seem to be getting a little less stupid about such things now!" I stood there watching them and I could see that they were at peace. It was simply a question of getting a little more life into them. That is the only way I can think of putting it. Somehow, I regained a little of my own peace by watching them.

VI

After a while I felt more like discussing things with Doreen, and I said to her, "Although I think that what you have been showing me is absolutely terrible and disgusting, and I do feel deeply concerned that such things are being undertaken in order to produce food for human beings who could very easily exist on something different, and I don't wish to turn my back on it all, I do feel that, for the moment, I can't really take much more of this."

"I did not really expect that you could," she acknowledged. "In fact, I am exceedingly pleased with you for having faced as much as you have done. At the outset of bringing you through the Animal Kingdom, I had intended to show you only the su-

128

perficial and happy parts of it, and only later on, when you had become more used to being here in this world, would I see whether or not you would be interested in seeing some of the darker sides. As it is, I have still not taken you to the very darkest areas of these poor creatures who come here from having been deliberately tortured and experimented upon and hunted and abused in so many different ways, because it would, indeed, be too much for you to experience and cope with at present.

"But, Judy, you have already shown so much interest and compassion for these poor creatures that I have been bringing you through far more diverse areas than I had intended at the outset. I had originally intended to take you only through some of the light and happy places and to then take you towards the city, where I know you will find lots of things that will interest you. But, as we gradually moved along and you became more interested and were prepared to listen to what I had to tell you about the ways in which some of these poor animals have been mishandled, I felt the time was right to continue you along this pathway. In so doing, you have not only extended your own knowledge, you have become, without realising it, more capable of protecting yourself here against the various vibrations. You have learned to tune in to thoughts and to read auras, and this is already preparing you for your visit to the city and the diverse characters you may meet there.

"Before we leave the animals for this visit, I would like you to leave them on a higher note than we have been just recently. So I am going to take you along to something that I think will give you a special delight. But, before we leave these darker areas, I have to tell you that there are very many far darker areas than those you have already experienced. There are similar dark, and even darker, areas where human beings exist who have been put through the most terrible experiences on earth by their fellow humans. There are even worse places where you will find the humans who have abused their fellow humans and also their other fellow creatures, such as those you have seen and those you have not seen, in so many despicable ways.

"Those people who have come here from having deliberately tortured and maimed and killed their fellow creatures for no reason other than their own brutal minds will have an exceedingly long time here before they even begin to emerge towards the light. Some of them spend the equivalent of many hundreds of years of earth time in making even one slight move towards the lighter areas. We do try to help every creature who arrives here from earth in a dark frame of mind, but it is impossible for some of these to be reached for a very, very long time.

"That, my dear Judy, is their 'hell' that you hear about on earth. Hell is created by their own minds and actions. It is not a place to which anyone else can send a fellow creature. Individuals, by their own thoughts and actions, put themselves into that frame of mind that holds them in those dark, and frequently evil-feeling, places. The average person, such as you or I, come here to a pleasant place, and we have to work our way to the higher realms that are, I suppose, regarded on earth as 'heaven.' But there is a great deal of misunderstanding on earth about heaven and hell, and this is something I shall have to discuss with you a little later on.

"At the moment I would like to take you to see something here that will, I think, send you off (and now I am going to quote *The Wizard of Oz*)," said Doreen with a smile, "along the yellow brick road towards our beautiful city and towards finding your father."

VII

Soon I was being led to a place that had the most beautiful hues that I could ever imagine. I used to sing about being "over the rainbow," but now I was seeing the most beautiful water and it reminded me of rainbows. I have already mentioned the translucency of the water I had experienced, but this water was beyond anything else I had seen previously or could ever have imagined. It flowed away from where I was standing to the distant horizon. It literally did have all the colours of the rainbow in it, and those colours seemed to be reproduced in the atmosphere above it. There were the most delightful emanations coming from the water, and I could see creatures leaping and bounding in and out of it in the far distance. I stood there feeling completely overwhelmed and uplifted by the whole atmosphere. I could "feel" rather than "hear" laughter, amusement, music, and intelligent communication without being able to completely explain to you why I felt there was communication.

Doreen took me by the hand towards a slightly darker area of this sublimely beautiful part of our world and said, "Now, come with me into the water here."

Where it was slightly darker, I saw a creature that looked to me like a porpoise. It was quietly reposing there, and slight bubbles rose in the water from the top of its head. It was not moving much, it just seemed to be floating.

"Put your hand very gently on its back," advised Doreen, "and leave it there and tell me what you feel."

The creature looked very gentle and docile, and I did as I had been asked. As I did so, I felt something vibrating through my hand, up my arm, and into me, which I find difficult to describe. "I'm getting the most extraordinary sensation," I said. "It is as though the animal is saying, 'Why did you do it to me? Why did you do it to me?' and I feel that I want to put my arm right around it."

"Well, why don't you?" said Doreen.

I stepped closer to what I felt sure was a gentle creature, and I put my arm around it. When its head slowly surfaced from the water, I gently stroked its nose with my other hand. Without knowing why, I laid my cheek on the top of its head and found myself saying to it, over and over again, "Don't cry, baby, it's all right."

I felt I wanted to love it, and I felt something coming from the creature to me. I went on talking to it and assuring it.

"It's all right, now. Nobody will hurt you any more. I assure you, nobody will hurt you any more. I've just been where I see that nobody gets hurt any more."

Gradually, I seemed to see a change in the area where the animal was. It began to lighten, and some colour came to it. It was weaker than the colour I had seen elsewhere in this place, but it was beginning to emerge. I just stood there, feeling that I could not leave this animal for the time being, that I wanted to stay with it and comfort it, and that it wanted me to stay. As I stood there talking and murmuring to it, it did not occur to me how stupid it might be to be talking to an animal who lived in the water in the same way I would talk to a human baby.

Gradually, I felt its whole being become stronger and more vibrant. I also felt an affinity reaching out to me. It was different from a conversation or a feeling of affinity with a human being, but I felt that, in some way, this creature had known what I was conveying to it, that it was responding and feeling assured, that it felt the affection I was extending to it, and that it was giving it back to me in return.

Suddenly it flipped its tail, slid away from my light clasp and began swimming around me in joyous circles. It dived and leapt and plunged and rolled over in sheer delight, and then came back to me, pushing its nose into my hand and waving my hand back and forth, as if to say, "Hello! Thank you for being nice to me. I feel so much better, now!" Then it calmed down again and floated quietly by my side once more. But this time the colours were so much stronger that I could feel life, vibrancy, and joy coming from it. At that point I realised that we were now part of the brighter light and colours. After a while some other creatures, looking very similar to this one, came up to it and nuzzled it, and it responded. It returned to me once more and nudged me with its nose before swimming away with his fellows.

I emerged from the water to stand beside Doreen. I said to her, "Of all the experiences I have had here, this is the strangest. I feel completely confused by it all. I seemed to feel the strong need of that porpoise to have some friendship and help and condolence. I felt it responding to me in a way that I never thought that an animal I had never seen before could respond to me, and I felt completely uplifted. This whole place is strange, because I feel there are sounds and music and laughter, yet I can't distinguish it as anything I can recognise."

"Well," said Doreen, "you thought that you were communicating with a somewhat basic fishlike creature without being too clear what it was."

"I thought it was a form of porpoise. We used to get them sometimes along the American coasts."

"It is part of the family, but it was, in fact, a bottle-nosed dolphin, which I had mentioned to you earlier as being highly intelligent. This one had not been in captivity. It had been swimming in the sea with its companions and had joyously followed a fishing boat. It loved to plunge and leap through the waves

132

with its fellows and to follow the humans. If a human had reached out to it, it would have responded in a friendly and trusting manner. This poor dolphin was caught and deliberately killed, in a most inhumane way, and then thrown back into the sea.

"I will not go into details, Judy, you have had more than enough, but that was the result. He had had a shock, and you found him in a state of confused shock. Because they give off very sensitive vibrations and thoughts, you were able to tune in to him and he was able to tune in to you. You were not getting words from him, but your mind interpreted what his mind was giving off and his mind interpreted your thoughts. Between the two of you, you have had a very special kind of communication. Your compassion for it has returned it from its state of shock and enabled it to rejoin its fellows in a comparatively easy manner."

I felt so completely overwhelmed by the whole experience that I did not feel able to comment any more to Doreen for a few moments.

"It really is extraordinary," I said to her at last, "how in tune I felt with the animal. I felt that I could have, if necessary, gone on talking to it. I don't mean that we could have had an intricate discussion, but I did feel that I could have continued talking to it in a fairly straightforward manner and that it would have known what I was saying, or thinking, in the same way as I seemed to know what it was thinking. I felt a surge of joy go right through it after I had been talking to it for a while. It seemed to shudder into a sort of vibrancy before it started swimming so happily around me, and I felt as though I wanted to join it."

"That is how you should feel, if you have any sensitivity, Judy, which you obviously have. Your reaction to it was perfect. You did exactly the right thing, and it responded to you. This is why I say to you that you are a natural here for helping the animals as well as the children."

"I do feel a strong wish within me to be able to do that," I told her. "Had you asked me at the outset, I would have said that I would love to be with children but that I don't know how to handle animals. I am still not sure that I would know how to handle some of the animals that we have seen. They seem to have been in such a terrible state that it is beyond me, but I would like to try."

"Some of it is beyond you at present, Judy. Not because you lack sympathy or understanding, but because you lack the experience here to know how to cope with the situation. I, for one, would never, ever advocate asking you to try and help some of the humans who arrive here in a very bad state, because I think you have too much sensitivity to be able to cope with the far more complicated, and more dense, mass of darkness that you would have to overcome. Because animals are less devious creatures in so many ways, you can cope with them in the same way as you can cope with children.

"I could not cope, at present, with helping some of the children who come here due to exceptional circumstances, such as that poor deaf and dumb child that we experienced. I could not, at present, overcome the deep darkness that surrounds some of the animals who come here because of the bestiality of some human mistreatment. But I hope, as I gather more and more experience here, that I may eventually be able to do that, as others are doing.

"Most people who undertake that particularly difficult work are very experienced and have had a very, very long time here before they become sufficiently experienced and developed. But I am so very pleased at the way you have faced up to everything here so far, and I do not want you to feel that you are failing in any way by not being taken by me to the even darker areas. I do congratulate you on coming as far as you have already done so soon after your arrival. There are some humans who have been here far longer than you who have never wished to visit the animals at all. There are others who have said they would love to visit the animals, but the moment I have suggested taking them to the darker areas, they did not wish to know.

"In both instances, they are failing in their own development as individuals. Eventually, they will probably come around to changing their minds and so extend their experiences. Those that do not will continue to exist in a state of ignorance of many of the aspects that help each one of us to expand here. I am not sufficiently experienced myself to be able to forecast how this will affect their development in the future, but I have been here long enough to know, from the teachings I have received, that such ignorance of mind does hamper them in a number of ways. I am so pleased, and even proud of you, that you have allowed me to take you this far."

"I have been very grateful," I said to her. "I do feel one should become aware of this sort of thing, and I think that if, when on earth, we could all give more time to considering how we affect our fellow creatures, the world would be a better place."

"It is too big a problem for us to try and unravel here and now, Judy, but, basically, I have been led to understand that, when life on earth began and different creatures began to emerge, the whole pattern was such that, although there was an element of primitiveness about it, because creatures did live off fellow creatures, it has, nevertheless, become completely out of hand because, as the more intelligent creatures came along and human beings evolved with their more complicated minds, so they had freedom of choice as to whether to use their intelligence for good or for bad. Instead of using that intelligence to live side by side with their fellow creatures, to give them as much help and as little hindrance and pain as possible, many human beings, unfortunately, veered towards the bad and the bestial as against towards understanding and sensitivity for each other and for their fellow creatures on earth.

"This is why the world of earth has become more and more developed in its technology but has become removed further and further from its original basic principles of all its creatures living together in as much harmony as possible. It is a vast subject, something that I have been studying in the many years I have been here and something that I feel sure that you will wish to study when you have been around a bit more and seen everything. But it is something I cannot possibly go into with you here, at this stage after your arrival."

"I do see what you mean," I said to her. "I always felt this at the back of my mind when I was on earth. I used to try and discuss it with people, but it was always exceedingly difficult for me to have a really serious conversation with most people. They always seemed to think that I had to be discussing show business. Each time I tried to start a discussion on other topics I found people veering away from it and trying to jolly me into what they considered to be a livelier frame of mind. They didn't seem to want me to be serious."

135

"We are aware of that, Judy. Some people tried to keep you as a child too long. There were others who steeped you in show business talk morning, noon, and night, irrespective of whatever else you had in your mind, and there were those who just felt that you had not got anything beyond shallow thoughts. They completely misconstrued you, and you have, indeed, been cramped in many ways. This is why I feel so certain that, after a period of being here, you will blossom out into someone that can be used here in so many beautiful ways, and you will feel happier for it."

"I think I will," I said to her. "I can't explain it to you, but even these very limited experiences that I have had so far have given me a different feeling inside of myself. I'm beginning to see myself in a different light and to have a wish that I could do so many more things here than I ever managed to do on earth."

"You will," said Doreen, "I assure you that you will. I also assure you that the music you will produce when you sing here—as you will do—will not only give you more pleasure than it gave you on earth—and you did feel pleasure when you knew you had sung well on earth—but it will also give even more pleasure to your audiences, even more than to those people to whom you sang your very best when on earth. Having told you that, I think it is time we left here for a while."

"Before we leave," I exclaimed, "I would like you to answer a few questions I have to ask, although I agree I don't think I could stand any more dark places for the moment!"

"Please do," said Doreen. "I think I know in advance what you are going to ask me, but please do."

VIII

"The main thought that has been concerning me as we have seen these different areas is about those poor animals that are used in laboratories. I have always been divided in my mind about whether or not such a thing should take place. I always felt that it was extremely disgusting that animals should be used for any form of surgical research that was for any reason other than the strictest medical reasons. Even then I felt that it was very unfair on those poor creatures who were treated in that way, although I am sure that a lot of human beings have cause to be grateful

136

that such experiments have produced certain surgical and certain other medical procedures that have cured many people of whatever was ailing them and helped to extend their lives. I realise it is possible that I may have received some sort of benefit somewhere in my life, without directly realising it then, and that various medicines I may have received when I have been dangerously ill may possibly not have been discovered had some poor animal not been experimented upon. But the other side of me always felt that such a terrible thing should not take place, that we should all take our chance in life, and if we cannot be helped to survive without having killed or maimed an animal in order to do so, that we should accept it as our tough luck.

"I feel this even more strongly from having seen some of the things I have seen here. It has been bad enough to see how those creatures have arrived here because of the various ways in which they have been handled. When I stop to think that cats and dogs and monkeys and possibly other creatures I am unaware of may have been operated upon or poisoned or had other terrible things done to them in experiments, I wonder how that affects their life here!"

"I knew that was what you were going to ask me," said Doreen. "It is a topic here that we regard as extremely loathsome in every possible way. No human being has the right to experiment upon any fellow creature for any reason whatsoever. *It is as final as that.* We are all born to live our lives as best we can. If something happens to bring us here, we have to accept it. There are certain herbs that have been provided on earth that can become antidotes or pain relievers and that help alleviate the more basic illnesses that can arise.

"The animals know how to find them, and they eat them. Many humans used to do the same thing, but as humans have increased in numbers and spread farther over the world and technology has come along, huge buildings and cities have been built, and all the natural vegetation is being destroyed. More and more things, therefore, have been created by man for man, and, too often, the plight of the animals is seen as being of lesser importance. *That is not so.* Although there are varying degrees of intelligence amongst life on earth, every part of that life has its place.

"I know there is a limit to what you can do to save life,

137

inasmuch as everyone has evolved to live off their fellow creatures. At the beginning of life, and even when human beings evolved, it would have been possible to live off the simple nutrients of the earth, such as vegetables and fruits, nuts, grain and food of that variety. Gradually, as life developed more, it began to live off its fellow vertebrates rather than off the more simple foods. Gradually, the animals who had eaten the fishes began to eat other animals, and so it has gone on through evolution.

"There was a time when a man ate a fellow creature only after hunting and killing it quickly, and he only killed again when he needed more food. Now it is 'mass this' and 'mass that' in farming. Creatures are born and developed and killed especially for human consumption. This is where it has got tremendously out of hand. Unfortunately, those human beings who were born during more recent times have been brought up to be used to purchasing whatever they want without stopping to think how those creatures have been reared and handled and killed.

"As human beings have got further and further away from the more natural environment into which they were born many centuries ago, before recorded time, so they have forgotten their natural way of life. They have come to live a very unnatural way of life, although it may be more highly intelligent. With it has come a lack of understanding, a lack of realisation, of what they are doing to their fellow creatures in killing them for food, especially in the mass way in which they are now produced for food. It is something we realise when we come here. We see the terrible pall which lies all around the earth, but everything has now come much too far away from its origins for it to ever be improved. In fact, from here, we see things going from bad to worse all the time.

"But, to bring you back to your original remark concerning animal experimentation and vivisection—that is the most appalling of all, because no human being has the right to experiment upon either a fellow human being or on any other living creature without its permission. In so doing, no matter how well intentioned they may think they are being, by deliberately inflicting that kind of treatment on a fellow creature, they reduce their own sensitivity and their own ability to develop in the right way. They also reduce the chances of that creature to come here in the kind of state that would help it to have an immediately happy life here.

They also put that creature through a number of terrible experiences, in many instances, that it should never have been called upon to experience.

"Again, this is an exceedingly complicated subject and one that I think you are going to have to consider in greater detail later on. Of course, it will not help your development here to know a great deal about it unless it becomes possible to transmit this knowledge to the earth at some future time for people on earth to think about. This is something we are always hoping we may be able to do eventually from here. We can communicate with certain human beings on earth, and those humans do their best to repeat and report upon our teachings. But too many people on earth think that communication between their world and ours is either wrong or else impossible, and so they do not care to listen to what is being told from here.

"That is another problem we are up against. We are constantly hoping that we may eventually succeed in reaching more and more people in this way. More minds are gradually beginning to accept the possibility of communication between the two worlds. The mass media are placing more of it before the public. Unfortunately, they often do so in a demolishing, demoralising way, rather than constructively, and people are misled about the possibilities of correct communication.

"But, irrespective of how many people we manage to reach eventually in that way, I personally feel that we shall always be fighting a losing battle. As mankind increases in numbers and gets further and further away from its natural life, and with the speed at which life on earth is now lived, more and more people with less sensitivity are being born. More and more are being born to live in overcrowded conditions. Some manage to remain intelligent and sensitive. Others who are intelligent are insensitive and often brutal and allow themselves to become more brutalised. I feel we shall always be battling with the results of this ever increasing problem.

"But I can say that from here, any kind of experimentation on animals, for any reason whatsoever, is abhorred. I know there are human beings who will say that some of the great surgeons have had to experiment on animals before they could operate successfully in so many ways on human beings and, therefore, prolong their lives. But we do all feel here that, while human life is regarded as precious and no human being should be deliberately deprived of it by the actual taking of a life, other creatures are just as entitled to live their lives. Although everything should be done to reduce pain by the use of the natural medicaments provided, no fellow creature should be cut about in order to preserve the life of another fellow creature.

"The current phase, as a result of operating on animals, is for one human being to be given a transplant organ from another human being. But, Judy, considering how many animals had been used and tortured and slaughtered in order to try and have success in that way and how few humans have really been given additional life as a result of it, we do not feel it has been worth it any more than it has been morally right.

"Humans tend to clutch at their earth life because they are afraid they will not continue to exist or because they are afraid of *how* they might continue to exist. If every human being could only be brought to realise that their life on earth is simply the beginning of a far more beautiful and extensive life here, provided they have the right attitudes, fewer people would be afraid of losing their lives and fewer people would be prepared to accept the extensive operations that they do accept in order to prolong their life. We agree here that every human being should do all they can to keep their life as active as possible and not to give up, but not at the expense of their fellow creatures. That, of course, brings me to suicides, but I would prefer to leave that for the time being, Judy, until I feel the time is right for me to discuss with you the different ways in which adult human beings come here."

"I realise you can only show me small parts of this world at present. It must be a vast subject and a vast place, and I realise that everything cannot be seen and understood all at once. But it seems that it must be, for any living creature who comes here, a tremendous experience of transition from one life to the next. Surely, whether we be human beings, animals, birds, or fishes, we must be coming here in our millions almost daily. I can't help wondering how it is that we never seem to see crowds anywhere! I am also wondering what happens to those family pets who come here from natural causes, not because they have been mishandled in any way, and who have been much loved by their owners. I also wonder about those who have been put down by the vet for reasons of kindness, because they were in pain or too old to walk properly, or blind and deaf, and so on. What happens to all of those?"

"Well, Judy, as you have said, it is a vast subject. I will try and explain it to you as carefully and as briefly as I can. First of all, let me say that, although human beings and animals do leave earth for our world at the rate of millions daily, their rates of progress and their states of being can be so very varied that they would not necessarily be on the same vibration as you or me. It might only be fractionally different, but it is sufficiently different for us not to, shall I say, get in each other's way. We do not meet with others on other vibrations unless we particularly concentrate on doing so. This is something that I intend to discuss with you in more detail as we continue our tour. When the time is more suitable, you will be able to understand and accept this more easily.

"With regard to the much-loved and well-cared-for pets of humans, they will each be received here, as is every creature, and helped to make the transition. When their human caretakers are already here, they will be taken to see them, and if there is a mutual rapport between the two, they may choose to remain together for all or part of the time for quite a long way ahead of them. There are others who are pleased to see each other, but there is no particularly strong wish to be together. Then the animal and the human continue on their separate ways.

"Of course, there are often animals who come here after having been despatched from earth through illness or blindness or some other problem, when it was considered to be a kindness to remove them from their pain or old age. They will remain here in a state of heavy sleep for quite a long while in order to help their etheric or spirit body to adjust and to gain the necessary strength to enable it to continue here in the proper manner. Every sudden ejection from the earth body, every one that is not by a gradual weakening of hold on earth life, necessitates a period of sleep in order to enable the spirit body to gain its strength. Experienced humans, often with the help of experienced animals here, can help those creatures to adjust to their change of place of existence. Then, when they feel stronger, much in the same way that you gradually stopped sleeping and felt stronger, they will

141

be taken towards their natural place of existence.

"Usually, you will find domestic pets in happy juxtaposition with each other in various parts of this world. When their human caretaker comes here, they will be given the opportunity to meet each other again, should they wish to do so, and they will then decide whether or not they wish to spend all of their time together, or part of their time together, depending upon how each of them feels. If there is a very strong bond between them, you will often find that they will continue together here for a very, very long time. When the time comes for a decision to change course, it will be a mutual decision and it will not hurt either of them.

"Believe me, Judy, it is quite often in this world that the human beings depend on the company of their domestic pets even more than the pets depend on them. As long as that animal feels a deep love and need coming to it from the human being, it will remain with that human being. But when that strong feeling from the human begins to lessen, as it eventually may if he or she decides to go in other directions, then the animal, quite happily, gradually moves further and further away until it becomes totally absorbed with its fellow animals and lives a happy and gradually developing life. It will still, I may add, have an individual mind, because most creatures who have been family pets, such as dogs, cats, horses, and even parakeets, who are quite intelligent little creatures in their own way, continue to have individual thoughts."

"Does that mean that I could find my Sam if I wanted to?" I asked Doreen.

"Yes, of course you could," she replied, "but I think it would be as well not to disturb him at the moment until you have seen all the different places I am taking you to see. It would be a pity to disturb him if you may possibly decide later on that you did not really need him to be with you. You may not, since you have had so many changes in your outlook. You may well find, after you have experienced the many areas here, that you will see things a little differently. This is especially the case as you never had him with you all the time even when he was on earth, since you had to travel so much and had to leave him at home."

"That's true," I said, "but I would love to see him again even if we don't stay together. Surely, if I've made myself clear to some of the other animals here, I should be able to make it clear to my Sam that I am pleased to see him, that I don't expect him to be with me, as I have other things to do, but that I would like to come and see him sometimes."

"That is entirely your decision, Judy, but I would suggest that you leave it for the time being because until you have got everything into perspective you will not be able to reason it through as clearly as you will later on. I do have a particular reason for saying this to you. I do not say this to everybody, because some people who come here have been so totally dependent on their pet for companionship that the first thing they want to do is to find that animal so that they can be together again. When that occurs, it is the first thing we help them to do. It gives them the companionship and assurance that they need. In your case, it is not such an obvious thing to do. As you have so much to encompass at the moment, I think it would be fairer to you both to leave that decision until later."

"Well, you have certainly guided me correctly so far," I told her. "I was not really wishing to cause any problems. It was simply a thought that occurred to me."

"I expected it to occur to you some time or other," said Doreen. "I am only surprised that it has taken so long. It is because it has taken so long that I am of the opinion it would be better for you to leave it just that bit longer until you have seen other things here that will possibly give you a change or perspective."

"My perspective seems to be changing constantly, anyway," I said, "so I do accept that, but it would be good to see him again eventually."

With that, we made our way towards the city that had been mentioned several times.

Chapter 3

I

Before long, I began to see the city again on the horizon. We seemed to be approaching it far more rapidly than I had been aware of moving previously, and, in what seemed to be no time at all, we seemed to be much closer to it. I commented upon this to Doreen, and she explained that, because we had spent such a lot of time with the animals, I had, without realising it, been gradually attuning myself to my new way of existence.

"You may not have realised it, Judy, but some of the animals were reached by a form of thought transference. We did not get there slowly, on foot, as we had been doing at the outset. It is a difficult thing to explain to you. Although our bodies in our present state of being are just as solid and natural to us here as were our earth bodies to us when on earth, they are, nevertheless, on a much more sensitive and quicker vibrational level. Once we get used to this, we can project ourselves, without any seeming haste, to wherever we wish to be, without having to take any form of alternative transport and without having to walk. We can, literally, take our being from the place where we are to the place where we want to be. Eventually, you will achieve this far more quickly and easily than you are now doing, but you are already on the way to reaching some places more quickly and easily than when you first arrived here. This is why we have now reached the city so quickly after having been with the animals."

I tried to absorb this explanation but I still felt a little confused. I had not been aware that I was no longer walking. In fact, I had felt that I had been walking. It had just seemed to me that, without any concious change in my walking pace, I had somehow covered more distance and reached somewhere more quickly than I had expected to do. Although it had not previously occurred to me, it began to do so now, as I saw the distance between us and the city, which had previously seemed to be so far away, being covered in such an exceptionally short time. I realise that the explanation

144

I am giving you may be difficult to understand, but I can only tell you that, in some ways, although I was walking, it was almost as though I had approached the city in the same way as something seems to be brought closer by looking through a zoom lens in a telescope. The only difference was that, instead of the city retreating again, as it had done during my earlier experiment, it continued to come closer, and before long we were walking in its streets.

I had been to many beautiful cities when on earth, although not to as many as I would have liked to have been, as there were many parts of the world that I had not visited. In most cities on earth, no matter how beautiful their facade may be, there is usually some dirt and squalor somewhere, some places that one has to avoid, some darkness or dinginess or too much noise, but this city was vastly different from anything I had ever previously experienced. The buildings changed in shape as we progressed along the streets. There seemed to be every possible type of architecture, yet they all blended well. Although the walls were solid and there were windows and doors, these gave off a light and an iridescence that was supremely beautiful. Doreen explained that all these different places were not made of bricks and mortar, as on earth, but were constructed in a special manner that produced this iridescent effect. When they were no longer required or else needed to be changed for any reason, they would be changed in a manner that totally avoided the messy demolition procedures and consequent rubble we knew on earth. Here, these buildings would simply change their shape or colour to suit whatever was needed.

"I hate to say this," I said to her, "because I have been trying so hard not to make any earth comparisons with Oz any more since I became so absorbed with all the things you have been showing me, but this does, to some extent, look like a very much more beautiful version of Disneyland!"

Doreen laughed and said, "I was waiting for something like that from you, Judy. In a way, Disney paints characters and buildings in colour, and he makes them go and come and be reconstructed very quickly. This is a much more complicated process of that very basic approach. After all, his buildings are created in imagination and the buildings that we have here are created by artistic people who have strong imaginations. Their imaginations work for us and create these beautiful buildings. When it is necessary for these buildings to be altered, the architects will recreate with their imagination, and the new building will be reproduced just as strongly as if it had been built with bricks and mortar."

I had to think about this for a long time. I had to test the buildings with my hands. To my surprise, I felt that I was touching stone or brick or marble. The beautiful iridescent light that emanated from each of these buildings blended with that of its neighbours without any jarring effect, despite the fact that there were so many different kinds of architecture to be seen.

As we gradually progressed around the streets, I saw that there were people walking and talking much as I had seen them in the countryside, so that, although they were there and certainly in larger numbers than in the countryside, there was still not a crowded effect. I cannot explain to you how this is, I can only ask you to believe that this is so. As we made our way along, slowly this time so that I could absorb everything and ask my questions, I was taken into various buildings. I was shown where people were learning music, where others were learning to paint beautiful pictures, where some people were singing, and where others were creating beautiful artifacts. In some places there were some beautiful flowers being encouraged to grow.

"What about books and television?" I asked Doreen.

"We do not have television here, Judy. It is not necessary. Everything is done by thought, and people can be creative here in such a way that there is no difficulty for anyone wishing to be entertained in getting to any of the public places we have here for that purpose. Therefore they do not need images to be brought to them; they simply tune in with their minds and go to the performance with just as much ease as it would take to turn on the television receiver. So we do not have television here, but we have concerts and we have people performing plays for those who wish to experience them. We have schools of learning, which are the equivalent of universities on earth, for those who wish to find out more about creation and human development. There are places where people can learn to help their fellows here that would, in effect, be regarded as our version of teaching hospitals, because we do have to learn before we can be let loose as it were, on those who arrive here from earth in need of help."

As we walked along the streets I saw there were flowers and trees and fountains. There was the occasional person with a dog walking beside him, but never on a lead. There were birds flying around, and there was a man walking along with a parakeet perched on top of his head. The parakeet was chattering happily to itself.

"I can tell from looking at those two," said Doreen, "that the old man had that bird for fourteen years and was devoted to it. When he died he was left undiscovered in his apartment for two weeks. By the time they found him the bird had also died. They have come here together, and they are staying together, at least for a while."

II

"When you come here from earth, it very much depends on your state of progress as to how long you remain the same as when you arrived," said Doreen.

I felt a little uneasy when she said that. "Don't tell me I'm going to develop into something that looks as though it has come from Mars!" I exclaimed.

Doreen laughed. "No, Judy! What happens is that, as we gradually shake off our earth problems and ill health, so we gradually gain a lighter body. We remain physically the same height and shape that we have always been, but we lose any malformations that we may have acquired. People who have lost limbs or eyes regain them here. The decrepitude and wrinkles of old age gradually leave us. Those who have been hindered in any way by, possibly, an accident or by arthritis, for example, gradually lose their handicap so that they feel and look completely rejuvenated. Eventually they will return to looking and feeling and being even better than at their best when on earth.

"Those who come here as children gradually grow towards adulthood and will eventually become sturdy young men and women, just as old people will return to being sturdy young men and women. The only difference will be that the older people will have had longer experience of earth life than those who come here young. This can usually be felt rather than seen by their approach to life here, but even this gradually recedes and everyone blends well together. Because of this, it often happens that two people can come here after having had vastly different experiences on earth, possibly having lived at different times as well as in different places and with completely different life-styles, yet, because of their rate of progression and development and understanding and because of the pathways to which their minds are taking them, they may meet on a certain pathway, find that they are exceptionally compatible in their current thoughts and interests and go along that pathway together for quite a long time, happy in each other's company. This can happen to two people who would never have expected to even look at each other on earth, because they were so seemingly unalike.

"This is how you may meet a couple who are friends, one of whom may have been here several hundreds of years longer than the other. Because life on earth is becoming, for some, more and more sophisticated, the one who came here later may already have a greater understanding of various matters then the soul who came here from a less developed part of earth some hundred years earlier. For instance, someone who was a gentle-minded philosopher on earth several hundred years ago might well find that an equally gentle-minded philosopher who had arrived more recently from earth was approximately on the same level of understanding only shortly after arriving here and that they could be compatible friends. I have to try and give this to you in an extremely brief, simple manner to help you to understand."

"Yes, I think I do understand," I said to her after I had thought about it for a while. "It's fascinating, really! I might even walk past Abraham Lincoln!" I said, laughing.

"Well, that's another subject again!" said Doreen, laughing in return. "But you will find yourself meeting people that you did not expect to meet, and of course you will be meeting people that you will not be particularly surprised to meet.

"Now, I think the time has come for me to take you to meet your father. Although you have been taken by a very roundabout route, I think that, even by walking around this city you have already absorbed and understood a lot that will help you to see your father in the right manner, to be able to judge more fairly for yourself how alike or unalike you may be. I will leave you with him for a while and will come back for you. We have not

148

got far to go before we find him. He has been given the message that you are on your way, and he will be very interested to see you again after all this time.

"But you have to remember, Judy, that when he last saw you, you were a little girl and you loved him very much and he was to you your loving daddy. He is now being greeted with someone who came here at the age of forty-seven after a very complicated life on earth. You have suffered and struggled and succeeded and failed. Your outlook has changed many times during those years since he came here, and it has even changed again since you came here. He has to face the fact that he is meeting you after so much happened to you on earth, as well as after some things happening to you here, and also after all the different things that have happened to him here since he left earth.

"You are already, before you meet him, seeing him differently from the way you did when he first came here. You have that confusion to overcome, and he will have his confusion to overcome. When you meet him he will be looking as he did when he was a young man of twenty years of age. He is of medium height, slightly built, and he has medium brown hair and brown eyes, as you will no doubt remember. But he will look much younger than you remember, and that is what you must be prepared to see."

"So I'm going to look older than my poor father!" I smiled at her ruefully.

"Well, Judy, you will not look as young as your father just yet, but you are already looking younger than you did when you arrived."

"Really?" I said to her, in some surprise. "I hadn't noticed any difference!"

"Perhaps not, but you are already looking much as you looked when you were around thirty to thirty-five years of age. Before too much longer, as you become more and more absorbed in your surroundings here, you will gradually resemble yourself at twenty."

I worked that back in my mind and decided, and I repeat it here for the benefit of those readers who know my film work, that I now look here much as I did at the time I performed in *Girl Crazy*. My hair is differently arranged and my clothes are different

149

and there is an element of experience in my facial expression, I am told, that was not there when I made the picture, but my features closely resemble the way they looked then. But, at the time I was approaching my father, I suppose you could say that I was looking as I had looked in my slimmest scene in *A Star is Born*. The one thing I have never had any problem with here is my weight. From the time I arrived here, throughout the whole of my experiences here, I have remained as slim as I always wished to be. I am sure that anybody on earth who has had similar weight problems will be happy to know that when they come here they will not have that problem any longer.

III

I found that we were approaching what looked like the old type of vaudeville theatre that I had known when I used to play the circuits with my parents and sisters. As we went through the front entrance and found ourselves in the stalls, I could see that, although it had the same lightness about it that the other buildings in the city had, it still retained the old-style architecture. There were the usual curtains in the proscenium arch, and although the seats did not look dark, a closer examination indicated that they were covered with what looked and felt like red velvet. I mentioned this to Doreen, who explained that they had been created to closely resemble the kind of theatres that my father and his friends here were used to seeing, but because they are in this vibration of existence, the building and its fixtures and fittings are of a lighter consistency and give off more light than on earth.

We made our way towards the stage, where several young men were discussing some kind of production problem. One of them turned as we approached and came towards me with a look of eager anticipation. I realised it was my father, looking very much younger than I had ever remembered him. We had had a few faded photographs at one time, which I had mislaid, but I remembered them, and this was how he looked as he came towards me. He took both my hands and held onto them long and hard, and he smiled at me. Then he put his arms around me and hugged me. He said, "I'd know it was you by your eyes. They've not changed!"

150

I hugged him back, but I felt a little bit lost. As we stepped back and looked at each other, I turned round to introduce Doreen, but she had gone. He led me from the stage to a room on the side that looked very much like a dressing-room, which it seemed to be.

"I was so surprised when they told me you were coming to see me. I had no idea that you had arrived here," he said to me.

"I haven't been here long," I told him, "but I've been looking around and seeing what life is like here. It is all very confusing at first, but I am beginning to get the hang of it. I had better explain to you that my friend, Doreen, who is showing me around, tells me that I am going to look to you as though I am about thirty years old, but I was actually forty-seven when I passed here, and it seems that as I have been going around and seeing places I have been getting younger looking."

"That's interesting to know," he said, "because that means I can work out how long I have been here, which I had not previously bothered to do. When they told me that you wanted to see me I realised that time must be passing. I wondered whether you were coming here from old age and whether I had been here longer than I thought I had been, because I don't really feel that I have been here any time at all. I seemed to have picked up almost from where I left off and not to have been doing my work here for very long. We don't have calendars or seasons here. We don't have day and night, and as we don't really need time as on earth, we seldom, if ever, think about it. We simply tune in to the thought as to whether something is ready or is not and that's it! So although my companions and I are working on a show here, we don't have to worry whether it will be ready on opening night. We put it together and when it *is* ready, we let everybody know and they come and see us."

"I have been told that I shall sing here, when I have been here a while longer," I said to him. "Are you putting on shows?"

"Yes," he replied. "You know I always wanted to be a theatrical manager, but I never managed to achieve it. This is what I am doing here. I put on musical shows."

"What sort of musical shows?" I asked him.

"Song and dance, mostly. We don't go in for the comedian's patter type of show here, but we have song and dance. We also

151

have musical comedy, and that sets people laughing because we have amusing situations."

"Is there anybody here with you that I would know?" I enquired.

"No, not really. These are all people that I have met since I came here. Have you seen your mother?"

"No, I haven't. Mother and I didn't get along too well after you left us, and I haven't seen her yet. But I understand that I shall be seeing her eventually."

"Your mother was a strange woman—a good woman in many ways, and I did love her in my own way. I tried to tell her that here, but she doesn't want to listen. She's got no love for me at all in her memory. She can be very hard when she wishes to be. I did hope that we could at least have met on friendly terms here to discuss our outlooks with each other and wish each other well, but she does not wish to know me at all. I know that my way of life here is, possibly, completely different from hers. I think it is a pity, however, that two adults cannot meet together and say 'I'm sorry for this' and 'I'm sorry for that' and then somehow part as friends. I think each of us would have been happier if we could have done that."

I found myself putting my hand out to him and holding on to his hand; but where, in the old days, I would have held his hand to gain comfort and love, I now felt *I* wanted to give *him* comfort and love.

"You know," I said to him, "when I was a little girl I loved you very, very much. You were my whole world, really. I felt safe with you, safe and loved. I'll always remember that and be grateful for it. When you came here my life changed a lot. I felt that mother did not love me very much. I found it difficult to find anyone to love me in the way that I wanted to be loved. Although I married several times, and each time I hoped I'd found the right partner, something always went terribly wrong. I felt very lonely many times in my life. I have been kept very busy all the time I have been shown around here, and I now realise that in many ways, I have been much luckier than a lot of others who have lived on earth. I still, however, feel an element of loneliness within me, and I can feel it within you. Unfortunately, I don't feel that I can give you anything that will help you, only my sympathy."

152

"That is a great thing to be given, my love." He smiled at me a little ruefully. "You're not my *little* love anymore, but you haven't grown all that tall either, have you?"

"No," I said, "I think show business shortened me off! It shortened a lot of us off, and it certainly shortened me off!"

Then I became aware that we were not alone any more. Several of the young men who had been with my father on the stage came towards us. He introduced me to all of them. They were pleasant and smiling and friendly, and we chatted. They were full of the show that they were going to put on. I was able to respond because I caught their enthusiasm and was able to enthuse back to them, but when I tried to tell them what I had been seeing and experiencing they seemed to shut me off. They did not want to know. After a while they began to draw my father away from me and towards them. He looked at me a little apologetically, a little diffidently, and said, "I hope you haven't been too disappointed in your dad. I did love each of you, and I have been so pleased to see you. I hope you'll come again."

With that, he was drawn away from me, and I found myself alone. It all happened in such a strange way. It was as if a force stronger then himself had drawn him from me, and I was left feeling empty and confused and somehow let down.

As I sat there, trying to get my mind into some form of order out of the confusion that it was in, Doreen reappeared. "I'm so sorry, Judy," she said, as she put her arm kindly round my shoulder. "I do feel for you."

"I feel very peculiar," I said to her. "I don't exactly feel hurt, but I feel empty and sad and lonely, lonelier than I felt when we were going around looking at the children and the animals. Yet I don't feel that I am lonely because I have lost my father. I think I've picked up some of his loneliness, and it has been transferred to me. It's all very confusing. It is as if he and his companions here are wrapped up in a sort of cocoon of theatre from which they have no wish to emerge."

"That is precisely what is happening here, Judy," said Doreen.

"But the thing that hurts me most is that he told me he had tried to tell my mother that he had always loved her in his own way and that he had loved us, his three daughters, but that she wouldn't listen to him. You know, Doreen, I can't help feeling that by not listening to him she has shut the door in his face and left him in this place. That is the only way I can describe it to you."

"Well, Judy, without realising it, you have just shown a great deal of understanding and perspicacity, because that is precisely what has been occurring here. We were hoping that it would not affect you badly and that your appearance might help him. It might still help him, as time goes by, when he thinks about it, or if you manage to approach him again at a later date."

"I would like to do that, if you think it will do any good," I said to her. "I don't like to see him in what I feel to be a place of limited experience. That is the only way I can put it. It's as though he is caught up in something that he can't escape from at the moment, as though in some ways he wishes he could escape but something is preventing him."

"You are quite right," she told me, "but this is something that cannot be rushed at the moment. I am now going to take you to see someone who will, I think, be able to help you a little concerning your confusion over the present situation."

IV

As I reconsidered again all the strange feelings that I had picked up during the whole period I was visiting with my father, and in particular while I was with his friends, I began to get a feeling of my own loneliness welling up within me. This happened despite Doreen's assurance to me that I would not be lonely here, that I would find the kind of friendship and affection and even love that I had always hoped that I would find. Doreen had now managed to convince me that my marriage to Mickey would not have been the permanent and close partnership that I had hoped it would be. The three children I had left behind on earth were not expected to join me here for a number of years. They would, in any case, be joining me with all their earthly experiences plus their own earthly connections and loves that they would have been experiencing in the years after I came here.

I began to think that part of the loneliness I had felt while I was with my father was my own and not just his, that it must have been a mutual disappointment that neither of us was really able to comfort the other. We seemed to have lost the rapport that

I had always thought we had. Doreen had already explained to me that this rapport was largely in my own mind, because although he had loved me and still did love me, he had not really loved me any more than he had loved my mother and my two sisters. So he was not the rock to which I was going to turn here.

All this went through my mind, and I went back through all my experiences here since my arrival from earth. Despite the kindness and help and even affection that I had received from Doreen throughout all our travels, which I had found exceedingly interesting despite their depressing moments, I still felt on my own, even here.

As this feeling began to close in around me more and more, Doreen took hold of my hand, looked me firmly in the eyes, and said, "Please, Judy, try not to dwell on that situation at the moment. I know what you are feeling, and I know why you are feeling it, but I have tried to explain to you that there is a happier future ahead of you. It does lie a little bit ahead of where you are at the moment, but I can only ask you to believe what I have already told you. When the time is right, you will find an enormous amount of happiness and love. I swear this to you."

I knew that Doreen was completely honest. She also seemed to know far more about me than I already knew about myself. I said to her, "Well, you haven't been proved wrong yet, so I will just have to go on hoping that you are right, but I still can't help feeling lonely at present."

"That is understandable, my dear," she said kindly. "But some of it has been brought about by your father's loneliness. When you become interested in other things here, you will gradually find yourself adjusting more and more to the attitude that we all have to come to accept here. We find that transition from earth to the world of the spirit does not necessarily bring instant happiness with it. That happiness has to be worked for, waited for, and truly earned. This, my dear Judy, you will earn. You have already earned it to some extent, quite unwittingly, by simply being your own true self."

"While you have been saying this to me," I told her, "I have again been getting the image of Lorna Smith. It really is quite extraordinary!"

"That is not as extraordinary as it may seem to you at present,

Judy. During the period of your time here, and this now amounts to almost two years of earth time . . . "

"As long as that?" I exclaimed.

"Yes, my dear, it has taken you as long as that to get this far. Meanwhile, Lorna has been constantly battling against the misinterpretations and misjudgments of you that are circulating widely on earth. You are already aware that many of your actions on earth were publicly misjudged even while you were there. We have discussed that. The moment you came here, there were those who began to write and speak about you publicly in a way that they would never have dared to do while you were on earth. Some people have done it in ignorance, because they presumed against you. Others, whom you had crossed at one time or another, have done it deliberately and with malice aforethought. One person, in whom you put a great deal of faith and trust, has added to it by misinterpreting you in his own way. This has led to a completely confused public reaction against you.

"Lorna has been doing all that she could to counteract it by writing to some of the people who have either made the most horrendous mistakes or who have deliberately lied. She also took the trouble to put together a comprehensive booklet, to be circulated amongst your fans, that tried to remind them of all that you had given in your life through your work.

"Now, in an attempt to counteract the many public articles and the books that are beginning to be published around your name, she has even commenced to write a book about you herself. It is intended to be as full a biography as she can manage. We already know here that it will fail to circulate as widely as the lies. It will also fail to be as detailed as she wishes it to be, because she is going to be told she cannot write certain things about some people who are still on earth, despite the fact that she knows they have lied about you. But she is doing it with a great deal of love and care and thoroughness.

"She is reminding people of all that you had to go through in order to survive all the triumphs and the disasters that you encountered in your work as well as in your personal life. She is going through it systematically, getting these events in their correct context. This means that she has been concentrating a very great deal to try and get it right, and she is getting it right, even though it will be drastically curtailed before it reaches the public. All the concentration on her part and the sincere belief and affection and love that she has for you have been reaching your subconscious. This is why, from time to time, you have been thinking of her. I have been aware that, during the journey around the Animal Kingdom, you had flashes of Lorna in your mind."

"That's true! I have! I thought it must be because you had mentioned her to me and I was so amazed that I could not get over my amazement. I knew she liked me a lot. She had always been very fair to me and very kind, and I knew she had always defended me in the articles that she wrote in the fan club magazine. I had no idea, however, that she would be capable of writing a complete book, and I had no idea that she would be concentrating so hard upon me now that I have come here. Nobody else seems to have been doing so, I gather."

"Your children have thought a lot about you, Judy, but *you* have also thought a lot about *them*, which is why you have not noticed any particular difference. The fact that Lorna has been thinking so much about you and you did not expect to be thinking about her has caused you to notice it more. Of course, her concentration has been much more intense than anyone else's, because it has included, on her part, a deep hurt for you that so many lies are being circulated and the frustration arising from not being able to say as much as she wishes.

"All this has reached you in such a way that, because you are far removed from the earth at present, you have received only brief flashes of her personality. She is, nevertheless, continuing with this work, which she would not ever have considered undertaking had she not become so deeply disgusted at what others were doing to your name. She is becoming very embroiled in it all, and although she is beginning to feel that many things are happening around her to try and defeat her, she has no intention of giving up on you in any way whatsoever. I hope that, although it is a little premature for you to understand, you will at least realise that someone is doing battle for you on earth as hard as she possibly can and with the sincerest intentions. So, you see, you are getting some back up, even though you do not yet seem to be getting very much here."

"Well, I do appreciate that she is going to all this trouble for me. I really do. I always felt, with Lorna, that she did try hard to put me across to my fan club members in the best way possible. She used to write articles in the fan club magazine that I always found immensely readable, and she did seem to understand me better than most. I always found her to be kind and considerate and thoughtful when we were together. She never stared at me or cross questioned me or wanted me to sign things, which everyone else seemed to do. I did appreciate that. I just wish now that she had not been quite so shy and reserved about me. Maybe I would have realised just how much she cared. But I did always feel that Lorna was kind and thoughtful and caring, and that was a good thing to know. We got our wires crossed a little bit from time to time when I was overworked, but she didn't seem to mind, and she always came back as though nothing had happened."

"That is what I am trying to tell you, Judy. Lorna will always come back as though nothing had happened. How many people in your life can you count on for that?"

"Nobody but my kids," I said to her ruefully.

"Well, there's your answer!" said Doreen. "Now, I am going to change the subject because I do not want to get you too far too soon. I am now going to take you to meet someone who will be able to understand a little of what is troubling your father."

"Yes, of course, I'd like that,"I said. "I don't know why, but I'm beginning to feel better already since you've told me about Lorna taking all the trouble to defend me. At the same time, I'm not at all happy to learn I have been so misjudged. I know there was a lot of rubbish going on around me. You've already discussed this with me—that people thought I was doing various things that I wasn't. But, somehow, although I am unhappy about that, I feel reassured that there is somebody there trying to do something about it. I don't know why I should feel this, when it is only one person against many, but somehow I do!"

"There is a reason for that, dear Judy, which we will have to go into later on. At the moment I want you to settle your mind a little bit about your father, because it will help you to see him, as well as other aspects of life here, more clearly."

V

Soon we were crossing a very beautiful square. There were fountains sparkling in the light and trees with birds singing. Some children were playing together, and people were walking about. We suddenly turned a corner, and I found myself facing what looked like a church.

"It is strange that we should come to this church," I said to Doreen, "because I was about to say to you earlier, but something distracted me, that I hadn't noticed any churches here."

"We do have churches, but they are not as numerous as on earth for a number of reasons. On earth there are an enormous number of religions, many of which are regarded on earth as being in conflict with each other. There have been the most enormous atrocities committed on earth in the name of so-called religion. Religion is something that has become completely distorted in the human mind over many, many centuries, and it is now almost totally unrecognisable for what it is in truth.

"When people have been here for a while, it gradually becomes clear to them that there is really no such thing as a world religion and that such a religion is not required here. There have been a number of good men born on earth who have been strongly psychic and who have endeavoured, each in his own individual ways, to transfer to the population in which they have existed the various teachings that they have received from some of the higher teachers here. They have reported to those around them what they have seen and heard and felt and, as a result, believed to be true. The teachings have been transferred into book form, often years after the original events and experiences took place. These books have, in turn, been translated and retranslated many times. It has always been doubtful that everything was ever recorded completely correctly, because human memory is very fallible. The accounts have often become coloured, however unintentionally, by the recorders' own thoughts and the clouding of memory. Others have felt the accounts not to be imaginative enough and have embroidered the facts to some extent. Thus, the various religious faiths all over the world have, without exception, come far away from the original basic truths.

"Our progress here when we come here very much depends upon how we have, or have not, been steeped in a certain religion while on earth. The strange thing is that, quite often, it is those who had no particularly strong religious beliefs but who had some faith that we continue to exist and that, somewhere or other, there may be a good God caring for us, who often are able to go forward most quickly here. Because they are more open-minded the teachers here can reach them more quickly and clearly and put them into the right attitude of mind to receive the truth. Many people who have steadfastly followed a certain religion on earth can become extremely narrow-minded and bigoted about their own religion, and it is ofen very difficult to prevent them from continuing here in the same beliefs that they have brought with them. It may take a long time before we can break through to them and begin to help them to see that their narrow-minded attitude is holding them back in a number of ways.

"Now you, dear Judy, did have your beliefs, but you did not follow any particularly hard and fast faith. You would have entered any Christian church that you had been asked to enter. Probably you would have been just as contented to enter a synagogue or a mosque."

"Yes, I would," I said to her. "I've often been very confused as to how much of the Bible was truth. I have discussed it with several religious advisers each of whom has tried to convince me of the truth of his own viewpoint. I have always had a deep belief in God. I have asked God for help on numerous occasions, and, although I was never a regular visitor to church, I did go from time to time, and I did try and read my Bible. I always hoped that there would be an afterlife, but I was a little unsure about it. I tried to instil in my children the belief that there was a good God looking after us and seeing that we didn't come to too much harm. When, however, I saw what happened to some people on earth who seemed to be leading good lives and who seemed to have a belief in God, I did wonder at times and my faith did get shaken. It was such a great relief to wake up here and find that everything was so beautiful and that we were all carrying on almost normally," I said with a smile.

"Well, Judy, it will be easy for me to explain to you how we see religion here.

"This church is for those who still need to come for some

form of consultation with the higher teachers. It does not conform to any particular religion. It is simply a place where people can come to consult those who have more experience than themselves. It is for people who are literally soul-searching.

"On earth, a church is often visited by those in need of a quiet place in which to be. In this world, it is so easy to find a quiet place almost anywhere that the churches are no longer needed for that purpose. We also realise that there is absolutely no need for hymn singing or for Bible readings. Nor is it necessary to have the kind of sermons that are given by church dignitaries on earth who have to try and find something within themselves for regular church meetings. It is difficult for them to find something new to say that will hold the congregation's interest. In addition, of course, they are of earth and, therefore, limited in their outlook to some extent, no matter how learned and sincere they may be from earth's viewpoint, because each one will have been indoctrinated with his own form of religion.

"When people come here, they find that all life is regarded as equal. They find there is no longer any fear of death. They come to realise that there are no true 'heaven' and 'hell,' only conditions of mind that are entirely up to them. They created their own heaven or hell. If they have treated any form of life brutally or cruelly when on earth, they will continue to exist here in their own private hell of the mind until they have learned true contrition and wish to contribute something towards those that they have cold bloodedly mishandled and destroyed while on earth. There are others who have done numerous good deeds on earth, who have lived as spiritually as any human being can possibly live, and who will, when they come here, come to an exceptionally beautiful state of mind and being and live in an exceptionally beautiful place here compared with even where you and I are at present existing. But they will still not be in as beautiful a place as those who have been here for many centuries and who have gradually been developing more and more spirituality, understanding, and knowledge.

"There are people, such as you and I, who come here from, shall I say, a middle-of-the-road kind of life. We never intentionally did anything vindictive or destructive. We never did anything exceptionally spiritual. So we have come to a place where the average person comes who has lived an average, well-intentioned life. Even here, I am being extremely basic, because those who have sensitive and loving natures will be in a slightly higher vibration than those who were slightly less sensitive, slightly less loving, but who were, nevertheless, sincere and straightforward in their approach to life when on earth.

"When people on earth claim they have had a vision of God or of Jesus as a result of their strong prayer or of some special experience somewhere, they will have probably seen a beautiful light and, possibly, a face in that light, because they have been reached by one of the higher teachers here. What we have here, we are told, is an overall ability to reach the highest possible spirituality. It is within us all to achieve it eventually, but we all have to work towards it. It is those who have achieved it who send us the beauty and the strength and the love that we need to help us to achieve it. In between those high beings and us are others who have gone very much further forward than we have yet gone, having been here for a very much longer time, and those that have almost reached perfection. It is the highest state of being which is the 'God Force.' In other words, it is a force for good. In its different strengths and vibrations it penetrates through to all of us, eventually even to those who are in the darker states of mind that we have been mentioning.

"Now, when anyone such as you or I need to be given some higher advice, understanding, or information, depending on what it is, we go to speak to someone who is in a better position than I am to help you. I am bringing you to this church because, here, you will be able to discuss with someone who is far more advanced than I am your own problems of the spirit and how your problems of the spirit can be affected by the problems of the spirit of others here. I will leave you for a while, and I will return for you. I think you will find that you will have a far greater understanding of your father and his problem, and possibly also of the problems of others that you may have met in similar circumstances while on earth, than you could ever have had before."

VI

The churchlike building that we entered was a very beautiful place. Light shone through tall windows in many different radiations of colour, but there were no altars or crosses or images or figurines. There was just a pool of light in the middle of what looked like a beautiful chapel, and there were two chairs. Doreen led me towards one of the chairs, and a gentleman in robes came and stood before us.

"Welcome, my dear," he said to me, taking both my hands in his in a kindly, fatherly fashion. "Please sit down. Your friend will be waiting for you when we have finished." With that, I noticed that Doreen had gone.

He reminded me a little of the paintings I have seen of St. Francis of Assisi, but I then realised that it was only a superficial look. When I looked again, I found that he had a very kindly expression, but he was not wearing a friar's robe. His robe was very beautiful, and it gave off a gold and silver light.

"I understand you have come here to ask for help in understanding your father and why it is you cannot feel as close to him as you had felt when you were both on earth."

"That's true," I said to him. "I realise that a lot of years have passed since we last met and that I have grown up and had a lot of things happen to me that he does not know about, but there seems to be more to it than that, and I can't understand what it is."

"Well, my child, you have to realise that I can only tell you a little about it, because your father is entitled to his own deepest, most private thoughts."

"Yes, of course," I interjected. "I wasn't trying to be inquisitive, only wondering how I could help him, because I would like to, if I could."

"I know you would. I was merely trying to explain to you that I will have to, in some ways, be somewhat superficial, but I hope that, when I have finished my explanation, you will be able to see his problem more clearly. I have to go back to when your father met your mother.

"He was a comparatively inexperienced young man with ladies. He was interested only in the theatre. He had been fascinated with the music and the lights and the action, and he had never felt deeply about anyone. When your mother came into his life, she gave him a feeling of reassurance. He was used to being mainly a solitary person. He could not explain to anyone why he felt as solitary as he did. When she came along and started to be chatty and friendly, he felt himself warming to her and feeling less solitary.

163

"Because your mother had a strong personality and began to feel attracted to him and spent a lot of time with him, he found himself being drawn more and more towards her, but it was your mother who talked him into marrying her rather than your father doing the persuading. Because he had become deeply fond of her and had come to rely on her companionship, he was happy to marry her, and he did love her in his way. But there was still this feeling within him that he needed periods of time to himself. He did not know why this was, but shortly after he had married your mother and your first sister had been conceived, he began to want to withdraw from your mother from time to time and to keep himself to himself. He tried to overcome this, because she could not understand why, from time to time, he seemed to shut off from her.

"As the years went by, your sister Susan and you were born. Over these years, your father managed to keep his marriage on a reasonably normal footing. But, as time passed—and marriages do tend to become more difficult to hold together in many instances—your mother became more and more domineering and your father shrank away, to some extent, from her domineering attitude. This increased his desire to keep more and more to himself and to be less and less of a husband to your mother. It was something he regretted in his heart, because he knew that it was contributing to the unhappiness that was creeping into the marriage, but to him it had become a vicious circle. The more your mother began to turn from him in anger and a feeling of being not wanted, the more he turned in to himself. He could be demonstrative to you three girls because he was simply giving you love and affection and interest, and it helped him in his separation from your mother.

"What I now have to explain to you is something that I wish the world of earth could understand and be more tolerant of. Each human being is born into a body with certain cells and genes. It is impossible for any human body to work in exactly the same way as another human body. Just as in any make of car or ship or train or aeroplane or engine, something quite small can go wrong that upsets its performance. The mind operates through the physical brain in all living creatures, including human beings. The brain controls the movements, feelings, reactions, and emotional reactions of the body.

"What happens to those people who have different reactions to their bodies than do others is that, in certain individuals, their minds work through their brains and reach their body in such a way that certain cells and genes in the body are impressed to work more than others. Some people who have a very high sexual urge are sometimes denigrated by those that do not, and vice versa. It is often something totally beyond the control of the person who possesses a high or low or a moderate sexual urge.

"When the human being has a particular urge, whichever it may be, it is up to him or her as to how he or she controls it. You might find that someone who has a moderate sexual urge marries someone with a strong sexual urge, and that can cause a lot of unhappiness to both individuals. One feels unfulfilled; the other feels too much emphasis is being placed upon the sexual side of their marriage and reacts against it. Neither of them can be blamed for their different feelings because that is how his or her particular body is being imprinted.

"Individual control comes into it when someone with a high sexual urge can see that his or her mate has not got such an urge and tries to be more considerate about it. The one who has a less strong urge will see that his or her mate is really trying not to be too demanding and in turn will try to be more responsive. It still does not make for a very happy marriage, but it does at least show that the two individuals are each trying to be more considerate towards the other. That is where sensitivity and control come into it, and it can sometimes keep a marriage going.

"You could also have people who have hardly any sexual urge at all. That is not something about which they should be derided, as they so often are. They just do not have it. In many instances they marry because they cannot bear to be alone on earth and marriage is usually the only way they can achieve a permanent companion. They try to achieve what is regarded by human society as a normal relationship. That is where disaster occurs again, because they and their partners have to try and arrange a sensitive understanding as to what is the most acceptable to them both. Neither of them can be blamed for the way they were born, but it is up to both of them as to how they react and handle their feelings.

"Now we come to those who are born in a confused state of mind because, through some inheritance from the parents, the

165

two cells that have joined together to form the human body have produced more of one kind of hormone than the other, so that they have a male body containing excessive female hormones or vice versa. This can produce a confusion in the mind that is operating that particular body. A male may find himself attracted physically to another male and a female to another female. That is something that is basically in their physical make-up and that can cause problems.

"It then depends again on each individual how he or she handles that problem. Some decide that the best thing to do is simply to cut themselves off from members of either sex in order to try and avoid any further problems. They might live a lonely life as a result of it, but they feel they have somehow managed to conform to what the world expects of them. There are others who decide they will try and form a regular partnership with one person of their own sex. Some achieve it; some do not. Just as in other male and female relationships, a highly sexed male or female will prefer to play the field, as it were, so will these play the field in many such instances, but among those of their own sex.

"I can only tell you that, from here, each of these sexual tendencies is recognised as not unnatural. We do, however, prefer to see all of them kept within reasonable limits and not allowed to take over a person's mind to such a degree that it coarsens and even distorts his or her general outlook on life. This is, regrettably, what can happen.

"Physical intercourse is something that each living creature on the planet earth is provided with in order to reproduce its kind. That is its basic purpose. The fact that it is performed for reasons of sensuality, out of a need for two people who are deeply loving to be as close as possible, causes different aspects to take over where humans are concerned.

"It can also be abused by those who feel that it is all they want out of life. Their relationships with others are reduced to the basic act of intercourse without any feeling of deep love and attachment. That, as far as the human race is concerned, is an abomination. When they come here, they have to find out for themselves that this coarsening effect has reduced their sensitivity and their understanding of spirituality to such a degree that it will take them a very long time before they can begin to reach the higher and more sensitive and, therefore, happier levels of existence that we have here.

"It is not easy to explain this subject to you in the few words that I am trying to give to you. What I am trying to explain to you is that you have a father who became largely misunderstood for his own relatively minor problem.

"Your father was a young man who would have gone through life as a bachelor without feeling that he had particularly missed anything in not having any sexual experiences. The fact that he wanted to have someone take an interest in him, as your mother was doing, led him into marriage. This created the problem that, although he tried to be a good husband and was, indeed, a good father, he did not always feel able to respond. He never let your mother down with any other person at any time. He simply felt, at times, unable to respond.

"Your mother saw him as someone who was deliberately cutting himself off from her, and she began to wonder whether he was being interested elsewhere. This was not so. He loved her as a person, in his heart, for many years. When she began to become hard and bitter, she drove him further and further away from her. Had she been more sensitive and waited, he would have continued to do his best to be her husband as far as he felt able. This was not a blameable fault within your father. It was simply that he took on a duty that he hoped he would be able to fulfil and, for the reasons I have mentioned, did not manage to do so. What we have still to get to the bottom of is why he was such a solitary person initially.

"He was born with fewer hormones than was necessary to provide him with what is regarded as a regular sexual impulse. Although he was unable to define it within himself, he became someone who just felt he could not respond as much as people expected him to do. He had not flirted with girls when he was in his teens, as his friends had done. It was not that he did not like their company. He simply was not interested in getting further involved than that. It was only because your mother was somewhat persistent and he was regularly in her company that he eventually decided he would try and live a normal life. He felt that with your mother he might be able to do that. The fact that he failed, the fact that she turned so bitterly against him in the last few years of his life, means that when he came here he was unable to overcome his feelings of having failed to make a proper life for the two of them. The subsequent failure to reach her with his explanation when she came here made it even more difficult for him. That is why we still cannot get him away from his feeling of failure.

"He is now working with other men who have had similar problems on earth. At the moment they are all deeply interested in their theatre because that was their main interest on earth. It helped to make up to them for what they were lacking in other ways. What we now need is some means of getting your father away from his feeling of failure and towards recognising what we all recognise here—that one can have a close and loving relationship here that is not in any way based on physical emotions.

"I believe you, yourself, are already realising that you can love your fellow creatures in the same way that you can love a child. Well, my dear, you can love an adult human of either sex in exactly the same way. You do not have to have a physical relationship in order to feel understood and loved here. If you have friends with a close affinity of the mind, they can be closer than any physical relationship was on earth.

"It can be far more uplifting, far more rewarding, because, basically, the physical relationship was, originally, *solely* for procreation. Unfortunately, it has become so distorted in human society on earth today that few people recognise it for what it is. They are given to understand that it is a failure within themselves if they restrain themselves from indulging in sexual relationships in a free and easy manner. In many instances it is ruining lives just as much as the extreme narrow-mindedness of some earlier times, when the male dominated the female to a horrendous degree. Both extremes can distort feelings and ruin lives.

"In your case, my dear, you were somebody who desperately needed to feel that one person loved you for yourself. You needed somebody to turn to on almost every issue of life, to discuss things with, to have children with, to be with, to love and to care for, and to cherish and to be cherished by. You felt that your partnership should be fulfilling in every possible way, that the physical fulfilment was part of your spiritual fulfilment. This is how you went into each of your partnerships, and, in almost each instance, you found that you were not being received and recognised in the way that you had hoped. In each instance you had to compromise, and in each instance you brought a higher attitude of mind to your physical relationship than did your partner.

"That is understandable in some ways, because on earth the male body is composed of a heavier substance than that of the female. It is a little more difficult for men to have such a spiritual approach to consummation. In some instances a woman may not be as sensitive as you were in that respect and may not feel any lack. In your case, you often felt lonelier than you thought you should have felt, and you wondered why. With your husband Sidney Luft, you had a closer rapport than with any other husband, but even he was sometimes not quite as sensitive as you would have liked him to have been, although you realised that it was unintentional and that he did love you. It was when he withdrew his love from you that you felt the biggest hurt that you had ever felt.

"Now, I think I will have to leave you to think this over. When you have thought it over, if you have any questions to ask me, please do so. The main thing that I wanted to get across to you, my dear, is that it is because your father had a physical body that was not able to live up to the physical body of your mother that he was misunderstood by her and by many other people. Because he was a solitary man in some ways, yet he could be responsive to all children despite keeping himself shut away from his wife, a number of people misunderstood him, and he knew it. That is what he is fighting to overcome here. You cannot help him alone; he has to be helped to help himself. It can only be little by little that he will see himself differently and be able to break away from his present cocoon of safety, which is how he sees it: 'I am here with people who know how I felt, and we will stay together here.' He has to be shown that they do not have to stay there together, that they can branch out and do other things, as you have already done."

"Well, I haven't really branched out into anything yet. I'm still finding my way around," I told him.

"Yes, but in finding your way around, you have visited the children and seen what can be done there. You have visited the animals and seen what can be done there. You have even visited

169

your father and seen a human problem there that needs to be reached and improved upon, and again you say you wish you could help him. Those men are all being negative. They are not looking around them and saying, 'How are others experiencing existence? Is there anything I can contribute to them?' They are all saying, 'I am going to keep myself where I know I am understood and safe.' All they are really doing is narrowing themselves down in the community instead of mixing with it and finding and expanding themselves.

"Anyone on the plane of earth who does not have what other people regard as normal emotions, normal physical feelings, tends to be derided, shunned, and put upon by their fellow humans. However extrovertly they may handle themselves on earth—some do and some do not—it is still in their minds that they are regarded as different from their fellows. They somehow acquire a shield that they put around themselves in almost every instance in order to come through life as completely as possible. Nearly all those people who come here have to overcome the shield that they have put around themselves. They may well arrive here in a higher spiritual condition than the so-called normal people who have either indulged or over-indulged their sexual activities on earth. But, because they have tended to wrap a shield around themselves, there is an emptiness about their existence here until we can remove that shield and absorb them into our more loving and spiritual states of existence. Can you understand, my child?"

"It is such an enormous topic, but I think I can. I am very sad to think that my poor dad found himself in that situation. Of course, in show business you tend to get a more open mixture of what are regarded as sexual deviations than, perhaps, in everyday life."

"Not really," my teacher interrupted me. "It is only that show business people are more extroverted in many instances and discuss it more openly amongst themselves. There are far more of these so-called deviates in the world at large than is generally realised. I would say that almost half of the world's population have a tendency towards being less sexual than the other half. Most of them try to hide it behind the façade of what society will regard as normal, and it can cause a lot of mental distress to the partners concerned.

170

"When they come here, many of these people feel free to be themselves for the first time in their existence. It is then that they find out whether or not they still have the partner with them that they had on earth. Many of them do not; some do. But some of the happiest partnerships here are those that would have been regarded on earth as abnormal, either because they refrained from sexual relationships altogether or else had them with another person of their own sex. They come here and they find that sexual relationships do not exist on this plane of existence where you are now or on the higher planes, although they do exist on the lower planes. They find they are loved purely for their minds, their thoughts, their ideals, their personalities, and for no other reason whatsoever. To them it comes as a joyful release from many restrictions and heartache and mental loneliness.

"We think that your father will not be too much longer in his present state. Your visit has made a small breakthrough, and eventually we see him turning into the creative, sensitive, and happier person that he is capable of being. So try not to be too sad about him, my dear, and try not to be too sad that, despite several marriages, you have not yet found someone that you feel you can turn to in the way you always wished to. The day will come when you will find such a person. I promise you.

"Most of us here feel the need to have someone with us as a special friend and confidant, for the additional assurance and interest that we cannot always obtain from our other friends, however kind they may be. Each one of us, and I have been through the process myself, needs to feel there is a special person with whom we can have an exceptional rapport. Of course even that changes as we come higher in our understanding. We may add others to that one person, so that we have a group in total harmony, but that does take time and experience, and one step at a time is necessary.

"After a period here and more experiences, you will find yourself preparing to take that one step that will help you to experience and expand beyond all your present understanding. But I do assure you, my dear, that although you have many things to learn, you will not be unhappy here, you will not be lonely, and you will eventually find that perfect happiness that you have always sought.

"I hope I have not confused you too much in what has proved to be a long explanation, despite the fact that it is still, necessarily, fairly basic. I have tried to keep it as simple as possible, but it is a very complicated subject. There are so many shades and gradations from one extreme to the other. If you do have any questions after you have had time to consider it all, I will be only too pleased to see you again. In the meantime, bless you and goodbye."

With that, he had gone and Doreen was by my side again.

VII

As we left the little chapel to return to the street, I felt, rather than heard, Doreen's reassuring presence. She did not say anything to me, and yet I knew, somehow, that she had already became acquainted with what I had been told and was giving me the opportunity to sort it out for myself. Doreen was always like that. Her presence beside me was kindly and caring and considerate, but never obtrusive. Yet, while I knew that she was being kind and thoughtful and helpful, I could not overcome the feeling, deep down within myself, that, although Doreen could not have been more kindly in her approach to me, this was something that she had undertaken for others before me and would also be undertaking for others in the future. Although she was someone to whom I could turn for counsel, hers would not be the kind of friendship I had often sought in my heart, where I could be certain that that person would always be there and would choose to be there because they were drawn to me and wished to be with me rather than having been asked to be with me to help me.

This was something that I had endured throughout the whole of my life on earth. Was the person that I thought liked me really with me because they wanted to be with me, or because they had been paid to be with me, or had been instructed to be with me, or had chosen to be with me only because they wanted to see what it was like to spend time with Judy Garland? I knew that Doreen was none of these things and that she was kind and sweet and genuine, but she was still, nevertheless, a helper provided for me and not there solely because she was drawn towards my company.

I had listened with great care to all that had been explained to me by the teacher I had met in the chapel. Some of it I had already realised before we met, because anyone with any caring intelligence would stop and reason as to why some people reacted in certain ways and some in other ways when it came to sexual inclination. Personally, I had always thought myself to be a middle-of-the-road person in that respect. When I married, I wanted to be as close to my husband as possible and to have children with him, because I felt that to be part of marriage. When I married Mark Herron, I had known that we would not be having any children, but I was happy in the thought that he did not need any and that I already had my three beautiful children—Liza, Lorna, and Joe. When I married Mickey, I felt that I should try and have a child for him, but I was concerned my age—forty-six—might make this impossible. We had discussed it together. He had not wanted me to put my life at risk, but I had said, and I genuinely meant it, that I intended to consult a gynecologist to see whether there was any likelihood of my being able to bear a complete and beautiful child and not one that might be born with any physical handicap.

While I was considering all I had been told, which had been in far greater detail than I have stated here, I was brought to think of all the various people I had met and often been associated with over the years—either as colleagues or acquaintances, and sometimes as friends—who had seemed to have a problem of one kind or another maintaining any sort of permanent relationship, no matter how pleasant and often seemingly kind they were as companions. I had accepted those who clearly had a problem associating with members of the opposite sex in any kind of a regularised relationship because I had felt it to be a difficult thing for them to have to live with and, but for the grace of God, any other person may have been born with a similar problem.

In many cases, I had found the young homosexuals that I had encountered to have been pleasant and friendly and even sympathetic companions, and I usually felt easy in their company. Much as I realised that women may be equally unfortunate in facing a similar problem, I always felt uneasy in their company and so tended to back away if any of them came towards me for friendship. Looking back from here, I began to feel there may have been a lack of understanding within me for these people who had, after all, just as much right to seek a loving companion as I had. I suppose the main reason for my mistrust was a feeling of discomfort in the kind of interest some of them seemed to be taking in me and my own strong feelings that I could never in any way respond to their less orthodox feelings.

As I considered all this I could not help feeling so very sorry that my poor father had apparently been misunderstood for his own actions, which were simply to keep himself to himself from time to time instead of doing anything that was disloyal to my mother. If more people on earth could put loyalty above all else, irrespective of their underlying problem, more people would have happier lives.

For my part, I had never felt able to indulge in any extramarital affairs with anyone. I always felt that the only satisfying relationship was within the confines of a loving marriage. It was only when my husband turned away from me that I considered divorce, and it was only when I was assured of someone's love that I accepted another marriage partner. Had I wished to have done so, I could have entered into various casual affairs. Such offers were often being hinted at to me by one person or another, and they were clearly surprised when I refused their advances. There was no way, however, that I could bring myself to accept their suggestions, no matter how deeply lonely I was feeling and no matter how much I needed a companion. Perhaps this may seem very old-fashioned and dull to the next generation after mine, who tend to see their sexual relationships from a different viewpoint, or even to my own generation, but no matter how much I used to wish to be accepted and regarded as a modern person, I could not manage to stretch my modernity that far.

I do not know how far Doreen and I went while I was turning all this around in my mind, but we had not been saying anything and I had not been noticing where we had been going. I gradually realised that we had reached a seat under a tree in what appeared to be a park. There were people enjoying themselves in various ways a little bit removed from us, but we were otherwise alone in our little area. As I looked at Doreen, I found her looking at me sympathetically.

"You have been a long way away in your thoughts, haven't you, Judy?"

"Yes, I have," I said to her. "The teacher explained to me about my father's problem and put it into its correct perspective. I have come to realise now why my parents' marriage was not a successful one. But, you know, I feel certain that, had I been in my mother's shoes, with a husband such as my father, we would not have had that sort of problem. I would have been quite happy to have him with me as long as I felt assured that I was the only one in his life and that there was not anyone else."

"Yes, you would have done, Judy, but there are many other women, such as your mother, who could not have handled that situation."

"But I also see now," I said to her, "where I may have misjudged others who tried to be helpful to me."

"It is not a very clear subject, Judy. It is even less clear to those on earth who are not prepared to think about it and who are prepared to misjudge almost everyone who does not think and feel exactly as they do. You may have misjudged others, but there are also others who have badly misjudged you.

"I must tell you that, amongst those on earth to whom you turned at one time or another with no stronger intention than sheer friendship, there are several who are using you, in their own minds, as a means of increasing and expressing their own egos. Although your approach to them was simply that of friendship, they have persuaded themselves that you wanted them as lovers. Although this is completely untrue, they are, nevertheless, convincing themselves that this is so, and in the stories that they are relating, they are succeeding in convincing others. As a result, the world at large will be given, not only now but in the future, a completely wrong impression of how you saw yourself and those around you. This is why so many biographies, not only of you but of many, many other famous people, have been giving those on earth an extremely peculiar and distorted view of the individuals concerned.

"One of the numerous misconceptions that Lorna is endeavouring to counteract in her book about you is that you were an inconstant and uncaring person who had various extramarital relationships, as well as five husbands. This had been implied to some extent in articles written about you even before you came here, which often misquoted you on the subject, but a great deal

175

more imagination has been brought to bear since then. She and I both know there will be a great deal more in similar vein, so that many people will feel disappointed in you. Lorna has actually seen some of the items that others are intending to publish, and she has privately challenged them as lies, but she cannot say so publicly. Some people consider her private denials on your behalf to be naive, whereas it was actually you who were frequently naive in your approach to certain people who are now intending to misuse your name for their own purposes. Unfortunately, they will probably succeed in convincing the world at large, which does not know you personally or very well.

"Now, although there is little that Lorna can do to prevent all these lies taking hold, she is doing her best for you. We feel here that, in order to give her the moral support and the interest and the friendship that we consider she deserves from you while she is endeavouring to counteract these lies, it would be a kindness on your part, Judy, if you would communicate with her and support her in what she believes to be the truth. She wishes to defend your attitude to your marriages and to confirm that you did not enter into any extramarital relationships."

My feelings had been very mixed while I listened to Doreen. I was angry, and I was hurt, and I felt disgusted. I also felt grateful to Lorna. Eventually, I looked at Doreen with the deepest astonishment I had experienced since I had arrived here.

"However can I possibly communicate with Lorna?" I gasped at her. "How can I possibly do that?"

"You would be helped, if you felt you would like to do so," said Doreen.

I gazed at her in total stupefaction for I don't know how long.

"Do you mean that I could actually speak to Lorna?" I said slowly and still unbelievingly. "I thought that could only be done through very special people, if at all!"

"Well, this seems to be as good a time as any to explain to you about the way in which we are able to communicate to certain individuals who are still on earth," she replied. "But before I go into all that complicated explanation, I would like to have your answer."

"I'd love to talk to Lorna! Of course, I would! I've always liked her, and I always appreciated what she tried to do for me.

I do realise, since I've been here and looked at myself more clearly, that I owe her a much bigger thank you than I ever got around to actually giving her. *Yes, I would* like to speak to her!" I said in a tone of complete finality.

"Right!" said Doreen. "But, before we go into that as far as you are concerned, I would like to explain to you some of the hazards in this kind of communication."

I found that we were emerging from the park in which we had been sitting and were returning to, of all places, the little glade that I had frequented so much in my earlier experiences here. Doreen explained to me, "This is the place where you are able to function the most clearly, at the moment, on your particular vibrational level. Although you did not realise it, while you were travelling through the city your vibrational level was adjusting slightly to enable you to make a brief contact with each and every person that you passed or spoke to. Your father and his friends were really on a different vibrational level to you. The teacher was on a much higher level than you, and he had to adjust his vibration to yours, but your vibration changed a little on entering the chapel. The fact that you were in the park and other people were not too far away from you meant another slight vibrational adjustment while in that area.

"But, in this little glade of yours, you are completely on your own true vibrational level of existence. I would like to explain to you, Judy, that even here the vibrational level in this glade has altered slightly since you first came to it, because each of your experiences here has slightly changed the vibration that is now the most natural to you. So, I have brought you back to where you will feel most relaxed. Here you will be able to think over what I am telling you just that little bit more profoundly than you would have done had we spoken about it all while we were still in the park."

VIII

"The first thing I have to explain to you, Judy, is that it is possible for the minds of people here to reach the minds of those who are still on earth. In theory, it should be possible for all minds on earth to receive communication from minds such as ours, that are no longer with an earthly, physical body. It does not work that way because, over the eons, human beings have evolved in such a way that the majority of the communities in the various parts of the world are completely oblivious of the other forms of existence that continue to operate around them in the same space but with a different vibrational quality to their own.

"Even while you and I are speaking here, there are an infinite number of forms of existence continuing to exist in this same space that we are using, but because their vibrational level is slower or quicker than ours, we cannot see or hear or feel them any more than the average human being who is still in the physical body on earth can see or feel or hear us. There are, however, people on earth who can tune in with their minds to certain communications sent—I could almost say broadcast—from here for them to pick up and interpret, just as a radio receiver on earth can pick up sound waves drawn from the electricity in the air and make these audible. Similarly, just as television transmitters can broadcast pictures on electrical waves, so can we, with a form of electrical energy, transmit to certain minds on earth that are capable of receiving us the thoughts and words and images we wish to convey. Such receivers on earth are usually known as mediums or sensitives or clairvoyants or clairaudients. As they receive us in so many different ways it is difficult to give a mass description of what takes place from here. There are those individuals who actually receive in their mind a very vivid image. There are others who do not see an image but get an impression of what is being conveyed. They could not explain to you how they get the impression, yet they seem to know they should be seeing, for example, a face or a car or a tree. There are others who are able to produce words beyond their own intentions without fully understanding how those words came into their mind to be spoken. There are some others who actually hear a voice that seems to them to be external to their own ear, and there are some who see things that are external to their own eyes. All of these forms of reception are equally creditable and acceptable. Some mediums are able to experience all these forms of communication, but others receive only one, or possibly two, such forms of communication.

"A problem arises with the different layers of the human mind and the positioning of that mind as it prepares to receive

178

messages from here. The human mind on earth has to operate through the physical brain. We could send out an impulse from here to convey a certain mental image or a certain word or a certain suggested action, and that impulse has to reach the correct part of the mind of the medium in order to create the image or the word that we wish to be singled out. It then has to be conveyed through the human brain to the human voice-box that is reproducing the message.

"If you have a really strong medium who is strongly linked to this world with his or her thoughts, then it is much easier for us to reach them with the correct message, because their psychic 'aerial' is strong. The psychic aerial of another medium may not be so strong. Then it is possible that a message sent from here might not be picked up quite so clearly. It becomes slightly blurred by the recipient's own subconscious mind, somewhat in the way you can get two radio programs coming together from close wavelengths on earth, and the message gets slightly distorted.

"Then there is the third problem of all the different layers of vibrational existence between the medium on earth and the communicator from here. Again, this may affect the medium's reception in the same way that having two or three radio wavelengths close to each other causes you to hear several programs at once, or to receive one radio station that completely obliterates what you are trying to pick up from another station. Other minds, in no way connected with the medium on earth or with the person who is trying to relay the message from here, can cut in with their own comments and images and completely confuse the reception. The poor medium is left floundering as to what he or she is getting and can then innocently relay an inaccurate message or image.

"This happens mainly to the inexperienced person who discovers that he or she is able to receive, who is not aware of all the complexities of such a procedure, and whose mind is wide open to receiving all those different channels. Such individuals have to learn to control what is being given to them. They have to learn that, in order to ensure that they are less likely to receive this kind of interference, they should broadcast to here the fact that they wish to communicate and then give those of us here with whom they wish to speak the time to adjust ourselves for this purpose. They should then sit quietly to ensure that their aerial is sufficiently attuned to receive the clearer channel—perhaps I should say the VHF channel—that we are preparing from here. Even with all these precautions problems can arise, but once the medium on earth has had sufficient experience to learn to overcome these hazards, then communication can usually be relied upon to be correctly achieved.

"I do not wish to become too complicated on this subject. There are other forms of mediumship that are possible, such as those practiced earlier in the present century on earth and the latter part of the nineteenth century. In these cases, people used to sit in their homes, holding hands in the dark in a circle, and various objects, including metal trumpets, would fly around the room. Some mediums would exude a substance known as ecto-plasm, from which forms could be created for a period of time. Although this does occasionally still take place in some places, the present-day medium usually relies on communcations of the mind, sitting in a brightly lit room and conversing with us here in order to receive and relate the information in a perfectly normal and natural way.

"A lot of people are fearful of communication from here. They should not be. It is a completely natural phenomenon. It used to take place and be accepted without any difficulty whatsoever very many centuries ago, before life on earth became so sophisticated and was taken over by cities and machinery and by so many destructive actions on the part of human beings. These have now surrounded the earth with a great black pall that is exceedingly difficult to penetrate in order to reach the average person in this way. It is still not unknown for animals or for very young children to see and feel and hear from us here, because they have not yet been surrounded with the sophistication of adult human life.

"Of course, there are the darker sides to be borne in mind. The fact that such as you and I can be helped to communicate means that we would only do so under the correct conditions and in the correct manner. But there are those earthbound spirits who, because of the lives they have led, have not yet reached the higher levels of existence that we are now in, and who are thus on different levels of existence between here the earth. Sometimes they find they can communicate with a person on earth who has a low attitude of mind. They can draw close to that person, and between the two of them, they create more evil. Or they can impinge on the mind of a developing medium and cause difficulties and confusion until that medium's mind has been trained to reach the higher vibrational levels of communication.

"Provided that each and every human being on earth who is endeavouring to communicate with us here approaches us in the right manner, with the right thoughts, the right wishes, and with the kind of regulated approach that gives us the opportunity to ensure that we are reaching them on their right wavelength, far from this communication being harmful, it can turn into a very beautiful and uplifting experience. I wish we could convince more unbelievers on earth, and those who consider it to be an evil thing, that there are few things more beautiful than for someone on earth who has lost a loved one to be able to hear from that loved one that he or she is alive and well and still loving the person on earth. The darker sides of communication are entirely the fault of those who have dark minds or who, in the earlier days of their mediumship, are unaware of some of the pitfalls that can exist between them and us.

"Now then, Judy, having explained that to you, I will also tell you, with respect to your wishing to communicate with Lorna, she has recently been attending various lectures and public demonstrations on the subject of psychic phenomenon. She has been doing this for two reasons. First, to enable her to decide whether or not she can accept that such communications are possible. Having come to accept that this is so, she is also hoping she may, sooner or later, receive a communication from here that will reassure her that she is doing the right thing in your eyes in trying to write this book. Although this is beyond her present knowledge, she actually has it within herself to become a most excellent medium. This will be made manifest to her very soon now, but at the moment she will have to rely on a communication through an experienced medium. We are hoping to arrange this shortly, when the time is right for her to go and see a medium.

"At the moment, she has only received, to her own complete astonishment, a brief message given to her in a crowded hall by a medium on the platform whom she had never seen before. It was a comparatively simple message from someone who had known Lorna's mother when Lorna's mother was nineteen years old. Lorna took the message to her father and asked, 'Is this correct?' Lorna's father was able to confirm it, and this has, of course, aroused *his* curiosity. Lorna's mother came here nearly eighteen years ago. Lorna's father did not remarry, and he is now in his eightieth year. It has given him more food for thought on a subject he had previously felt unable to believe. We are hopeful that it will give him some sort of interest during his remaining years on earth, because it will be so much easier for him to make the transition here, directly to his wife and family, if he has that kind of belief firmly instilled in his mind.

"We believe that Lorna will shortly be seeking the help of a particularly excellent medium on earth. It is through this lady that you will be making your best communications, but this is a bit premature. We want to give you time to understand the possibilities and to consider them for yourself before taking you towards this action that will involve you, to some extent, in a considerably stronger change of vibrational level than you have so far been expected to achieve. I do not think you need spend a great deal of time pondering these complexities any further, Judy, but it is better that you have them in your mind. When we consider that it is a suitable moment for you to speak to Lorna, I will let you know."

While Doreen had been speaking to me, I had been receiving some strong images of Lorna sitting in a chair and writing and getting up and crossing the room to a cabinet that seemed to have records in it as well as books. She kept pulling out a certain volume—I was not quite sure what it was—and retracing her steps to the armchair. I found myself wondering whether it was the book about me that she was writing, but I could also see her in a state of mental confusion. I told this to Doreen.

"You are quite right. There are a number of reasons for Lorna's present confusion, but I am not going to tell you about them at the moment. I would prefer you to learn more about those later on. I think the thing to do now is to take you back to the city to meet some of those people who you will have known on earth. Having sent that thought ahead of us, I feel certain that, amongst those friends, you will find your much respected and liked President John Kennedy."

Chapter 4

As Doreen took me back towards the city, I looked forward to meeting again some of those people I had known and liked when on earth. I was curious as to how they were reacting to their existence here. I wondered whether they had been through as many seemingly peculiar experiences as I had met with during my recent travels. I was longing to discuss my hippopotamus and dolphin experiences with those I thought would appreciate them. I had so looked forward to telling my father and had been somewhat disillusioned to find there was no way in which I could have even begun to get him to understand how I had felt about those creatures.

Doreen and I chatted happily together as we made our way along the streets. Even here I was experiencing aspects of the city life that I had not encountered previously. I commented again to her that, apart from the fact that she had already told me there were no television programs, I was also not able to see any movie houses or, for that matter, theatres, although I had experienced one when visiting my father.

"I think, Judy, I had better try and explain to you the different ways in which people here keep themselves amused and entertained, one could almost use the word 'occupied' because our approach to our activities here, while in some ways not dissimilar to those on earth, are nevertheless influenced by our reactions to things, by our own deep down inner feelings, as well as by the depth of our interest in the activities concerned.

"If we take your father as an example, we have to realise that he has really not progressed very much at all since he arrived here. This is partly his own doing and according to his wishes, because he feels more secure and safe in the background in which he now is, but it has also been partly due to the lack of any person to whom he could turn for some sort of interest and affection."

"What about his own parents?" I enquired. "It has just occurred to me. He would have had parents, although I never knew them. Would he not be able to turn to them?"

"Well, Judy, how much have you been able to turn to yours?" enquired Doreen.

"Yes, that's true," I told her. "What a stupid thing for me to have said! But he did have some brothers and sisters."

"They grew apart the same as your sisters grew apart from you. You do have a sister here whom you have always liked and who still likes you, and you will be pleased to meet each other shortly, but you have not really got anything in common, have you?"

"No, that's true, we haven't really. I used to see more of her when she was married to Jack Cathcart and he became my musical arranger and orchestra conductor for a time. We seemed to get on quite well then. When she and Jack Cathcart were divorced, I went towards a different part of my life and towards other musical arrangers and conductors. I didn't really see much of Susan in the last years of our lives. She then became very ill, and I tried to take a sisterly interest in her, but I was going through a very bad period in my life and I guess, although she was pleased that I went to see her and I was glad to feel that I had tried to contribute something to her, even then we didn't really have a great deal in common."

"And you will not have much in common here, Judy. You will like each other and be pleased to see each other, but you will not have a strong bond with each other, because her ways are not necessarily your ways. Here again, we often find that brothers and sisters, just as much as husbands and wives and parents, do not always have a strong bond here. They are born into a family group and they share the same environment for part of their lives, sometimes for all of their lives on earth, but deep down they can be very different individuals. When they come here and they are no longer hidden behind the facade that many have had to live behind on earth, they blossom and move in different directions that are not necessarily the same paths as those taken by other members of their family. They will usually, eventually, find themselves moving towards a group of people here who are similar to themselves, who have had similar experiences and who react similarly. You will probably do that eventually, although you have

184

got a long time ahead of you before you can come to that decision. I do assure you that you have a very, very great deal of experiencing to do here before you will feel in any way inclined to move towards a group of people with whom you may work and live together in close harmony."

I pondered on what Doreen had said to me. "I keep coming back to my own kids," I said to her thoughtfully, "because, although we all did love each other very much indeed, I never felt that I had the right to keep them by my side unless they truly wished to be with me. It was always a source of happiness to me that my Joe and Lorna chose to be with me each time their father tried to remove them from my custody. They always said that they wanted to stay with mama, despite the fact that they loved their daddy. When my Liza got to be around seventeen years old, she began to want to be far more independent from me, and I let her, and I never tried to draw her back to me. I left it to Liza to decide for herself.

"There were some occasions when we had rows. Looking back now, I realise it was partly my fault because I used to get so easily overwrought, but it was also partly Liza's fault because she didn't want to listen to what I was trying to explain to her. I knew where I had made some of my biggest mistakes in life, through letting my emotions carry me away, and I wanted to try and stop Liza from making the same mistakes.

"Now that I am here and see it a little bit differently, I realise that the part of Liza that is like me is the part that over-reacts time and time and time again. When I over-reacted, I shouted at people and regretted it afterwards. When Liza over-reacts, she does precisely the same thing, and we both of us end up hurt in our own different ways. I used to feel so hurt that I kept myself back from actually speaking to the person about it later on. Liza tells them precisely what she thinks and then shoots off and refuses even to listen to that person again and makes a life for herself elsewhere. If I had a spat with someone who I loved very much and they came back to me, I would always be glad to try and sort it out. Liza decided she is not going to be the one to be hurt, and she goes off and specifically shows them they are not going to hurt her in any way by starting her life again elsewhere. I never found it easy to do that.

185

"When Liza and I had our spats, she didn't come back and say, 'Mama, we both acted like fools, let's make it up.' She usually waited to see whether I was going to say anything. Because it was Liza and not anyone else but one of my three kids, I did make contact with her, and sometimes she agreed that we'd been foolish and we made it up. But during my last year on earth, I didn't succeed in making it up with Liza, and I do feel so sorry about it. Although, looking back from here, I feel it was probably mostly my own confused and silly attitude to life, I think it was also because Liza did not understand why I was behaving the way I was. I sincerely regret that we didn't make it up before I came here. I was in touch with Lorna and Joe shortly before I came here, and they understood I had not deliberately left them in America while I was living in England and that I was trying to get things sorted out, with Mickey's help. I feel sure that they both loved me, but I am a little unsure about Liza."

"I do assure you, Judy, that Liza loves you just as much as she ever did. She shed many bitter tears over you when you came here. She would never have admitted it to the world, but she said 'Oh, Mama, Mama, Mama, why and how did it happen? Why did I not telephone you? I could so easily have come to see you. I should have been prepared to listen to what you wanted to say!' And she is speaking very beautifully of you now, Judy, in her own way, to those who try and speak to her about you.

"Liza is like you inasmuch as she always tries to laugh off her sorrows. It is unfortunate that, in trying to turn some of your sorrows into a joke because she knows that is what you always tried to do, she has unintentionally given the world a wrong impression of you. The world thus does not realise how deeply hurt and hard hit you have been over some of your experiences. All of your children see you as someone who laughed it all off, and that, of course, has contributed to the misconceptions in your world. Everyone thinks that you took everything lightly, although you did not. It was that part of you that tried to turn everything into a joke, both for your own sake and for the sake of your children, that sometimes gave them a misunderstanding of how deeply hurt you had been and how terrible you were really feeling underneath it all. But they do all love you and, deep down inside your three children, there is a strong resemblance to the way you

186

have often felt about things. It is not superficially obvious to any of them, but I assure you that, within each of your children, there is a truly deep love for you and a deep similarity.

"You will have them with you here, but not quite in the same way as on earth. As I tried to explain to you when we were previously discussing them, they will come here as adults who have experienced their own problems in life. This will have rubbed off on them, in some ways adversely and in some ways to the good. They will have changed in their ideas and outlooks, and they will have to work their way through themselves here, as you are having to work your way through yourself, to come to their true selves. Once they have done that, you will all find a great wish to spend time together. Because you will have made affiliations here and they will have made affiliations on earth as well as some affiliations here, you will not be together as mother and children. Not that you ever were, really. Quite often you were just like four kids together, were you not?" asked Doreen, with a smile.

"Yes, that is true." I smiled at her, a little ruefully. "I guess I never did really grow up! I did like being one of the kids with them!"

"Well, I can put your mind at rest concerning your children, I do assure you, Judy. You will be here quite a while before they are able to join you, and certainly before they are able to work their way through their life experiences and see themselves as clearly as you will, by then, be seeing yourself. But I assure you again that you and your three children will be a happy little group here in due course, although not necessarily all of the time.

"Now, we seem to have got away from what you started to ask me. You were talking about cinemas and theatres.

"On earth, you would have a liking for a certain type of play, or film, or music, and you would go along to see whether or not you could like whatever was being performed. Here it is a little different. Because your emotions are so highlighted here that you have to live on certain vibrations, and you have to protect those vibrations should you wish to enter a different level of vibration, you generally only tune in here to the kind of entertainment to which your soul will be able to react in the right way. Therefore, although people are performing plays and musical entertainments, you will not tune in to that particular level unless it is reaching you in your highest mind.

"If a piece of music or the words of a play would react badly against your vibrational level, you will be unaware of the existence of these unless you try hard to tune in to the item. In this case you would have to adjust your vibration. So, although concerts and plays are going on in the city, you will not be aware of them unless they are reaching your particular vibrational level, and then you will probably decide that you would like to go and hear them. But if you had already set your mind on going elsewhere, you could very easily keep your mind on where you are going and reject going towards the music or the play that may be taking place. If you were not particularly anxious to be occupying yourself in any other way, you could equally easily drift towards the sound and become part of the audience. Because of this situation, because nothing is actually taking place on your vibrational level at the moment, you are unaware of such activities that others may be attending.

"Should you meet a former colleague here who says to you, 'I am going to perform such and such shortly,' you will be able to decide vibrationally whether or not it is likely to be something you wish to see or hear. If it is, they will say, 'I'll let you know when it is ready.' So then, if you are likely to be too far away to easily tune in to it, they will send you a strong thought that you will be able to receive. Then you can say, 'Thank you, I will be coming,' or 'Thank you, I cannot come at the moment.' But, if you do go to such a performance, you will find that, whether it is music or whether it is a speech, the performances will normally take place outside in beautiful surroundings and the sounds that are given off by the music produces beautiful colours that change with the vibrations of sound that are being produced by the music. This is why, so often, people who had an unmusical ear on earth are able to enjoy music more easily here, because the sounds produce the colours that enable them to understand the meaning behind the music.

"On the world of earth, Judy, you sang the kind of songs that people could react to because they understood the words and they were normally quite straightforward melodies. Here those melodies can be performed in a more complicated way that will give added beauty to the sounds that will produce the beautiful colours. People who felt overwhelmed by, and involved in, the emotional force of your performances on earth will be even more caught up in the emotion here. The kind of person that you are was what you so often poured into your songs, and these songs will produce here the most beautiful sounds and colours. People will soar up with you into all the beautiful vibrations. When you were working well on earth, and sometimes even when you were not, you took audiences away and upward with you in exceptional tides of emotions that few performers have achieved in that particular way. Here it will take place even more beautifully and ecstatically.

"We also have the music of the great composers from earth, such as Mozart, Haydn and Beethoven. They continue to compose here, and their music, as you can imagine, produces other beautiful emanations of sound and colour. Again, people who were unable to understand and like their kind of music when on earth will be able to understand and respond to it here, because they now see in their minds precisely what the composer is trying to express. This is something that a lot of people, when on earth, are unable to do. But, again, their souls have to have reached the kind of vibration where such sounds can reach them in total harmony. Have I made myself clear?"

"Yes, I think so," I said to her. "I'm gradually getting adjusted to this description of 'tuned in' and 'vibrations,' and so on. I think I know what you mean. It certainly sounds as if one can go on and perform in the knowledge that one's audience is going to be with one, even before one starts," I said to her hopefully.

"There were many times in your life, Judy, when you knew your audiences were going to be with you even before you had started to sing, because you had already brought them to you in their hearts over the years, so this will not be altogether new to you. I can assure you that those years of hurt and sorrow and confusion for you on stage are definitely in the past. The moment it becomes known here that Judy Garland is going to perform a concert, there will be a considerable convergence to the area where you will be singing. I cannot tell you that it will be a sell out, because we do not sell tickets here, but it will be exceptionally well attended, even by your best standards on earth."

"Well, I sure hope I don't have to face all the hazards I had to face in my open air concerts on earth," I said to her. "Birds, bats, insects, aeroplanes, rain, fog, cold—you name it, I got it!" I said to her laughingly.

"No, Judy," she smiled back at me. "You are free of all those hazards here. You are free of bronchitis and laryngitis and influenza. You are free of drunks and bullies and misunderstandings, and you will soon be free of your feeling of loneliness," she assured me.

II

We eventually arrived at the front door of a house that was quite palatial compared with others I had seen en route. It was very similar to the modern houses in some of the more luxurious areas of California. The façade had the beautiful light appearance of most of the buildings here, and there were some trees and a small lake, or pool, nearby. As we stood by this door, I could not see a bell or a knocker, but, after a few moments, the door opened and, to my greatest possible delight, I found myself facing a smiling Jack Kennedy.

"Hi, Judy!" He beamed at me, coming forward with both hands outstretched. "I was told you were coming to see me. Please come in."

He motioned me in and also shook Doreen's hand, and we went inside to a place that looked very similar inside to the Kennedy residence I had visited at Hyannis Port. The more I looked at it the more I realised that it had a lot of those features but certainly not all. There were some very comfortable chairs that Doreen and I sat on, and Jack sat down opposite us, bright-eyed and cheery. It was so good to see him again after the shattering experience of his assassination. As I looked, I realised he was much younger than when I had last seen him, although I had, of course, immediately recognised him. I began to realise that he looked very much the age he had been in the photographs I had seen of him when he was in the navy, and I suddenly became aware, subconsciously and without him mentioning it, that he no longer had the back injury that had caused him so much trouble and pain when on earth. He must have caught that thought, because he immediately assured me, "I am completely fine here, Judy. I have no after-effects whatsoever of anything."

We chatted for a while as if nothing had happened since we had last spoken together on earth. He told me what he had been doing since his arrival here. Then he said, "I can see that you've been through it, Judy, but I'm glad you've come through it in one piece!"

"How do you mean, 'in one piece?' " I asked him.

"I knew things were going badly for you when you were telephoning me after you started that television series. It was something that could have been so beautiful and it was going so horribly wrong for you. I did feel sorry, because you were a great performer and a great lady and I always liked you and respected you. That is why I was so proud when you spoke up for me and performed for me when I was campaigning to be president. I thought it was rough that you were going through what you were going through. When I came here so suddenly, I didn't really know what was going on on earth, but when they told me that you had arrived here and wanted to see me, I made a point of finding out a little more about it. I found out that you survived me by nearly six years, that you had been through a terrible crisis of emotional upheavals, and that you had got to a point where you didn't really know what the hell was going to happen to you next. I was so sorry, indeed I was so sorry, to learn this. Looking at you here and now, I can see that whatever you went through, you have come through it as the Judy I always knew. That's good to know, because so many people come here with the darker side of life showing on them. You haven't, and I congratulate you."

"Thank you," I said to him. "How did *you* get on when *you* first came here?"

"Well, of course, it was a terrific shock. One moment I was sitting next to Jackie and then, suddenly, everything had gone. I didn't know what had happened, and I didn't know what continued to happen around me and Jackie. I just found myself floating. I didn't know where I was floating, or why. I just seemed to be in space. I felt sore, literally sore, all over. It was terribly confusing and also alarming, really. I thought, *How could I have been sitting with Jackie in the car and suddenly I'm floating and sore and I can't see anything clearly?* It seemed to be a helluva long time before I began to focus. I gradually realised that I was coming towards what I could recognise as countryside. There seemed to be grassy hills and trees and water, and I seemed to drift down slowly towards a pool and down into it. It had a very strong blue colour, and it was warm. I floated in the pool, immersed in the water, for some while, but I couldn't tell you how long. I began to feel less sore, but I suddenly realised that my head felt numb. On one side, I felt as though I had been hit by a blow, but I didn't know what sort of blow. After a while, I began to feel more like myself, and I had a strong urge to swim around under the water. It reminded me a little of the heated swimming pools I had swum in to try and help my back trouble. I thought that maybe that was what I ought to be doing. I swam around under the water for a while and then realised that I did not have to come up for air, which I would normally have expected to do. There didn't seem to be anything of any interest in the water. It was just a beautiful blue colour. When I finally surfaced, I felt very, very much better, and my head felt back to normal. In fact, I felt completely back to normal, except that I still felt slightly confused and 'floaty.' I waded out of the pool and sat on the grass, and to my amazement I realised that I was completely dry!"

"I know!" I said. "The same extraordinary thing happened to me! What were you wearing?"

"I was wearing the suit I had been wearing in the car, but there wasn't a mark on it, as though I had just stepped out of the tailors!"

It was then that I stopped to look at Jack again, to notice what he was wearing now. I had been so pleased to see him and so amazed at his youthfulness that I had not really stopped to consider what he was wearing. Then I saw that he was dressed similarly to myself. Yet, although he was wearing a robe of variegated colours, which sounds feminine, it was in no way effeminate. I later asked Doreen how this could be, and she explained that in the area in which such people as Jack and myself exist, we all wear robes that reflect our particular souls and personality. As we gradually move through our various experiences, however, on our individual vibrations, so the gender of masculine and feminine becomes less necessary and less obvious and all such differences fade away. This made sense, as Doreen had already explained to me that we do not have any physical "husband and wife" relationships in our area of existence. But to return to when we were visiting with Jack at his house, he wanted to know whether I had seen his family and Jackie since he had come here. I told him that I had not really seen them at all, because my own life had changed so much, as had theirs, that there had been little reason for our paths to cross.

He nodded understandingly and said, "When I had been sitting on the bank for a while, wondering how I had got there, I suddenly saw a man coming towards me who looked very much like my grandfather, which he turned out to be. He held his hand out to me and said, 'Well, Jack, I didn't expect to see you here so soon!'

" 'Where am I?' I asked him.

" 'I'm sorry to have to tell you that you've been killed and you're in the Spirit World,' he told me. *My God! Jackie and the children!* was my first thought."

"That's exactly how I reacted!" I told him. "I thought of my husband and the children!"

"Your husband? Sid?" he asked me.

"No, Jack! That's a long story. I'll have to tell you another time," I said to him, "but please tell me about yours."

"Well, he took me away to his house and we sat down and had a long talk. He told me precisely what had happened and that there was absolutely nothing I could do about it, that Jackie and the children were being taken care of and that I wasn't to worry about having left the president's chair vacant. 'They'll miss you, Jack. You were just the sort of president your country needed, but they'll have to get along without you. And they will, possibly not as well. Whoever sits in that seat has a thankless task in the end, because the earth will never be at peace, it will always be struggling. So try not to worry about that. Just bear in mind that it is in the past, that Jackie and the children will be taken care of, and you have now got to get yourself adjusted to life here.'

"I stayed with him for a while, until I got a little more reconciled to being here. Then I suddenly felt terribly tired, so tired that I felt unable to move, and I think I drifted off to sleep. When I woke up, I wasn't in grandfather's house; I was here. I wasn't wearing my suit; I was wearing what you see me in now," he told me. "I've had a number of people helping me to adjust to life here, explaining to me what life is like here and showing me some of the places."

"Have you been to the Animal Kingdom?" I asked.

"I had a brief visit there, but I also visited the children's area. I was particularly interested in the mentally handicapped children, as you can imagine, and I am being trained now to help some of them. I think that is something I would very much like to do."

He asked me what I had been doing, and I gave him a brief outline of my travels to date and how shocked I had been over my poor father.

"I understand how you feel about him, Judy, because I know you always loved him very much. But I'm sure that, now you are here, your interest in him will help him a lot. I've found that out since I've been here. If you show any kind of loving interest towards anybody, they will automatically take a step forward. That is something I have been able to do with the children here. But in order to help the mentally handicapped children, you have to be trained. So, although I've taken an interest in some of the children who have had a rough time, I have to be taught how to help the others. Not that they are mentally handicapped here, of course, but because they have led a restricted life on earth they have to be handled in a special way here in order to help them progress. I've seen them being helped, and I have seen them taking the most gigantic steps forward in a very short time. That is what I want to help them to do."

"I'm going back to the children when I have been around a bit more," I said to him. I spoke a little hesitantly and looked at Doreen, because I was not too sure when that would be.

"Then I am sure we will meet again there, Judy. I can tell from the way Doreen is looking at you that she has other things in line for you at the moment, but I am so glad to see you again— and I shall be there at your concerts." he said to me laughingly.

"I am told I shall sing again here, but I haven't made any plans yet," I said, smiling again at Doreen.

"No. But I shall be the first to hear when you do, because we are going to meet again and we will see a lot of each other, Judy, I am sure," he said to me smilingly.

I found we were making our way back to the door. "I am

sorry I have to ask you to leave now," he said, "but I have just had a call to go to one of the children who seems to need me. That has to be my first consideration once I have given a promise, but I am so pleased to see you," and he gave me a bearlike hug. He put his arm around my shoulder and his other arm around Doreen's as he went with us towards the door. He stood there waving to us as we left, with that bright, eager look on his face that I had known so well.

I felt quite buoyant as we walked away. After a while, Doreen commented, "That has given you quite a lift, hasn't it?"

"Yes, it has," I replied. "Jack always made me feel like that, because he was always such a positive person. It didn't matter how many demands were made upon him by all sorts of people, he still always managed to find time for his friends, and I always felt better for having been in his company. That is why I was so grateful during that awful time I was going through in 1963, when he told me I was to telephone him at any time. I always felt better for having talked to him, and I am so very, very glad that after having that atrocious thing done to him, when all he was trying to do was to help his country in every way possible, he is now so well and obviously enjoying life here to the full."

"He is enjoying life here only to a limited extent," she said to me. "He is a very positive person, as you have said. He was delighted to see you again, and he is doing all that he can to help the children, but he still feels, somewhere inside himself, that he did not complete what he set out to do for his country. In his heart, he still wishes he could do something about that. You did not feel that from him because he and you were so delighted to see each other again that his innermost thoughts did not reach you any more than your innermost thoughts have reached him. But I am so glad that there is at least one person here, so far, who has come up to your expectations," she said with a little smile.

"*I'm* so pleased to see him well and young and vigorous and enthusiastic," I replied, "because that's the Jack I knew on earth and that's the Jack that seems to be existing here. After the demolishing, demoralising effect I received from my poor father, I am so relieved to see that Jack appears to be not only normal but blooming."

"Well, I'm glad for both your sakes." Doreen smiled.

III

As we proceeded, discussing the situation generally, Doreen suddenly said to me, "Judy, I would suggest that the time is now right for a visit to your sister, Susan. She has been told of your arrival here, that you have had to adjust to your arrival and have been taken around various parts of this world, and that this has included a visit to your father. She would like to see you again, and she says that she is exceedingly fond of you, although she was never able to be as demonstrative towards you as you always wanted to be towards those around you. I think it would not be a bad idea for me to tell you a little about your sister's character while we are on our way to see her, if that is, you think it would be a good idea to visit her."

"I would love to see Susan again, Doreen," I told her. "I can't really imagine why I didn't suggest it earlier, because she is a nice person and I was always very fond of her. It was just that, after a while, we had little in common and it was sometimes difficult to know what to say to her. I suppose that seems a strange thing to say about one's own sister, but she was always a little more withdrawn after her divorce from Jack Cathcart. I think it made a big hole in her life. She clearly loved him very much. I felt deeply sorry for her when she told me that the marriage was breaking up, but not through any wish on her part for it to do so. I understood that feeling all too well.

"I suppose, now I stop to think about it, I seldom discussed my innermost hurts in any detail or depth, so why would I expect Susan to have expressed hers to me. The point was that, whenever I had had a shock like that, although I didn't talk about it to other people, I did try and seek companionship and I did like to talk about all sorts of other things. Maybe I was talking a lot of rubbish on other subjects, but I still liked to talk! Susan tended to be monosyllabic, and no matter what I tried to talk about, it nearly always ended with Susan saying 'yes' or 'probably.' In the end, I used to get annoyed and fed up, and I'd decide it really wasn't worth the effort of trying to get in touch with her. Often I didn't, particularly when I was feeling miserable over my own problems, until she became so very ill. Then I felt that, although I was up to my neck in my television series and all my own hurts with my separations from Sid and the court cases over the children, the very least I could do would be to try and see Susan for what might prove to be her last months on earth. In the end, I was glad that I did, because I did at least feel that we had finished up as friends."

"Well, Judy, she sees you very much as someone who was always far more loving in your heart to anybody than was the rest of the family put together. Because, although your father was demonstrative to you he was not particularly demonstrative to her or to your other sister, Virginia, any more than he was to your mother. But he used to respond to you, as I told you before, because you gave a lot of love to him. Susan always saw you as the demonstrative one in the family, and she did feel affection for you, but she just did not find it so easy to show it.

"She used to see and share some of your troubles when you saw more of each other in the 1950s. She saw that you had some troubles with Sid that were not always of your making by any means, although the world at large tends to think that it was all your fault when things went wrong with your marriage. She saw you as someone who was struggling to keep the family solvent. She saw you as someone who loved your children very dearly and was loved by them and she wished that she had had a family, which she had not managed to do. She felt that had she had children, her marriage might not have failed or that when it failed, she would have had more to fall back on. The fact that she was often silent when you tried to talk to her about all sorts of things was mainly because she liked to listen to you."

"Yes, Susie was a good listener," I admitted. "She was a kindly listener, the sort of person you felt you could talk to if you wanted to. I did sometimes tell her what was in my heart. I told her how, although I loved Sid very much, I wished he could be more reliable with our financial situation and that I wished I could do something to stop his gambling. She was sympathetic and understanding, and I think it was because she was so deeply hurt when Jack left her that she felt unable to be as good a listener as she had been at one time. She became so much more withdrawn that I felt I could no longer tell her any more of my own troubles, and I kept them to myself. There could be some awkward silences between us. I felt it was not because we did not like each other, but because there was a barrier that I could not reach across."

"That is precisely what it was, Judy. Each time you got hurt you did always try and hide it from the world. You always went out and about to meet other people almost all of the time, except when you had that big shock from Mark Herron, which came so swiftly that you withdrew for a while. Even then, you eventually tried to go out again to meet other people. Susan withdrew and stayed withdrawn and has never been quite the same person again. It did something to her, deep down inside, and she was never able to cope with life again afterwards. You always tried to cope, even if you did not always succeed and, in so doing, made many mistakes and confused decisions.

"Susan was inclined to back away from the world and to stay backed away, in an effort to keep herself as intact as possible. Unfortunately, it turned her into a depressive to some extent. That is what made it more difficult for you to communicate with her. You used to get emotionally worked up, so that you would over-react in anger or else laugh a lot in order to try and overcome the rising hysteria within yourself. You would sometimes burst into tears at what you often felt to be a most embarrassing moment, and then try to recover yourself. You were never, however, in any way a depressive. That is why we felt so sorry for you here when individuals on earth tried to convince the world at large that you were suicidal. That you never were and never would have been. You had too much get up and go to have ever contemplated suicide."

"I would never have seriously contemplated such a thing," I assured her. "There was just that one foolish occasion when hysteria overcame me when Vincente and I had our clash. It was only, I felt certain, a spontaneous over-reaction and nothing I would ever have planned or ever truly intended. The whole thing took only a few moments before Vincente followed me."

"It was never in you to consider taking your own life, Judy. We know that here, and we have admired the way you tried to face up to world opinion that had been discoloured against you by such abominable insinuations being placed before the public. Now then, Susan is different to you. She did, on more than one occasion fall into such deep despair in her loneliness that she did consider such an act. She never succeeded, but it lowered her deepest emotions so that, when she discovered that she had a serious illness, from which she might or might not have succeeded

198

in recovering had she had a little more wish to do so, it was not long before she got into such a deeply despairing state that she contemplated removing herself to here sooner than she would have naturally come to us. This means that, although she never did come to us prematurely, she nearly did on more than one occasion. That, plus the exceedingly debilitating illness that she had on top of her own despondency, means that she has not completely recovered herself yet, even here, although she came here some years before you did."

"Well, she came here at least six years before I did," I calculated, "because she died when I was ill in 1964. I was in London, in June of 1969, when I came here."

"Although Susan is all right and recovering," continued Doreen, "she is in a less happy place at the moment than you are, and so I have to warn you to be very careful and to protect yourself against the area where she is at present. This is not because it is in any way physically harmful to you, but she is not as happy and positive as you are. There will be an element of unhappiness from her, and I want you to protect yourself against it so that you do not absorb it into yourself."

"Am I particularly happy and positive?" I asked Doreen.

"Yes, you are, Judy. I know you still feel an inner loneliness, and I know you still feel within you that you have failed your children by coming here as soon as you did. I also know that you are even beginning to realise that you may have failed your public, in some respects, in your last few years and that they have been given a very distorted view of you, which has taken hold. But you have, nevertheless, come through everything that I have taken you through with the right attitude and with a hope in your heart for the future. That is something which your sister has not yet found. Now that you have visited your friend John Kennedy and seen how positive he is being, we hope the positive attitude you will bring to your sister will help her to come out of her present mood and prepare her to face her future here in a happier frame of mind."

I was regarding Doreen in some dismay while she was telling me all this. "The Gumm Family don't seem to be making a very good job of it here, do they?" I said to her.

"Except for you, Judy."

"Well, you have yet to convince me, Doreen, that I'm making

as good a job of it as I should be able to do, because I still have, from time to time, this feeling within me of having failed. You have just mentioned my audiences. Yes, you are right. It has begun to filter through to me that maybe I did fail them too, in a way, although I am unclear in my mind as to why I am beginning to think that I may have failed them. I know I wasn't working as well in my last few years. I know I sometimes did not manage to complete a performance, and I sometimes did not manage to work as well on stage as I wanted to do. But it is only recently that I have begun to see it this way. I can't really understand why it is so prominent in my mind and why I'm thinking about it so much. Until just recently, I seemed to have been thinking more about my kids than anyone else and now . . . there goes Lorna Smith again! I've suddenly seen Lorna, writing!" I exclaimed in astonishment.

"That is one of the things she is struggling with, Judy," Doreen told me. "She knows you did not intentionally let down your public. She knows you had good reasons at times for wishing you could cancel a performance and that, for one reason or another, you were told that you could not. She knows there were other times when you went on stage and tried your hardest to perform, only to find that you were being misunderstood and that people assumed you were either drunk or on unorthodox drugs, when you were actually trying to pull a performance out of a totally ill nervous system and from a physical weakness that people did not realise or understand. She is trying to explain all this to people."

"I know that people used to presume that I was drinking heavily when I wasn't. That was due to those lies that were put out about me in the court hearing. I knew people thought that about me, and it wasn't fair, because I was never a heavy drinker. I used to drink at parties, and I would sometimes have some drinks at home, but I always made them last. As for drugs, I only ever took those prescribed by my doctors. There wasn't anything abnormal about them, although I did sometimes have to take more than at other times. I guess I did get very confused, otherwise I wouldn't be here now!"

"Judy, you will recall that, when you were working at the film studios and were so frequently too unwell to work properly, the gutter press began to imply that you were taking various

unorthodox and illegal drugs that were causing your erratic behaviour. You were able to get some of those stories publicly rescin-
ded. Nevertheless, the image remained in some quarters, and it
began to spread during your final few years, when you were again
behaving erratically and sometimes irrationally. Few people
realised or recognised that you were actually really very unwell
in several ways, and they misunderstood the cause of your irra-
tional actions. Therefore, there is a strong leaning today towards
regarding you as addicted to unorthodox, and even illegal, drugs
that produce hallucinations and distorted frames of mind, instead
of the legal and widely prescribed and used medicinal drugs that
were the only ones you ever took," said Doreen, speaking slowly
and carefully.

"Good God!" I said in horror. "My God! What must my poor
kids be facing? Doreen, this is terrible. I would *never, ever,* in my
whole life, under *any* circumstances, have gone in for *anything*
like that! I know that when I was at the studios, I swallowed all
sorts of medicines that were prescribed for me for my various
nervous conditions. I know that when I left the studios I had to
stay on sleeping pills and sedatives until I managed to stop these
in 1960, after being warned by the doctors that these could be
damaging my health. I had to go onto Ritalin to get me through
the television series in 1963, but that was prescribed simply to
give me some energy to overcome the physical exhaustion and
distresses I was going through. These were all prescribed for me
by proper, registered doctors. I *never, ever* indulged in anything
such as you have just mentioned. I would *never, ever* have done
so. I would not have abused my own body in that way. I certainly
would not have put my children's future at risk by lumbering
them with that kind of a mother. I would never have felt that I
had any faith in myself or that my audiences could have had any
faith in me if I had lived that kind of life. I know I failed in a
number of ways to keep myself going as well as I had hoped to
do in the last years of my life, but, Doreen, I would never have
gone in for anything like that. It's filthy. I think it's degrading,
and I just feel completely appalled and demeaned that anyone
could have thought that about me, let alone put it out as a public
statement!"

Doreen looked at me kindly, sympathetically, and understandingly. "That seems to have aroused you even more than the

201

wrong accusations about alcohol and suicide attempts, Judy."

"It has! I've seen people get into trouble over alcohol. Thank God, I never did, but I could see how that sort of problem could arise. I have seen people, people who I worked with, who didn't set out to become intentionally dependent upon alcohol but did. Sometimes their lives became a strain for them in one way or another, and they would take a drink to keep calm. Then they would need two drinks to keep calm, and so on, and it became an unfortunate habit that grew on them. Then, of course, it got out of hand, and they had to have treatment. That I understood and sympathised with. I was so thankful that I had, at least, managed to not do that.

"My own problem arose from the sedatives. I sometimes came to need more sedatives than I had needed originally. Then the normal glass of wine that I liked taking because it was thirst-quenching and relaxing began to slow me down and to affect my timing. I didn't notice this until I was warned, and then I tried to be more careful. That was what I struggled with. So, because I knew my own problems with the sedatives and the sleeping tablets, I could understand other people's problems with alcohol, and I sympathised. I'm just grateful that alcohol did not ever become a big problem in my life.

"But I think that anybody who deliberately goes onto any kind of hard drug is foolish and must be limited in his intelligence. Surely people must know there is only one way you go when you begin anything like that, and that's down, down, down. To think that my kids and the ordinary people who liked my work should be faced with this kind of filthy insinuation, on top of all the other lies that I engaged in free-wheeling love affairs, is the most degrading thing that I can imagine. Doreen, you have just told me how positive I am, but this makes me feel so completely demeaned that I have seldom felt less positive about myself at any time."

"Well, Judy, let me put it to you like this. I feel I have to tell you precisely what is being insinuated about you because it is all this, which has been piling up and piling up, that Lorna Smith is fighting against in her book about you. She knows how cruelly unkind and untrue it all is."

"Thank God for Lorna Smith!" I said to her. "Thank God for Lorna!"

"Exactly," said Doreen, "and that is why some of this has been coming into your mind and why you have been seeing Lorna. She herself is so shocked and horrified for you that your memory is being so debased by some individuals who have chosen to do this that she is spending a great deal of time and effort in writing and rewriting to try and get this across in a way that people will believe. She is already hampered by the knowledge that she must not openly accuse certain people of lying. She has to work around it in a different way, and although she does not know it yet, we know that she is going to be prevented from even saying as much as she is now trying to say for you. But her deep concentration on the subject, her deep hurt on your behalf, is reaching you and that is why you are getting flashes of it.

"Now I want you to know precisely how bad the situation is, because, if you get your mind adjusted to it now, we can take you forward more easily in the future. We can get you to see this whole—I agree—degrading situation as we see it here and as you will shortly be able to see it from here. Once you become absorbed in your life here, as you will be, you will be able to put the whole of your earth life into a better perspective than you can do at the moment, and you will be able to put it all behind *you*. That is what we want you to be able to do, really, before you meet Susan. If you can demonstrate to Susan all that *you* have put behind you, you will be able to show Susan what *she* can put behind *her*. Between you, you will then be able to do something constructive towards persuading your father to realise what *he* can put behind *him*."

I looked at her silently for a while, trying to get my mind sorted into less of a turmoil. Eventually I said to her, "You tell me Lorna is fighting to save my name from all these filthy lies, all this garbage. Why is it only Lorna? Sid Luft knows that the allegations are untrue for the time up to our separation. Mark Herron knows they are untrue for the period I was with him. Mickey knows they are untrue. My children know they are untrue. To hell with anybody else! They all know it is untrue. Why aren't they saying something?"

Doreen looked at me again with sympathy and understanding.

"There are several things that you have to bear in mind here,

Judy. I am going to tell you something you should have realised for yourself sooner than you have done. Even when you were with Sidney Luft, there were times when you got out of hand in public. Your nervous system would reach breaking point, and it would not take much for you to become overwrought. A doctor would be called in. He would give you some sedative to calm you down, and you would have to go out on stage to work. Even then there were occasions when you were not able to work as well as you normally did. It would not necessarily show when you were on stage, but when you came off, it would be apparent to the management that you were not quite yourself. You would say things and do things that you would not normally say or do. Because you had had a row with Sidney Luft, he would not always be around to help to shield you from some of those managements, and they would see you acting in a strange fashion. They would presume that you were drunk, or under some other influence, although you were simply trying to hold together a nervous system that was easily over-agitated and easily misunderstood.

"That sort of thing fed the rumours that had even started in your earlier years in the Hollywood studios for similar reasons. Nobody, or very few, put it down to the straightforward medicines you were taking to try and support your already shattered nervous system. They put it down to drugs and drink because that is what people thought they were seeing. They saw it in others, and they presumed it in you.

"That was what started it all, and of course those rumours were resurrected after you left the earth and came here. They were embroidered upon and exaggerated. People who wanted to write articles or books about you took up the rumours and the scandalmongering, often unaware and not caring that these assertions failed to fit the true context of events. They even added some embroidery of their own when they were not sure how to make things seem to fit together. They interviewed people who claimed to have known you at one time or another in your life. They listened to what they were being told and embroidered into the fabric of what they were writing. This has already taken place.

"We know, and Lorna knows, that there are other books coming along by other people who did not know you very well, but who are, nevertheless, writing books about you. These will be published and will relate all the rumours as though they were facts. Once the books are in print there will be little that anybody can do to prevent this sort of attitude escalating. That is why we know, from here, that Lorna is fighting a losing battle on your behalf, but we admire her for at least trying to do something about it."

"I do, too," I assured Doreen. "I really do. I always liked her. I always felt that she tried to be sympathetic and understanding towards me, but I still think it is appalling that the only person who knew me who seems to be doing anything about defending me is Lorna. I come back to what I have just said to you: What about the others?"

"Sidney Luft," said Doreen, "is about to organise a biography about you. It will be written by someone who is well known as a writer. He will be making a lot of material available to this writer. It is this book that will have the largest influence of any about you, because your children will be asked to contribute to it on the understanding that it will be as correct a book about you as anything that is likely to emerge. They will think that they are doing the right thing in helping their mother's memory. In fact, the whole responsibility for the contents of the book will fall upon the writer, who will be swayed, in his turn, by others. Therefore, the way the book will be completed will misrepresent what was originally plain truth and ultimately will contribute to the misunderstanding about you.

"The situation will be worsened by the fact that it will appear to have had your childrens' support, whereas, in the end, they will come to regret that they ever contributed towards it. Because Lorna and Joe were so young when you came here, it is not possible to expect them to express themselves as clearly about you as an adult would be able to do. Liza so frequently feels that, whatever she says, she is likely to be misquoted anyway that she does not feel it worthy of any further comment. She tends to let the whole thing go. Mark Herron usually tries to avoid saying very much about you because, in his own heart, he knows that he failed you. He thinks that the less he says about you the better.

"Mickey Deans is still very confused about you. He is at present writing a book about you that will, again, confuse the public even more. Because he only knew you for a short time, and because your last few years on earth were very confusing years for you, he never saw you as you were when you were well. He only saw the very confused condition you were in during those last years when your whole physical system was weakening. You spent a large part of your time with him under adverse conditions, which immediately rubbed off on you and made you more difficult to handle and more difficult to understand. He misunderstood and misconstrued you in a number of ways. He was exceedingly unclear about why you said and did a number of things. He had no real background knowledge of you before you met. He had no idea of the illnesses that you suffered, the set-backs and the hardships, the emotional destructions that your soul had been through. Because he is young and healthy and takes a basically straightforward view of life, he failed to understand you in many ways. His book is going to be just as destructive to your memory as all the others will be.

"The reason I am mentioning all this to you now, Judy, is because we are going to take you to speak to Lorna before too much longer. Before you speak to her, at which time you will probably be able to tune in to her mind quite clearly, you will have had to overcome your present reaction to this situation, so that, when you talk to Lorna, you will be able to do it in a way that reassures her that you are all right. It would not do for you to try and speak to Lorna through a medium if your mind was careering all over the place because of this situation. You have got to get everything completely clear to yourself. You have got to overcome it, to some extent, in your own mind before we can give you the opportunity of speaking to Lorna. Her own mind is already in a turmoil for you over this whole subject and situation. She feels for you so very deeply and sincerely. She is telling anyone who mentions your name that 'if Judy had been the sort of person they are speaking and writing about, I would not have wanted to know her. But I did know her, I respected her, I was very fond of her, and I am going to do my best to try and not let them all get away with it.' "

"Well, thank God for Lorna," I said again. "Thank God for Lorna."

"One of the reasons she was able to understand you so well, Judy, was the fact that she saw her own mother suffer through many years of nervous troubles. She saw her own mother so weakened that she hardly knew how to put'one foot after the other. Lorna saw her not eating, day after day, and losing weight, and becoming confused and hardly able to stand. She saw her mother saying and doing things she would not normally have said and done. Some of this behaviour was brought about by the fact that, because she had had a nervous breakdown, her nervous system was confusing her mind. The lack of food was also confusing her mind. As Lorna is telling so many people, 'My mother was not on drugs or alchohol, but many times she reacted in the same way that I saw Judy reacking and behaving. There were many times when I was with Judy that I was reminded of my mother, and that is why I understood her and sympathised with her. They were both sensitive people, they both had a sense of humour, but at times they became difficult to cope with. I could understand that an outsider who did not know anything about it, who saw my mother swaying in front of them, might have thought she was on drugs or alcohol, but she wasn't. I knew she wasn't. I knew Judy wasn't on anything that she shouldn't be on.' "

The more Doreen talked to me about this, the more I thought about it, the more clearly I began to recollect some of the conversations that Lorna and I had together. She had tried to tell me this several times in different ways, but someone had always come into the room in the middle of it, and we had never finished what we had started telling each other. But I could, when I stopped to think of it here, realise how it was that Lorna was able to understand me a little bit better than some. She never did slam out of the room when I got worked up. She always stayed and tried to calm me. She did not always succeed, because there was usually someone else arriving and her efforts got cancelled out, but the more I thought about it, the more comforted I felt. I still could not understand why I felt comforted by this, but I did. I felt the calmness descend upon me again that had been abruptly shattered by Doreen's latest revelations. I thought to myself, *If Lorna could understand me, and now I see very clearly that she did, then I could not have been so awful. Surely, if the others misunderstand me now, it must be mainly because they want to do so, and, if they want to, that is their look out and not mine!* I began to feel much sassier about the situation.

I had always said, when I was on earth, that I was responsible

207

only to God for my actions, and I did mean that. If you spend your life in the public eye, you come to realise that you cannot please all of the people all of the time. There are always people who are staring at you and waiting to pull you apart at the least possible excuse. I had always faced great adulation on the one hand and demoralisation on the other throughout my whole career in show business, which was nearly all my life on earth; but in the last years of my life, I became more and more aware of the negative attitudes against me rather than the positive attitudes for me. At one time, the positive attitudes for me were very much stronger and brighter than the others, so that the negative attacks had not really mattered so much. The last few years, however, I did not always know how I was going to manage to get through a performance, or even each day, and I was aware that I was losing a lot of the audiences that I had always had, and I had also lost all of my love in my private life except for my kids. This had demoralised me a very great deal. I still said, "I am responsible only to God," but I did sometimes find myself saying, "but where the hell is he?" Yet, deep down inside myself, I felt that I had not let Him down, even if I had sometimes let myself down, because, in my heart, I wanted to live a good life and give a good life to my kids. I just wanted to be given the strength to do so.

As I thought of all this, a great calmness descended upon me, and I felt as though I was drifting away in a pink cloud. I stayed in this cloud for some while. When I gradually emerged from it, I found myself back with Doreen in my usual quiet little glade, but I could not remember coming here. I looked at Doreen, almost drowsily, and asked her, "How did we get here again?"

She explained to me, "When I first gave you that shock, Judy, we were in a fairly quiet spot by some trees. Then you became very agitated and hurt and angry and confused, and I thought the best thing to do would be to bring you back here. So I sent out a thought to those others who are helping me to help you, although you have not met them yet, and we transported you back to your little place of rest."

"Well, I don't know where I've been," I said to her. "I was beginning to see things more clearly. I thought over all that you've told me. I found it very demoralising and demolishing, but I think I have talked myself into a better frame of mind about it. I was beginning to feel that I was overcoming it to some degree when I seemed to drift off into a pink cloud."

"That pink cloud, Judy, was all the love that we were putting around you to reassure you that, here, you are loved and will be loved. Here you are seen as you truly are."

As Doreen spoke, I felt myself drifting back into the pink cloud.

IV

I awoke from what appeared to have been a comparatively heavy sleep and became aware that the whole of my little glade was filled with the most beautiful light and sounds imaginable. The flowers seemed to be tinkling little tunes. The birds were singing, seemingly to me. There was a beautifully perfumed atmosphere and the light was diffused with tinges of pink and blue and silver and gold. I lay there very dreamily, going back in my mind to what Doreen had told me. For some reason that I could not explain, it no longer seemed to matter to me what people thought of me on earth. I said to myself, "It is because I am here now, in a far more beautiful world. I am still sad that people have misunderstood me and are being given the wrong information about me, but I guess it doesn't really matter just as long as I know who I am and what I am and how I intend to be for the whole of my future life here.

I still felt sorry for my children, that they should have been given such a poor public impression of their mama to face up to. I may have failed them in a number of ways—by being ill so many times and by being away from home when they had to stay in school—but I had never let them down badly in my morals or in my outlook on life, however unwell and confused I may have been at times—or sometimes bad tempered! Looking back over my life with my children, I felt that none of them would ever be able to accuse me of having been cruel or ill-natured towards any of them, and I felt that was something to my credit.

I had cared, earlier in my life, what the public felt about me. I suppose that even in my last few years, I cared to some extent, although I had come to care far less. I always told myself that I had an obligation to work for people on stage with everything that I had got in me, but that my obligation ended when I stepped away from the footlights. This is something that many public figures are not allowed to believe. It seems to be generally accepted that if you do something in public, whether it be as a performer or a politician or anything for which you become famous, you are then owned by the public at large. Many people feel that they have the right to criticise you and demean you or adulate you, however they happen to feel at that precise moment. They cocoon themselves away from any criticism, yet feel thay have the right to criticise public figures.

In my last years on earth I began to feel exceedingly bitter over the way I had been publicly criticised, demoralised, and demeaned by the media and by certain members of the public who felt they had the right to send me disgustingly accusing letters or approach me in a public place or building or even on the stage and shout rude comments to me simply because of what they had read about me or heard about me. So I had gradually been turning further and further away from my original love and devotion for my audiences. But in the earlier days of my career, both when I was in the movies and when I returned to the stage, I did always love and respect those audiences, and I worked hard for them.

There were still some people who I believed were genuine in their approaches to me, but in my last few years I had come to the strong feeling that, no matter what I did in my life, it really did not matter any more what people thought of me. I would just have to pick up the pieces of my life and go along the best way I could manage. I still went onstage hoping that I could be successful and please an audience, but when I found that I was not pleasing them as well as I used to do, I was not always clear in my mind that maybe I was failing them. I usually put it down to the adverse publicity. It was only now, as I had been going back through my life and considering some of the things that Doreen had told me about myself, that I came to realise that my ill health had affected my performances far more than I had ever previously understood. It was this as well as the adverse publicity that had caused some of my performances, in the latter years of my life, to be less successful than those that I had performed previously. I had not been too clear about this when I was on earth, and I was only beginning to see it more clearly now.

I would, at this juncture, like to say to those people who came and enjoyed my work and who stayed faithful and loyal to me over all the years that I was on earth that I did always, originally, mean it most sincerely when I said that I had a deep love for my audiences and that I could never cheat on them. I did mean it and I never intentionally cheated on an audience. I do realise now that, in the last years of my life, my ill health got so on top of me that I did fail you on stage. For this, I am sincerely and abjectly sorry. I ask you to forgive me and to excuse me, and I ask you to remember that, when I was well and happier than I had been latterly, I had always striven to please you. I did give back to you the love that you gave to me. I would ask you to remember that I tried to give you beauty and joy in my work and to try and remember me that way.

I am so happy to tell you that that is how I am remembered and recognised here. I am now, once again, performing in the way that I had always wanted to perform, and even far better than I ever managed to perform on earth. I am creating joy and beauty for those who come to hear me sing here, and I would ask all of you who reacted with pleasure to my work on earth to look forward to the day you can come and hear me here. I assure you that you will once again be able to recognise me as I always wanted to be, and not how I sometimes seemed to be on earth during my last years. Having said all that I had better return to the point where Doreen had come back to collect me one more time.

"Are you feeling better, Judy?" she asked me in her usual kindly way.

"Yes, I am, thank you. I'm seeing everything so much more clearly. I feel completely relaxed, and somehow I am able to accept that whatever happened to me on earth no longer really matters any more. I am so sorry that people are being given the wrong ideas about me, but I can accept it now. I feel as if it is all completely in the past and it has nothing to do with me because it wasn't really me. I am not the kind of person that they think I am, and what really matters here is that I am what I am. What I have to do now is to go forward and prove it to myself and to everyone else here."

"That is exactly what we were hoping you would be able to

211

see, Judy. That is why we took you into the healing rays that we have here, to give you the opportunity to sleep again in a way that you have not done since your first awakening from leaving earth. While you have been sleeping, we have been reaching into your deepest mind and discussing it with you. Although, now that you are awake, you do not remember it all that clearly, we have been through it with you, and you have now been able to accept the situation in the way you now see it, because the main thing to remember here is that nobody on earth is seen truly by their fellows as they really are. It is only when a human being comes here that they are seen in their true colours, and they have to come to see themselves in their true colours.

"What other people on earth think you are makes no difference to your life here. What you think you are and what you actually are can, in many instances, prove to be two very different things. We have had to peel away from your mind some of the misconceptions you had about yourself and others, but you are seeing yourself clearly now, and you are seeing where your faults lay. We feel here that, of all the many faults that you had during your earth life, none of them were irretrievably bad faults. They were minor faults that were played upon by others. They were deeply affected by your reactions to others and by their reactions to you, so that they became more prominent as the world gave you some bad knocks and you found it increasingly difficult to overcome those knocks.

"*None* of your faults cannot be removed from you in a very short passage of experience here. Those people who have chosen to put such vicious and degenerate-sounding lies around your name, however, whether they have done it deliberately or because their own minds are too low to be able to see you differently, will have to face themselves when they come here, and it will take them a far, far longer period of experience to overcome their own faults and failings and attitudes than it has taken you to overcome yours.

"As I was coming back to you I caught the thoughts that you were feeling about your audiences. I assure you there are a great many of them who still love you deeply and sincerely for what they remember that you gave to them in your better years. They have not forgotten. They do still love you. They are confused by all the lies and the stories. In their hearts they cannot always make the lies fit with what they remember, but of course these are beginning to rub off on some of them to some extent. There are always those who prefer the cheaply sensational to the quiet truth. There are many others who went to your concerts in the latter years of your life who were exhibitionists, and they prefer to think of you as exhibitionist. They will always be prepared to believe the worst and to put it around you as 'The Garland Legend.' Because they see life in that way, they will prefer to see you as a highly coloured lady in all the various nuances that have been placed around you."

"To hell with those," I said to Doreen. "I want no part of them, but I am grateful to know that a lot of people still love me and remember me as I always tried to be. I do want to send them my love from here and my appreciation that they continue to remember me with love. You tell me that I can tell Lorna these things. I shall tell her that. Maybe she can use it sometime."

"She will not be able to use it in the book she is writing now, dear. We do not think it will be an appropriate moment for her to reveal the fact that she has been hearing from Judy Garland in the next life. She is going to have enough problems, as it is, getting the book accepted and published, without confusing the issue at this stage over something that will, in any case, be confusing her for a number of years yet. We do hope that she will be able to tell people your feelings eventually, but that is quite a long way in the future.

"Now that you are feeling so much better, so much more positive, and you have got the right ideas about it all, I am going to take you to see your sister, Susan. Only after that can I begin to make plans for you to speak to Lorna through a medium. She has been going to a lot of public lectures about the possibilities of communication from our side of life. She has by now become convinced that such communication is possible, and the time is getting to be right for her to seek the sort of medium whom she hopes will be able to give her the information that she has been seeking about your continuing survival.

"Now, then, I have already warned you that your sister Susan is still in a comparatively unhappy frame of mind and, therefore, you must protect yourself against the unhappy emanations that she may have around her. We are hoping that the sight of you will bring her forward into the light much more quickly. You may even find that, as a result of your visit, she will soon be feeling much better. This is something we cannot completely predict yet, we shall have to wait and see. I can assure you she is very much looking forward to seeing you again. She was so sorry to learn that you had come here so suddenly, without any real wish to do so. She feels sorry for you because she knows how much you loved your children, and she feels sorry for them. She does not know what has happened to you since she came here. She knew you were having your troubles with Sidney Luft and your television series; but by the time you became seriously ill with bronchial pneumonia and pleurisy in Hong Kong, she was too ill herself to really know what had been going on. As you will know, she came here while you were recovering from having nearly passed here at that time."

While Doreen had been telling me this, we had been emerging from the little glade and were on our way once again.

V

The countryside around my little glade was beautiful and very much like the countryside you see in New England, in America, at its most beautiful. As we went along the path, the light became darker. We came to a place where there was a large house in what seemed to be a glade that was in shadow, as it would have been had the sun gone in on a summer's day on earth. It had the feel and appearance of a summer's day without the sunshine.

We arrived at the door of this large house, and it was opened by a smiling, welcoming nun, who seemed to be expecting us. Doreen introduced me, and the nun smiled and nodded and told me, "Susan is feeling much better at the knowledge that you are on your way to see her."

The building reminded me a little bit of the hospitals I had seen on earth where the nurses were nuns, but I had never seen Susan nursed in such a building, or nursed by nuns, and I felt a little confused.

"This looks a little bit like a hospital," I said to the nun.

214

"It is the reception centre, dear, for people who have come here in a very unhappy frame of mind, the emphasis being on 'mind.' Your sister Susan was exceedingly weakened physically by the illness that she had, but she was also in a very, very deeply unhappy frame of mind. We have been nursing her here."

"But for such a long time!" I said to the nun. "My friend, Doreen, has warned me, but it does seem such a very long time."

"Well, as I expect you have been finding out, dear, time is not really relevant here. Time is not weeks and months and years, as it is on earth. It was a very long while, shall I say, before your sister even awakened to this world, because, you see, she had come to doubt that this world existed."

"Yes, that's true," I recalled. "We discussed that on one of my visits to her. I told her that while I could agree there were lots of times when I did wonder where the good God is who is said to be looking after us, I still felt that, somewhere or other, we continued to exist. In fact, it was that part of it that sometimes worried me. I wondered what it would be like if we did!"

"Well, your sister had convinced herself that there was *no way* in which she wanted to continue to exist. It was this difficulty that we had to overcome when she came here, and we have only recently started to overcome it. It is not that her progress here has been slow, it is simply that is has only recently started."

"So, she hasn't really been having a terrible time of it all these years?" I said, hopefully.

"Not really. She has just been in a deeply comatose condition. She would have been vaguely aware of shapes moving around her but without the incentive to find out what they were. She was not in any pain. Nothing was happening to her. She tended to just stay in what she thought was a peaceful sleep. We are now managing to rouse her."

"How did you manage to do that?" I wanted to know.

"By thoughts. We continuously poured kindly thoughts towards her. When you arrived, we knew it would take a while before you would be able to meet her, but it was then that we were able to say 'Your sister, Judy, will be wanting to see you.'

"Your name reached her, and gradually she came awake. When she awakened, we explained to her what had happened to her and that you had also arrived here. We explained that she had to get better. We told her that you were already being shown some of the beautiful parts of this world and that when you had been here long enough to be able to be brought to see her, you would be brought, so she must try and liven herself up to see you. We have told her that this is a beautiful world and that you have been seeing some of it. We have not told her any more than that. She still feels very deeply that, no matter how beautiful the world may be here, she still does not particularly want to be a part of it. Yet, in her deepest heart, she is looking forward to seeing you. She is in a strange state of mind, Judy, and we are hoping that you will be able to pull her through it."

"I'll do the best I can," I said. I looked at Doreen. "Doesn't it strike you as being a little ironic? You have been sorting me out, and now I am expected to sort Susan out, and I even have the nerve to say, 'I will do what I can'!"

"That is another big step forward on your part, Judy," said Doreen with a smile. "In the latter part of your life, you had so many things happen to you that, although you wanted to be sympathetic towards other people and you did try to be, there were other times when you said to yourself, 'I have enough of my own troubles. I can't worry about other people.' "

"That's true. I did feel like that. I would probably feel like that now if you hadn't talked me into being able to put all those troubles behind me."

"Yes, well that is why I waited to raise this moment," said Doreen. "You had to come through all that exceedingly difficult period before you would be in the right frame of mind to be able to face and to help Susan."

With that, we reached a room that was set aside from the general hospital area. "This is what we call one of our convalescent rooms," smiled the nun as she ushered us in.

There was Susan, sitting up in bed and smiling at me with her arms outstretched. I rushed towards her, and we hugged each other. Then I sat on the bed and kissed her.

"Judy, darling, it is so good to see you again," said Susan. "It's so good to see you!"

Susan and I gazed at each other, in this first reunion for some while and in such an unexpected manner for each of us. Neither of us, when we had last been together, had ever envisaged that

I would be coming to this side of life for very many years ahead. I saw her looking at me with an element of puzzlement, but also with an infinite compassion, and she said to me, "I have no idea how you came to be here, Judy. I don't seem to have been here very long. It must mean that you followed me quickly, and I can't imagine how that came to happen."

"I didn't follow you all that quickly," I said to her, trying to choose my words carefully. "I was alive on earth for five years after you came here. Because you had been so ill and so tired, you have spent a very long time sleeping, or so I am told. I don't think I spent too long sleeping, at least not as long a time as do a lot of people when they come here. I came here sort of accidentally, but partly due to the fact that my health got very shaky shortly after I last saw you, and then various things happened on earth that made it even shakier.

"In the end, what seems to have happened, although I don't remember it clearly, is that I did what I had sometimes done in the past from time to time without realising it and took an extra dose of my sleeping pills. Because I hadn't been eating, the effects of the dose on an empty stomach and the fact that I had, in any case, been getting into a weak condition, seem to have tipped the scales and brought me here. It wasn't anything that anyone on earth, including myself, would have expected to happen at that time, and I've been so deeply concerned for my three kids and also for my husband whom I had married only a few months before I came here."

Susan looked at me thoughtfully. "I knew you were going through a terrible time with Sid Luft and his court cases," she said to me, "but I didn't realise that you had remarried, Judy."

"Yes, I did. Twice!" I informed her.

Susan's eyes grew round in astonishment. "*Twice* in five years! That doesn't sound like you, surely!"

"Well, I always did have a great way of making stupid mistakes in my decisions about people. In the last few years of my life, I think I made more terrible mistakes than I had ever made during the rest of my life put together, and as you well know, I was pretty good at making terrible mistakes even then."

"Yes," said Susan, with a smile, "you were never the calmest of sisters. But you were always loyal, Judy, and it seemed so surprising to me when you said that you'd had two husbands in five years. It didn't sound like you."

"It wasn't really my fault that it happened. I did make a wrong decision, but I did not break up the marriage that I went into after Sid, and this last marriage of mine had only been in existence a few months."

"Were you happily married this time?" asked Susan.

"I thought I was," I replied, "but the lady who has been helping me since I came here" (I looked around for Doreen, so that I could introduce her, which I had forgotten to do, and then saw that Susan and I were alone) "the lady who has been helping me—her name is Doreen—has been taking me through various parts of my life on earth, including my marriages, and showing me where the faults were on both sides. I have now been brought to realise that, although I thought that I was happily married, it would not, apparently, have been as successful as I had intended and hoped that it would be. So although when my husband comes here, we shall meet again on friendly terms, it seems that it will not be the close relationship I might have expected it to have been."

"Poor Judy!" said Susan sympathetically. "You always seemed to me to have more love in you for the person you loved than they ever had for you."

"It isn't so much that," I said slowly. "It seems as if, although I loved Mickey and I think that he loved me, we came together at a difficult time in my life so that I wasn't seeing things clearly. As a result, he couldn't see the sort of person I really was underneath all my illness, and so he did not really understand half the things that I was doing and saying to him, which I now realise it *would* have been difficult for him to do. Really, we would not have had a great deal in common, as two people living together for a long time need to have to keep them together. So when he comes here, he is likely to be thinking and viewing things differently from the way I think and view things. I believe and hope we shall be pleased to see each other, but we will not be constant companions. That is something I have come to realise since coming here. Apparently this is something that happens quite often with couples. When we come here to this world, we see each other differently, and we see ourselves differently, and we tend to form different kinds of relationships. Certainly, from what I have already seen and heard here, I can now find this very easy to understand and accept, something I found less easy to do when I first arrived. I am hoping that I could, maybe, explain to you some of the things that I have discovered since I came here, and be able to help you," I said to her smilingly, holding her hands again. "They have told me that you were so weak and weary that you have been sleeping all these years—like Rip Van Winkle!" I added.

Susan smiled at me quietly, but I could see that I had not really reached her too well with my explanations.

"Anyway, that's enough of talking about me. How are *you*, now that you are awake?"

"I don't really know," she replied. "I had this feeling that I was in the midst of a strange, dreamlike situation, but I didn't particularly feel that I wanted to wake up from it. Now that I am awake and look around this room, I don't feel any incentive to get up, although the nuns tell me that physically I am completely healed and that there is a beautiful world waiting for me outside."

"It *is* a beautiful world." I assured her earnestly. "I haven't seen much of it, but what I have seen so far *is* beautiful. It can be beautiful, but the main problem seems to be the way we arrive here. People who have had a bad time on earth, who have got into a deeply gloomy state of mind, tend to see only gloomy things here. They only have to remain in these gloomier places because the kind of 'body' we have here cannot stand the brighter light unless our attitude is right for it. I have seen some people who have come here in unhappy conditions still remaining, at present, in unhappy conditions, but they are on the way to getting to better places. I have seen human beings, and I have seen animals, and I think that that is your problem at the moment, Susan dear. You were very unhappy even before you got to be physically ill, and then you got to be even more unhappy. I am told that you have remained in an unhappy state of mind here and that that is why you took so long to wake up and why you are still not feeling happy. Yet you seemed pleased to see me, and you actually held your arms out to me, which you would never have done on earth!"

"I was very pleased to see you, Judy, and I guess I just acted instinctively. I've always been pleased to see you, but I've never been demonstrative. I don't know why I did that just now, but

I'm glad I did, because I realise that I must have seemed off-handed to you at times when you took the trouble to come and see me."

"I did sometimes feel that I hadn't been wanted, and I wondered whether my journey had been worth it," I replied ruefully. "But I've had all that explained to me, and they've told me that you *were* pleased to see me, after a fashion, as much as you could be pleased about anything at that time," I told her. "I hope, now that we are both here, that we will be able to do something positive together for a change. After all, we are sisters, and we ought to see whether we can behave like sisters."

Again, Susan gave me one of her quiet little smiles, but without much response behind it. "Have you seen Mother?" she asked me.

"Not yet, but I've seen Dad."

"I wonder what Virginia is saying about the two of us both coming here!" said Susan.

"Did she visit you when you were ill?" I asked.

"She came once with her husband, but they didn't stay very long, and I felt she came out of a sense of duty rather than wanting to see me."

"I hadn't seen her for some years before I came here," I said. "She seemed to have a different attitude to you or me. I think she is Mother's daughter, really. I'm not quite sure what *I* am! I was looking forward to seeing Dad, and I'm sorry to say that he isn't in a very happy state of mind, either. I understand this is for two reasons. Apparently, when he was on earth with us, he did still love Mother, although he was not always able to show her. Now she won't see him here, and he is feeling he is not wanted by anybody. So he's staying in his shell and not coming out of it. I wish I could do something to help him."

"Well, he did give Mother a bad time, Judy. There's no doubt about that. She did have good cause to complain about him. We both know that, don't we?"

"We both thought we knew it, Susie, the way Mother explained it to us later on. But I have seen it very differently from here, and believe me, he is not nearly as bad as Mother painted him to us. In fact, I feel very sorry for him. He did a lot to keep our family going in a happier direction, because he did make us laugh and was kind. He wasn't doing the things behind Mother's

220

back that she thought he was. He was only trying to keep his moods to himself. Let's face it—we all get these in different ways in life. If Mother had been a little more understanding and a little bit more prepared to listen, they could have had a happier marriage together than they had.

"I can see it all much more clearly from here than we were ever able to do with Mother's version given to us on earth. I'm hoping that when you feel a bit better, you'll come with me to see him, because I am sure he will be pleased to see you. I could see that he was pleased to see me and regretted that he could not be a little bit livelier. I was hoping that, if you could come with me, we might manage to brighten him up a little."

"I still seem to need brightening up myself, Judy, at the moment. But, if what you tell me is true, I would like to see him again and get his version of things. Maybe, as you say, if we all get together again, we'll feel a little happier, the way we all used to do as kids."

"That's what I mean," I said to her. "If you stop and think, we were all happy when the five of us were travelling around together. It didn't matter that other people didn't like 'those theatrical kids' because we were together as a family. When Dad died, everything fell apart. It did for me. You and Ginnie went away and got married. You didn't get stuck with being with Mother the way I did. She was very hard and unkind to me, and I still see it that way, despite having had things explained to me a bit more. I still don't think that I got much love from her any more than Dad did. I can understand now why he feels that he has been really turned against unnecessarily, because she won't even listen to what he wants to say to her. That's typical of Mother!"

I found Susan smiling at me again. "Well, Judy, there were times when nobody could say anything to you about some people!"

"Yes, I suppose that's true," I admitted. "I didn't always listen when I should have done, but I would usually listen eventually, after I had cooled down. Then I would listen. But, by that time, half the people I knew wouldn't bother to explain themselves. Anyway, I've seen a lot of my faults already, so, with you around to point out a few more to me, it shouldn't be too long before I get myself onto the right road!" I said to her, beaming. "So, how about it, Susie? Are you going to stay in this place indefinitely, or are you going to liven up and come round with me and see a few places?"

"If the world outside is as beautiful as you say it is, I would like to have a look at it with you, Judy. Have you seen anyone else since you arrived that we know?"

"Only one, and that's Jack Kennedy. He's just as bright and lively and positive as ever, I'm pleased to say. But I've been very busy being shown what this world looks like. My friend Doreen has been helping me to get myself and my life into better perspective, because I got my mind into a complete twist in my last years on earth. I wasn't seeing things at all clearly and Doreen has been helping me to unravel it all before I meet most of the people that I knew on earth. The first person that she took me to see that I had known was Dad, and he was a disappointment to me, really, at the outset. He seemed so sad. But I am beginning to put that into better perspective now and to realise that he will be all right eventually. Then I met Jack, and he was so positive and cheerful, as usual, and now I've met you. I'm told I am going to sing again here, which is good. I feel I want to start doing something positive again."

"He must have had a terrible time," said Susan, "Jack Kennedy, I mean."

"Apparently not," I replied. "The fact that he came here so suddenly caused him to feel very confused, but he soon got over that and he's fine."

"I'm very pleased to know that," said Susan. "I always admired him—his positiveness. I think he would have made a good president."

"I always felt he would have made a good president," I said to her, "and I still think it is terrible that he came here the way that he did and when he did, but it is at least good to see him looking so well."

It was while we were discussing all these topics that I noticed a slightly lighter glow around Susan than there had been when I first entered the room, and I began to get the feeling that she was coming back to a livelier interest in things. She was asking questions and listening to what I was telling her, and this seemed to have brightened her a little. Then the nun and Doreen came into the room.

222

The nun advanced towards the bed and stood beside Susan. Doreen came and stood beside me, and I was able to introduce her to Susan. They smiled at each other, and Susan said, "Judy's been telling me about the places you have taken her to see and that you have helped her to straighten out a few things in her mind." She looked at the nun standing beside her, took her hand, and said, "Perhaps you'll be able to do the same for me."

"We have someone who is waiting to do that for you, my dear child," said the nun kindly. "I have to stay here to nurse others who arrive here in the same way you did, but there is a lady waiting to help you, and of course, you will be able to see your sister quite frequently as well. I am sure she has already told you of the beautiful world that waits for you outside these doors, and I am so glad to see that you are looking a little brighter already as a result of her visit."

"I do begin to feel better and more cheerful," said Susan, "so I will be very grateful to be shown around. I hope that Judy and I will be able to see more of each other than we were able to do in our last years on earth."

"I hope so, too, Susie," I said to her, feeling brighter for knowing that she wanted to see me more frequently, because I had always felt fond of Susan depite feeling that we had little rapport in her last years. With that, I felt a great surge of love come towards me from Susan, and I felt that I wanted to give her all that love in return. We hugged each other, and I said, "I think we're going to be far better friends again here, like we were as kids, than we have been for a long time, and I'm so glad!"

Then I began to feel that I was getting the signal to go, so I said to her, "I think Doreen and I have to leave you now, Susan darling, but I'll be back to see you soon and I hope it won't be long before we're seeing lots of beautiful places here together."

"Somehow, I think you will," said the nun, smiling at us both.

Susan smiled back, held onto my hand, and said, "Years ago, Judy, you always did me a heap of good. I know I turned into a misery during the last years we saw each other, but you've done me a heap of good again today. I do love you." With that, she turned over in bed and seemed to go back to sleep.

"She'll be a different person when she wakes up," said the nun as she escorted Doreen and me to the door. "Your visit has done what we hoped it would do. She is over the worst now, and it will not be long before she is in a very, very much brighter and happier place."

"Thank goodness for that," I said, "and thank you for looking after her."

As Doreen and I walked away, I began to feel a burden lifting from me.

"I'm so pleased that Susan was so glad to see me," I said. "One of the things that concerned me when on earth was the lack of family. That's why, no matter what was happening to me, no matter what sort of spats I was having with my husband—when I was with Vincente and Liza, and when I was with Sid and Liza, Lorna, and Joe, and even later when I was on my own with them again—I always tried hard to keep a feeling of family. I felt it was important to have a family atmosphere. It was something I lost when my dad died and my sisters married. I never regained it again until I had my own kids. I had to fight hard when the four of us were on our own, to keep a feeling of family, but I did always try. I felt that I was lacking a family from my Mother and both of my two sisters. I think Virginia is very much like Mother in her attitude. Although Susan was a bit more like me, she was only a little bit more like me, and we never seemed to have a great closeness. But somehow I felt closer to her today than I have ever felt. It would be good if we could keep that closeness."

Doreen was silent for a while as we walked along. Eventually, she said to me, "Judy, the last thing I want to do is to seem as though I am throwing a bucket of cold water over your hopes. Susan is a kindly person. She has been more than pleased to see you again, as you have been pleased to see her. You brought with you your usual feeling of warmth and joy, which you do bring when you are feeling more yourself, and that reached out to Susan and she was able to return it to you. You will see each other here, and you will be much friendlier here than you were able to be on earth, but do please bear in mind that despite the fact you are fond of each other and were pleased to see each other and will enjoy being together from time to time, you are still not destined to be really close together. Some of your ways will be different to Susan's. She will have to find her own pathways, make her own decisions, and develop her own interests, as you will. Yes, you will be happy friends, but it will not be a close family relationship any more than you will ever regain a close family relationship with your father, although, again, you will be pleased to see each other from time to time.

"The only reason I am saying this to you now is that I do not want you to make the mistake of thinking, 'this is where my future lies, to get the family together again,' because it will not be that way. The main thing to you, I know, is that you feel loved again because Susan was so pleased to see you in the warm, sisterly way that you had missed for a very long time. This is something that will adjust itself to its proper level after a while. By all means see Susan, by all means be happy friends with Susan, but do not believe that it is going to be a close partnership, a close regular existence together here. We know enough of you and Susan to realise there are many differences inside each of you that will take you onto different pathways.

"We are very glad that you were so pleased to see each other and you have done Susan a great deal of good, just as your presence on earth, when you were feeling well, often brought a great deal of warmth and vitality and laughter to those around you. But, you see, although Susan is a gentle and kind person, she will always be drawing more from you than you will be drawing from her, and we do not want that to happen too often. Do you understand me?"

I realised, while Doreen was talking, that she was trying to tread warily and not to stamp all over me. I listened to her in the way that she was meaning me to listen. I took it all in my stride and said to her, "I know you are right to tell me this. I did always go towards somebody the moment I thought they were coming towards me, and I would later find out that I had made a mistake. You have probably just prevented me from making another one and then feeling hurt later on. It was good to know that Susan loved me, that I wasn't the unloved person that I had begun to feel that I was, but I understand what you are trying to say, and I will be a little more circumspect in my approach." I smiled at her. "And I promise you I will not let anything like that hurt me here."

"That's good," said Doreen with a relieved smile. "I am glad I have got that across to you without too much difficulty."

VI

We stepped out of the woodlands through which we had been walking into the bright light of the open countryside. It was a blinding light compared with where we had been. As I adjusted to it, I realised that we were coming back to where we had left the children.

"I thought you might like to see how Sally is getting on," said Doreen.

"Yes, I would," I replied. "How long will she have been here now, in earth time?"

"We calculate she must have been here about six months, Judy. Her mother will be getting more reconciled to the child having come here. Sally will have woken up from her sleep and been learning how to play and to fit in with the other children. We thought it would be pleasant for you to pay her a visit and see the progress she is making. I am sure she will remember you."

"Yes, I'd like to," I agreed, "but I was wondering whether it would be possible to meet a few more of those people that I knew on earth before I get involved with helping children, which is what I would like to do, and you did say something about me singing again."

"Judy, dear, this will only be a brief visit. We have a lot more for you to see and do before you settle into working with the children, but I thought you would like to see Sally again while we make our way towards another part of this world."

We were approaching a little group of children who were playing together with two young nurses. In the midst of those happy, smiling faces, I caught sight of Sally. She had lost the confusion and shyness of that earlier meeting when I first met her, and she had turned into a very positive little girl, directing some of the others in their play instead of being the one who stood there quietly watching. They all looked over to me as I approached the group, and Sally ran forward and caught hold of me. I bent down and put my arms around her and kissed her.

"Hello, Sally. You remember me, then?"

"You are my other mommy," she said to me.

"Well, for a little while," I laughed at her.

"My mommy knows that I am alive and well here," said Sally,

looking round-eyed and solemn.

"Does she darling?" I said to her, keeping my arm around her.

"Yes, 'cos I went and spoke to her," said Sally.

"I'm so glad. That must make her feel a lot better," I said, giving Sally another kiss.

With that, Sally pulled me towards the group of children. "This is my friend, Judy," she told everybody. "She's my other mommy. She's going to sing for us."

That was the first I had heard of that, but I decided I would try, so I sat down in their midst and asked, "What would you like to hear?" There was the usual barrage of songs being called out, while I foraged around in my mind to recall one that I might be able to sing to them, because I had no idea of many of the songs they were calling out to me.

"Why don't you sing the song you sang before?" said Sally helpfully.

"What a good idea!" I told her with relief, falling back once again on "Ten Pins in the Sky." That went down well, and I decided to leave it at that because, try as I might, I could not immediately think of anything in my past repertoire that would have been suitable for a group of three and four-year-old children. Even "Over the Rainbow" did not seem very suitable lyrics, now that we were all here. "The Trolley Song" seemed incongruous. Somehow, nothing seemed to fit. It was at that point that my mind began to wander towards my concert repertoire. I had to jerk my mind back to where I was with the children before I wandered too far away from what we were all doing there.

I stayed and played with them for a while. Doreen sat at the side and watched. Finally, I said to them, "I've got to go now. I'm so pleased to see you again, Sally darling, and I'm so glad you have been able to speak to your mommy and that she knows you are well and happy."

"I speak to my mommy lots of times," said Sally complacently, putting her arms round my neck. "Will you come and see me again?"

"Yes, of course I will, darling," I assured her. "It is just that my friend Doreen and I have somewhere else to go at the moment, but we will be back, I promise you." I blew a kiss to all the children before joining Doreen and leaving the spot.

VII

"Doreen, a thought struck me while I was with the children. You said I am going to sing again here. While I was trying to think of a suitable song to sing for the children, my mind was rapidly going through all the songs I have ever sung, and somehow even those that I had sung in my younger days in pictures didn't seem to fit too well with where we were. Then I began to realise that most of my adult repertoire for my concerts really does not fit in here. How can I sing about a trolley when we don't have or need trolleys here? So many of the songs I sang don't really seem to fit this atmosphere. How extraordinary!"

"That is something you will have to think about very carefully when you start singing again, Judy. You have some other experiences ahead of you before you actually start singing. It will give you an opportunity to think about it and to turn over in your mind what is likely to be suitable to sing here. We're not really all that different here, you know!" she said to me laughingly.

"No, I know, but there is this subtle difference in the way we view things here and the way we viewed things on earth. Looking back over my songs, they are mostly love songs of a sort. I've either found somebody, or lost somebody, or I'm looking for somebody. You tell me that those sort of relationships don't exist here. I don't suppose I could even fit in something like 'Forget your troubles, come on get happy,' could I?" I said to her in smiling desperation. "I'll have to think about it, I really will! I suppose I could sing 'That's Entertainment,' " I said to her, brightening a little.

"You could always try some new songs, Judy," said Doreen, smiling at me.

"That's my line!" I smiled back. "I used to joke about occasionally learning a new song. But so often it was the old ones that my audiences seemed to want. I had to learn a lot of new material for the television series, but the producers kept changing their minds about what we were all supposed to be doing, and I hardly ever felt these were as well rehearsed as they should have been. Anyway, that's all past now. I will be completely responsible for what I do here, won't I?"

Doreen nodded smiling agreement, and for the first time since my arrival here, my mind began to turn towards singing again. Before this moment I had been told by Doreen that I would sing again. Now I was beginning to turn the idea over in my mind, considering not so much *when* but *what* I should sing. I suppose it was at that moment I began to move once more towards what had always been one of the most important things in my life—putting together in my mind a concert program that I hoped would bring pleasure to audiences.

Doreen looked at me a little quizzically. "I know what you are thinking, Judy, and I know why you are thinking it. You have now adjusted to being in this world. You have seen how, in certain circumstances, some people handle it in one way and some in another. You have always been a positive person, and you have remained positive. Now your confusion is behind you. You have met again three people whom you had known on earth and seen how differently they have reacted to being here, and you have seen how the children are reacting, as well as the animals. Your positive side thus can now turn more towards the thing in your life that gave you a great deal of pleasure—to be able to perform to give pleasure to others. Although you sang for your supper, as it were, and although it often brought you some heartache in its wake, simply because of the other things that were happening around you, you always had, deep down inside you, a sincere wish to sing for the sheer pleasure of singing and for the sheer pleasure it often gave to others. There were some people in your profession who, whenever they went to parties, would be prepared to perform, if asked, and who hoped to be asked, and they often performed for the sheer pleasure of showing off. In your case, you felt a sincere pleasure at being asked, for the sheer pleasure that it gave you to sing. Now, you are beginning to get that kind of pleasure coming back to you. Is that not so?"

I had to stop and consider for a moment. Quite frankly, although I had been absorbing all that Doreen had been telling me and I had been going through each of my experiences here in awe and wonderment and confusion and sometimes sadness, I had not become aware that I had in any way adjusted. Nobody could be more surprised than I was to find myself tentatively thinking now of what sort of concert program I could possibly put together.

"I wouldn't have agreed with you that I was beginning to get *that* adjusted," I said to her. "I've been interested and intrigued. I've sometimes been concerned and worried. I know you are telling me the truth when you tell me I can be much happier here in due course. I am sure I can. I do accept it is only a question of time and that a lot of the responsibility for finding that happiness lies within me and my approach to other people. I do believe you when you say I will sing again, but I still do not understand why I am thinking more about it at this point, because frankly, I can't see myself getting around to it until I have had much more opportunity to see other people and do other things."

"I could not agree with you more, Judy," said Doreen. "You are quite correct. The main thing, as I see it, is that you have begun to think about what you will sing. That is a big step towards accepting that you have a future here and that singing will be part of your future—an important part, in some ways, because of the joy it will give to you to see the joy that you are giving to others. It will help to reinstate and reinforce your belief in yourself as a person and as someone who can give pleasure to others. So, although it does still lie a little ahead of you, in my view it is a very positive step towards adjusting to your life here."

"Yes, I see what you mean, now," I told her. I suppose I said it with a feeling of relief that although I had begun to ponder what I should sing, I had not yet got to get around to actually doing it. I still lacked something that would enable me to go out to an audience and be as positive as I would like to be, particularly since I had come to realise how easy it is to pick up other people's thoughts and feelings here, if you are not very careful. I knew that I had to handle that part of myself far more securely than I was so far managing to do if I was to become a successful entertainer here.

VIII

While we had been talking, we had come back to a familiar place where we had been before. We were back on the shore, looking at the waves twinkling in the bright light. In the distance there was a bright haze with an extra bright light shining from it.

"Now then, Judy, you are about to make your first experiment in conveying your thoughts to someone on earth."

I looked at Doreen in some bewilderment. "I know you told

me that I was going to do so, and Sally made it sound extremely easy. In fact, if she had not been so young, I would have asked her how she managed it, but I felt the time was not right for that. I never expected to be told such a thing while I was standing here in a place such as this," I said to her.

"Well, first of all, you have to bear in mind that Sally is such a young child that her thoughts have to be conveyed through a medium to her mother on her behalf. When she is a little older here, she will be able to do it herself. But now, to ensure that her mother will recognise her and know that she is definitely hearing from her little girl and that this is not being imagined by the medium, pieces of information have to be conveyed to the mother that she will recognise and that only she and Sally would know. Sally is a little young to think of that sort of thing on her own. You will have help from here from other people, but basically you will have to be the person who is sending the thought to reach the medium who will transfer it to your friend, Lorna."

"You mean Lorna Smith," I checked, knowing in my heart that that was who she meant.

"Yes," said Doreen. "She has finally made up her mind to see whether she can get some definite proof of your continuing existence."

I began to feel some excitement welling up within me that I was going to take part in this kind of experiment.

"Now," Doreen began to explain, "you will shortly be joined by some friends of mine, and also yours, although you have not met them before. They will surround you with their own power of thought to help you convey to the medium what it is you wish to convey. Think about it carefully, Judy. What can you have passed along to Lorna that will help to convince her that it is you who is sending the message?"

That question completely confounded me. I stopped to consider how Lorna would have recognised me on earth if I had been on one side of a closed door and she on the other. I could have shouted through the door, I supposed, and she might have recognised my voice. I could have picked up the telephone . . . "

"Ah!" said Doreen. "Now then, that is what you are doing now, aren't you, Judy? You are picking up the equivalent of a telephone."

"Yes, I suppose I am," I agreed.

231

"But the problem," said Doreen, "is that you are speaking to someone on the other end of the line who will not necessarily know what your voice sounds like or even what you look like. So you have to try and show that person something that will help them to convey to Lorna what you are giving them. I would suggest that you try and pass along part of what Lorna knows you to have been as a person. Also, is there any incident you can remember that you shared with her and nobody else shared, that could be related to her and that she is likely to recall? More important still, Judy, is there something you can tell her that you know about her from here that nobody else would know and certainly not the medium?"

This kind of discussion went on for some while and in some detail before I was primed as to what I might try and tell Lorna through the medium. We were then joined by several people with smiling, pleasant, friendly faces, to whom I was introduced and who told me that they were part of a team who would be helping others, as well as myself, to reach those on earth. They said it was something that they often undertook for people who were trying to reach earth for the first time. We discussed the points I had to try and make and Doreen explained to me that it was very much touch and go as to how much we would succeed in conveying. "There are so many elements between us and the medium, so many points at which the message could go astray, particularly when there are others with the medium who are also waiting for messages from here. There can be so much static interference, where lines get crossed in the same way that telephone lines can get crossed on earth. If the medium is feeling tired and not so strongly psychic or clairvoyant as on other occasions, things can go wrong. I can only assure you that we will help you as much as we possibly can to reach Lorna who is by this time more than anxious to hear from you."

I was instructed to stand there, on the shore, and to look towards the extra bright light that I could see in the distance. I had to try and think across to that light what I felt in my heart about myself and about my life and to keep on concentrating like that until I saw an answering flicker in the light. This I tried hard to do. When I got this answering flicker, which seemed to take some time to reach me, I continued in the way that we had planned.

232

I became aware of a feeling around me that seemed to indicate that I had succeeded in conveying one part of what I was thinking, so I went on to convey the next part. What I tried to convey to Lorna was my personality and that I had not ever thanked her enough for what she had tried to do for me and that I was doing so now. I gave her the names of my children, rather than my own name. I gave her the image I had previously received of her, where she was sitting down and writing and getting up and going across to the cabinet, which seemed to be full of records but from which she was pulling something that had nothing to do with the records and that she kept referring to. I put forward an image of the scarf and also the pearls that she had loaned to me on two occasions. I found myself sending her a great loving wave of gratitude, because I felt the need to do so, and I suddenly felt I wanted to put around her neck a whole host of flowers. I felt, rather than actually heard, the medium say to Lorna, "I know I have got someone here who was a very famous performer, and I feel I ought to know the name, but I can't quite catch it. She is sending you a great deal of love, and she is putting a garland of flowers around your neck." At that point, I felt the joy that came from that side of life, and that joy was reflected to me, but, suddenly, the contact snapped, and the light steadied again. It did not go away, but I knew that contact had stopped.

"You did exceedingly well for a first effort," said Doreen. "I am sure Lorna will feel much happier for having known, beyond any shadow of a doubt, that it was you."

"But how strange," I said to her, "that I should have been trying to give my name, Garland, and he described my flowers as a garland of flowers and not as my name."

"That is the sort of thing that happens, dear. We have to be prepared for these little idiosyncracies," said Doreen, "but I think you have made a very good attempt for your first effort. I think it will help Lorna to know that she has heard from you and that you are all right. It will not be too much longer before you will be able to speak to her again in a different way, but this is at least a beginning."

Our friends surrounded me with their congratulations that I had done so well. "Thank you for all the help you gave me," I said to them, because I had felt a strange power around me while

I was sending those thoughts. They smiled and nodded and went their way. Doreen and I were left to ourselves. I found myself looking back again across the water to the pinpoint of light that was beginning to recede further and further away. I felt very drawn towards it, and I felt that I wanted to follow it. Doreen put her hand on my shoulder. "You cannot do that, dear. Not for a while."

Not for a while? What did she mean, *not for a while?*

"It is too early to go into that yet," said Doreen, "but now I think I ought to take you to meet some other people that you knew on earth."

I brightened a little at that suggestion, because, for some reason that I could not understand, I felt lonelier seeing that light recede than I had felt since before meeting Jack Kennedy and my sister Susan. I could not understand why I suddenly felt lonelier again shortly after I had felt a great sense of achievement at reaching Lorna successfully.

"You are bound to have these mixed feelings at the moment, Judy. You have just made your first contact again with earth. You have spoken to someone who loves you very much, and you have probably picked up her confused reactions, a mixture of pleasure at hearing from you and unhappiness that you are no longer there to speak to. You mentioned your children, which would bring back to you your feeling of being away from them. You took the trouble to assure Lorna that you had not taken your own life, and she was sending you back the thought that she knew you had not. But, you see, you each knew that some people had tried to imply it. So, although you and Lorna have not had direct contact as yet—that will come later—you have been linked through a medium, and you have each picked up the other's confused reactions. Lorna will be going home feeling happier than before she came but still in, shall we say, a mood of sensitively mixed feelings about it all. You are having similarly sensitive mixed feelings. Now then, just as she will have to return to the hurly-burly of life on earth, so you will be taken along to your next step here."

Doreen turned away from the shore towards a path that led across some fields, but I turned back to look again at the light. I still felt drawn towards it, and I felt as if a little piece of me was leaving me and going towards that light. "For some reason that

I can't explain, I feel like bursting into tears," I told Doreen.

"That is a natural reaction, dear," said Doreen. "Lorna, like your children, has been shedding many tears over you. She has been delighted to hear from you, but now she has to cope with her own emotional reaction to it. There is nothing more you can do for her at the moment, so come with me and meet some more people."

I turned reluctantly away from where we were and joined Doreen in a walk across the fields. These seemed to be full of the kind of flowers that one sees in the springtime, all sorts of beautiful colours—yellow, red, pink, blue, mauve, white—all dotted amongst the green. The birds were singing, the air was perfumed, and my heart began to rise again. I began to take more interest in what Doreen was saying to me. She explained that we were now on our way back towards the city.

"Is this the same city we've already visited?" I asked.

"It is not exactly the same city, it is *a* city, but if you bear in mind, Judy, that once people get completely adjusted here, they can go from place to place very quickly and speedily, it is as good as being in the same city. But I am bringing you to it on foot because I think the atmosphere that we are going through will help to cheer you up again."

"It isn't that I feel sad," I said to her, "I just feel very drawn towards that light. I feel I want to have said very much more than I managed to say and, somehow, although this may sound silly, I almost felt a little bit of me, for want of a better phrase, going towards that light."

"It is not too surprising, Judy, when you stop to realise that Lorna has been writing about you with a great deal of concentration over many months and this is the first time you have managed to speak to her. That 'little bit of you,' shall we say, is already within Lorna. She has been trying so hard to convey on paper the person that she knew you to be. That is really what you were tuning in to. When the communication stopped and you had to go your individual ways, she took with her what she felt for you within herself and you felt that going towards her."

I could not help my mind going briefly back to the scene in *The Wizard of Oz* where the Scarecrow has been pulled apart and scattered around and says "There goes a bit of me again." Doreen laughed and said, "It's a long time since you came back to *The Wizard of Oz.*"

"I know," I said to her. "It must be because I've been talking to Lorna!"

"That is not impossible," said Doreen. "You see, that is one reason why we think that she could be such a good friend to you in the future, because so many of the things that were part of your career on earth will be known to her. That quick thought, that you have had would be something that she would be able to quickly recognise and acknowledge and know precisely what you mean. You would not have to explain it, as you would have to explain it to others. Yet, at the same time, she will not be treating you as 'Judy Garland.' That is why we feel that, when Lorna eventually comes here, you will have the kind of friend that you always wanted, someone who loved you for your work but who also loved you for yourself. When I say *for yourself,* I mean the kind of person she knew you to be, not the person she thought you to be or wanted you to be or imagined you to be, but the person that you are, with all your faults and failings but with all your positive attributes as well."

I was silent again for a while after she had said that to me. "I am beginning to wonder whether you may be right," I said slowly. "I must say that, although I had always liked Lorna, it had never occurred to me that we had all that much in common, but I am beginning to find it more easily believable than I did at one time." Having come to that decision, I suddenly felt more positive again. "Anyway," I said to her, brightening up, "what interests have you got in store for me now?"

IX

Before long, we were approaching an area that looked like the Californian ranches that I had visited occasionally. We were approaching a very palatial ranch house with a swimming pool close by it. As we came to the pool, someone was climbing out of it. To my amazement, it was Clark Gable.

He came towards me, took one of my hands in both of his, smiled at me with that very familiar, quirky smile of his, and said, "Well, Judy, I didn't expect you to be joining us yet! How are you?"

236

"I'm fine," I replied, smiling back at him. "How are you?"

"Couldn't be better. Come over and meet Carole."

He led me across to where a smiling blonde lady was sitting. I recognised her as Carole Lombard. She smiled in welcome, I introduced Doreen, and we were invited to sit down.

I had not known Clark well on earth. Our names had become linked in the song that I had first sung when I was fifteen. "Dear Mr. Gable." I had been asked by the heads of the studio to sing it at a party they were giving for him, and later it had been put into a movie that I had made. Over the years at the studio, we had met from time to time and chatted briefly. I had known how deeply shocked and unhappy he had been at the death of his wife, Carole Lombard, in a plane accident, after a comparatively short and apparently happy marriage. I knew that he had had many amours and several marriages after Carole. Although I did not know him well enough personally to know, people had told me that he had never really got over the loss of Carole. It was a very pleasant surprise for me to see them happily together here.

"Carole and I have a lot of lost years to make up," said Clark. "And that is precisely what we are doing, isn't it, dear?" he said to her. Carole quietly smiled and nodded back.

"It must have been a terrible way for you to come here," I said to her, bearing in mind the plane crash.

"It was hellish at first," she replied, "because we knew we were crashing. We didn't know what the pilot was doing or how he was coping, but we could see we were heading straight downwards. I felt a terrible panic and a terrible feeling of constriction in my lungs and my head, as though everything was going to burst. Then I must have blacked out, thank God. I woke up here in a hospital. For a while my brain felt confused and cloudy, and I couldn't move. People kept coming up to me and reassuring me and telling me that all I needed was a good sleep and I would be very much better. I did drift away into a sleep, and when I woke up again I felt quite all right. They explained to me that, although I had become unconscious before the plane had actually crashed, the impact of the crash had so damaged my physical body that it had, for a while, damaged the spirit body that I am using here. My spirit body had to be given time to recuperate before I could move normally here. Of course, it was a great shock to me to realise that I had come here without Clark, and I knew that he would be in a terrible frame of mind over me. It took me a long while to attain a more positive attitude about our losing each other like that. I never did really, not properly, until Clark came here."

They instinctively reached out towards each other's hands, and he said to me, "I came here pretty quickly, as I expect you know. I'd got a son due to be born to me and my wife, but, when I woke up here, the first person I saw was Carole. I had a heart attack and I woke up here, in the hospital, and found Carole sitting beside me, waiting for me to wake up. It was the most wonderful feeling I can ever remember having, when I realised I wasn't just dreaming about her, as I had often done on earth, but she was really there and we were together again. It's a marvellous feeling, Judy, a marvellous feeling, I assure you," he said to me. "Don't worry, you'll be just as happy as we are."

"Well, thank you for the reassurance," I said to him. "I've already been getting quite a lot from my friend, Doreen."

"How did you come here?" he wanted to know.

"Doreen tells me that, because I hadn't been eating, and because I was generally undernourished, and I had mistakenly taken more sleeping pills than I had intended, my body couldn't stand up to it, although it probably would have done, had I not been in such a weak condition," I told him. "It came as a bit of a shock to me, too, to go to bed on earth with what I thought was a sore throat and to wake up here when I had only been married for three months."

"Oh, you poor kid!" said Clark sympathetically.

"But I'm all right now," I said to him. "I've had it all explained to me."

"I'm pleased to hear it. How long do you think it will be before you'll be giving us a concert?"

I looked at Doreen. We smiled at each other, and I said, "I don't know. Doreen is gradually encouraging me along that way, but I have a little more visiting and experiencing to do before I actually give a concert. I've seen Jack Kennedy already, and he has said that he'll come along."

"We'll be there, too," said Clark positively. He turned to Carole and said, "You don't know what you've missed, by coming here when you did. You've never seen Judy perform a concert.

Boy! That's really something!" He grinned at me in the way I'm sure all his fans will remember!

We chatted for a while, on personal matters of his and Carole's before Doreen and I left them both in their happy state by their pool.

As we walked away, I began to feel a little bit curious. Doreen had already explained to me that many marriages do not survive a transition to the spirit world, yet here I had just seen a very happy and contented married couple living in the kind of surroundings I would have expected them to have lived in when on earth.

Doreen caught my thought and said to me immediately, "That is why I brought you to see them, Judy. I wanted you to see how it is that, in certain circumstances, people can reside happily together here after having been man and wife on earth. In this instance, what you have to remember is that Clark and Carole were very happy together on earth for only a short time before they were parted by Carole's accident and very sudden departure here. They both felt they had been left unfulfilled in their life together by being parted so abruptly in the midst of their happiness. That is why they were so pleased and delighted to meet each other again here and why they are so happy together. Only after a period here will they be able to see completely clearly just how truly compatible they really are. At the moment they are thoroughly enjoying being together again, and good luck to them."

"I agree with you," I said to her warmly. "I hope we will see some more people as happy together here."

"You will, quite often. But, you see, after people have been here for a while and they start to look around them and to enquire more deeply into things generally, they often find themselves coming out with different sorts of answers to the person that they are used to being with. That is when the test comes as to whether or not those people are truly compatible here. I am not saying for one moment that Clark and Carole are not compatible or will not continue to be compatible. In view of their present happiness, I sincerely hope, for both their sakes, that they will prove to be so. But it is something that neither of them will be able to be certain about until they have completed their experience of living together again here and have begun to look around them at the different directions where they wish to go for their next step forward. Some people take a very, very long time indeed before they decide they want to look a little bit further, and it may well be that your two friends will not come to that decision for a long time. Some come to it sooner than others. For example, the couple I am now going to take you to see are in very different circumstances to Clark and Carole. They each came here as individuals who had never met on earth. They had both had unhappy marriages; they were both exceedingly lonely while on earth. They felt as though there was no particular person who loved them or who was taking any interest in them, and when they came here they were very lonely indeed. Both of them had someone to help them to find their way through their different experiences here, much in the same way as I am trying to help you. Because their problems seemed to arise from the same set of emotions, because they seemed to be of similar natures and similar outlooks, they were brought together here and introduced to each other, and some of their experiences with their teachers were shared. Gradually, they formed a very close companionship here that is not in any way a physical relationship. But they are deeply fond of each other and are exceedingly happy together. This is why I want you to meet them and hear from them how they have reacted to this somewhat unexpected situation."

X

Doreen was drawing me towards what looked like a small landing stage by the side of the lake. Farther along there was a cabin, the sort of cabin you might see in the Canadian Rockies. It was small and very basic-looking, yet it gave the impression of being cosy. As we walked up to the door, there were sounds of singing from inside. When we drew nearer, the singing stopped, the door opened, and, to my astonishment, I found myself looking straight into the eyes of someone I had known in my early days at the film studios. She had been a bit player. I doubt whether anyone on earth would remember her name as a performer, but she was someone that I had liked because, although she never seemed to have the kind of spark that the studio would have required to turn her into a star, she had always been pleasantly smiling. Whenever I spoke to her, she was always open and friendly. I had liked her and would have liked to have had her as one of my friends, but she was not among those that the studio chiefs would have picked for that purpose, probably because she was too honest, I suppose.

Her eyes grew round and her jaw dropped in amazement when she saw me standing there. She seemed to recognise me, which surprised me until I realised that, after all, *I* had recognised *her*, too! The two of us must each be considerably older than when we had last met, but I was probably looking almost as young again as she was now looking. At least, I hoped I was! I gathered from Doreen, afterwards, that I had been continuing to lose my years and that I now looked as I had when I was around nineteen or twenty years of age. I think I was as astonished as she was, because I could not imagine why it was that Doreen had brought me here. Anyway, Peggy, as I now recalled her name to be, overcame her astonishment and invited us in. We sat down on some comfortable chairs that were covered in some brightly coloured, homely material. There were pretty curtains at the windows, and there was a dog sprawled on the floor. He wagged his tail in welcome but otherwise remained uninterested in the visitors. There was also a sink and a cooker. I thought to myself, *How strange. I haven't eaten since I've been here and I haven't felt a bit hungry! What are they doing with a cooker?*

Peggy obviously caught my thought because she laughed and said: "I know what you are thinking, Judy, but I always wanted a little cabin like this, and it would not have been complete without a cooker. We don't use it, but it is there as part of the surroundings to make the cabin look like home. I always spent my life in big cities, trying to earn a living in the hardest possible way. I always felt deprived because I had never been able to get out into the countryside, as I had always wanted to do, and live like this. That is what I am now doing and why I have got my cooker!" She laughed at me again. "But I am surprised to see you here!"

"You can't be any more surprised than I am," I told her. "I've just been taken by my friend, Doreen, here, to meet Clark Gable and his wife, Carole Lombard. I had no idea where I was being taken next, and I must confess that the last person I had expected to see was you!"

"I suppose I could tell you the same thing," said Peggy, "but it is great to see you. I always liked you, and I was always so pleased for you when you were a big success."

"When did you come to this world?" I asked her hesitantly.

"I was only twenty-five. I got hooked on drugs," said the girl. "You know how easy it was to get hooked on such things in Hollywood."

"Yes, I know," I replied a little lamely. "It must be a terrible situation to be in."

"It started quite innocently," the girl replied. "I was at a party one night and everyone decided they were going to try some marijuana. I was not particularly interested, but I did not want to be the odd one out, so I tried it. It was very pleasant, and I was feeling very lonely and dejected, so I went along with it. Before I knew where I was, I was getting far more involved than I had expected. Eventually, I got involved in so many other things and problems that I was arrested on a narcotics charge and went to prison for it."

My God! I thought to myself, looking at this happy, smiling, childlike person. *However could that have happened?*

"Anyway," she went on, "I got into a really bad state, and in the end, it brought me here. I was in a bad way here for a very long time. That's because it does something to you deep down inside of you. It affects your mind. I had a long, long haul to get out of it again, a very long haul. I was given a great deal of help here by various people, but it was a long, drawn out experience for me, and I haven't been here in this lovely place for very long. It was while I was gradually surfacing from it all that I was introduced to my present companion. He had been in a similar situation, but not in Hollywood. He had been in Japan, where various drugs were easily obtainable. He got into opium and then onto heroin, and he got into a terrible state. We are both recovering together. He is out on the lake at the moment. He had an equally grim time when he came here, and we are both beginning to find our real selves again."

I looked at her thoughtfully. I did not quite know what to say. Eventually, I said, "Doreen has been telling me that, because I spent the larger part of my life on earth being supported to some extent by a number of medications prescribed for me by doctors because I had several nervous breakdowns and illnesses, the world at large on earth considers that I have been on the kind of drugs that you have been mentioning. When she told me this, I was horrified and disgusted. I said very strongly and adamantly that I would never, ever, have gotten myself involved in anything as depraved as that and that I had too much respect for my own body and for my children to have ever done such a thing. I felt very righteously indignant about it all. Looking at you and hearing what you have said and remembering you as I knew you at the studios, I would not ever have considered you to be a weak or depraved person. I liked you. I think you were probably one of the few genuine and truthful people that I met during those years, and I am so sorry to hear how involved you got and how difficult it became for you. I can see now that maybe it was arrogant of me to feel so rebellious against those kind of drugs when I was accepting the other drugs handed out by doctors because I regarded them as medicine, which I thought they were. I still think they are, but I can realise now that, possibly, there is a very thin line between the two."

Peggy looked at me seriously. "No, Judy, there is a difference. I got into hard drugs because I said, 'Yes, all right, I'll have a go,' and I did not want to be regarded as a bore by those people I was spending time with. I did it out of loneliness, and I got myself into a state. After so much therapy, both on earth and also here, to get me back to my present state of mind, I can tell you from personal experience that there is a vast difference between being given something by the doctors to keep body and soul together and taking something to deliberately keep you in a different frame of mind, which is what those other drugs do. They erode the mind and, in consequence, the body. From what I have heard, particularly since I have come here, doctors on earth often give sedatives and pep pills much too easily to their patients, and people become dependent upon them far more easily than they had ever realised that they would. In my view, that is the fault of the doctors. They should tell the person to whom they are giving it, the full medical purpose of the pill and that it can become addictive. To my mind, it is the doctor's fault more than the patient's, in many instances, and I imagine that is what happened to you, Judy."

"Well, yes, it did. But I got myself off all the sedatives and the sleeping pills when I had a very severe attack of hepatitis and the doctors told me they thought it had been promoted by those. After that, I was far more cautious for several years, and healthier for not having anything like that. Then I got hauled into a traumatic experience with my television series and my marriage turning sour and court cases and overwork. I was put back onto sedatives and sleeping pills, and I was also put onto a drug called Ritalin, which helped me to keep working longer than I would have otherwise been able to do. I accepted that these were all necessary in order to complete a totally exhausting contract. I did know what I was doing, and I did wonder whether I was putting myself at risk, but I felt I had no alternative. The moment the series ended, I tried to cut down again. Then I nearly died with bronchial pneumonia and pleurisy. This weakened my physical condition so much that, forever after, during any period of intensive hard work or strain, I always had to return to the Ritalin and the sleeping pills and the sedatives. It does become a vicious circle. So, who am I, really, to criticise you and others who have found yourselves in a vicious circle?"

"Judy, dear, it is very sweet of you to say that to me. I do appreciate it. I appreciate the way you are trying to see my viewpoint as well as your own. I can only say to you that, possibly there is only a thin line between the two, but there is a very definite difference between them, as I have found. I went through an exceedingly bad time on earth, and I continued to go through an exceedingly bad time here for a long while. What sort of bad time have you had?"

"Well," I said, "I know that I lost a lot of friends in the last few years of my life on earth. I have come to realise most of that was not due to the pills that I was taking but due to my general debility from lack of enough food (because I was not eating), my lack of energy, and the fact that my nervous system had taken so many shocks that it had affected my mental outlook. I wasn't mad, thank God—I don't want to say that—but I sometimes had a distorted outlook, and I didn't always see things clearly. I was never depressive.I used to cry sometimes hysterically, and probably for unwarrantable reasons, but I used to get over it again. I used to feel sad and lonely, but never depressive as such, and, since waking up here I've had no problem, really. Doreen just started showing me round, and I must say it has been fascinating."

"There you are!" said Peggy. "A vast difference, my dear Judy."

"Anyway, you're both over it now," said Doreen. "But I wanted Judy to meet you, Peggy, because I have had to tell her that the world at large on earth is being given a picture of her as a drug addict. That 'thin line' between *medicines* that go under the heading of drugs and the other kind of drugs, such as heroin, cocaine and marijuana, has become so muddled in public minds that, unfortunately, Judy's public image has been damaged and distorted by people presuming that she kept herself going on alcohol and the kind of drugs you have been discussing. I wanted her to hear from you the kind of differences that arise from the two. I also wanted her to know this because we have plans for her for the future where it will help her to have this kind of information. I am grateful to you for being so honest with her."

"It's no good trying to be dishonest in this world," said Peggy with a smile, "and if I've been able to help you, Judy, by telling you about my past problems, I'm only too pleased. I used to feel sorry for you when I saw you at the studios. I could see you were a property and not a person to so many people, and you so much wanted to be seen as a person. You always seemed so pleased just that I stopped to speak to you."

"I was," I said to her. "I would very much have liked to have had you as a friend, but, somehow, it didn't seem to be possible."

"I always felt I would liked to have been your friend," she replied. "Maybe if I had been, I wouldn't have got into the kind of situation that I got into."

"And maybe I wouldn't have got into mine!" I smiled back at her.

At that point, the door opened and a giant of a man walked in. He was well over six feet tall, very broad, with blond hair and a blond beard. He looked like a Viking, I guess.

"This is Darren," said Peggy, introducing us. "And this is Judy Garland. We knew each other slightly at the studios, when we were in our teens."

He smiled at me and shook hands and sat down. "This *is* a surprise. This is the first time we've had a visit from anyone that Peggy knew on earth, especially a famous person. I saw you in *The Wizard of Oz*. Have you been here long?"

"I'm not quite sure how long I've been here," I said to him a little hesitantly. "I came here a good thirty years after *The Wizard of Oz*, but I'm not sure how long I have now been here in earth time."

"About three years, dear," said Doreen helpfully.

"Thank you," I acknowledged.

"The reason I asked that," said Darren, "is because we've completely lost track of time, as such, here. As time doesn't matter here, we tend to drift and drift and drift. I was interested, when I saw you, as to how long we had all been existing here. Peggy and I went through such a bad period when we got here that we're late starters. I don't really know why I even asked you about the length of time, because it doesn't really matter."

"It *will* matter to you," said Doreen. "That is probably why you felt impelled to ask it."

"Will it?" said Darren, in some astonishment.

"Yes, because I get the impression that you and Peggy will eventually be working to help some other people who have come here from earth in the same situation in which you came. You will be supporting each other with your common experiences and affection in helping other people unravel their problems. Then you will have to be concerned, to some extent, with earth time. I think that is why, without realising it, you were already subconsciously trying to work that out in your mind."

Peggy and Darren regarded Doreen in open-mouthed wonder. "We haven't heard anything about that," said Darren.

"You will not for a while," responded Doreen, "because you both still need the rest and respite and pleasure that you are sharing together at the moment, but it is there for you in the future should you wish to volunteer. It is only by keeping you a little bit in touch with earth that you will be able to find within yourselves the kind of attitude you are going to need to come to the right decision as to whether or not you wish to help others in the way that you and Peggy have been helped."

"Yes, I suppose we do owe it. A lot of people spent a lot of time on us. I suppose the least we can do to repay their goodness to us is to help someone else who has been in a similarly unhappy state," said Darren thoughtfully.

He and Peggy had been drawing closer together while he had been saying this. "As long as we don't have to make that decision right now," said Peggy, putting her hand in his.

"No, you will not, dear," said Doreen kindly. "You have got a lot of time ahead of you to relax and see things here before you are going to be asked to do anything like that. Even then, you do not *have* to. It is your decision. It is just that I think you will probably find that you will want to."

Peggy brightened at the thought that there was no immediate decision to be made, and I felt relieved for her.

"I think it is time to leave now," said Doreen.

"Goodbye, Judy dear," said Peggy, impulsively reaching out to me with both hands and putting her cheek against mine. "I am so glad to see you, and I am so glad," she said, looking at me earnestly, "that whatever else you went through in your life—and I can see from looking at you that you've had some very deeply unhappy moments—I am so glad that you never got hooked on my kind of drugs. I respect you for it, because I feel quite sure, that in the position in which you were, it would have been so easy for you to have fallen in the wrong direction, and you didn't. God Bless you."

"God Bless *you*," I said to her. "I wish you every happiness." I smiled at her and at Darren before turning away and walking outside and back to the lake.

Doreen followed in silence. I walked a little way by the lake, turning over in my mind what I had seen and heard. After a while I said to her, "Doreen, I thought it was a little unkind of you to have started pushing them towards helping other people when they've clearly only just got over their own problem."

"I knew that was what you were thinking about me," said Doreen, in her usually quietly kind way.

"I know you're not an unkind person," I immediately assured her, "and that is why I was so surprised when I heard you say that."

"It was necessary, Judy dear. You see, although they seem contented enough in their little cabin, it was, as you could see, somewhat basic. The very fact that they feel the need to have a stove there to give it a homely look, although it is not really necessary, shows that they still have a long way to go in their development before they can begin to approach life here even in the way in which you have already approached it from the first moment you opened your eyes and set foot outside the spirit hospital where you had been sleeping. They have got to be given a push in the right direction. They do not realise it yet, but they will need to help those others in order to find their own way. It was necessary for me to put the thought into their minds because, once it is there, it will start to turn over and over, and, gradually, they will come to realise that helping another person is a positive thing for them to do. Once they have taken that positive step forward to help another who has been through what they have been through, they will be on the road to a more positive life here. Can you understand that?"

"Yes, I think I can. It is just that, when I first heard you say it, I felt so appalled. Peggy had already told us what a terrible time she had been through, and I thought that she had hardly got over it before being pushed into helping someone else who had been in the same state. I saw it as a backward step, not a forward one, but I guess I see what you mean now."

XI

We turned away from the lake and went towards a brightly coloured chalet which looked very much like those I had seen in pictures of the Swiss Alps. There were brightly coloured flowers on the balconies and around the door. Little children of around three or four years of age were playing outside, and, somewhere, someone was yodelling. I looked at Doreen. "I don't believe it!" I said, laughing. "This looks like something straight out of *The Sound of Music!*"

She smiled at me and took me towards a blonde-haired little girl who was playing on the grass with a puppy. The little girl looked up and smiled. "Don't tell me her name is Heidi!" I said. "That would complete it!"

"No, it isn't Heidi, it is Morganny and the puppy's name is Hans," said Doreen.

I sat down on the grass and stroked Hans's sleek, chubby little body. "Hello, Morganny. My name's Judy." She looked at me for a moment with round, solemn eyes and then thrust a ball at me. I found that I was supposed to throw it to her and to the puppy in turns.

"Does she understand English?" I asked Doreen.

"No, and she has not been here long enough to transfer thoughts, Judy, but the fact that you smiled at her and seemed friendly has prepared her to be friendly with you."

"Where are we now? What's happening?" I asked as I continued to throw the ball. I threw it somewhat absentmindedly, but the child was quite happy so long as I kept the ball coming to her and the puppy.

"This is the equivalent of an orphanage in Switzerland," explained Doreen. "It was suddenly destroyed in an avalanche. It was swept away, and the children and their nurses were all killed and they are all here, recovering."

"Good God! How extraordinary!"

"They are all right, but they are slightly dazed by it all. They all seem to be continuing together, as they will do for a while, but they have needed this respite here before they can completely adjust to what has happened to them. Some nuns have moved in with them and are taking care of them, but it is taking a period of time to get them used to their changed circumstances. I am not going to take you inside, as that would disturb everybody at present, but I wanted you to see it and to see this little girl, so that I could explain the situation to you. It is because they have not completely adjusted that you are feeling somewhat on the outside, aren't you?"

"Well, yes, I am. I don't feel I am responding to this little girl in the way I responded to Sally."

"That is the difference. First of all, there is the language difficulty at present, as thought transference has not yet reached them. Also, this little girl is still feeling dazed by it all and so is not responsive. Although Sally came here suddenly, she came on her own. So she turned to you instinctively because she could not find her mother. This child is with the people she had been with before, and so, you see, she is only in a partly transitional state."

"My goodness!" I said to Doreen. "All these different states are very confusing."

"That is why I thought it would be good to show this to you."

Feeling that we were about to leave, I placed the ball down between the little girl and the puppy, put a hand on each of their heads, and left them there, playing together.

XII

As we wended our way along the pathways, we came across a pretty little stream with fishes swimming among the stones and the water plants and flowers. It gave off the merry little musical sounds I had heard during similar previous encounters. We walked alongside the stream until we came to a decrepit, broken-down old water mill. I viewed it in some amazement, as all the buildings I had so far encountered had always looked so bright and beautiful in their various ways, even those that had been somewhat basic. This looked such a wreck and not like something that belonged to this side of life. As we approached it a little old man came out and came towards us. He had the red, weather-beaten complexion of the countryman, with a stubble of beard. He was wearing a battered old hat, leather waistcoat, and well-worn trousers. He touched his forelock and bobbed his head at Doreen. "Hello, Joseph. This is Judy."

He acknowledged me in a similar fashion and said, "Pleased to meet you."

"I'm pleased to meet you," I replied, feeling as confused as usual by one of Doreen's surprise encounters.

"How is your wife, Joseph?" enquired Doreen.

"A bit better, thank you, when I saw her yesterday. She'll be coming along, I reckon, before too much longer. I've been doing things to the inside of the place, and I'll soon be starting to improve the outside and get it back to work. Would you like to come in for a cup of tea?"

"Not this time, thank you, Joseph," replied Doreen. "We are on our way elsewhere. I just thought I would see how you are."

Joseph nodded and bobbed his head to us again before turning and walking back towards his home.

"What was all that about?" I wanted to know. "I have never seen such a battered place here, and he said he saw his wife yesterday, and I seldom know what day it is here!"

"He and his wife did not believe in an afterlife. They lived together in England in this old mill. She was a very narrow-minded, bitter woman, and he was a heavy drinker. He neglected the mill and the house, and she ranted and nagged. They were each to blame for the other's extremes. One night, the whole place caught fire. As neither of them had believed in survival and had each got into such dark attitudes of mind, they did not realise that they had actually left their earth life. Their minds continued to exist close to the earth for very many years of earth time. They saw and heard each other but nobody else, and nobody from here could reach them. They were like that for about fifty years of earth time.

"Basically, he was not an unkind man. He had turned to drink more than he would have done due to her bitter tongue, and she became even more bitter as a result of his drinking. Eventually, we did manage to reach him and to get him to understand and accept that they had both died and were now existing on a different level. He is gradually getting things more clear in his mind, and he is now trying to help us to reach his wife. He has been helped to understand there were faults on both sides, and he is trying to improve. But he has to start with his original home and rebuild from there, as that is as far as he understands. He and his wife had little or no education and few people to give them a wider understanding. They lived a very narrow and basic life. Therefore, any advance they make will be on the level of their original understanding until we can clear away the debris of their past life together."

"I got so confused when I saw such a wreck of a place and then he said he'd seen his wife *yesterday!*"

"That is because that is how he sees it. He probably recalls being with her recently, but not immediately prior to our visit, and so, to him, it seemed like yesterday."

"How terrible to have been hanging around so close to the earth all those years and to not know you have come here!" I exclaimed.

"They did not do any harm to anyone. They were not evil. But, because they had not expected to die at that time nor that they would continue to exist if they did, and because they had such a dark and narrow existence, they could not easily be reached. Some people who come here suddenly with a fixed notion that there is no continuing existence, but who have otherwise extended their minds and lived a reasonably happy and constructive life on earth, are reached far more easily and can be led forward here more easily. But Joseph has, at last, been reached and has made the decision that he intends to improve his home and make a better life for himself. That is a big step forward for him, despite the fifty years it has taken him to take it," said Doreen.

XIII

As we wended our way, discussing the various ways in which people arrive here and all the many difficulties that can arise for some and the ease for others, I began to feel that I had been exceptionally lucky. "Not *exceptionally*, Judy. You arrived a little bit ahead of your time, but unintentionally and not with any great hindrance to your mind, so you were easily helped to rest and to recover. You also have a genuinely friendly and open-minded attitude and a positive approach."

"I'm still not sure about being as positive as you keep telling me I am. I always considered the Jack Kennedy type of person to be positive, and I was not like that. I always had to feel there was someone to whom I could turn for help and support, and I felt lonely without it."

"That was one of your problems, Judy, in some ways. You did always need and expect that kind of support from your husband, and that was very feminine of you. Where you did make some mistakes was in hoping that other gentlemen could be safely approached for advice and support when you were unable to rely on your husband. People such as President Kennedy understood and respected your reasons for turning to them for some friendly support and advice. Unfortunately, others presumed you were approaching them for other reasons and, in consequence, have been damaging your reputation with their grossly untrue insinuations. I am repeating this to you because we shortly hope to arrange for you to speak to Lorna again. She is finding it more and more difficult to complete her own book amidst all these insinuations. She is correctly stating that these make little sense when considered in the context of true events, but she is also now encountering a further complication she had never, ever envisaged at the outset.

"I have already told you that she has been attending lectures and public demonstrations and also reading books on the possibilities of communication between the two worlds of earth and spirit and that she intends to visit a clairvoyant from time to time to try and hear from you. She has been devoting a great deal of time and concentration to completing her book about you as accurately as possible.

"The outcome of all this enquiry and concentration has brought about something which she never expected would, or even could, happen. Her own mind has opened to the thoughts being sent from here, and she can 'hear.' She is not hearing very clearly because, due to not having had any past experience nor any means of learning any proper control, she is hearing anyone and everyone who chooses to approach her. The fact that she has been taking a general interst in the subject has drawn many minds from here towards her. Many of these are people who have stayed closer to earth, and they are telling her that they are you and her mother and various other relatives speaking from here. We are trying to send her some help from the better areas, but the results are only confusing her more.

"Having originally felt that she may have been heading for a nervous breakdown, she has come to realise that she has been receiving some verifiable truths amidst a lot of misinformation. She has, therefore, very sensibly, tried to obtain some help and guidance from some of those she has seen working as professional mediums. Sadly, they have not seen her problem clearly and their advice has been hopelessly muddling.

"Now she is on the brink of trying for better sense elsewhere, but this will take a little longer. In the meantime, she is afraid the contents of the book she is writing about you will be jeopardised by these intruders. She feels she may, possibly, have to delay it for a while, or even abandon it altogether, unless the situation improves. The problem is that some of those who are sending her their thoughts are telling her they are you and they are trying to persuade her to change parts of the manuscript. Fortunately, she is questioning it all, over and over again, and denying that it sounds like you, but she is feeling very unhappy and confused as well as very despondent over the delay all this is causing."

"I can well imagine," I interjected at last. "It must be absolutely terrible for her *and terrifying!* I would have been terrified if such a thing had happened to me. I would have thought that I was going mad! How awful!"

"She is handling it all exceptionally well in the circumstances, but she does need a lot of support to get her through it all. She asks all the time for you to be helped to give her the truth."

"I wish I could!" I replied. "I wish I could."

"We are preparing to help you to do that, but the time is not yet suitable. This is why I want to prepare you for what lies ahead," said Doreen.

We continued to discuss this for a while, this whole, for me, amazing situation, and I suddenly felt Lorna with me. I cannot explain it, but I suddenly felt her presence, and so I said, "Lorna, darling. I am so grateful to you for what you are doing for me. I do so appreciate it!" I felt her coming towards me, and then she was gone and I was left with a feeling of confusion. I turned to tell Doreen, but she was clearly aware of what had happened.

"Doreen, how do you know all about this latest development with poor Lorna when you have been with me all this time?" I asked at last.

"I heard of it a while back, when you were thinking over your visit to Peggy and Darren. It has not come as a complete surprise, because we have known all along that Lorna could be mediumistic. It was simply that this had not previously been obvious to her, and we had been hoping that we could introduce her to all it entails at the right moment and in the right manner. Unfortunately, her intense concentration, as well as the intense concentration of various souls gathering around her, have caused her psychic centres to open up unexpectedly and brought her this further problem. She will overcome it all eventually, I am sure, but it is going to take a while for her to do so."

"I am sure I spoke to her just now," I said. "I can't explain it, but I almost felt her beside me!"

"You were probably both concentrating on each other at that precise moment, and so it happened," said Doreen.

XIV

The path we had been taking broadened out towards a road on the other side of which was a wide path leading towards a very palatial mansion. It had the same iridescent quality of the buildings I had seen in the city, but this seemed to be standing alone in a park and reminded me of the kind of mansions that can still be seen in the state of Virginia, in America. There were wide steps leading up to a spacious verandah or porch, with elegantly tall portals and an elegantly tall front door. The windows were all large, and there was an air of the past about it, so that I could almost visualise a carriage and pair drawing up to the door. But instead of reaching back into the past, I was surprised to see the front door open and a youthful Spencer Tracy descended the steps to greet me.

"Hiya, Judy! It's good to see you!" he exclaimed as he approached me with both hands outstretched to clasp mine. He leaned forward and kissed me on the cheek. After smiling at Doreen, he turned back to me and said, "I was very pleased to hear that you were being brought to see me but also very surprised. How come you are here so soon? I was getting along in years, but even I came here too soon, and I wasn't expecting you!"

As he led us both towards a seat under a tree, I explained my situation to him and recollected he had come here on my birthday, June 10, 1967, two years ahead of my own arrival. "Yes, well, I'd been feeling so very tired for a long time, Judy. It was no great surprise, although I guess I felt cheated. I was no boy, but I hated to admit that I was getting old. I sure think you got a raw deal. I'd heard you were having some problems, but I'm sorry about the pills. You had put up such a good fight over those and were in great shape when we did *Judgment at Nuremburg*. What happened?"

I gave him a brief outline, and he nodded. "It's still tough luck. You deserve better."

I told him a little of what I had been seeing since I arrived and that I'd met Jack Kennedy and also Clark and Carole.

"Yes, I'd heard those two are together. It must be a good feeling—to find someone again when you've lost them. I guess I'll be glad to see Kath again. She's quite a gal. I miss her."

I knew he must be referring to Katherine Hepburn, but I felt, somehow, that it would not be appropriate for me to make any comment. His eyes had changed as he spoke, as though he felt something very deeply but preferred not to say anything more on the subject.

"What d'ya think of this place?" he suddenly asked me, turning towards the house.

"It's big." I smiled at him.

"Yes, well, I always did have extravagant tastes, and I thought I'd like to try something like this. I always wondered what it would be like to live in one of these places! Come and have a look at it."

He led us inside. I was surprised to find that, although it had numerous rooms and was beautifully proportioned and was also very light inside, only two of the rooms were furnished. Spence must have realised my amazement because he turned and smiled that roguish, little-boy smile he had at times. "I guess that when I'd got it, I ran out of ideas. It seemed a bit silly to use all the rooms, so I really only use these two."

I began to realise there was a feeling of emptiness and loneliness about the house, as though it was not really a home.

"You're right, Judy. I'm not happy here, really. It was something I thought I'd like to try, but it isn't working. I'll be changing my ideas soon. What sort of place have you got?"

"Well, I haven't got anything yet," I told him. "I've been touring around with Doreen, and there doesn't seem to have been any reason for thinking about it. But, of course, I was without a place of my own on earth for so long that I guess this isn't new!"

"You'll have a place of your own here, Judy, I do assure you," interrupted Doreen. "It is just not yet the right time for such a decision in your case."

"What about concerts?" asked Spencer.

"I'm told I'm going to sing again here, but I've not got around to it yet. In fact, I'm not sure what to sing."

"You've got to do 'A Couple of Swells.' I insist." He smiled at me. "I'll even be the other hobo if you'll do it."

"I might just take you up on that!" I laughed.

"Done! I always wanted to play it!" replied Spencer. That is how it came about that, when I did eventually perform again here, my very first duet was "A Couple of Swells" with Spencer Tracy as my partner!

After some more conversation, Spence accompanied us to the road and waved us off. "See you again, Judy—and don't forget our concert!"

"It's a date!" I called back.

As we walked away, I explained to Doreen how much I had always admired Spence as an actor and that I had been especially pleased to have a part in *Judgment at Nuremburg* when I realised he was to have the leading role. "It was fantastic to see him work."

"He seems to have admired you in it, too, Judy," said Doreen smilingly.

"Just two hams admiring each other!" I laughed back to her.

By this time, to my surprise, I found we were back on the shore and looking across the waves to the distant light on the horizon.

XV

"I now have to tell you, Judy, that Lorna is being encouraged, by certain mediums on earth who should have more sense, to listen to what is being told to her from here and to write it all down. The effect this is having in her currently confused state of reception is that she is attracting more and more people around her from this side of life who are in no way connected with her and who have not reached the better regions that you and I are in. Some people from our part of this world have been trying to give Lorna some of the clarification that she needs for the book that she is writing, because other have tried to bring in conflicting aspects that she feels are completely incorrect. Her faith in what she is writing has begun to be shaken because people claiming to be you are telling her it is wrong and are giving her different versions. We, in our turn, have been trying to confirm the right version. Because she is so inexperienced at receiving messages from here, it is all coming through to her in a jumble, and she is utterly confused. Because she knew you personally, it would be possible for you to reach Lorna in such a way as to give her the conviction that it is you. If you concentrate extremely hard at a time when she is also concentrating, you can reach her and she will be able to feel your presence. She may even see you in her mind and also get the impression of your personality and so be able to decide that it has to be you and that it has to be right.

"We are going to have our friends back shortly, those who previously helped you project to the medium, but this time you are going to project your thoughts directly to Lorna. What you have to do is to think of Lorna very hard and very long, with deep concentration, and keep sending the thought *This is Judy, this is Judy* until you feel her response. Then you can talk to her. In order to do that, you must have what you want to say to her clearly in your mind."

Doreen and I discussed this for some time before our friends arrived and gathered around me. With their power to help me, I concentrated on the pinpoint of sparkling light that I could see on the horizon and on Lorna.

After a surprisingly brief period of time I felt her answering response, but, at the same time, she was holding back. I continued with my concentration, and, to my astonishment, I was able to see and to feel that I was with Lorna at her daily place of work in an office. I began to realise that I had approached her in the middle of a hectic part of her day at work. Although she was acknowledging me and was delighted to hear from me, it was difficult for us to converse, but it was quite clear that I had reached her. When someone approached her to discuss a client and the client's name was *Garland*, we both felt convulsed with laughter while she struggled to remain serious and attentive to her colleague. She was frantically sending me the thought: "It's great to hear from you, Judy, but I can't really stop and talk now." In the end, I said to her, "I'll come back later." I stopped concentrating on her, and, as my concentration lessened, I felt her presence going away from me.

I stared at Doreen in amazement. "That seemed so easy! I felt that I was with Lorna in her office, and she said to me, 'It's great to hear from you, Judy, but I can't speak now.' It seemed as though we were almost together!"

"That is how it can be between two people, once the link has been forged," explained Doreen. "She has been thinking about you; you have been thinking about her. The fact that her psychic centres have now opened means that you can reach her quite easily with some concentration. Where the difficulty arises is that, because her psychic centres have opened, almost anyone can communicate with her. Because many of those others who are trying to communicate with her are closer to the earth than you are, it is still possible that, while you are talking to her, someone else could cut across the communication and alter it. What we now have to do is to try and get Lorna to control the situation so that this interference cannot so easily happen. But that was a very good beginning, and we shall have to persevere as much as we

258

can to help Lorna get through this very difficult phase of her psychic develpment and to get her onto a clearer pathway. It is unfortunate that we chose a moment when she was busy elsewhere. The next thing we must try and do is to see whether we can reach her at a less busy time. It has to be trial and error for a while, but you made a very good beginning."

What had impressed me the most was the way Lorna had acknowledged my effort almost immediately, accepted who I was, and had tried to explain to me why she could not talk at that moment and how sorry she was that she could not talk to me then. I had been made to feel extremely welcome, and it was a good feeling.

Doreen said to me, "I think we will have to keep ourselves free from any other form of occupation for a while so that, as soon as I get the information of a time that is likely to be more suitable, we will try again to reach Lorna."

For a while, that is precisely what we did do. Whenever the time was right, or seemed right, I concentrated on Lorna and managed to reach her mind. We had a number of interesting and illuminating conversations. She was able to tell me the problems she had been encountering in trying to complete the book and all the confusions that had been arising from all the other spirit people talking to her. She told me how she had tried, without any success so far, to get it all sorted out and how the confusion had been delaying the book. But, apart from this, we were able to have friendly discussions concerning each other and I began to look forward very much to those moments of conversation with someone who was still living on the world or earth.

The thing that I appreciated the most happened when, at one point, I said that I hoped I was not intruding on her life too much by suddenly turning up unexpectedly and mentioned that, if it was not convenient for her to talk to me, she should say so. She replied that it would never, ever be inconvenient for her if I tried to speak to her. It was only that, if she happened to be talking to someone else on earth, she could not always respond to me as well as she would like to be able to do. But any time at all that I chose to visit her I would always be welcome. I knew from the way that she said this to me that she was speaking to me as one human being to another, that she liked me for myself and not just because I happened to have had a famous name. This was something that had brought me many problems on earth—not knowing whether or not I was liked for myself or only as a famous name. Lorna clearly liked me for myself and was also clearly relieved to know that I was still around somewhere and still talking in the way I used to do, which I still found it easy to do then. It became less easy after I had been here longer, but that is another story and came much later. During these visits together and our various conversations, neither of us actually left the spot where each of us had our individual existences, yet we heard each other and felt each other's presence very clearly. In between these visits, Lorna was continuing her full-time office job, and I was having long discussions with Doreen.

XVI

It was during these discussions that I began to think of where I was now going in my present world. I knew I had more experiencing ahead of me and many more explanations, but I did begin to wonder where my life was leading me. It was true that there had been little time previously to stop and consider where I was going or what I would be doing, but I was concerned that I would not continue to drift before finding some place that was home. Yet, what sort of home would this be and who would be in it with me? I discussed all this with Doreen, and she explained to me that it was necessary for me to see the whole of my earth life clearly and get my personal feelings into their proper perspective before I could decide what sort of home I wanted to have here, what sort of work, if any, I wanted to undertake, and where I wished to look for my friends.

"Some people, Judy, come to those decisions much sooner than others. Let us go back to your friend, Spencer Tracy. He arrived here after a comparatively lengthy time on earth, not as you have done in your middle years. He had had a certain life pattern that had not been really disturbed. He had been going along in a certain direction on earth, so that when he came here, he kept going in a positive direction. The one thing he is aware of is that he does not have any one special person here as a companion. He has no particular ambitions to fulfil here at the moment. So he is letting himself take it all slowly and quietly.

260

His little experiment with the mansion is obviously about to change, and with his change of home there will be a change of attitude and a change of direction.

"You came here after an extremely disturbed life pattern in many ways, and you are also a highly sensitive person. You have needed careful handling and careful steering all the way. You are now facing the additional complicaton of being told by me of the way your name and memory are being mishandled on earth and of the one person who is doing all she can to try and improve that situation. It is clearly not the right moment to be able to settle down anywhere."

"You are right," I agreed ruefully. "It is just that I am beginning to wonder whether I ever will be able to settle anywhere."

"Yes, you will, dear. I do assure you," Doreen replied firmly. "It is simply that there is a long way to go yet before you are out of the woods in a number of ways. It will not be an unpleasant time for you here, but it will continue to be unsettling until we have got a lot of aspects cleared up. There is a lot of interest lying ahead, but one thing at a time is necessary. One of the things to be borne in mind is that, in order to keep you fairly easily available to communicate with Lorna during this exceedingly difficult period for her, we cannot afford to get you too deeply involved in whatever else is happening in this world."

"I do agree it is essential to give Lorna as much support as possible," I agreed. "And I am enjoying talking to her, I really am, and she seems to enjoy talking to me."

"I have been telling you all along, Judy, that you two have a natural rapport, far more than either of you ever realised when you were together from time to time on earth. You liked each other before either of you had the opportunity of discussing some of the things you have now been discussing together."

"That's true," I said, "but how is it that, when one reaches someone through a medium, with all that effort, only the odd bit gets through, yet I have long conversations with Lorna?"

"That is because you have got the advantage of talking to someone you knew on earth. The link is already firmly established. All you have to do is to tap into it. It does make it easier for communication in that way, provided the person on earth is a medium. Fortunately for you, if not for Lorna at the moment, that is what she is. It took certain circumstances to bring that medium-ship to the fore, but it does have to be refined and controlled and extended in the proper manner and not in the way in which it is being handled at the moment. Lorna has tried to establish, through several mediums, the best way of handling this situation, and none of them has given her the correct advice. This she is still seeking, and we are hoping that, before too much longer, she will find it."

During my conversations with Lorna, I had mentioned to her that I had found my meetings with my father and sister to be very disappointing and that I really had no wish to meet my own mother as she seemed to have been particularly hard on my father as well as on me. Lorna had asked me, "So, who *are* you with, Judy?"

I replied, "I'm not especially with anybody. I'm being helped by some very kind people but I don't feel I've got anyone here that I can call my own." It was clear from Lorna's reaction to that statement that she understood how much I needed to feel that I had someone from whom I could receive some personal friendship rather than simply some kindness. It was at this point that she suggested to me that I might try and find her own mother. She told me that her mother had had several nervous breakdowns and that she had also had trouble eating enough, just as I had done at the end of my own life. As a result, her mother had become exceedingly weak and confused and had also come here unexpectedly as far as the doctors were concerned. She told me that her mother had always liked me as a performer and that they had often discussed me sympathetically when I left Metro-Goldwyn-Mayer accompanied by a gale of unfortunate publicity. Her mother had passed here in 1954, without ever seeing me perform on a stage and several years before Lorna and I had first met in 1957.

"But," she said to me, "I am sure my mother is the right kind of person for you to talk to. She would sympathise with you and understand you and be very pleased to see you, Judy, and she has a sense of humour that you will like."

Shortly after Lorna told me this, Doreen informed me that it had been decided that I should no longer communicate with Lorna until after she had completed the book and it had been published.

"The reason we are telling you this, Judy, is because, despite the fact that you are now reaching each other very clearly and I know that you are both enjoying the conversations, it has not in any way helped to improve the situation with regard to those others who are talking to Lorna. They talk to her day and night, and she is now faced with the fact that the publishers want her not only to reduce the manuscript considerably in length but also to avoid any public criticism of any individual who is still alive on earth. It is difficult enough for Lorna to accept that pill and to reduce the book in the way she is being asked to do without also having to decide who is telling the truth or not. Provided we can say to her, 'At no time at all will Judy be speaking to you until after the book is published,' she will know that anyone else who is trying to speak to her is not the right person. That will, at least, give her the freedom to ignore everyone and concentrate solely on finishing the book in the way the publishers have asked her to. We will be explaining this to her, and we are asking you to stay right away from her for the time being. You will be able to return to her later on, after the book is published."

I accepted what Doreen told me without a murmur. I realised that Lorna and I had been exceedingly privileged to have been able to have so much time together, considering we were living in two different worlds. I also did not want to do anything to add to the problems that she had already got, so I willingly agreed to Doreen's suggestion. It was only after we had left that place and the question arose as to where I would now be going that I began to feel extremely unhappy. I felt I really had lost an exceedingly good friend and companion. I had looked forward so much to our conversations, as I knew Lorna had also done, and we had both got a great kick out of them and a lot of laughter. I suddenly felt there was a void. To the void of lacking my children and my husband, was now added the void of not being able to speak to Lorna.

"Why don't you," said Doreen, "do what Lorna suggested? We will try and arrange a visit to meet her mother."

That seemed a good idea, but I felt a little hesitant as to how I would approach this unknown lady out of the blue and say, "Hello. I'm Judy Garland, and I know your daughter!" But, strangely enough, that is precisely how it happened.

XVII

Doreen told me that it could be some while before a meeting with Lorna's mother might be arranged, as many efforts needed to be made in order to find someone who I had not known on earth and who had been largely unaware of me and certainly not expecting to hear from me. So it was suggested that we spend part of the waiting period trying to complete the experience I had yet to perfect, that of not letting my thoughts and emotions reach others around me unless I specifically wished them to do so. Doreen explained that I had already come a long way towards achieving this, but, when she would no longer be with me all the time to help and prompt me, I would need to be able to do this altogether by myself. We worked on this for a while, and then I began wondering whether Doreen was preparing to leave me.

"Not completely, but you will be needing to experience things for yourself and make more decisions and also decide what areas of activity you wish to explore. Although I shall be available to discuss anything with you, should you have any problems, it is better that you begin to make more choices and decisions of your own. There will be many more people for you to meet, and I would expect you will wish to meet your own mother eventually."

"I have thought about it, but I don't think I'm ready for it yet," I said. "She seems to have treated my father badly. I still feel she was unkind to me, and even Susan does not seem to be that fond of her. I think I'd rather leave it for now."

"Since you still feel like that, I agree. It is no good you and your mother trying to meet until you both have a wish to do so. In the meantime, you seem to be going to meet a kindly and sensitive lady with a sense of humour, if Lorna is a good judge of her mother."

"That is how she spoke of her to me, and she said she thought we'd get along well. I'm really looking forward to meeting her, although I still feel a little bit foolish at approaching her like this!"

It was then that I found myself wondering more and more about my future here and where I would be going, whether with or without Doreen.

"It is necessary for you to see how one thing may lead to another, Judy," Doreen explained. "You will probably be seeing a different area and meeting other people as a result of meeting

Lorna's mother. You will also be pursuing your music and meeting people through that, and each experience will lead to another."

"My mind does still keep returning to singing," I admitted. "When I was on earth, I always loved to sing, apart from getting paid to do so. It was only in my last years that I lost the wish to do so, because of the way I was feeling and the way everyone else seemed to be reacting. I'm beginning to feel that I very much want to sing again here, for the sheer pleasure of singing and for the pleasure I hope it will give others."

While we had been talking I had found that we were again entering the city. Before long, we were approaching a little house that reminded me of the Japanese houses I had seen in paintings. As we approached the door, it opened and we were greeted by a pretty little Japanese girl who looked like Madame Butterfly! She had the same elegantly combed black hair and the brightly embroidered kimono, as well as the spirit colours emanating around her. She bobbed a little curtsey at us and smilingly invited us to enter.

Doreen explained to me that this young girl had been a part of a singing and dancing group, that she had been carefully groomed and trained to perform this art in a completely pure way, and that her life had been a very narrow one. Now, she was learning to live her own life in her own little home but still using the art of singing that she had learned on earth, and she would be able to show me how to project my singing here.

Although I had no knowledge of Japanese and she knew no American, we got along surprisingly well. I began to realise that the main art is to convey the intent behind the words and to convey that through the music rather than through the actual words. Although I found the Japanese style of music strange, I was well able to understand what she was conveying.

I recollected that, when singing on earth, it was not unknown for performers to forget the lyrics of a song they knew very well. I would sometimes forget the lyrics of a song I had been singing for twenty years! Then I would try and fill in some words to fit the music. How, I wondered, was I going to find thoughts of actions and intentions to fit the music? Then I thought of "A Couple of Swells," which Spence had urged me to perform, and I thought, *How ever do I convey that?*

I turned to Doreen and explained my problem. "I always had great fun singing this number, and it was always a great favourite, but how can I go on stage here, wearing a tramp outfit, a fright wig, gappy teeth, and a dirty face?"

"Remember, Judy, that your friend wanted you to sing it. There will be very many other people here who will remember you singing it and also many others of the same period of time on earth who will be able to understand it and enjoy it. You will be performing it for them. When you have been here longer and had many more extending experiences, you will be able to perform the kind of songs that encompass that element of experience and will please others of similar experience. At present, you will perform for those of similar experience to your own. There will be many composers here who will be able to provide you with suitable melodies for the thoughts you wish to convey."

Reassured, I turned back to my new Japanese friend and managed to convey my problem. Amidst a lot of laughing, we worked our way through some strange approaches to my song until we felt we had made some headway.

I don't know how long we were together before Doreen returned to tell me that Lorna's mother had been found and, although exceedingly astonished to learn that I wished to see her, would be most pleased to meet me.

I took my leave of my new friend and set out to meet someone who turned out to be exactly as Lorna had described her to me—a most kind and sensitive lady who had, indeed, seen some sad times of her own and who sympathised and understood why I had shared similar experiences. We were to become staunch friends, and, before long, we had established a completely friendly rapport which led her to invite me to stay for a while and to meet other members of the family who were in close and regular touch with each other.

XVIII

"Lorna's family are nearly all here, now," her mother, whose name is Lilian, told me. "There is really only her father and one aunt, my sister, left on earth, apart from a few cousins. None of us here realised that Lorna could receive any communciation from

266

us. In fact, I always felt that such things were better left alone."

I gave her the general situation, as it had been explained to me, and she was very concerned. I told her that I had been speaking to Lorna most easily, but there were so many others causing interference that I had now been asked to remain away for a while. "But I do intend to try and speak to her again, as soon as I am allowed to try, and I am sure she will be pleased to hear from you," I told Lilian.

"I'm so pleased she still thinks so well of me," she replied. "I was such a misery for years, with all my troubles and illnesses. I wonder that either she or her father put up with me so well."

"She told me she always realised you were not behaving like your true self of years before and therefore did not blame you, and that is why she did not blame me, either," I told Lilian.

That paved the way for our exchanging many of our personal experiences and hurts and discussing why we felt the way we did. Before long, we had put all our past woes behind us and were simply enjoying each other's company. She told me a lot about Lorna as a child and how I had always been a part of their lives since they both first saw me in a picture I made in 1938. I told her about my own children and all that they had meant to me.

"I was blessed with a very good husband," said Lilian, "because he always remained steadfast and loyal to me throughout the whole of my life, but I would not blame him if he had got fed up and left me, because I got so depressed."

"I seldom stayed depressed, but I used to get angry easily and then I'd get confused and blame someone else for the confusion I had caused." I laughed. "But I still feel some people could have waited around a little longer to find out where we had got confused. At least your Lorna always waited until the next time we met, and we usually stayed friends," I said.

"Lorna was always very loyal if she liked someone very much. And God help anyone else who said anything against them. But she only chose to be as close as that to a few, and she was very sparing in her speech, even to those she liked," said Lilian.

"Yes, I found that out," I replied. "But she always did stay with me when others left me alone, and we've recently agreed there is something to be said for being silently loyal in preference to those others who fell all over me one moment and then lied about me the next."

By the time we had exhausted all that we found to say during our initial meeting and I had agreed to stay for a while, Doreen had decided to leave me for the time being. I was to send out a strong thought for her when I felt I needed her.

Lilian's home was a small but exceedingly well-kept little house. It had a generally well-cared-for atmosphere, as though all the items of furniture and ornament had been carefully chosen. There were a few comfortable chairs and a table. The doors from the main room led out into a well-kept garden that had a pink brick wall around it and roses climbing in profusion over the walls.

"My sister, Nell, was the gardener in the family when we were on earth, but I've taken to it here and really enjoy encouraging everything to grow. Of course, it is always so rewarding here. If you love what you are tending, the plants and flowers respond to you. One of my few attempts on earth was frustrated by Lorna's tortoise biting off and eating the new shoots." She laughed.

"Lorna's still got that tortoise. Her father's looking after it," I told Lilian. "She told me she has had it at least forty years!" I exclaimed.

"Her father used to call it a few choice names when it ate all the best plants, but he's a good-hearted man, and he would never have hurt it. Does her father know she has been speaking to you?" Lilian wanted to know.

"I don't think so. She has told him she has been taking an interest in the subject, but she is still too confused about all that is happening to her psychically and she doesn't want to worry him, so she hasn't told him everything."

"I'm very worried about her," said Lilian. "I wish we could do something to stop it."

"I'm not sure she wants to actually stop it. I think she would simply like to get it under better control. We thoroughly enjoyed being able to talk to each other, and we also straightened out one or two misunderstandings. It is a wonderful thing to be able to do, provided it can be handled properly, and I am told she will handle it properly eventually and be able to do a lot of good with it."

"I hope you are right," said Lilian, and we let the subject drop for a while so that she could take me to meet some of the family.

The time I spent with Lilian, meeting various members of the family, was a very happy one for me. For the first time since my arrival, I truly began to feel part of the world in which I was now living, being accepted by others simply for the person that I was and am. Doreen, of course, had always treated me like that, but I had always been aware of the fact that she was my official helper. Others that I had met were people whom I had never met before and had been taken to meet simply because it was part of my adjustment to a new life, in order to see different aspects of existence here. This had even included some of those people that I had known as a performer. Even Clark Gable and Spencer Tracy were not people that I had known really well as personal friends, but simply as people in my profession.

Here, I was being accepted in an ordinary, friendly manner by people who had led ordinary lives far removed from show business. Although Lilian remembered me as a child performer on the screen and had apparently later enjoyed my "Couple of Swells" number when she saw it in the film *Easter Parade* just as much as had my subsequent concert audiences, she still told me, nevertheless, that she had always felt for me as a human being and not just because I was a famous name. She said that she knew her daughter, Lorna, had always felt about me in the same way. When she took me to meet other members of the family, a few of them also remembered me as a child performer, but none of them had been so enraptured by show business that they had in any way put me on a pedestal as, I regret to say, some people on earth had done, only to try and pull me off that pedestal at a later date. Lilian's family all treated me as though I really was the girl next door and I revelled in their friendly companionship. None of them asked me any questions about myself, but if I volunteered an anecdote, they always greeted it with friendly interest and often laughter.

I soon learned who they were and how they fitted into the pattern of Lilian's existence. She told me that she had always been on friendly terms with all the members of her own family and her husband's family, and that they all intermingled here on a regular social, friendly basis. They each have their own individual interests that they follow, but they enjoy the same kind of background and are always happy to meet together, just as they had always been pleased to do when on earth. "It is much easier here," said Lilian. "On earth, we always felt we would have liked to have been able to meet each other more than most of us were able to do, because there was always the problem of the journies that were involved in order to meet each other, but here we can get together whenever we like—and we do. I see a lot of my sister and brothers and my parents, and I also see a lot of my husband's parents and brother and sister and my sisters-in-law. We all get on so well together, sometimes even better than when on earth, when we did sometimes find differences creeping into our attitudes. Here, of course, we tend to have a wider understanding of each other, so we all get along exceedingly well."

It was because I was accepted into this happy group of people, as though I was one of them, that I at last began to feel as though I belonged. I told this to Lilian and said, "It must seem very presumptuous on my part to say that I do, at long last, feel that I belong with a group of people, but that is how everyone has made me feel."

She told me that it was something of a surprise to her to realise how well I had fitted in. "Because," she went on to explain, "although Lorna and I had always liked you very much as a personality on the screen, one has to bear in mind that you have come from a completely different environment to any of us. Without meaning this in any way to be a derogatory comment, I would have automatically assumed that your interests and feelings and attitudes would be very different to ours, but I am surprised how well you seem to adapt to our way of existence here."

"I suppose it is because, in some respects, I always found myself having to adapt to those around me rather than having others adapt to me," I replied. "Looking back on my life, I did enjoy being a performer in many ways. I loved my work, and I loved my children, but I would have loved to have had a family around me in addition to my children, and this never seemed to be. It was something I always wanted to have and never did. Although I had my problems with my career at times, and I do now accept that I sometimes may have been difficult to work with, I still wished to have a normal home and family background. I didn't wish to have an extravagant life-style, and I didn't want always to be regarded as 'Judy Garland'. I wanted to be treated, in some ways, as though I was still 'Frances Gumm,' despite it being such a terrible name." I laughed. "But, somehow, I was never able to achieve the two. I was always 'Judy Garland,' and I was always a public 'thing.' I was put on a pedestal one moment and knocked down to the depths in another, simply because I did not always manage to live up to my public image—an image that people created around me in their own minds.

"Here, I feel I am allowed to be an ordinary, normal human being. The only way I feel I do still differ is that all of you seem to be very contented people and to just go along happily with whatever you are doing. I still feel somewhat restless and feel that I ought to be doing more than I am. I begin to feel that I should be trying to go back to help those poor children and the animals who arrive here in such a poor state, and I also feel I want to do something positive about singing again."

Lilian was very sympathetic and understanding about this restlessness within me. "I think you have to bear in mind, Judy, that you have not been here as long as the rest of us have been. All of us have been here much longer than you, and some longer than others. We also come from the kind of life where we didn't do anything spectacular. You obviously have this talent to do something that is particularly uplifting for people. I always felt uplifted seeing you on the screen, and Lorna told me that you were a far more exciting performer on the stage than on the screen. You must have had a very special talent to be able to produce those feelings within people. I can understand that, if you've got it in you, you need to use it, otherwise you are going to feel very confined and frustrated here.

"As for helping the children and the animals, you've made me feel suddenly guilty that I haven't been doing anything much in that way. I have been contented to stay in my little home and garden and be with my family and my friends who have come here. I have been so happy and contented to be with everybody again, to feel so well after many years of ill-health and sadness on earth, and to be able to be with everybody whenever I feel like it, that I confess I haven't really thought of doing anything else."

"I hope you don't think I am trying to stir anything up," I said to her, feeling guilty myself.

"Not at all, my dear. In fact, the shoe is on the other foot. I suddenly feel guilty that I have been a bit too contented in my background here when I might possibly have been doing something a little more constructive."

"I've been thinking about going back to the children and also some of the animals," I said to her. "Why don't you come with me?"

"I'll have to think about that. I've got a little dog here that I have not yet introduced to you, as well as a cat. They are here, and I have been talking to them, but I have not previously thought to introduce you to them because I had not realised, until you just mentioned it, that you are interested in animals."

"I never knew much about animals until I came here and Doreen took me round the Animal Kingdom. I was so fascinated by it all that, apparently, she took me further round than a lot of people get taken. It is fascinating to find how we can communicate with them, but I was appalled at the condition of some of the poor creatures, and I learned that human beings here help them to recover. I would like to be able to help them in some way, as well as to help some of the children." I told her of some of my experiences.

"I will think about it," said Lilian, "although I won't make any decision at the moment. But do come and meet our own little family menagerie. My little dog, Laddie, was actually Lorna's dog, but I call him my dog because he was the family dog. My cat, Fluff, came here before Lorna was born. They live together here in a little group with all the other dogs and cats that shared their lives with the rest of the family on earth. We contact each other whenever we feel like it. We are not together all of the time because the animals are just as much entitled to their own lives and their own wishes about things as we are. I would not want to go a long way away to do something else for a while without discussing it with my two pals and letting them know what I am going to do, so that they would not worry about not hearing from me."

With that she took me to a little area where there were a number of dogs playing together. Amongst them was a little black dog. Lilian told me he was a Scottish Terrier and that he was named Laddie. She introduced me to Laddie as "This is a friend of Lorna's." His eyes immediately sparkled at me, his tail wagged, and he woofed at me, as if to say, "I'm pleased to see you if you know Lorna." Then a large, tawny dog with a long tail and of very mixed ancestry joined us. He put his head on my lap. "Oh! This is Chum," said Lilian. "He's the softie in the family. He always was, and he doesn't like to feel overlooked. He was my sister's dog, but he and Lorna were great friends when she was a little girl, and we both missed him when he came here." I put my hand on the friendly head, and I almost felt him smiling at me.

"Laddie came here after having cancer. He came here four years before I did," said Lilian. "We had to make the terrible decision whether we would keep him with us, with the possibility of him suffering pain, or whether we should help him to be released from his earth life. Lorna was away at the time. When she went away, she had been very concerned about him, and I had asked her if, should it come to it while she was away, I would have her permission to do something about Laddie? It was with the greatest reluctance that she agreed that I should. It tore me apart emotionally when I had the vet visit him and she said that he was in such a bad state internally that the kindest thing would be to release him. I worried for months afterwards if I had done the correct thing. It was a closed subject. But each of us felt we had lost a dear friend.

"As I became more and more ill and depressed, I seemed to think more and more of this little chap, although I never mentioned him to Lorna or her father. You can imagine the joy I felt when I woke up here, and, there sitting next to my bed in the hospital, was Laddie on one side and my little cat, Fluff, on the other. They had been brought along by my parents to greet me as I woke up. I thought at first that I was dreaming, when I saw all four of them sitting there, but it meant everything in the world to me to know that I had woken up in a new world with people that I loved around me, including my pets.

"It did not take me long to shake off all the depression and the physical debility that I had had on earth and to become absorbed in my loving family. When my sister Nell came here after what would have been two more years of earth time, I really felt as though everything was back to normal. We had always got on well together as sisters. We were sad we had left our third sister and our brother still on earth at that time, but we were so happy to be together again, and we knew that, one day, we could look forward to seeing the others, including my husband and my daughter. After nearly twenty-five years of widowhood, Nell was reunited with her husband, Charlie, who had been drowned at sea only two years after their marriage. They are still close companions, as they like the same things."

"That's how I feel now," I said, "at the thought that I shall see my three children again eventually. I have, however, been warned that, although we shall always love each other, they will be different when they come here, as they will have had many experiences since I left them and these will change them to some degree. I don't seem to have the same rapport with my own sister and father and certainly not with my own mother," I said to Lilian, and I began to tell her some of the things that had been worrying me.

"I can understand how you feel, my dear," said Lilian, "but if I may venture to make a suggestion, I think it would be as well to try and see your mother again. You never know—if you can get through to her to explain how confused you have been and how confused Susan is as well as your father, you may get a better understanding. If you like, I will even come with you to give you a bit of support. If I could explain how we all are as a family, having come together here, perhaps it will help you to establish a better and happier relationship with your own family."

"That's very sweet of you," I acknowledged, "and I really do appreciate your offer, but Doreen has already told me that it is unlikely we shall ever be a close-knit family unit, as we are all so different from each other. But I think I take your point, and I should try and see Mother before much longer. At least it will be something to have made the effort and see whether or not Doreen is correct. She is, usually!"

XIX

Shortly after I discussed my family situation with Lilian, Doreen came back to see me.

"Lorna is about to visit a well-known medium," said Doreen, "in an attempt to get her various confusions sorted out. She has completed the book as far as she can, and she now has to wait to see when they are going to publish it. She feels the time is now right to try and get more sensible help than she has so far managed to do. I think it will be a good idea if you and Lilian come with me to try and reach her through this medium."

I was delighted to be given the opportunity to communicate with Lorna again, even if I had to do so indirectly. So was Lilian, although she was still a little doubtful as to whether this was something she ought to be doing.

"Please do," I urged her. "Lorna's in such a difficult situation. She can hear so many different people, anyway. Your staying away won't make it any better. In fact, it might make it worse if she feels that she isn't hearing from you at all, although she is hearing from everyone else!"

Eventually, Lilian made up her mind that it would not be such a bad thing to do after all, and she agreed to come with us. Ironically, after all her doubts as to whether or not she should attempt such a thing, much as she loved Lorna and much as she wished to be able to speak to her, when it came to the point of meeting, she was put forward to speak first, and the medium managed to convey her personality and her message to Lorna very clearly. It was only when Lorna tried to explain to the medium that one of the reasons she had come along for help was because she had been receiving voices and she wished to get the confusion sorted out that the medium went along a completely wrong pathway. When Lorna tried to tell her that she thought she had been hearing from a friend who was now in the Spirit World, the medium told her that it was all in her imagination and that she was not hearing from the Spirit visitors at all. Lorna did not name me, but she and I both knew to whom she was referring. We were equally devastated when we heard the medium saying, categorically, that Lorna could not possibly have been hearing from me and that it was all in her imagination. Lorna's emotions flared up, as did mine, and we both dissolved into tears. Doreen and Lilian were trying to console me. Poor Lorna had nobody to console her.

Eventually, she calmed down sufficiently to be able to tell the medium certain things known only to the medium about herself. She told the medium that she was getting this information from a London cockney in the Spirit World who was giving her his name. At his juncture, the medium had to admit that this man

275

was among those who helped her with her clairvoyance and that the information that Lorna was now relating to her was completely correct. This caused her to backtrack on her original, hasty assumption. She told Lorna that this showed her that Lorna must be receiving certain information from the other side. "But," she said, "it is all jumbled up with your subconscious, and you have got to get it sorted out." She then went on to tell Lorna that she did not have the time or the opportunity to help her but that Lorna should try another medium who might be able to do so.

By this time Lorna's faith in a number of mediums that she had seen working well at public demonstrations of mediumship was beginning to be largely demolished. Each time she had turned to one of them for help, she had ended in a worse situation than before. This time she had faced someone who had presumed too much and who had demolished what little faith she had got left by telling her that she could not possibly be communicating herself with a Spirit friend. It was after this shattering experience that Lorna decided to leave everything alone for a while before taking her enquiries any further.

I came away from that meeting, which I had gone to with such joy, with a feeling of complete depression and disillusionment, after having told Lilian what a beautiful experience it could be. Poor Lilian ended up in a far more worried frame of mind than she had been at the outset. "My poor Lorna! My poor girl! What are we going to do about it? We can't leave her in this state!"

"It is because of all this confusion that she hasn't told her father," I said to Lilian. "She doesn't want him to feel worried."

"He would be enormously worried," said Lilian, "but I feel so concerned for her that she cannot seem to find anyone to help her. That is why I always said it was a subject that should be left alone. We shouldn't try and dabble. It is foolishness to try and communicate between the two worlds. I always said I thought it was possible but that we should not try and dabble."

"Well, she's not dabbling," I explained. "It just came upon her. She told me that she feels she has got no alternative but to continue to try and go forward. She can't just sit and let it all happen around her. She had got to find a means of controlling it so that, when she has got it under control, it will be better for her. She would then try and use it more positively to help other

276

people. She feels it is better to try and develop correctly, now that she has found she has the beginnings of clairvoyance and clairaudience, than just to leave it in the muddle that it is to her at the moment. She really has little choice," I said to Lilian. "She can't go back because the door is already open, so she now has to try and learn to control who gets through the door!"

"I suppose you are right, really," admitted Lilian with some reluctance, "but it is a terrible state to be in."

We both felt equally concerned that so many people who could speak so glibly in public about the subject should prove to be so unhelpful in private. However, it was not long before Doreen was telling us that Lorna had decided to take one more chance with a medium she had recently seen working on a public platform. She was going to make an appointment to see her. "I think you should both be there," said Doreen, and we both agreed.

XX

By the time Lorna was actually sitting with this medium, whose name is Doris Collins, Lilian had got her own mind sufficiently organised and geared for the fray. It was not long before we realised that, at long last, Lorna had come to the right medium. She gave Lorna a graphic description of her mother and her personality and of her anxiety at the muddle that Lorna was in. She also gave Lorna a very vivid description of me, my personality, my life, and some of the things that I had been telling Lorna from here. She told Lorna of the impression she was getting of the terrible muddle that Lorna was in and said that Lorna's mother was asking Doris whether she could possibly help Lorna out of this muddle. We heard Doris Collins confirming to Lorna that she had indeed been hearing from the Spirit World and that she had been talking with me, but that she needed to learn proper control. She told Lorna that she had only a few weeks left for her training class and that the class was already full, but that she would make room for her for those few weeks, if it would be of any help. Lorna very gratefully accepted, and her mother and I began to feel happier for her.

Indeed, it not only proved to be a great help to Lorna, but it also gave me the opportunity I had been awaiting for such a long time, to find out more about this subject of communication. Although I was still being asked not to speak to Lorna directly on a day-to-day basis for the time being, I made sure that I was present on each of these occasions when Lorna sat for one hour a week in Doris's training class. I worked hard to communicate through Lorna and also to Lorna through the others in the class, as well as through Doris.

When Doris asked Lorna to give her some clairvoyance and Lorna said she did not think she would be able to do so, Doris replied, "You don't know until you try." I was the one from here who helped Lorna with that clairvoyance, and we had a surprising amount of success, so that Doris said to her that I was an exceptionally good communicator. This pleased us both, and I said to Lorna through Doris that I hoped I would one day be able to help Lorna to help others in the way that we had been helped. Doris had agreed to Lorna's request that my name should not be given to the class, because she preferred me to be given privacy here that I had seldom had there. It was at that period of time in our communications that we agreed that, when Lorna was through all the confusion and she had got her psychic faculties more clearly established, I would be one of those who would be giving her as much help as possible from here. It was something that I wished to do more than anything else I could think of, including my singing.

It was to be a number of years before we were able to work together again in this way, because of all the other complications that arose along the pathway, but Lorna and I have established a very firm relationship. It is something that has drawn us closer together than either of us had ever envisaged at the outset, and it has developed into a beautifully spiritual association and friendship. I have helped many people from here to communicate through Lorna to their loved ones on earth. She does not work professionally or even regularly, but she has been able to help some of her friends and their friends, and even some strangers who have approached her in conversation with their problems, by receiving information from here to pass along to them. This has sometimes been news of loved persons here, but has also included advice she has received to pass along, as well as some of the explanations she has received from us as to life here.

278

In the years that followed her sessions with Doris Collins, Lorna was able to gain sufficient control and confidence to tell her father much of what had been happening. She was able to gain his interest in the subject, which he told her he would never have believed from anyone else. She was able to tell him things about his own parents that he confirmed as correct. He, in his turn, passed along some information to one of his neighbours who had been recently widowed. She came along for help when Lorna next visited her father, and I was the chief communicator to help this lady's husband and brother-in-law to reach her very clearly indeed. Both Lorna and I felt that we had done something worthwhile. We shared a feeling of achievement that we had helped one soul to feel a little bit less lonely and bereaved. However, that took place a number of years after I received permission to return to speak to Lorna on a regular basis, after her book about my life on earth was published in a far shorter form than we had hoped, in August 1975.

Let me go back to the point where Lilian and I had at last managed to communicate with Lorna through the right medium, Doris Collins, and I was still being asked not to speak to Lorna at any other time until the book was published and the possibility of any more rewriting was ended. It was then that, on Lilian's advice and with Doreen's agreement, I set about trying to meet my mother in a reasonably friendly frame of mind. In the end, I chose to go along only with Doreen, although I told Lilian how grateful I was for her offer to come with me and I would probably like to return and discuss it with her afterwards.

"You do whatever you think is best, my dear," she said to me, "but I'll be thinking of you and hoping everything will go well for you. I know that if it had been my daughter that had been estranged from me, I should be most grateful that she was trying to make it up with me."

"You are a very different person to my mother," I told Lilian. "If I'd had a mother like you, I wouldn't have had the troubles I had in my life."

"I always tried to be a good mother to my daughter," said Lilian, "but you have to remember, Judy, that I started having nervous breakdowns when my girl was only fourteen years of age, and I continued to have those troubles as well as physical

279

illnesses until I came here when she was twenty-seven. Although, as my normal self, I was careful and caring and we shared a similar sense of humour and even similar interests, I was very often a complete misery to be with and unable to rouse myself from it all. It caused a lot of unhappiness to Lorna as well as to me, and yet I felt unable to overcome it. It is possible your mother may have had some problems of which you were unaware when you were younger."

"That is what I shall have to try and find out," I said to her, "but you seem to have been more like my sister, Susan, than my mother."

XXI

"You seem to have had a very happy time with Lorna's mother and family," said Doreen, as we made our way along.

"They made me feel most welcome and I really feel part of their family. It is extraordinary, really, because we come from completely different areas on earth and we've had completely different existences. They have mostly had quiet and comparatively straightforward lives, although they have had their problems, whereas I've been pushed into the public eye throughout the whole of my life. Yet, I found it a very pleasant and easy place to be. The only thing is, I do get a restless feeling of wanting to do other things, and I still feel I have to seek to fulfil myself. It was Lilian's suggestion that, before I do anything else, I should try and get my mother into the right perspective in my thinking, because she feels I will then do everything else with a clearer mind."

"I think she was very wise to suggest that to you, Judy. I would have suggested it myself, had you not felt so unhappy earlier when we told you that you could not talk to Lorna anymore for some while. As Lorna had already suggested that you meet her mother, I thought that seemed the best idea for that time."

"Oh, it was! I'm so delighted that I did go and see Lilian and meet all those people. It has given me a clearer insight into what family life could be. It has also given me a clearer insight into Lorna, because her mother told me a lot of things about her that I never knew. And it has given me somewhere to go when I feel

I want to be quiet but not necessarily alone, because I have been told I am welcome to go anytime and to stay as long as I like, and that's a good feeling."

"I am very happy for you," said Doreen. "Now then, we are about to reach your mother's home. We have told her you are on your way, and she is pleased to be seeing you, despite your qualms. So try and take it easily."

At this point, we arrived at a low-lying building of white clapboard with a white picket fence. There was an apple tree in the garden and a few flowers around the door. The door opened, and my mother stood in the doorway, looking as she had done in photographs I had seen of her when she was around twenty years of age. She leaned forward and kissed me on the cheek and invited me inside. We sat down, and Doreen said to her, "Although I have come with Judy to show her how to find you and to help you meet each other, I am going to leave you to discuss this between you. I shall be back for Judy presently. Before I leave you both, I want to say something to you. Judy has had a very bad time on earth in many ways since you came here, not the least of which was feeling that she had never had any love from you. Since she has come here, she has met her father, who has also told her that he has not had any love or understanding from you, although he did still love you and had tried to explain it to you. Judy has also been to see her sister, Susan, who has only recently woken up after being here quite a long while. All three of them feel a little doubtful that you have any interest in them. I am explaining this to you before I leave, because before you and Judy become involved in any sort of explanation, I want you to look back into your heart and ask yourself, 'Why do my former husband and my daughter feel that I have no love for them? Did I have any love for them? If I did, how was it that they think I did not?' I want you to question yourself while you are talking with your daughter. I feel it is something I should leave you to work out between yourselves, without a third person intruding on what I know is going to be a difficult time for you both. So, I will go now, and I will be back for Judy presently."

With that, Doreen left us together, and Mother and I stared at each other in silence for what seemed an interminable period.

It had been all of seventeen years of my earth life since I had last seen my mother, and, by the time we now faced each other, I had gathered from what Doreen had been telling me that I must have been here for approximately five years of earth time. The fact that my mother and I had been somewhat estranged when she came here meant that the unpleasantness of our last meeting remained predominant in our minds. It was true that she had kissed me on the cheek when we first met here, but I wondered how much of this was spontaneous and how much was due to her regarding it as the correct approach. Eventually, it was I who spoke first.

"Well, Mother, it is a long time since we met. A lot has happened to me, both here and on earth, and I expect a great deal more has happened to you here. I have seen Dad, and I have seen Susan, and I thought it time to come and see whether or not I could make my peace with you."

Mother looked at me for what seemed a long time before she answered me. Even then, I felt that her response was something that could be taken either way. She was not giving me any indication of her feelings. It was all very superficial.

"I always considered you to be your father's daughter and not mine," she told me. "Susan was a little of each, and Virginia was very much like me. Although I tried to feel the same about all three of you, I resented the love you gave to your father without apparently considering my feelings in the matter. Later on, when you became a big name at the studios, I just seemed to be very much in the background, and I never felt that we had anything to say to each other, especially when you married and moved in such different circles to those in which I felt comfortable. It was very difficult for me to remain friendly with you or to feel motherly towards you. You never seemed to want to listen to my opinion about anything, and I very much resented it when you went against my wishes in leaving Vincente Minnelli for a man like Sidney Luft."

"First of all, Mother," I corrected her, "I did not leave Vincente for Sid. Vincente left me in his heart in a number of ways before we separated. I did not get friendly with Sid until Vincente and I were separated and I was completely on my own again, without any kind of loving interest coming from you or from anyone else, so far as I was aware. He was the only person who seemed to be taking any positive interest in the fact that I did not know what to do next in my life. Although Sid and I did part eventually, after twelve years of marriage, I still feel that Sid gave me a lot in those early years of our marriage. I don't truly know what went wrong in the end, even now, but we had two lovely children together, and I loved him very much. I still think we might possibly have worked something out if my nerves had not given way again and put me into such a confused frame of mind, with the press giving me such awful publicity that everyone got the wrong ideas about me. I'm not going to blame Sid for everything. You didn't even know him. You didn't give him a chance.

"As for me not being friendly towards you, or taking any notice of you, I turned to you desperately after we lost Dad, and at no time did you seem to want to be bothered with me. You passed me over to the studio chiefs, and you let them rule my life. When I separated from David and was deeply unhappy, you did not seem to want to know how I felt. That is partly why I married Vincente, because he seemed to care for me, but he wasn't really the right kind of person for me. His ideas of marriage were not the same as mine, and the kind of people we had visiting the house all the time were not my kind of people. But there was no time at all that I could ever go to you and discuss it. You were not interested in me, so I don't see how you can say that I never told you anything or never listened to you. The only time you gave me your opinion was when you thought I should be going to someone else for advice, never to you. That's why I grew so resentful and hurt."

Mother listened to me, seemingly unperturbed by my outburst, and said, "Well, I can only tell you that I considered *you* not to be interested in *me*, so I stayed back from you. Now you tell me that *I* was not interested in *you*. You always found it easy to be demonstrative to people. I never did. I just wish, in some ways, that we had been able to remain just an ordinary family, not continuously travelling around from one place to the next so that we could never have a proper home. Then, when we moved to Hollywood, I never felt that I fitted with any of those people at the studios. They always made me feel that I wasn't anybody of any account. They never consulted with me, although I never felt I could cope with any responsibility, anyway. I resented the fact that I seemed to be put continuously in the background of your life."

We continued in this vein for quite a while without getting very much further. Eventually, I said to her, "I think we'll just have to agree to differ, Mother. I had hoped we could clear the air a little bit if I came to see you. I can only assure you, from my point of view, that I always felt that Dad loved me more than you did, and that's why I gave him my love. When you seemed so cold and bitter against him when he was so ill and after he had died, I did try to be loving to you but you just withdrew from me. I felt very hurt inside. I never felt I could ever go to you with any of my deepest feelings. There was nobody with whom I could discuss my problems. I think that is why I married David, who was so many years older than I was. Then, when he left me and, later, Vincente seemed to be taking a loving interest in me and I still had nobody to turn to, I married Vincente. He was far too old for me in a number of ways. His sophisticated ideas of life did not fit with mine at all. Then when I found a man like Sid, who seemed to be closer to me than either of the others had been, you didn't want to know him. I just don't feel you and I had any rapport at all, and I don't feel we have any here. I had thought that, possibly, having both experienced what life is like in this world, we might find that we have more to talk about, but I don't think that we do. I am so sorry you are still not prepared to speak to Dad. I was hoping, when I came here to see you, that you might consider seeing him again. He tells me you haven't forgiven him for what you think he did to you on earth, but he tells me he never did do what you blamed him for, that you misunderstood him completely, and that he never let you down with anyone else in any way whatsoever. He also said that he did still love you."

At that, she seemed to withdraw even more within herself. I felt as though her whole being tightened up.

"I have no intention of trying to meet your father again. We have nothing to say to each other. But I would like to see Susan. I did not know she was here."

"She came here six years before I did," I told Mother, "but because she was very sad and depressed for a long time and had been physically ill for some long while, she has only recently managed to begin to emerge from her depression here. I think she might be pleased to see you. I had thought that we might go and see her together."

"I'll think about it," said Mother.

I began to feel an emptiness and a sadness creeping over me again as I sat there trying to decide whether I should try for any further discussion or whether I should consider leaving. Then I began to realise that part of the emptiness and depression was coming to me from Mother, although some of it was within myself because of the disappointment I felt at not apparently getting anywhere, despite the fact that I had not really expected to get very far.

"Mother," I said to her, somewhat desperately, "I have just come from spending time with the mother of a friend of mine. She has been in this world approximately the same amount of earth time as you. She tells me she had many years of illness and sadness of outlook before she came here, but she is now living a very happy life with other members of her family. She has been more than kind to me and so have her family, and I have felt more of a kinship and family feeling with them than I have ever felt since Dad died. I came to see you to see whether I could find any hope of feeling some sort of affection and friendliness from you. I haven't found anything at all, but I do get a strong impression that you are not happy yourself and I am wondering why that is, because as you have been here all this while, I would have expected you to have found a little more happiness within you than you seem to have. I don't feel as unhappy as you seem to be, although, God knows, I have had enough unhappiness on earth, and I have nobody close to me here who was part of my own family. Even Susan is wrapped up in herself, and Dad is still sad and withdrawn. What sort of family are we, that we are all in such unsettled frames of mind?"

"I don't know what I am expected to do to please you, Judy," she said to me. "When I came here, I felt very bitter against you and against your father. I haven't got anybody here, any more than you have. I've made myself as comfortable as possible in this little house, and I am going about my daily tasks."

"What about your husband?" I said to her.

"He has got his own interests, and I've got mine. We don't see much of each other."

"What are you doing with yourself?" I asked her.

"This and that," she said abruptly. "What is there to do?"

"Well, there's a hell of a lot," I said to her. "I've seen a lot of things to do here. I'm just biding my time to getting around to doing them."

"Well, I've had it up to the neck with show business," she said to me. "I don't want to do anything like that. I just want to lead an ordinary life in an ordinary way and that's what I'm doing."

"Mother, I've been spending time going around and looking at a lot of the beautiful places that are here. I've been meeting children and lots of different animals. I've also met people who I have known on earth and who seem to be adjusting quite happily here in their different ways. They all seem to be positive people. I've just met this family who are all happy together, with their various interests and hobbies. I'm just so sorry that, of all the people I have so far met here, I seem to be the least able to reach *you*. Susan is a little bit difficult at the moment, but I think she is getting better. You and Dad, who should be closest to me, I can't seem to reach. I hoped that, by discussing it with you, we might be able to find a way around it all."

"Well, I am pleased that you took the trouble to want to come and see me," said Mother, relaxing a little. "I was pleased to see you when you arrived. Perhaps I have been a bit rigid in my attitude. I will think over what you have told me, and perhaps you would like to come and see me again after I have thought about it in my own way and in my own time."

For the first time since my arrival, I seemed to get a glimpse of the mother I had known when I was a little girl, before she became so much harder on me.

"I suppose," she said to me, "I did try and discipline you too hard at times, for the age that you were, but I thought it was the right thing. Show business is full of pitfalls for the unwary, and I wanted to make sure that you grew up to be a responsible person. I did love all three of you at the outset. Mind you, it was not all my fault that we didn't get along, but I am at least pleased to know that you felt enough about it all to come and see me. I will go and see Susan, but I'd prefer to go on my own. When I have seen her and had time to think about it all, perhaps we can meet again."

"All right, Mother," I agreed, "if you feel that is the best way to go about it, but I would like to try and see, if possible, where we may have both been wrong. I would still ask you to think about Dad and whether or not you could manage to see him again and be prepared to listen to him this time and to discuss it with him."

"One thing at a time and first things first," said Mother, withdrawing within herself again, "but I'm glad you came, and I'll think over what you have said."

With that, Doreen came back for me. Doreen always seemed to know the right moment to reappear. Somewhat thankfully and relievedly, I took my leave of Mother and departed with Doreen. I came away with the feeling that I had made a tiny breakthrough, but I had no impression that I had brought any feeling of affection or friendship with me.

XXII

Doreen looked at me understandingly. "I know what you are feeling, Judy. It is an uphill struggle, but I think you will find that, although your mother has not been ready to capitulate immediately, she will think about your visit and will eventually be prepared to see you again with a revised attitude. Although you will never be close, because you are unlike in too many ways, you will, I think, at least be able to be more amicable towards each other. It is better to be amicably neutral than actively resentful, which each of you has been until now. You will find that, if you can be a little bit patient and give her time to work on herself, which is what she has got to do, and if you will think over some of the things that she has said to you, you will eventually, each of you, reach a feeling of neutrality that will, in its way and in some extraordinary fashion, give each of you the additional peace of mind that you both need in order to go forward in your individual ways."

"Yes, I do see what you mean," I acknowledged. "I'm not as stupid as I was when I first arrived." I smiled at her. "And she has at least agreed to see Susan, which should help Susie a little bit. At least, I hope it will."

"Susan has got to work her way through her own problems,

Judy. Seeing your mother again will be a contribution towards it. It is better that you do not get involved again until Susan is ready to take the next step forward. So, let her meet your mother, and let them work on each other in their own ways. In the meantime, you can continue to experience things here and to settle more and more into the happiness that we know lies ahead for you. Then, when you return to meet your mother and Susan again, and also your father, you will be stronger and happier and more reassured than you are at present. Any problems that they may still have will bounce off you more easily. When they see the radiance around you, who have not been here for as long as any of them, they will begin to realise that they have not made much of an effort on their part. Now, I am going to take you back to your Japanese friend to ask her to help you to put a concert together. You will have to carefully consider what you want to do and whether you want to seek any new songs, and then she will be able to help you to project it all."

I hesitated at that suggestion. "I've always projected myself in my own way, Doreen. I was happy to have her help in order to show me how to get thoughts across, but I think that I now need to work on myself for a while, on my own, until I have got each song clearly in my mind and then to go to her for the final instructions."

"Whichever you think best, dear," said Doreen. "It is just that I am getting the impression that you are anxious to do something about your singing."

"Yes, I am, but I would like to see Lilian first and tell her how I got on with Mother. Then I am going to start thinking about my concert. Will you come back with me to see Lilian? Then we can continue to wherever I have to go to get the concert work under way."

We returned together to find Lilian anxiously awaiting news of my visit to Mother. I gave her the general gist of it, and Doreen was able to assure Lilian that she felt I had made more of an impact on Mother than was evident to me at the moment. "She has promised Judy that she will think it all over," said Doreen. "It will take a while, but I think Judy's visit has sown a few seeds for thought so that the next meeting will be a little easier."

"I hope so, for everyone's sake," said Lilian. "In the meantime, Judy, you know you will always have a home here for as long as you like and whenever you like."

"I know I have," I assured her gratefully, "but I have now decided that it is time I gave my first concert. I am going away to work on it, and I will let you know when it is ready. If you or any of your family feel they would like to come along I would be very happy to have you come," I said to her.

"I will most certainly be there," Lilian assured me. "I always liked you in your films, and I had such glowing reports from Lorna of you on stage at the Palladium that I would love to come along. I think I might get my sister Nell to come with me. She used to hear Lorna enthusing about you, and I think her curiosity will get the better of her!" she added with a smile.

"I'll let you know," I confirmed, "and I do love being with you here. I really do."

XXIII

Doreen and I having taken our departure, I asked where I could go in order to find what songs might be acceptable here. "I feel that most of my previous material may not be suitable, although Spence seemed convinced that 'A Couple of Swells' would be well received."

"Well, dear, I think I'll take you along to the Musical Academy here, our equivalent of a musical learning centre. There are a number of composers working there. Some were composers on earth, and some have become composers only since their arrival here. Most of the people who will be coming to hear you sing, although they may have been of many different nationalities on earth and of different generations, will be people who are now more or less on your present level of existence, although they may be staying in different places here. You will thus be able to reach their hearts and feelings in a similar manner to the way you reached your audiences on earth. What you now want are composers who are writing songs for your level of existence. I will leave you with them. When you need me again, just think hard that you are ready for me and I'll return for you."

She left me in a beautiful building in the middle of the city, where I recognised several song writers that I had encountered in my life on earth and others that I had not. Because of the way my career had begun, in the vaudeville theatres of the mid-1920s, and because I had then gone to the film studio where many of the movies had reintroduced songs that had been made famous from the beginning of the century right through to the 1960s, my repertoire had already spanned a number of generations. I was also used to very mixed age groups in my audiences. I found that, although some of the songs that I had sung on earth were not necessarily completely suitable for here, there were a number that were remembered by people with affection and would be most happily received here. I also found, however, that I should intersperse those popular favourites with some new compositions. The whole idea appealed to me enormously. When I had finished discussing the different aspects and problems with the various composers, I began feeling more assured about my performance. It certainly meant a different approach to when I had sung on earth, but it appeared that the essential quality would remain unchanged.

I worked hard with the musicians and found that, with their help, I did not even need to return to my Japanese friend for any further help, although I did eventually send her an invitation to my concert. She came along, and we have remained friends. She has, in fact, made herself known to Lorna through two different mediums, and a psychic artist has drawn her portrait for Lorna, who was very confused at first as to who she was and where she fit in. At the outset, she simply accompanied me out of interest to see how to communicate with those on earth. She had not intended that the artist draw her. Lorna was aware of my presence and hoped that I would be drawn, but it was my companion's face that the artist saw more clearly, and an astounded Lorna received this Japanese portrait instead of mine. This is where extrasensory communication can sometimes be confusing.

However, to return to the period when I was working for my first concert, I found that new songs were more easily learned and absorbed here than on earth, because the whole approach was mental and not physical. This meant that, once I had decided on the feelings that needed to be conveyed, I could think the note and its colour and its impact,and this all came winging through without any of the vocal problems often encountered on earth.

Basically, I remain the same kind of performer, because I usually did bring my emotions into my work. Although I know a lot of people criticised me for this, there were others who appeared to prefer me to do so, and I found that I usually could not avoid doing so, anyway. I believe anyone who reads this who liked my work at those times when I was singing well during the 1950s and early 1960s will enjoy hearing me sing here.

When the time arrived for me to make my first concert appearance here, I was allowed to visit the area ahead of time to see the kind of area where I would be singing. I found it a little bit awesome. I had sung in some vast areas on earth, including stadiums, and even the Astrodome at Houston in Texas, but never had I seen anything as vast as this arena. I say *arena* because it is difficult to explain it in any other way in earth terms. It was a vast, ascending stairway of beautiful light and softly diffused colour, mainly a pale gold tinged with pale blue. There was almost the feeling of a very beautiful, open air cathedral, if you can imagine such a thing. I was told that it was kept specially for the kind of performance I would be giving, as it provided the correct atmosphere and also the best vibration for me to work within. There would be, I was assured, a vast audience there who would be able to hear me and even to see me clearly despite the seeming vastness. This was because the individual members of the audience would be able to tune in to my work and to my personality and to receive this just as clearly as though I were right in front of them and singing directly to them. I could not help remembering that, during my happier singing days on earth, many in my audience used to say that they felt I was singing to each of them personally, and so I began to feel better and better about this whole new process.

Spencer Tracy had already been to see me. We decided that, for my very first concert, I had better not attempt "A Couple of Swells." It would be best for me to get over the initial strangeness and to get the feel of the audience and their likely response before attempting anything with anyone else. But he was happy to come and hear me sing again after such a long time. He gave me a lot of friendly interest and support during the rehearsals of some of the new material. By this time, he had changed his house for a smaller version of the home in which he had once entertained me in Beverley Hills during the 1950s when I was still in Hollywood.

"The best thing I ever did was to come to see the idiocy of that mansion, Judy. I feel far more a part of this world now, and I'm looking forward to having some folks along more often. I hope you'll come along and bring your friend Doreen, or anyone else for that matter."

"I'd love to, Spence," I assured him, and he beamed at me like a schoolboy.

Lilian and her sister came to see me shortly before the concert was to take place. They said there had been a concerted effort by the entire family to come and experience my performance. They all sent me their love and expected great things from me.

When I had sung on earth, even when I felt well and happy, there had always been an element of tension within me before I actually walked out on stage. Sometimes it quickly dispersed if the audience greeted me with a huge wave of loving applause, as so often happened. Sometimes, if I was singing somewhere for the first time, it lasted a little longer, until I began to win their approval. Here, for some inexplicable reason, despite the new approach I was using and that I felt I still had to get used to using, I felt completely calm. I hoped everyone would like me, but I no longer felt it would be a total disaster if they did not.

Doreen was by my side as I stood a little outside the arena before walking out to face the audience. "I have every confidence in you, Judy. They will all love you just as much, and possibly even more, than your very best audiences on earth. On earth, some members of your audiences used to feel that you were singing with your soul, and that is why they loved you so much. Here, everyone will know you are singing with your soul and love you even more for what they see and feel and hear. Good luck, and God bless you!"

I took her hand and held it tightly in mute gratitude for all the help and confidence she had been so instrumental in giving me in so very many ways. Then I walked out into the beautiful light and atmosphere of the arena and towards the greatest wave of love that I had ever felt coming towards me at any time in my entire life. When I was on earth, I had been used to hearing audiences call out to me "We love you, Judy," and I would respond with "I love you, too." Here, it was as though all the hearts of all the people present were reaching out to me in all sorts of different ways. I could clearly sense that many were already familiar with my work and had looked forward to seeing me again. Their love meant so much to me, after those last years on earth when so many things had gone wrong, and I knew that I had come home at last.

When Lilian and her sister Nell came for me afterwards, to take me back home with them for a while, they were both smiling happily and told me "Now we know what Lorna meant—and she was *so right!*"

How good it was to be going home to the family afterwards and to feel so welcome, both as a performer and as a human being. I was finally, I felt sure, over that damned rainbow!

Chapter 5

I

The time I spent with Lilian's family after I had given my first concert here helped me to begin to see more clearly where my own areas of activities since my arrival differed almost completely from theirs. Mostly at my enquiry, we all discussed how we had arrived here and how we had fared since. It soon became clear to me that there were many different ways of getting adjusted, as well as many different attitudes as to how and where to exist in this beautiful world where there is such a freedom of choice. Here, if you wish and work for it hard enough, almost anything is possible—a far cry from our many experiences on earth.

Lilian and I discussed many topics together that, she told me, she had been unable to discuss with the family simply because they all felt so contented in their present life and in their present areas. They felt no strong wish to take themselves into the many deep subjects that would have probably removed them from each other's company for long periods. Lilian also felt she would prefer not to remove herself from her family and so was content, at least for the present, to simply wonder about those things. Then she found that I also wanted to have answers to many questions, and we became involved in many interesting discussions. I told her that I had already asked Doreen for answers to some of these and had been told that they were too complicated for me to fully understand at my present stage of experience. Although I had accepted that Doreen was probably as right about this as she usually proved to be, I had still wondered about the where and why and how.

One thing that became more and more clear to me while I was discovering so much about the family was how much I needed to feel a part of it. Much as I had enjoyed giving the concert, much as I had enjoyed the pleasure I could still give to those who recognised me and who still so obviously loved me, much as I had felt glad to find that I could also give pleasure here to many who had never previously experienced my work, I knew that the most important thing for me was to have such a genuine and sincere group of people to be with, to laugh with, and to share ideas with in general activities. It was during this visit that I learned more about how a close family life can still be experienced here and more than I had ever known before. Yet, I also found that my journies with Doreen had taken me to many places and had raised many questions that appeared not to have occurred to Lilian or to her family. Most of these new-found friends of mine had been met on their arrival here by members of their family group who had taken them, after their period of rest on awakening in this world, straight to the family area. There they had remained, happy and contented together. Because of this there had been few questions raised about other parts of this world and little inclination to remove themselves elsewhere.

Lilian told me there had been a number of occasions when she had broached a subject to her sister Nell, who would normally have been the best person to accompany her on any journies because they were very close in their attitudes. But Nell was so happy to be reunited with her husband after so very many years of being apart from him, because he was drowned at sea after only a brief marriage, that she felt reluctant to leave his company for any length of time. And *he* was still staying within easy reach of *his* family.

The outcome of all my discussions with Lilian was that I

suggested that we should seek out Doreen for her·advice as to where we could now try and find the answers to at least some of our questions. Except for the one teacher who had spoken to me about my father, Doreen was the only person I had experienced here who had provided any explanation to me. She had certainly opened my eyes to many things here that Lilian had not yet experienced. I felt she would be the best person to ask since Lilian said there had been no attempt by anyone to lead her beyond her present area.

Doreen was immediately helpful. She explained that my experiences had been unusually extensive and varied so soon because I had shown immediate interest each time she had attempted to show me something. She explained that, because there was no one who was close enough to me to greet me and to take me into our world here, and also because I needed a great deal of careful psychological treatment to unravel me from my confused state of mind, she had been appointed to help me. Because she was comparatively experienced here, she had felt able to lead me towards more varied experiences than many others experience so soon after awakening in this world. "Some of those experiences were very much more necessary for Judy at that time in order to help her—and she was such a good pupil!"

Doreen then said to Lilian, "I am also aware, my dear, that apart from your natural reluctance to remove yourself from your family, you wish to remain in the area where you are most likely to be easily reached by your husband, Stanley, when he comes to this world."

"That is true," Lilian acknowledged. "He was such a kind and considerate husband to me, and I was so ill and unhappy for so many years. I want to be available to make it up to him in any way that I can when he comes here. Lorna has told Judy that he still loves me very much, so it seems that the best thing for me to do is to stay where I am."

Doreen agreed and added that, for many reasons, it would be better for Lilian to leave things as they had been, since she was so contented at the moment. "Judy has had to face a very different arrival here. She is going to need a lot of activity to keep her contented until later on, when other aspects will arise to change her path again."

Lilian and I returned to our discussions in the knowledge

that we were clearly not ready for any more deep experiences at present, and, therefore, we should simply let everything take its course.

Lilian's admission to Doreen, that she was waiting for her husband, Stanley, to arrive before she made any decision about extending her experiences here, was something she had not mentioned during our discussions. "It was just that, knowing all the disappointments you had faced with your own husbands, I did not want to rub salt into the wounds and put too much emphasis on looking towards my future with Stan."

"I understand and appreciate your thoughtfulness," I told her. "It is sweet of you to have thought about it in that way. I guess it does give you a different outlook to know you have a person coming here to be with you. Doreen has assured me there will be someone, in the future, with whom I shall have a very close and sincere rapport and resultant companionship, because it is not necessarily the marital partner from earth that turns out to be the most satisfactory companion here. I am sure you are doing the right thing to wait for your husband. He seems to be the right person for you to be with. I have to wait and see whether Doreen is correct in the ideas she is putting to me as far as my own future goes. In the meantime, I guess I'll settle for some of her ideas as to what I might be doing now!"

"I am sure you should!" Lilian agreed. "I am only surprised that you have managed to stay with us as long as you have without feeling more restless than you have done."

"Oh! It's such a joy!" I assured her. "And it will continue to be a joy, providing you can put up with having me whenever I feel like turning up!"

"It is always a pleasure to see you come back to us," said Lilian. "We all love you very much. You have got the sort of personality that I always thought that you had and that Lorna always told me she thought that you had, although, of course, she had not met you when we were discussing you on earth."

"Yes, well, I think Lorna realised during my last few years that I did not always manage to keep it going, but that, underneath all my problems and confusions and peculiar reactions, there was the real me, and that, when I got broody and morose and yelled at her, I didn't really mean it."

"If she had thought that you really meant it, she would have told you precisely what she thought of you," said Lilian. "My daughter does not mince her words when she feels someone deserves to be told what she thinks. If she kept quiet about it and stayed with you, she must have had her reasons. If I know my daughter, it was because she believed in you and did not want to let you down."

It was at this point that I began to go back in my mind to all the conversations that I had been enjoying with Lorna and to Doreen's insistence that it would be with Lorna that I would be travelling around more extensively in this world of ours when she arrived here. I told this to Lilian, who immediately looked as surprised as anyone could be.

"I know that you like Lorna, and I know she was always very fond of you and greatly admired you as a performer. I can certainly see that, when she comes here, you and she will get on well together, because you have got along well with the rest of the family, but I must admit that the last thing I ever expected to hear from you, or from Doreen for that matter, was that you and Lorna would be travelling together here. It seems to me that that is a very difficult decision to make when you are on one side of life and she is on the other!"

"I couldn't agree more," I assured Lilian, "and that is what I have been telling Doreen. Doreen tells me that Lorna would be just as amazed to be told such a thing. Nevertheless, she predicts that, when Lorna and I get down to discussing things more deeply, we shall each of us recognise that we have far more in common than either of us could ever realise at present."

"Well, what an extraordinary thing!" said Lilian, smiling at me good-humouredly. "Whoever would have thought it, all that time ago, when I took Lorna to see you in *Everybody Sing*, when you were both so young, that you and I would ever be sitting here, *where we are*, and calmly discussing the possibility of you and Lorna becoming close friends here and travelling around together! I suppose I am still seeing Lorna as I knew her on earth and so am not in any position to assess the situation clearly, but it does seem to me that you are wise to regard it as something you cannot really decide until you have spent time together here amidst other people."

"I realise that," I acknowledged. "It is only Doreen's insistence that has brought me round to considering whether or not it might be at all possible. Certainly, there is nothing that I have encountered here, at the moment, that would lead me to think that this possibility is necessarily right or likely. So I am going to keep an open mind about it. I am just wondering what Lorna's reaction will be when I tell her what I have been told!"

It was then that I realised that I had a sincere wish to discuss this with Lorna and to find out what she really thought about it. Then I thought, *Judy! Why have you suddenly got this wish to discuss such a thing with Lorna? If you have so many doubts on the subject, and Doreen has already told you that Lorna would be equally doubtful, what is to be gained from this?*

I sat and pondered this extraordinary situation very carefully. I told myself that it really revolved around the fact that I had enjoyed talking things over with Lorna and with her mother, and that I was looking forward to the time when I could return to discussing with Lorna some of the things that I had discussed with Doreen and with Lilian. "But, why," I said to myself, "should I be so anxious to discuss these topics with Lorna rather than with anyone else?" It was while I was muddling my way through this in my mind that Doreen approached me with the suggestion that it would be as well if I kept myself more occupied than I had been recently, because, although I had not realised it, I had been so concentrated in my mind on these thoughts, so deeply immersed, I suppose, that I had been withdrawn from her and everyone else for quite a long period. I gazed at her in astonishment. "How do you mean, that I've been withdrawn from everyone?" I asked her.

"Well, dear, in this world, if we start concentrating on something very, very deeply, to the exclusion of everything else, it literally takes us inside ourselves, and we literally withdraw and shut off from everyone who might be trying to speak to us."

"There have been occasions on earth when I have been thinking about something quite deeply and have not heard when someone has been talking to me. I suppose you have just described that *sort* of thing but on a larger dimension?"

"Exactly," said Doreen, "but the reason for approaching you at this time is that I feel you are getting to a point where you need some form of activity. Otherwise you will be continuously falling back into these reveries that cut you off from Lilian and the family more than you wish and also possibly take you further away from me than is best for you at the moment. I have only just managed to catch your attention to bring you back to me," said Doreen, smiling. "And this could become something that is not good for you at present."

"What plans have you got for me now?" I smiled back a little uncertainly. *My goodness!* I thought. *How strange that I can cut myself off in that way. I'll have to watch it!*

"Would you like to go back to the children and spend some time helping them? Not those who need a lot of difficult attention, but those who are already adjusted here and still need a guiding hand to keep them occupied and happy."

"I would love to!" I said to her. "I'll just go and see whether Lilian would be interested in joining me. If not now, she might like to come later on. She doesn't want to leave her dog behind, or even her cat, despite the fact that the cat seems to be pretty independent of her, as far as I can see. But her little dog does love her very much, and she might not wish to go without him. Perhaps she could bring him along?"

"That would be up to her and also the dog," said Doreen. "Surprising as it may seem, she would have to discuss it with him and see what he feels about it."

I thought to myself, *Even in* The Wizard of Oz *I didn't expect to get any replies from Toto!*

Doreen laughed at me and said, "Here we go again!"

"Well, you must admit," I said, "that it does seem rather strange. Although, after all you have shown me and explained to me and all that I experienced in the Animal Kingdom, everything should be acceptable to me by now."

At this point, Lilian joined us, and I told her of our discussion. She laughed and said, "Well, believe it or not, even when he was on earth, Laddie had very definite ideas of his own. Lorna and I had to work hard sometimes to get him away from them." She told me of several amusing incidences. "I will come along with you later on, but not at the moment. Just give me a little more time. I'll tell my Laddie and let him see what he thinks of the idea. I do believe it would be possible for us to go together. I shall have to see how things go. But I wish you all the luck with your trip, dear. Do come back and see us again before too much longer, because we do love having you with us."

"I don't honestly think that I could be going to the children with such a happy and light heart if I hadn't felt, very strongly, how welcome I would be here at any time," I told her. "I am so grateful to you, I am grateful to your family, and I am even more grateful that Lorna had enough insight to suggest to me that I might come and see you."

With that I left Lilian and set off again with Doreen.

II

As we made our way towards the children, Doreen told me that she would be leaving me there for a while.

"The time is nearing, Judy, when you will have to take most things on your own responsibility. You will soon learn to find your way back to wherever you wish to be without me necessarily taking you. You are almost doing it now. It is just that you have got used to turning to me to take you to various places. You will soon be able to find your way around. I believe that, by the end of the period with the children, you will easily be able to make your way back to Lilian without necessarily calling upon me. I do want to assure you that you are welcome to call for my help and attention any time that you wish, but you are through your difficult period now. You feel far more assured and happy and you know you now have friends with whom you can discuss things if you wish to do so. Nevertheless, if you need me at any time, I will do my best to be with you. I shall be free of any other particularly involved work for quite a long time now, so I shall be available if you need to speak to me. But I feel the time has now come when you should be left to your own devices to make your own decisions and to follow your own wishes.

"I will be back to see you as soon as it is possible for you to speak to Lorna again. It should not be too much longer now, and this may well be why you found your mind turning to her again recently. The book is almost published, and, when this has taken place, we will be helping you to be reunited with her. She is still having problems with people talking to her who ought not to be doing so, but she has got it under slightly better control now, and I know that she is anxiously waiting to hear from you again. We have tried to tell her that you would be staying away until the book is actually published, but this did not prevent others embroidering on this information. They have made it seem to her that you have been forcibly removed and forbidden all access to her. She is worrying about where you are and how you are and how long it will be, if at all, before you manage to communicate again from here."

"Oh, my God!" I said to Doreen, looking at her in horror. "Poor Lorna! What she must be going through! I complacently thought everything was going to be all right the moment I stopped speaking to her."

"We had hoped that that would help the situation," said Doreen, "but it has put her through a lot of additional confusion and unhappiness. I know that no one will be more delighted than will Lorna when she hears from you once more."

"Wouldn't it help if I went to speak to her now?" I asked cautiously.

"Not really, dear. We have told her that you will be back after the book is published, and I think it is better that we keep to that arrangement. If we tell her one thing and then do another, it is going to break her faith in us."

"Don't you think that faith may have already been broken, if others have been telling her different stories and she has been getting worried about them?" I asked.

"You may be right, dear, but I have been asked to handle it in this way, and this is what I will have to do. We often find here that things are suggested to us in such a way by the higher teachers that we do not always understand why we are being asked to do something. It is better to do as they suggest, because they often know far more about these things than we do."

I had to be content with that explanation for the time being, but it began to sow a seed of worry in my mind as to how Lorna had been faring in the period of time since we had last been together. It was not too much longer before I was able to find that out for myself. Meanwhile, I was on my way back to the children to spend some time with them. These included Sally, who was now more than competent to direct the more recent arrivals with suggestions as to what they might do to keep themselves occupied. Despite the fact that, by this time, Sally would be approximately five years of age by earth time and she was still not very tall, she seemed to have advanced in her mind to well beyond that age and to have the attitude of a ten-year-old child on earth.

"That is because the mind of a child here can be advanced more quickly than on earth," explained Doreen, who had worked with children during her earlier days here. She explained how it is that the less-impinged-upon mind of the average child can be led forward more quickly than the mind of a child who is encompassed in the heavier physical body on earth. "The children who come here very young have gained rather than lost, because they have often managed to bring with them the innocence and the laughter that life on earth has not yet had the opportunity to distort or destroy. It is the children, my dear Judy, for whom you will have the greatest affinity. Despite your problems on earth and the fact that you often got confused and sometimes got angry and sometimes became a little bitter in some of your verbal exchanges on earth and in some of your hurt reactions to what you saw as a lack of any loyalty or love or understanding, none of this was truly you in your innermost feelings. Your soul still retained your childlike approach and your laughter, and you brought these with you here. Now you are going to share these qualities with the children."

She kissed me on the cheek before she left me, Sally and her friends already crowding round me. "God bless you, Judy dear. I want you to know that, although you and I had to spend a lot of time discussing all your earth world problems in order to get you disentangled from them, I never, at any time, found this to be a difficult or depressing assignment, as some of mine have proved to be. I took to you immediately. I enjoyed our discussions together. I am grateful that you accepted me so easily, that you did not, really, provide any difficulties for me. I've grown very fond of you, and I wish you every happiness here. I hope that we will still meet from time to time as friends, apart from any other reason for which you may wish to contact me. But I leave you where I feel you most belong, with the children. I am sure that I will see you again before long. God bless you again, Judy dear." With that she smiled at me and walked away.

As I thought over what had just been said to me I told myself, "Well, if Doreen could have felt that about me, having gone as deeply as she had to do within my soul in order to help me, I couldn't have been such a terrible person, could I?" With that feeling of comfort, I turned to Sally and the children and we went off together.

III

I spent a long time with the children, learning the ways in which I could be most helpful to them. I soon found that in addition to being one of their more adult playmates, I had to learn to handle various attitudes here. Much as I had always felt that a child brought with them a wide-eyed, shining approach of innocence, I soon learned that many of these youngsters who were coming here from earth had not been given the sort of example by their parents that they might have been given and had already had their thinking distorted by some very low-based attitudes and ideas. I felt hurt and upset by these attitudes instead of feeling, as I had expected to feel at the outset, nothing but joy in mingling with young children. Sally had brought with her the unsmirched innocence of a young child with loving parents who had been teaching her the correct attitude to life in a way that all children should be taught.

It was not long after my return to the children that I began to find that I had to teach some of them not only the ways of existence here but also how they should, as children, have seen their life on earth. I had many barriers to break down, particularly with some of those children who had been on earth for five or six years. During this period, I was not expected to take on any child who had lived on earth for more than that time. Later, I was asked to help those who had arrived here at an older age, between ten and twelve years. Some of them had been handicapped by physical accidents to their bodies. One girl I helped had been stricken by polio at the age of six and, for the second half of her life on earth, had had to cope with having her legs in irons and spending the larger part of her time in a wheelchair. I found that she had reacted to that experience with a great deal of courage and fortitude. In fact, she was a great deal of help to me with the others. I was able to show her as a shining example to those other children of her age group who had come here without any kind

303

of past physical or mental handicap but who had taken an exceedingly bitter, rudimentary, and even cruel attitude towards others on earth.

I was somewhat surprised to find that I was handling this kind of child, because it had not occurred to me at the outset that I would ever be any good at that sort of thing. I must admit I had visualised myself as mostly helping those of Sally's age group and type of outlook. Now that I am able to look back at it as it happened then, I suppose it is really very gratifying to find that, after such a comparatively short period of being here and no previous experience of such work, I was able to help these more complicated children to unravel their minds to the full beauties of this world and the correct ways of existing here.

I was to find, during those periods I spent with the children, that I had succeeded with them exceptionally well. I was told by others who had been trying to help them that I had really made the most astonishing progress with some of the more difficult children that they had experienced there. Therefore, I feel that anyone on earth should be capable of bringing up their own children with the right attitudes.

I have been assured here that I had the correct attitude to my own three children and that, because of the attitude that I had towards them, they have each grown up with the right attitude to life, despite making their own emotional mistakes as human beings are likely to do. None of them has any cruelty within them, and they would never intentionally hurt a fellow creature. They are aware that there are still a lot of beauties to be found on earth, providing they are prepared to look for them.

I know that my daughter, Lorna, is now a proud and happy mother and that she is trying to bring to her little boy the kind of loving understanding that I always tried to give to her and to my other two children. The very fact that she has learned from me in that way is, in itself, a gratifying thing.

When I was on earth I always loved being with babies. I would have been only too happy to have had many more babies of my own. I had a very difficult time when giving birth to my Joe, and I decided against risking the likelihood of giving birth to a malformed child, which is why I had not intended to have any more children. It was only after I had married Mickey that I wondered whether I should take that risk one more time for his sake. But to return to when I had decided against having any more children of my own, I had laughingly said to my three children on a number of occasions, "I can't wait for you to grow up so that your Mama can have some baby grandchildren." They had laughed with me, but I would like my Lorna to know that I am aware that she is now such a good and loving mama, and I sympathise with my poor Liza, who has failed in her many sincere attempts to become a mother.

Having said all that, I think it is time to tell you of one experience here that remains vividly in my mind.

Shortly after I had been asked to leave Sally's group of children in order to try and help a child who had come here under very difficult circumstances, I faced something that was not unlike the kind of experience I had had on earth, which I mentioned earlier in this book. This time it was with a little child who had been so tormented by her parents that her mind had been very badly affected. She had been in a state of abject terror on numerous occasions because she had been beaten by a brutal father. This had damaged the child's mind because, in punching her head as hard as he had on a number of occasions, he had caused her to suffer the same kind of brain damage that a boxer can suffer after many traumatic bouts in the ring. This had addled her brain to such an extent that she became very slow thinking. She was unable to speak because her brain could not pick out the words to pronounce. The more addled she became, the more she was abused by this terrible man who called himself a father. Although the mother tried to protect the child to some extent, she was totally dominated by the man and did not really do very much towards protecting the child. It was after one of these bouts of brutishness that the child's head was banged so hard against some furniture that it brought her here after a very serious concussion. Her nose had been broken, and one of her arms was badly damaged.

As a result of all that she had been through on earth, we found it difficult to reach her mind clearly here. It might be difficult for you to understand, despite all the past explanations from Doreen that I had previously tried to repeat to you, how it was that, when she came here, she was not immediately restored to her right mind, now that she was no longer blocked by the physical brain. But, you see, because the brain had not been functioning correctly, she had not been getting the correct impulses into her mind so that, when she came here, she remained, for quite a while, in a state of shock and terror, incapable of communicating her thoughts clearly to anyone. My task was to try and reach through that child's terror and confusion and try and explain to her that she was no longer going to be beaten or in any way harmed, that she had reached a beautiful place where she would find nothing but love and kindness.

I have been told by many people here that I have an impulsively loving nature. I guess it is difficult for anyone to see themselves clearly or to understand how they are seen by others. I cannot understand how it is that I seem to affect people in this way, as I am only reacting as it seems normal and usual for me to react. Nevertheless, I am told this about myself and I have also heard mediums on earth describe me to my friend Lorna as "someone who has a great deal of love to give." So, possibly, that is why they asked me to help this child. It seemed to me that I had not been long with her before she began to show a tremendous change in her outlook. I could almost see the greyness turning to a glow as I concentrated on her. It was not long before I was able to communicate to her the fact that she was now in a beautiful and loving place. This child emerged from what I can only describe in earth terms as a grey coma towards being a beautiful, warm-hearted, loving, laughing little girl. We had a lot of fun together, and she was devoted to me. This, of course, made it very difficult to know what to do next. I knew from what I had already been told when I first arrived to help the children that I would not be able to remain completely with one child for an indefinite period because it would not be good for either of us. So, what I then had to do was gradually introduce the child to her playmates and to the other teachers. I would be with her at the outset and then, slowly and carefully, withdraw myself from her in such a way that it was imperceptible to her that she was gradually losing me and moving towards those children and the teachers who would now take her forward to instruct her in the ways of the spirit generally.

Afterwards, I was congratulated at having had such an exceptionally speedy success. My subsequent success rate with the various other children I was asked to help became the laughing, smiling talk among those others who were also trying to help the children here. I came to realise that I was succeeding unexpectedly well in a field I had not expected ever to attempt. Then I was approached by Doreen with the news that Lorna's book was now officially published and that I could begin to speak to her again.

IV

Doreen told me that I need not remove myself completely from the children in order to speak with Lorna, provided I did not undertake to become deeply involved with one child at that juncture.

"I know you will wish to be available to speak to Lorna at every opportunity, at least for a while, until you two readjust to the present change in circumstances, and it would not be fair, either on Lorna or on the child, if you found yourself torn between the two."

"I realise that," I said to her. "In fact, I've already been through the kind of experience where I felt I had to stay alongside a small child for quite a while until she was well and happy enough to leave her with others. But I'm so pleased to hear that Lorna's book has been published, and I hope it will be a big success."

"Well, dear," said Doreen, "I have to remind you of what I told you before. It will not be the success that it deserves to be, because that is the way of life on earth. It has not been handled particularly carefully by those who should have looked further afield with regard to its future. I already know from Lorna's thoughts that she has been exceedingly frustrated to find that it was left to languish unpublished for nearly eighteen months after she had reluctantly reduced it in accordance with all the various requests and requirements, and that it is now being issued alongside two other books about you by two well-known writers whose books have both had a great deal of publicity and are twice as long as Lorna's. She recognises that hers does not now stand much chance of success, and she feels her sincere wish to defend you and to explain you to the public will fail. It is because she has been feeling very frustrated about it all that I am warning you of this before you actually speak to her, as it will guide you as to what to say to her from here."

307

Before long, we were back on the shore, looking across the waves to the gleaming light in the distance. The light that I saw seemed to be fluctuating and flickering. Doreen explained that I was, once again, approaching a medium. It was someone whom Lorna had seen lecturing in a public hall and who had given the impression that she was exceedingly good at receiving regular communications from here. Because Doris Collins was not available, Lorna had decided to try this medium. I later learned that the flickering light was the somewhat muddled mind of the medium. In certain circumstances, she could be very good indeed, but she was feeling very tired and somewhat agitated, and her own mind was leaping about all over the place. She was linking erratically with several people here and getting very confused, so that Lorna was getting a little of one and a bit of another and not the whole of anyone!

I soon realised that Lilian was also there, having been brought along by Doreen's thoughts, and it was Lilian who eventually managed to make herself understood by the medium. It was Lilian who managed to convey the names of certain people that Lorna knew on earth. I then searched my mind and dragged in a few more, since this seemed to be what the medium was seeking. Between us, we were at least able to give Lorna the names of people we knew she was meeting on earth, but there was very little comfort coming to her from here, because we could not find the way to get it across. Eventually, I heard Lorna say, in some desperation, "I was hoping to hear from a certain friend of mine who is in spirit. I wonder whether you can reach her for me!" It was at this point that I managed to give a great surge of strong thought towards the light, and I made a very minor breakthrough. Lorna was able to recognise me from what the medium said, but received little else. So that attempt on Lorna's part to straighten things out tended to drop away into confusion as had so often happened in the past.

Shortly after this she made her way to another lecture. When she arrived, she found the lecture had been cancelled and in its place was to be a demonstration of clairvoyance by a medium she knew nothing about. Having come this far, she decided to stay. Because I had kept myself available, Doreen was able to arrange for me once again to try and send Lorna a thought. I managed to reach this medium's mind much more successfully. I remain eternally grateful to that lady, whom neither Lorna nor I had experienced before, for telling Lorna so much about me and what I knew about her book without actually divulging the details of who I was or the actual nature of the book to the other people in the hall. Although we were still not talking together, we were both able to come away from that meeting in happier frames of mind about the whole situation than we had been in for a long while. Lorna was reassured that, at last, I seemed to be around again!

It was after that experience that I learned from Doreen that the teachers agreed it would now be better for Lorna's frame of mind if I returned to speaking directly to her. That is how I next spent a period of time here, thoroughly enjoying the freedom I had to speak to Lorna whenever I wished to do so. She was both happier and relieved to hear from me again. She told me what she had been going through, not really knowing what was happening. We both felt very strongly how much better it would have been had I been the one to tell her that I would not be talking to her for a while.

She had received advice from several mediums to the effect that she should not, at any time, be endeavouring to speak with anyone from this side of life unless she was sitting with a group of people who had met together specifically for this purpose. She was told that, if she remained as open to the Spirit World as she had been all this time, she would be spoiling her chances of good mediumship and running an element of risk. She discussed this with me very carefully, and she told me that, try as she might, she had not been able to in any way close down from those who were surrounding her. She had managed to get it under an element of control, so that they no longer seemed to be shouting at her, and she no longer allowed them to tell her what she ought to be doing. She knew she was not yet completely free of confusion, but she did feel that, as she had not yet found a way to completely close down and not hear to some extent, I might just as well avail myself of the opportunity of also speaking to her whenever I felt like it. My presence did become very clear to her, through and over and above everyone else. She seemed to know when it was me and felt that we should enjoy being together for a while.

She said, "I'd much rather have you amongst all the others,

309

Judy, than to have all the others without you. But I want to make it clear that it is only if it is convenient to you. In no way do I want to drag you away from your beautiful world to come and talk to me through what must be a very difficult area."

I hastily assured her that I was having a ball and, if *she* did not mind, I would love to continue our meetings. So, we thoroughly indulged ourselves with lots of happy conversations. I soon found that Lorna's enquiring mind was asking all those questions that I had told Lilian had been concerning me and which, we had been told by Doreen, we had not yet been in this world long enough to truly be ready to enquire about or to completely understand. I explained to Lorna why I was being so unhelpful, and we laughingly agreed that, when she comes here, we will have a go at it all together! And that is precisely what we intend doing.

I have already made up my mind from here that I would love to have Lorna as my travelling companion, exploring all the many, many varieties of existence here. I would love to have her to discuss things with, to enquire with, and to laugh with, as well as to discover what lies beyond the present beautiful areas of my experience and to decide whether we will be able to explore other places together. Neither of us will be able to do so for quite some while after Lorna and my children have arrived here. In the meantime, we feel that we can be travelling a similar pathway and asking similar questions. Possibly, when the time is right to do so, we can make the next step forward together, secure in the knowledge that we have beside us a faithful friend and companion to laugh with and to talk with and generally have a fun time with, as well as to enquire with about the more serious aspects of life here.

Once Lorna had got over her own surprise at this outcome of our discussions together and I had succeeded in convincing her that I had very many reasons for feeling this would be a very successful arrangement and that she was not being fooled by her uninvited and intrusive local communicators, I told all this to Lorna's mother. Lilian was delighted.

She said, "I always felt that I should have had more than one child, but I had such difficulties at Lorna's birth that the doctors advised me against having another in order to avoid the risk of having a deformed child. I felt that Lorna led a somewhat solitary existence as an only child, particularly as there were not many children near us in the family with whom she could be. For various reasons, she has not found a suitable partner on earth and has decided to live life on her own. So I feel more than pleased that despite the fact that you had a number of disasters in your life in one way and Lorna had some disasters in her life in another—and I count my many years of miserable illness during her young years as one of them—that you two have managed to reach each other's minds sufficiently to be certain that you are doing the correct thing to take the same pathway here. I am truly pleased for both of you."

I soon found that even those members of Lorna's family who had never known her on earth—such as her father's parents, who had passed here before she was born but who had taken an interest in her progress on earth once they had realised that she could communicate with us here—were as pleased as Lilian that Lorna and I had made this decision.

Lorna became very confused at first, of course, when a medium described her grandparents to her and the dog that they had brought with them to visit her through the medium. Lorna recognised the dog from her father's descriptions of their family dog when he had been a boy, and she recognised the grandparents from various things that were said to her. She was able to relate all these details to her father, who was duly amazed and also impressed. It was this information that kept being given to him from here, about various members of the family, that finally convinced him that everyone was continuing to exist and that he, in his turn, would be able to meet them all again. This helped him considerably during his last few years of life on earth, when he was reaching his middle eighties and was unable to walk as far as he had before. He was then largely restricted to his own home and spent several periods in hospital. He had this information stored in the back of his mind, and he would sometimes lie there and think about it all, so that when he eventually passed here—as he did in the year 1980 on earth—it was a comparatively easy transition. His family were ready and waiting for him, and it was no time at all before he was able to be brought to his loving family and Lilian.

It was during the last period of his time in hospital that Lorna was able to be reached many, many times by various members of the family, all assuring her of the way to handle the situation. She seemed to know precisely when she ought to be going to the hospital and precisely when it was not necessary. When he did actually come here, she had a strong feeling of the presence of the family for the whole of the week before his funeral, and, shortly after that, he was able to speak to her himself. This was all done with the strong wish and help and determination of the whole family group to work together. They concentrated their thoughts upon Stanley and Lorna, so that he was brought here quickly and carefully and lovingly, and she was given the information and the confirmation that she needed to know that he was well and happy and glad to be here. To her amazement, she received instructions as to who should be offered various items that he had left behind on earth. She received a lot of joking comments both from him and from his brother and other members of the family, so that, instead of feeling sad and bereaved, she felt calm and relieved and happy for him.

He had not been here long before he was telling Lorna good humouredly, "Judy and I are firm friends!" This astonished Lorna to some extent. She had already learned how friendly her mother and I had become, but she had not envisaged that her father and I would have much in common. But, shortly after his arrival here, my time had come to visit the family again, and I asked that I might be introduced to him, as I had heard from Lorna that he had arrived. He was surprised and delighted that I had taken the trouble to ask after him. He told me that he had heard a very great deal about me from Lorna and that he was so proud of her for having written the book about me, which he had read several times. He said he had felt that he had come to know me very much better from reading the book than he had ever felt before, and he told me how pleased and delighted he was that I had taken the trouble to come and see him.

I found him to be a very sincere and kindly man. I could see what Lorna had meant when she told me that, although he had a lot of laughter in him, he did not always see what was amusing her and her mother. I, nevertheless, found that he did like to laugh, and we were able to exchange a lot of joking remarks together. I found that I had made another friend in Lorna's family group.

He and Laddie were delighted to be reunited. He was also

pleased to be reunited with the dog he had shared with his parents on earth, as he had been equally devoted to the beautiful Patch, who, to me, was a replica of the famous dog film star Lassie.

It was not long before he was telling Lorna, "I feel completely rejuvenated. . . . I feel eighteen again," despite being eighty-six when he had come here.

V

Lorna's and my decision to be companions here in due course was not as precipitate as it may appear. Admittedly, I had been dubious when Doreen first approached me with the idea, but I had not been here long at that time, and I was used to thinking of partnership in earth terms. I knew that neither Lorna nor I would have ever considered the suggestion to be likely on earth. Later, when I saw how others here were happily enjoying companionships that were somewhat unusual by earth standards simply because earthly partnerships usually seem to have a sexual connotation of one kind or another, I began to think differently. It was certainly a very big point in Lorna's favour that she had known and understood me on earth, with all my earth world faults and failings, yet was prepared to defend me so strongly and despite such continuously mounting odds against succeeding.

During my conversations with Doreen I had repeatedly found myself having to face myself as various people had expected me to be when I was on earth and how they had subsequently thought me to be, but seldom as I had actually been. Most of my dealings with those who had claimed to be my fans and who had wanted to be my friends had ended in disaster. Usually, it was the more pushy or pernicious of those who had succeeded in gaining my attention. They were also the ones who, when I was so much more alone and uncared for during my last years, had succeeded in becoming a closer part of my life. Because I was no longer able to keep myself well, I was not seeing anything or anyone in the correct perspective. Otherwise, I would not have accepted such offers of friendship so easily. Even those whom I had known better from earlier days let their attitudes be coloured against me when the press stories and the hangers-on had their field-day with my reputation.

That is why I am so especially grateful that Lorna came forward to be helpful to me in 1969, when I had arrived in London after so very many troubles. I am also grateful that she stayed faithful to my memory even when I came here six months later, after we had recently seen each other for what had proved to be the very last time on earth.

When Doreen kept telling me that Lorna would prove to be my best friend here and future companion, I began to compare her in my mind with all those others who had been around me at various times over the years. I had already agreed with Doreen that I had always liked Lorna and had appreciated her attitude of quiet kindness towards me instead of the emotional reactions I had received from others who had subsequently rejected me. Doreen had told me that Lorna was as sincere and thoughtful about me and for me as I had felt her to be, and that this had stemmed, right at the outset, from a deep similarity to me within her own soul. Neither of us had recognised this similarity at the time but nevertheless, it had always been there.

In addition to this unconcious similarity, Lorna had experienced her mother's own struggles with a strained nervous system, and she had also been able to see my own emotional disturbances and confusions and over-reactions for what they were. This was the firm and solid basis of Lorna's deeply sincere affection for me, together with the fact that she could respond sincerely and affectionately to my true personality as well as to my talents as a performer.

This has all been related elsewhere, I realise, but I feel it is necessary to repeat this here as a way of ensuring that you realise where the original basis for our now accepted and agreed friendship for the future was conceived. I discussed all this with Lorna because she had told me that she was, herself, often surprised that she was able to feel so devoted to me over all the years. We only met occasionally and seldom had much opportunity to get to know each other all that well until the more recent times before I came here. Even then, I was usually too involved or too unwell to really see our association all that clearly. "I used to regard myself as a Garland nut," Lorna has since told me laughingly, "but no amount of straight talking to myself seemed to make any difference. I still remained one!"

314

"Thank God for that!" I was to reply for her from here, and I truly meant it.

Lorna has asked me how it is that certain souls of such diverse backgrounds on earth can be so similar deep down inside when there is no obvious soul link between them. That is one of the many questions to which we both have to await an answer during our future experiences and evolution together here. It is not something to which I have found the answer at present. I am just thankful that it is possible.

Some people are fortunate enough to be able to have a close friendship or partnership with a similar soul when on earth, but they are more rare, I am told, than those who have to wait to find their true soul mate here.

Lorna is close to her mother's soul also, and that is why I share such a close friendship with Lilian. There are other factors, however, at this stage, that cause Lilian still to feel close in outlook with her husband as well as some members of her family. Lorna, on the other hand, is linked with the family less closely and mainly through Lilian, although she recalls some of them with affection.

Much as I appreciate and enjoy the many sincere friends I have made here, and much as this has led me towards a happier life, I now recognise and realise that it was Lorna's undoubting faith in me, which was reaching my subconscious mind during all those periods of doubts and revelations concerning my earth life that I had been discussing with Doreen, that had so often helped me to overcome the sadness and feeling of failure that I still had within me. I later felt that, surely, the very finest friend I could have here would be the one who had remained steadfastly on my side—one might almost say "by my side"—even during those troublesome days on earth and even when she was still uncertain whether or not I continued to exist in another life.

It was all these aspects, of course, that Doreen and the teachers had in mind for me, but I needed the time and the opportunities to see it all more clearly for myself. In this, I was greatly helped to make the right decision by several extraordinary events that the teachers here helped to arrange. All these happened several years before Lorna's father, Stanley, came here, so I must now return you to the period shortly after Lorna's book had been published. We were once more speaking to each other regularly,

315

with the blessings of all my friends and helpers here and with what would probably have been the consternation of those who were occasionally trying to advise Lorna on earth concerning such matters!

Having already established our firm friendship, I was approached by Doreen with the news that it had been decided to try and bring Lorna and me closer together for a brief period by having her mind brought here while she was asleep. In saying this, I had better briefly explain there are many different layers of consciousness in the human mind, few of which are actually used while on earth and many of which often remain unused here for eons, until we gain the necessary experience to reveal the next layer, as it were. Lorna's everyday mind would remain with her body while asleep, and the higher, more sensitive, part of her mind, which is normally used for her more spiritual decisions and attitudes, would be brought here to visit me in my area of existence, which, at that time, was mainly with the children. It is a complex subject and not one that I can explain deeply here, but the fact is that, on several occasions, Lorna was actually brought to visit me here. She literally stood beside me as a living being who was as substantial and real to me here as she had been when standing beside me on earth.

We laughed together and said how glad we were to be together and seeing each other again. We spent time with the children, and, on one occasion, Lilian also came along, and they spoke together. Lorna was able to tell stories to the children, something she would have felt completely incapable of doing had she been asked to do so on earth at that time. She also found that I was just as clever with the animals we had there as with the children, something she would not have expected me to have been particularly good at when on earth.

There was one occasion when a loud noise woke her and drew her away from me so suddenly that I rushed after her and called out to her. She woke up in her bed on earth feeling very confused, yet strongly aware of my calming presence. I managed to stay with her until she had readjusted.

She was very confused about each of these several visits because, although we both derived enormous pleasure from them while they were taking place, I was the only one who recalled them clearly afterwards. When Lorna awoke, she usually had only a very muddled recollection and felt somewhat unhappy without realising why she had such a strong feeling of "loss" and unrest. We realised it was unsettling her concious mind on earth. So, after a while, Lorna's visits here were discontinued, but not before she had been used, at her own request, to help a friend of hers to pass here more easily than he would have otherwise done.

She and her friend, Marion, had met Fred three years earlier when on holiday in Austria. Fred and Marion had become engaged shortly afterwards and had married in the following year. Sadly, Fred was found to have terminal cancer, and he came here after only a little more than two years of marriage. He and his wife had discussed his impending passing, and he was exceedingly unhappy at the thought of leaving his wife alone on earth after such a brief period together. Lorna had asked Marion whether it would be of any help whatsoever to read anything on the topic of life here, and Marion and Fred decided to read and discuss the literature that Lorna sent. Although it was a little difficult for them to grasp it all in such a brief time, they did at least feel it had helped a little. Fred derived more help from it than he realised at the time. Lorna had felt deeply sorry and shocked for them and had asked to be used in any way possible if it would help to ease Fred's passing here.

The result was that, when Fred left the earth, he was in a coma and drifted slowly towards where there would be those waiting to try and help him. Lorna's mind was brought towards his mind, and he felt her presence. He was surprised to see her but confident that he must be all right. She and his helpers were able to transfer him safely to the hospital here until he was rested and recovered. When Lorna awoke, she felt very strongly that her friend had actually passed here at that time.

My part in the story came later, after Fred had been here for approximately six months of earth time and was still feeling very unhappy without his wife and even without all the various ac-tivities that he had taken part in when on earth. It can sometimes be difficult for someone who is as exceptionally active mentally as Fred has always been to approach life here a little differently, especially when he is missing a loved companion. He had loved his wife very, very sincerely, and he missed her exceedingly, while also knowing that she felt very despairing over his loss.

I was suddenly asked by Doreen whether I would be prepared to visit this friend of Lorna's to see whether I could help him to understand where he could be most active here. They knew he had a fine potential, but he was feeling listless and disinterested. "We think, if you could tell him some of the happy places here and perhaps ask him whether he would like to send a message to his wife through Lorna, it might be helpful."

I was glad of the opportunity to be useful to one of Lorna's friends, and I willingly agreed. I wondered how I would make out with an adult problem, having only, so far, struggled with those adults of the Gumm family! I later discovered that Fred's main problem was simply that he was finding it difficult to see how he might manage to pursue some of the numerous interests he had enjoyed on earth in a way that fitted into his new environment.

To my surprise, Fred's face lit up in pleasure when I arrived. "Judy! I never expected to ever meet *you!* What a very great pleasure!" He went on to say he had always enjoyed my movies. He and Lorna had discussed me at some length, and he had read her book about me. He said he had not read very much about me in the newspapers in Shetland, where he had lived all his life, but that he could recognise the problems I had faced in my life simply by hearing about me from Lorna, as well as by reading her book.

"But you're looking very well, now!" he told me. I was able to assure him that life here could be a great healer in many ways, and we had a long and very serious discussion. At the end of it all, we were laughing heartily together, and I could see the true Fred begining to emerge. He gratefully accepted my offer to help him to send a message to his wife through Lorna, and we set to work on it.

It was not much longer before we confronted the amazed Lorna, who happened to be watching television at the time and wondered why the person she was watching on television had suddenly reminded her of Fred when there was clearly no resemblance! Anyway, we managed our visit extremely well. Lorna was delighted to hear from Fred and be able to transfer his message to Marion. It gave Fred the incentive he needed to take the same very positive attitude here that he had always had on earth. He set about exploring the territory and eventually linked up with a friend of his who had passed here not so very long after his own arrival. They had shared similar interests on earth, and they helped each other to become active here.

Fred is now as busily and happily active as ever. He had suffered from a severe physical disability when on earth, as a result of having had polio, and he was so pleased to be completely free of it all here. He is now one of our very active people, helping others who arrive here in some form of distress to take positive steps forward in a happier direction. He and his friend take care of those who arrive here from Shetland and who are in need of help. Fred has also managed to reach the minds of some of the conservationists on earth and has often, without those concerned always being aware of it, managed to work constructively on their minds with ideas for the conservation of nature in Shetland, something which was dear to his heart when on earth.

By this time, my own family were beginning to make better progress. Susan had met both our parents and had also sided with Dad against Mother's still unbending attitude towards him. She had become a much happier and much younger-looking person by the time I next met her, and we were able to meet each other occasionally. Strangely, our next meeting was, in some ways, a little less successful than had been the first one shortly after she had awakened here. Then she had been sad and wan but seemed so loving towards me. When she next awoke, she was still pleased to see me but a little removed from me again. Doreen said this was natural, really, as she had to admit there were many weaknesses in Susan's attitude to life here that needed more positive thinking. However, she stood up to Mother and defended Dad, who is now getting a wider attitude here himself.

Mother has at last admitted to me that she is now very sorry that she did not realise how harshly she was sometimes treating me after Dad died, and she also regrets that she let the studio chiefs rule my life. She had seen there were faults in their attitude towards me, but she felt she was unable to make any other suggestions. She let it happen, and she now regrets that she had not taken a firmer stand for me. The outcome is that we have been able to reconcile and not feel bitter against each other any more, but we remain apart and are unlikely to ever be close.

Susan is gaining some help now by being used to help people who come here from some sort of physical handicap, as she always had sympathy for those who suffered such handicaps on earth. It gives her the support she needs to realise that, in some ways, they had more cause than she had to feel unhappy. In feeling so sympathetic for them and so pleased to see them soon get well again here, she is gradually brightening up to be the Susan I had known when we were young.

VI

It was soon after I had begun meeting Lorna in her sleep that I began to wish I could, somehow or other, reach my children. The wish to be able to speak to them had originally taken root in my mind when I had learned of Sally's messages to her mother and when I had found I could speak so easily to Lorna. On the other hand, I had to recognise there could be difficulties in sending messages through the wrong medium, even should my children decide to visit one, which they had not chosen to do. I recalled there had been one occasion when a medium had described me to my friend Lorna quite well, without actually knowing who I was, but had then completely turned around what I had been hoping to convey. Fortunately, Lorna was aware of it and challenged the comment, so that the medium tried again and came up with the correct answer.

By this time, Lorna was beginning to realise all the pitfalls that can arise from such occasions, and she was always careful in the way she accepted or disputed what she was being given as a factual piece of information. Too many mediums, we have both now learned, try to give a fuller statement than they have actually received. Their own minds, often unintentionally, add interpretations that can give a wrong impression of what is actually being conveyed from here. This is how I came to realise how important it is for the medium and his or her helpers here to be in complete accord. I always ensure that Lorna and I are completely adjusted to the correct vibration before I tell her anything important. My sincere wish to be able to help in this way is being fulfilled here, but I will return to that later.

I must now return you to the period when Lorna and I had

been talking together regularly after the publication of her book and after we had been spending the special times together here. It had been such a joy to speak easily to someone who still loved me on earth that, more than ever, I felt I would like my own children to realise how well and truly happy I now was.

I approached Doreen and explained that there was this strong wish within me but that I hesitated how to try and go about it. Doreen said she would make an enquiry and let me know whether any possible link could be found. I had to be content with that for some while. In the meantime, I had decided to take more interest in meeting with the show business people who meet together here from time to time. On earth, much as I liked parties and fun and laughter, I had not always felt comfortable with some of the attitudes I had encountered in some people. I had tried hard to seem to be fitting in, otherwise I would have been considered a snob and a bore, but it had been difficult at times. I guess I did feel foolish, also, on those occasions when I was not accompanied by my husband during one of our periods of separation and was asked out by one or another person whom I had liked as a friend only to find out that they wished me to take them as a lover. This had never been my intention at any time, and I always found it difficult to explain this satisfactorily. It had made it difficult to be alone at a party and often equally difficult to accept an escort.

Having found that the attitudes here were likely to be easier in this respect, and after singing my first concert here and having found a happy background with Lilian and her family, I felt I could now also try and find some friends among those who had been in show business when on earth, although I was not seeking out anyone in particular. However, it was during this period that I again met John Hodiak with whom I had worked in *The Harvey Girls*. He had always been kind to me when I became a little over-tense during the filming. It had been an exceedingly difficult picture to make for everyone in the cast, as the script kept being changed and rearranged and we never knew from one day to the next what we were going to be expected to do.

There were also lots of horses around in this production. I was so scared of them that I had great difficulty in completing some of the rehearsals when they were standing all around me.

John had realised my fears and had taken these seriously and tried to be as unobtrusively protective as possible. I had liked his quietly calm company, and he seemed to be such a polite person. So, when he approached me here and said he had enjoyed my concert, I was pleased to see him again. We only met a few times after that, but he seemed unchanged from when we had worked in the picture.

When I had been visiting the show business area from time to time for some while, I met Carmen Miranda. She and I had hardly spoken when on earth. Here, we seemed to find more in common. She is not at all like the personality everyone who saw her in pictures remembers as the "Brazilian Bombshell," as she was described in her publicity for the pictures. She is really a very quiet and serious person. We shared a lack of height, which we discovered we both felt to be a little bit demeaning when on earth, and we discovered we both felt we had spent the larger part of our lives on earth in supporting others, with little gratitude in return. We had some long talks together and she was intrigued to learn of all my talks with Lorna.

It was during this time that Doreen informed me that she thought there might possibly be a way of getting a message to at least one of my children. I was delighted, and when Doreen explained it all to me, I asked Carmen if she would like to come along with me. She was very excited at this suggestion, so we made our way to our usual area for communication. Here I should explain that I no longer needed to return to that area for my direct talks with Lorna, as we had formed a sufficiently strong link for me to simply find a quiet place and then concentrate upon her. But, for the purpose of this link, we needed the usual support from those who provide the power for such occasions.

Doreen had explained that some people I had met in London, who had also met my children at that time, would be visiting a medium. As my daughter Lorna would shortly be visiting London, it had been thought that, if I could convince these people that I had communicated with them, they might, possibly, tell Lorna. It was only a possibility, but it seemed to be the only possibility that was likely to arise at that time, as far as Doreen's "explorers," for want of a better word, could see.

During the several visits that I made to the meetings these

people had with the medium, I did manage to convey who I was, and I was well received. This encouraged me to make several other approaches to those in the group through other mediums. In so doing, I even went so far as to experiment a little in order to show them how easily I could reach people and how easy it is for some people on earth to be influenced from here without actually being aware of it. Unfortunately, none of this was ever conveyed to my daughter Lorna, and I eventually gave up. Despite the interest that Carmen took in it all, I somehow felt defeated and even empty as a result of all those efforts. I told this to Doreen, who immediately diagnosed the trouble.

"Even apart from the disappointment in not reaching your daughter, you have also had to be 'Judy Garland' again for those whom you visited. It was from 'Judy Garland' that they accepted the messages. With your friend Lorna, you are her friend Judy, and that does now make a very big difference to your reaction."

"I guess you are right," I admitted, "but it was worth a try."

It was not too long after this that I found I was able to reach my daughter Lorna, to a limited extent. She never actually sees or hears me, as does my friend Lorna, but she can be made aware of my presence, if I try hard, and she does feel me with her from time to time. It gives me a lovely feeling to be able to let her know I am still very much around as a person. Although Lorna is not normally mediumistic, I think this contact is possible because we were so close in our feelings for each other when I was on earth. I love all my three children equally strongly, but Lorna is closest in her soul to my way of feeling things.

It was some while after I had made these attempts to send a message to my daughter that I actually told my friend Lorna. I guess I put it a bit badly. I simply said, in reply to a comment she made to me, "Yes, I *have* been through to others. I went with Carmen Miranda."

At the outset, Lorna decided she had either misheard me or else another communicator had cut across! At last I convinced her that I had become friendly with Carmen and told her why I had decided to try and send messages to others. Lorna was angry with me at first.

"How could you, Judy, after I have always tried not to let any medium, other than Doris Collins, know you are communicating? Can't you just imagine the headlines? Especially if someone gets it all wrong!"

I did agree with her, but I also felt I had been correct to try and get a message to my daughter. Lorna agreed with my wish and need to reach my other Lorna, but she felt that I had not chosen the best time and place. Indeed, I did agree there would probably, at that time, have been a better opportunity if I had let her know of the problem beforehand and not afterwards. By the time I did so, it was too late.

Not long after we had discussed this, Lorna told me that my communication to the others had now become the topic of an article in a psychic a newspaper. "It makes you seem very silly and shallow in your approach, and the writer is clearly unaware of your true reason for communicating!"

She was obviously angry again, and I really did feel so sorry that I had undertaken the whole thing. "I promise faithfully I will never do that again," I assured her, "unless one of my kids actually goes directly to a medium in the hope of hearing from me, although I don't think they will."

"That's a different thing entirely, and I would understand your need to do that, Judy, but for God's sake be more careful in the future! If you must say something to somebody, try and clear your name! Don't sound so frivolous!"

I was completely told off, and I felt very sincerely sorry. We were able to laugh together afterwards, when Lorna had cooled down, that we had even managed to have a disagreement from two different worlds!

It seemed no time at all after this disagreement that Doreen told me that my friend Lorna was on her way to a lecture to be given by Doris Collins, the medium in which both of us had much faith, and that, although Lorna was unaware of it, Doris intended to illustrate her lecture with some actual clairvoyance. "We cannot guarantee it, Judy, but we thought you might like to be there."

I very much wished to be there, so I went along to see whether I could manage to speak through Doris. I had always found it very easy and straightforward to communicate through her, but I had never before had to try and reach her through a barrage of other minds who were all trying to speak through her to others in a crowded hall. This time, I had to wait to see whether Doris's main helpers on this side of life would allow me to speak, or whether others would be considered to have priority. It had all happened so suddenly, and I was uncertain as to whether or not I would have a chance to say anything. To my delight, I was signalled to send my message. As others were waiting, I kept it brief and to the point! "This is Judy Garland. I'm not going to say much. I just want to tell you that I did not take my own life. I had a very happy life, and I lived it to the hilt, and I don't regret any of it. Goodnight!"

There! That's said! I thought to myself as I happily made my way towards Lorna, only to find that she was far less than happy!

"Judy! How could you? How could you?" she was demanding of me. "How could you?"

Before I could speak to her, the lecture had ended, and Lorna was approached by excited members of an enquiring audience, all asking her whether she thought it was really me. She assured them that I had spoken to her on a number of occasions through Doris and others, that she had known me well on earth, and, yes, she was positive I had not taken my own life. She left the hall knowing that a number of people there seemed to have been pleased and relieved to know that I had not taken my own life, as many had been led to presume, but she was clearly not at all happy at my sudden announcement. I gathered that even her companion was a little bit dubious. I heard Lorna trying to explain to her that I had tended to have this unfortunate habit of rushing into things when on earth and saying something in a way that could be misconstrued. "And she's done it again!" I heard Lorna say despairingly.

I stayed around, apologetically, for some while. Lorna tried to acknowledge my presence while having to speak with her friend. Eventually, I left and I returned later when Lorna was alone again. She was clearly aware that I was full of apology—and I was! I realised that, in some way, Lorna felt my message to have been a disaster, but I could not see why.

"Judy, it was 'Sunday Night at the Palladium' all over again," she said, recalling one of my public disasters towards the end of my life on earth, when I had rushed on stage unprepared, due to a backstage misunderstanding, and had suffered very bad publicity as a result.

325

"But I thought you wanted me to say that!" I told her.

"Not like that!" she replied. "Judy, I have spent a great deal of time and trouble explaining to readers of my book, as well as directly to people, that you always tried to overcome all your difficulties, but that you did have difficulties. I have also tried to explain that your life was not lurid as others would like the public to believe. Now, just consider what you have said and how you have, in a few brief sentences and in public, cut across all that I have tried to say for you!"

It was some while before Lorna simmered down from this event. Eventually, I saw why she was so mad at me. "You have done what you always did," she told me. "You have turned on the public face of Judy Garland rather than let the public see you as someone who has faced unhappiness. You have, as usual, succeeded in contributing to the wrong public image."

I had to admit that she was right. Eventually, of course, Lorna forgave me and accepted that my intentions had been good. "Doreen is right, Judy. You have always been a positive person, even when you have been positively wrong!" She laughed with me.

We discussed where my two attempts at communication other than directly to or for her had put us and what could be done to alleviate what Lorna saw as my two disasters.

Eventually, we agreed that she would provide a very carefully worded article that would explain my various communications to her and would also endeavour to give a better indication of the sort of person I truly am. The article would also explain that my worth has been recognised here, where I am very happy and succeeding exceptionally well. My helpers here all approved the completed article before Lorna approached the psychic newspaper in which the other article had appeared. She told the publishers that they could only have it if it went in completely unchanged. Should it need to be shortened, she would be responsible for any cuts. This was agreed. When it appeared, the article had not only been reduced from what had, in any case, not amounted to an inappropriate length, but words had been changed, and the previous article that had, to some extent, prompted it, was reproduced in part alongside. When Lorna received a telephone call from a journalist who wished to know the manner in which I "manifested" to her, she had to assure him the word was not hers, that it had been introduced into her article by the publisher, and that the only way she sees me is as a brightly coloured image imprinted on her mind. At no time does she see me standing in front of her! We were both angry that the readers might get the wrong impression of me as still being to some extent earthbound. Later, Lorna received a telephone call from the man responsible for the other article about me. He told her his article had been very much reduced, that my seemingly silly and shallow actions were not really like that at all, and that I had a serious reason behind them. Lorna was able to let me have this piece of mollifying information, but we both felt frustrated that each time something was attempted to try and clear my name, it was always bungled in one way or another.

It was while all these experiences were taking place that I realised a friend of mine had arrived here from earth. This was Beatrice "Bumble" Dawson, who had been a theatrical costumier, as well as sometimes designing clothing for other ladies. We had met during one of my earlier visits to London, and she had been one of the few people who had continued to be my friend during my last visit to London, in 1969. She had visited me at the hotel a few times and also at the theatre, and had helped me to prepare for my wedding to Mickey.

She and Lorna had met from time to time during those months in London in 1969, and after I had come here and was trying to help Lorna get her confidence back to complete her book about me during all the confusion around her, I kept telling her to "ask Bumble." Eventually, after I had removed myself for a while and Lorna was still confused, she did, I later learned, "ask Bumble," who assured her that what she had written was correct but also warned her against publishing it, as she might be sued. Poor Lorna felt that to restrict it all would be letting me down, and she hoped to at least get some of it accepted.

Meanwhile, Bumble had respected Lorna's hopes but felt that she had little chance of succeeding. Then she read Lorna's book and was so moved and impressed that she wished she had taken it all far more seriously and given Lorna the firm support she had needed when she was clearly the only person speaking out firmly for me. "I saw Lorna was sincere, Judy," Bumble was to tell me here, "but I felt she lacked the experience necessary to complete a full book about you. I felt so sorry later on, when I saw how much more she seemed to know about you than I had ever realised."

I assured Bumble that I had been equally astonished but exceedingly grateful. I was able to tell her how much I had somehow managed to contribute to it, even from here, even though, like some of my best scenes from *A Star is Born*, much of it had ended up on the cutting room floor. "They publish all the lies and cut out the truth," I complained.

Bumble sympathised and added that even she had put her foot in it about me with Lorna on one occasion. She had been carefully put in her place with what Lorna felt to be the better explanation. "Yes, she did know me better than I realised," I told Bumble.

We agreed it would be a good idea if Bumble joined me on one of my visits to Lorna, and we managed to explain it all to Lorna quite clearly. Bumble was recognised, and she managed, with my help, to describe how she had come here as a result of a car crash. She had found herself lying on the side of the road, but not in any pain. She simply saw that there was a crash and she was lying there. Then she blacked out, so far as she could recall, and woke up in the hospital here, where she was soon sufficiently recovered to begin her life here.

She does not really know whether she saw the roadside in her mind when her physical body had already been left behind or whether she came here later. Anyway, she felt no pain whatsoever and felt it had been an extremely lucky sort of passing, because she hardly felt any ill effects when she woke up here. Some people have a feeling of soreness when they are unexpectedly removed from their earth body, but Bumble only recalls waking up here and feeling well after being beside the road without any pain.

She told Lorna how very sorry she now was that she had not helped her more with her book. Lorna said, "Yes, I had hoped for more, but I also understood you would not realise how much I needed your support then, and I felt I could hardly tell you I had been hearing from Judy!"

Bumble agreed that that would have really made her think that Lorna was unlikely to be a reliable biographer, and we all agreed there was not really any recrimination necessary. Bumble later joined me on two more visits to Lorna, but she is now involved elsewhere and we seldom meet. I believe she still sees a lot of Vivien Leigh and Noel Coward and others she knew through living in London. Noel Coward visited me here once, coming with Bumble, and he told me he was amazed to see me in such unsophisticated surroundings. I suppose it is surprising to the average show business artist that I really am far happier in the company of those who have never been famous performers.

VII

Before long, Lorna and I were again facing two more literary destructions of my character. One was by someone I had regarded as a very sincere friend for a number of years. We had some misunderstandings, but we had always, I had thought, remained friends. We had laughed a lot together, and yet we had serious discussions. He had remained in my mind as a friend, even during the several years since we had last met on earth. There had been several occasions when Lorna and he had spoken together about me. He had seemed to retain his affection for me and had even encouraged Lorna in her idea to write a book about me: "Let all the rubbish about her subside and then bring out your book."

Eventually, several years after Lorna's sincere attempt on my behalf had been largely overlooked and not even published in my own country, his book appeared and provided yet another titillating example to the public at large as to what an exceedingly peculiar person Judy Garland had been. Admittedly, I had been difficult at times, and often more difficult than I had ever actually realised when I was on earth, but there is a very big difference between being a person who becomes easily temperamental when under stress and strain and the sort of person he has depicted in a number of incidences.

I found it extremely difficult to accept that the person I thought I had known as my sincere friend could have written so abominably about me. There was no way I could have behaved in the way I have been depicted as acting in various episodes.

Doreen tried to explain to me that there were several reasons for his change of attitude towards me. It had seemingly started when I had been a little bit highly strung and over-sensitive at a period when a number of things had been distressing me and I had been dieting during work on a picture. Then he had read various other accounts of me after I had come here, on top of the bad publicity I had been receiving during the last years of my life on earth. Instead of rejecting it all, he had allowed it to play on his subconscious mind, so that, when he had decided to try and write about me and had spent many, many hours alone and thinking about it all, his judgment had become impaired, his memory had played tricks on him, and it all became distorted in his mind. His imagination had become involved without his realising it, and the result had been an inaccurate account of the way in which certain events had taken place, although he had been genuinely convinced at the time that his recollections were accurate reconstructions of what could have taken place.

I had already realised that Lorna was being upset again by it all. Although she usually tries to avoid reading all these destructive accounts of me, people who know of her interest in me nearly always send her these items for her to see, and she finds it difficult to avoid them. "I've sent him an explicit letter, Judy, telling him that, in letting you down so badly, he has also let himself down, but I don't know what else I can do."

I told her the same as on previous occasions, which is that the truth is known here, and that is what really matters. I did, however, feel hurt that someone I had liked, and even felt affectionate toward, should have even felt that I had been capable of such actions, and that he had thought it right to provide such an account of me for public reading. I felt sad for the person I thought I had known as a jolly and sincere friend, and I felt sad for myself that I had, one more time, not made the friend that I thought I had.

Having faced this demeaning letdown with even less equanimity than some of the others, I decided that nobody could possibly stoop any lower than the writers of various accounts of me had already done, so this would probably be the end of all the destruction of my public reputation. However, more was to come, and that proved to be the last straw which eventually caused this book to be written.

There had been a number of people in my life at one time or another who claimed to have loved me. Few had truly loved me.

They had loved spending time with "Judy Garland." This man was no exception. He had come into my life when I was deeply unhappy and lonely and also very broke. I had been staying in Boston in order to spend more time at the hospital where I had gone in the past to try and get well after a period of strain, but I had returned to New York to discuss some forthcoming television programs. This man was introduced to me as a new writer. I agreed to listen to his material, and, when I liked it, we worked on some of the preliminaries together. He told me that he had always liked me as a performer, and said how grateful he was that I had agreed to perform his material. Then he invited me to have dinner with him.

I was pleased to accept, as he seemed genuine, and I later accepted an invitation to meet his family for dinner. They were all very pleasant to me and invited me to stay with them as their guest. I did actually stay with them for a few days and was made to feel most welcome. I felt uncomfortable, however, that they were all working and away all day, although I had some very pleasant talks with the grandfather, so I left and, shortly afterwards, returned to Boston.

I had mentioned in passing that I was having some confusing tax problems and this man had offered to check them over for me, but the papers were in Boston. One day, after I had returned to my apartment, I received a telephone call from him. He told me he was in Boston on business and asked if he could call and discuss the tax problems and then take me to dinner. I was happy to agree. When he arrived, we sat and talked for a while. Then he went into my bedroom to get the bag that was holding the tax papers. He was only there a few moments. When he had looked at all the papers, he said these were beyond his understanding, and he felt I needed more professional advice than he was able to give me. Then he took me to dinner. He seemed genuinely concerned. Later on, after I had returned to New York, he did make some enquiries for me concerning some of my trunks that had most of my clothes in them and were being held in California.

Even after the television shows had been taped, he never acted otherwise than very courteously, and I had no reason to believe that he was feeling otherwise. Yet, the detailed material that he has since presented about a very few minor incidents in our acquaintance consists of a few simple, bare facts that have been used as pegs on which to hang a whole series of imaginary situations. He has succeeded in abusing me in a way that no one else has done to quite that extent, simply as a result of my believing that he was being a true friend.

Doreen has since helped me to try and get his attitude, as well as mine during this period, into better perspective. We are agreed that there was no justification for his writing about me in the way that he has chosen to do. We were never more than casual friends, even though I believed him to be sincere in his liking for me. Although I am always demonstrative to those who I think like me, I never gave him any cause to think that I might have had any interest in any association with him beyond that of simple friendship.

We were never anything more than very casual friends, and I had only known him a short while when I met Mickey again. I had been acquainted with Mickey for some time before we had fallen in love and decided to marry. Mickey met this man several times and, when we married, sent him a wedding invitation. We both thought of him as a pleasant and friendly person, and this was the impression that Lorna had received when I introduced them. Imagine our reaction when, of all the books that have appeared in print abusing my name in various incredible ways, this has proved to be, in my view, the most degenerate and debasing account. I would never, ever, in any way whatsoever, have spoken and behaved in the way in which I have been depicted. It not only demeans me below anything that anyone who truly knew me could ever have imagined, least of all believed, but it also throws dirt on my truly sincere love for Mickey during the months we had together before I came here. I told Lorna that it was the filthiest, most degenerate attempt that could ever have been concocted to thoroughly ruin what little was left of my reputation on earth.

When I asked Lorna about some of the other accounts that had been written about me, she said she had not by any means seen them all. From the extracts she had read, however, it did appear that almost all of them, whether intentionally or unintentionally, provided distorted accounts of my words and actions, and they invariably placed some events many years out of their correct context in order to make their versions of me appear to fit. She considered most of them to be either arrogantly presumptuous or colourfully imaginative. We discussed some of these, and I found it helpful, because she was often able to give me her own views of what she had actually seen and heard happening at some of the times that had been written about. Through our discussions, I was helped to see myself and some of the others more clearly. I often took these aspects back to Doreen, and we had further discussions that I also found helpful. In some ways, I was able to see myself and others even more clearly than I had done in my original discussions with Doreen. Then I would take my findings back to Lorna and get her further opinion.

Before long, I was again seeing myself as not having been as bad as I had begun to feel from all this unpleasantness. Judging from all that I have been told about myself from here and from Lorna, I could be extremely exasperating and often a little bit annoying. I would not always listen to something I should have listened to, and I sometimes got angrier than I should have done. I also, however, too often did not get given the correct information from those to whom I would have listened for an answer and for support. There was no way that any reasonable person could honestly have seen me as either destructive or amoral. If they did truly think this of me, then there must be something extremely peculiar about their own way of thinking.

Lorna agreed with me that she also saw this latest account of me as being the worst of many that she already regarded as despicable. Yet, even as I attempt to defend myself to you from here, I am advised to refrain from mentioning the names of my detractors who are still on earth in case I cause Lorna some of the legal problems she encountered when trying to complete her original book on my behalf.

Apparently, because I am officially dead I am legally regarded on earth as public property, but my public denigrators are not so regarded because they are still officially alive. Somehow, I always felt that I was public property when I was officially alive on earth, so I guess things have not changed all that much, except that I now know how few people have remained loyal to me.

I accept I was often quick-tempered and high-strung. I often got the wrong impression of a situation and, as a result, got overwrought and said things I did not truly mean or even clearly remember afterwards. I guess, when you get into this frame of mind you also get to be a little bit selfish at times, but I was never intentionally unkind to people, and I was never vindictive. I never acted immorally, and I never intentionally lied to, or about, anyone. Least of all would I have ever allowed any man other than my promised husband to make love to me, and even then, both with Sid and Mickey, only because we were so sure we were to be married as soon as we could legally be so. I had a sincere respect for the marriage vows, and the insinuation that I had an affair with anyone, and in the appalling manner described, is the one that repels me the most.

Lorna has justly reminded me that, when I was on earth, I tended never to explain myself to anyone. A few timely denials on my part at certain times in my life on earth, when the publicity got out of hand, might have helped things a little bit more than my usual attitude of answering public questions as lightly as I could. There is a good reason here for finding out that that is where I failed, more often than not. At least, I tell Lorna, *she* tried to stand up for me on earth in my absence, even before she realised that I still continue to exist. That is why I hope she will decide to remain my friend when she comes here.

We both felt incensed about this latest abomination in a long line of defamatory literature. Although I had tried very hard to follow my previous procedure of assuring Lorna that it no longer mattered to me here, I found that it did matter, very much, especially for those I still love on earth and who still love me. Eventually, Lorna said, "Judy, will you help me to write a chapter about your present life and include in it what you feel about all the lies and the misinterpretations that are being put around your name? If you agree, I will make another attempt to get my book about you accepted in America, with this additional chapter included and with an explanation of how I can hear from you."

I felt this to be a wonderful idea, and I said I would see what could be done. With Doreen's help, I asked the higher teachers here. It was agreed that I could be helped to provide this information to Lorna and that I could assure her that it would be published in America. I rushed excitedly to Lorna and made the dramatic announcement: "I have been given permission to tell you that

334

'our' book will be published in America!"

"Well, before we go to all that trouble, and to avoid sending manuscripts back and forth across the Atlantic and probably losing them, I'll make some enquiries," said the faithful Lorna, somewhat cautiously and dubiously in view of past disappontments.

The upshot of all the enquiry was that, having narrowed down the field to those publishers that seemed likely to be interested in the psychic element of the book as well as the show business aspects of my life, she approached eight possible publishers. All sent polite reasons for not being able to consider it. We seemed to be back to square one until Lorna saw an advertisement for an American publisher who published manuscripts for a payment but with the promise of all the usual outlets. "This is our only chance, Judy. Let's go for it. I don't know yet whether or not I shall be able to afford it, as they only quote the cost after reading the manuscript. Are you game?"

I felt more than "game" and raring to go! It was then that I learned the answer to something that had been perplexing Lorna and me for a very long time. During those earlier days of speaking to Lorna through Doris Collins, Doris had twice told Lorna that she was being told from here that Lorna would write another book. Lorna was so fed up with all the trouble she had already encountered over her first book about me that she was adamant against writing another. "Anyway, I wouldn't have anything else to write about," she said. We were even more mystified when Doris passed along the further information that "I feel it will be about a professional person, and you will get a lot of help from the other side, and you will not have the legal problems you had with the other one."

This had remained a mystery for what I later realised from Lorna was ten years of earth time. It was only when I asked for help for the additional chapter that I learned it was my account of my life here that was to be the second book it had always been intended for Lorna to write! Apparently, the teachers here are always pleased when someone such as I am comes along and am able to communicate clearly with those on earth. It helps them to provide details of life here that some people on earth would otherwise not bother to read. They feel such accounts can be enormously helpful to those who may have doubts about what life is like here.

335

"But we had to wait for you to be ready, Judy. We do not like to force the issue in any way. Now you truly want to get things clearly stated on earth, and we are more than willing to help you."

I took this information along to the incredulous Lorna, who felt that, somewhere or other, communication could have been a little clearer than it frequently turned out to be! When we had discussed the arrangement at the outset, I had told Lorna that I felt I could probably hold the vibration for approximately fifteen minutes, if I tried hard, but no longer. When it came to actually doing it, I was advised by those who were to help me that it was proposed to provide far more details and explanations than Lorna and I had originally envisaged and that the sessions for the book would last much longer. "You will not have to hold it alone. You will mingle with us to keep the information on the correct lines, and we will all transfer it to your friend."

It was with certain misgivings that Lorna found that the original fifteen minutes was stretching to thirty minutes, forty-five minutes, and even, occasionally, to an hour. She could not always feel my presence amidst it all, and she was being given a far more detailed account than envisaged. Eventually, she was given the full explanation that I felt we should have both been given at the outset, which was that we would, between us, provide a full-length book of my life here and not simply as an additional chapter to the original book covering my life on earth. It was also explained to Lorna that, if she was unable to be sure of my presence during the dictation, because of the mass thought concentration being used, I would visit her more directly afterwards and be able to reassure her. So, this is how this book has been produced, and we all hope, from here, that it will be of some help to those who are enquiring about what life is like here. I also hope, as does Lorna, that it will go at least some way towards helping me to clear my reputation on earth of some of the reprehensible and truly unfair allegations that have been placed around it.

VIII

Looking back at my life on earth from here, I now do see where my own prejudgments of others' actions led me into situations where I tended to over-react against them. I then usually shouted in order to avoid becoming tearfully emotional, but I sometimes failed abysmally and did both. This unfortunate reaction usually led me to deeper problems and troubles. Doreen has explained that this was all part of the emotional insecurity that I had struggled with since childhood. My own children realised I was not a mean person at heart and so did my friend Lorna. In fact, I recall something she wrote about me in a fan club magazine, some years before I came here, which seemed to sum me up pretty well. It is this attitude of hers that I feel more of those who have written about me publicly could have tried to understand. I have asked her to reproduce it here exactly as she wrote it then, as follows:

> At first it was difficult to see past the public image to the Judy that ticks underneath—the person of many moods who is constantly struggling with her nerves. Photographed, quoted, reported upon, followed—it is soon easy to see how, she can be happy one day and sad the next; one day exuberant and another drained of all energy. Things are made more difficult for her by those of her fans who mistakenly let admiration and affection develop into hysteria. They dog her footsteps relentlessly, fling themselves upon her, wallow in emotion, and refuse to accept it is not always convenient for Judy to speak with them. Quick to anger, but usually quick to forgive; friendly and demonstrative by nature and never condescending; this is Judy Garland as I know her—a Judy for whom I have an unshakeably warm regard.

Lorna tells me she already realised, a good while before I came here, that some fans from whom I had accepted friendship had chosen to distort my actions to others around them simply because I had been too ill always to be able to behave in the way that they had expected me to behave. This makes me even more grateful to her for her continuous defence of me during the last years of my life on earth and also since I came here, just as I am also grateful to my three children for their continuing devotion.

Many people whom I have met here have shared a similar problem of misunderstanding when on earth and have often, in consequence, found themselves less well loved by those they left behind on earth than they had thought and hoped themselves to have been. Like me, they have been helped to see themselves, as well as others, more clearly. Yet, the disillusionment of finding out what others have thought and said about you can be both hurtful and saddening. It has made me realise more than ever how exceedingly fortunate I am to have retained the devotion of my three children, as well as to have managed to find such a very true and loyal friend.

We all care here what people have felt about us on earth, and we all need to review our lives when we come here. My personal review was undertaken more thoroughly than some are so soon after arrival simply because I needed to find out where my few true friends had been and where I had been misled as well as verbally abused in public accounts of my life. I have worked hard on myself since I have realised my faults more clearly, and I am now happier than I have ever been. Doreen has explained to me that those people who have deliberately lied about me or have chosen to genuinely believe me to have been the sort of person they have depicted will take for longer than I have done to reach this happy state and to progress in the right direction. They are all seeing me through the filter of their own minds, and these are clearly not happy minds or even fairly placed.

Finding someone like Lorna was something that I badly needed. I would never have seen her so clearly had I not been shown where others whom I had believed in and trusted had badly failed me, not only on earth but in their memoirs of me. Even my last husband, Mickey, failed to understand me properly, although I still do not blame him for that. What I do regret is that he chose to write about it all publicly and to even give a very wrong impression of my dependency upon pills during our marriage. During our months together, at the times I was not working, I really did reduce my sleeping pills and those I needed to help me work hard. It was because of this that I was not sleeping properly or regularly.

After I had settled down here, I even made further enquiry concerning the night I came here, as I still could not understand how I could have taken the six sleeping pills it was decided that I had taken. The first two I do now recall taking, because I thought that a good night's sleep might help me to lose the sore throat and headache and make me well for the next day. I can accept that I may have awakened, and, not being too clear in my mind as a result of the first two, I could have taken two more without recalling the first two. Doreen says she has no further information either, so I have to leave it there. It was because I wished to avoid such possible confusion that I asked Mickey to take charge of my pills. Although he meant well when he told me that I should continue to be responsible for them, I had only meant it to be a safeguard and not a weakness on my part.

The pills I used to take in order to help me to complete my performances during my last five years on earth were called Ritalin. I took two of these before I performed, or sometimes during the performance if not before, but I seldom used them otherwise. I relied on my sedatives to help me to stay calm, as Lorna has been trying to tell everyone for me since I reassured her of this fact soon after I first spoke to her from here. I am very sorry that Mickey did not say this. My doctor of that period also made it clear to Lorna that malnutrition was the main problem at that time. That was why I had been taken ill in Spain. Mickey chose to fly back with me to London so that I could get more rest in my own home and also avoid the bad effect the heat always had on me when I was so weak.

During our months together, Mickey often tried to get me to eat more. He even tried to get me to take more interest in going out with him, because he felt I had been spending too much time in the house. But I have learned from here that my whole internal system had been weakened so much as a result of my not eating properly for the last three years—on top of the weaknesses left by the hepititis I had in 1959 and the pleurisy and pneumonia in 1964—that there was simply nothing to prevent this minor overdose of such a strong sleeping pill from taking its toll. So, you see, I would like to make it clear that I was not so bad at keeping myself clear of medicines as it may sometimes have appeared to people. I also want to say how sad I am that few people have realised this.

Despite wishing that Mickey had expressed himself differently concerning our months together, I have been assured that he did, and does still, love me and recalls our months together with happy thoughts rather than otherwise. I still remain very grateful that he came into my life when he did and I still hope we will meet again here as friends.

My life here is a very happy one. I still like to laugh a lot, and I do. I have many interesting discussions, which I enjoy. I can honestly say life is never dull or boring or even uneventful, provided you make the effort yourself to ensure that it is not. I am told that I am much happier here as a person because I am able to see that people truly like me a lot and to not have to simply hope that they do. This makes me very even-tempered, because I no longer continuously need to defend myself, nor am I getting suspicious about some peoples' actions. I am still a little bit impulsive in my decisions, and some of these have ended in minor disasters, but these are never too serious and have usually ended in friendly laughter. Mainly, these disasters arise when I assume I have made it all very clear only to find that I have missed out the vital explanatory link in a chain of events. Again, Lorna seemed to be not at all surprised to hear this from me, but at least people here recognise it is simply impulsiveness and not intentional.

I sing concerts regularly and find that some of those songs that were favourites in my concerts on earth are also favourites here. These still include "Over the Rainbow," "Swanee," "Just in Time," "San Francisco," and "Chicago." Spencer Tracy has performed "A Couple of Swells" with me on several occasions, and we have great fun with it. I also sing songs that others sang on earth but that I never did, as well as material that has been composed here and never sung by anyone on earth. My audiences continue to include many people who knew my work on earth, some of whom have come here years after my own arrival here, as well as many who are several generations "older" than I am if judged by earth time, although we have no such divisions here.

I now have a little home of my own, which is small and cosy and not unlike the style I chose to have in California with my children, but I seldom spend much time there, preferring to stay with my new family and friends. But I can spend time there alone, something I felt unable to do when on earth.

When I want to think very carefully, I still find my way to my original little glade.

I continue to spend a lot of my free time with Lorna's parents, Lilian and Stanley, and they are my best friends here, quite apart from the gratitude I feel to Doreen for all her help.

Although Jack Kennedy is still my friend and comes to my concerts, we are usually working in different areas and only meet occasionally for any length of time. He still wishes he could have done more for his country before coming here. Much of his time is spent, at present, trying to influence correctly those on earth who are responsible for the many decisions that have to be made to try and keep the world progressing along in a correct way. It is becoming increasingly difficult for all those concerned, so he feels that, as it is possible here to be more far-seeing than those on earth, he should try and give guidance to those whose minds can be reached from here, even though they usually fail to realise it is coming from beyond their own thinking.

In the years since I have become interested in mediumship and the various ways and means of communicating with people who are still on earth, I have also become one of those who help to contribute this kind of service. Lorna and I are agreed that it is better that I remain anonymous in this work, so I only make myself personally known to Lorna or to friends of hers. I undertake this work from time to time with others, however, and it is very fulfilling to take part in helping to bring about this form of reunion between people who have been parted from those they love. The upliftment this can give is something to cherish.

Lorna has asked me about a news story in which it has been reported that someone who knew me when on earth believes that they have clairvoyantly seen me dancing on stage alongside them. It is not impossible that they may have had this image provided by minds beyond their own, in which case they could very easily have been misled into thinking that it was me, but I wish to assure you all that I have never been so close to the earth that such a phenomenon could actually be me. I have not even danced since I have been here, other than to play with the children, and I shall never be so close to the earth that I could actually be seen in this way.

This reminds me to mention that I still like to watch fine dancing, and we have dancing here by those who were talented dancers when on earth. Sometimes, I go with Lilian to watch the great dancers who are here, including Pavlova. Lilian says she feels she would have enjoyed ballet when on earth if there had been more opportunity for her to see it. We go together here, and she now enjoys it as much as I always did.

There are very, very many different ways of progressing here, and I have been helped in this way far beyond my original expec-

341

tation. I am now learning to help the teachers here to communicate with and through mediums on earth. This has included using Lorna to pass along to others some of the communicators who are far more experienced here than I am likely to be for a very long time. Because I have a close link with Lorna, I am used as a mental bridge between the teachers and Lorna. We have had some very successful results, so it will not be too much longer before she will have learned a number of things she would not otherwise have learned until she had been here for a while. All this has had a somewhat unexpected effect (at least it is unexpected as far as I am concerned) on my own vibrational level of existence here, so that I am no longer able to give Lorna such a very strong feeling of my presence as I did at one time. We have, however, learned other ways to help her to know that it is me, and our friendship continues to flourish.

Although there are very many other experiences here that I would like to be able to tell you, especially now that we have already gone much more into my life here than I had ever originally expected, one has to know when to stop. So I have to leave it all at that for the present. Lorna and I are already concerned that you may find some of what I have already told you to be a little difficult to follow. We are also both concerned that the explanations are not always couched in terms that I would have used on earth, or even had I been left entirely to my own devices here. Of course, had I been left to work on it and to phrase it all on my own, you would not have got it at all!

I am aware there may be many faults in the way it has been presented, because Lorna has been raising regular objections to me, which I have, in turn, referred to those responsible. It has to be understood that there are many problems for those trying to communicate with earth when we have to work as a team. We have to try and be all together when picking out the words that we can imprint into Lorna's mind in order to produce a complete paragraph instead of simply a brief phrase. The result can sometimes be a little bit rambling, and possibly repetitive, as Lorna has so constantly complained to us. So I ask for your understanding and forgiveness if it does not always sound like me, although Lorna laughingly admits I could also be a little bit rambling when telling a story on earth!

We have both felt very strongly that it would have been extremely unwise to have arranged for this book to be attempted through anyone but Lorna, because of the pitfalls and misinterpretations that can often arise between communicators here and an unfamiliar medium on earth. It has sometimes, however, placed Lorna in an embarrassing position to be asked to act as a channel for so many references to herself and to her parents. She feels there is already a likelihood that she will be accused of letting her own imagination take over, and the references to herself and her parents may even seem to support this contention to those who find it difficult to believe that such communication is possible. Yet, surprising as it has been for all of us, she and her parents have been such an integral part of my present happiness that it is necessary to make this clear. Without the exceptional friendship that I have now found, my happiness would not now be so secure, and this book could not have been written.

Despite Lorna's increasing concern over the length of my story, it is necessarily episodic, and a lot of my experiences here have had to be left out, but I want to assure you that everything that has been related did actually take place and that I truly am happier now than I have ever been.

As there are so many experiences that I have not been able to tell you, perhaps, one day, I shall be allowed, if not encouraged, to speak to you again. For now, I will simply, once again, send my love to all my fans on earth who have continued to be loyal to my memory and to love me as they always did despite the systematic attacks that have been made against my reputation both before, and especially since, I passed here. Life here can be infinitely rewarding and far more fulfilling than life on earth, so that, before long, the troubles of earth recede and become largely forgotten. It does still matter to me, however, that those whom I tried to entertain and uplift in my work should have had to face all that has been alleged against me, so that all the joy and beauty I always endeavoured to give you should have become so tarnished. But I also realise there are many who, although they are confused by the lies and the insinuations, still steadfastly refuse to let these change their love for me in their hearts. To all those people, I send my gratitude and my love from "your Judy" and also the assurance that, should you wish to do so, when you come here in your turn, you will still be able to hear me sing in much the same way that you remember me singing at my best on earth—but far better. To all of you, and also to my three darling children, Liza, Lorna and Joe, I say, "God bless you."